Pentecostals in Britain

Pentecostals in Britain

William K. Kay

First Published in 2000 by Paternoster Press

06 05 04 03 02 01 00   7 6 5 4 3 2 1

Paternoster Press is an imprint of Paternoster Publishing,
P.O. Box 300, Carlisle, Cumbria, CA3 0QS, UK
and
Paternoster Publishing USA, P.O. Box 1047,
Waynesboro, GA 30830-2047, USA

Website: www.paternoster-publishing.com

British Library Cataloguing in Publication Data
A catalogue record for this book is available from the British Library

ISBN 1-84227-011-7

Cover Design by Mainstream, Lancaster
Typeset by WestKey, Falmouth, Cornwall
Printed in Great Britain by Bell & Bain Ltd, Glasgow

Contents

Foreword

When Professor David Martin published *Tongues of Fire: Conservative Protestantism in Latin America* (Blackwell:1990) it was refreshing to find a scholar who could write about Pentecostals without either rancour or condescension. On the contrary, Martin sees the Pentecostal churches as an evangelical engine of social and economic enterprise that revitalise decaying cultures as well as enliven moribund liturgies.

Such a positive rendition of the Pentecostal tradition is not yet typical of European scholarship, and in the light of this it is a pleasure to welcome this new book by Dr. Kay that I think is the most important study of British Pentecostals since Donald Gee's classic *Wind and Flame* (Assemblies of God: 1967).

In a way, the study of British Pentecostals may be thought to be one of failure. Before the 1930s were out, no doubt as their South American counterparts do today, British Pentecostals expected to carry all before them in the power of the Spirit and in the light of an expected Second Advent. In the event the Lord stayed his hand, and Pentecostals have had to settle down – albeit restlessly – to become principled Christian communities.

Of course one could say that Pentecostalism was born in sectarian delusion. If we were to say this, however, the same would have to be said of Christianity itself which began as a sect of Judaism and expected to labour industriously, but briefly, in God's vineyard till the Lord's imminent return. One reading of the early church is to say that it sold out to Constantine and state religion and in so doing forgot its calling and lost its revival fire. While not wishing to endorse Constantinianism, I think a more generous account of early Christian leadership is that it came to terms with reality, and recognised that the people of God needed nurture and succour as well as fervour and excitement. Similarly British Pentecostals, while not reneging on their millennial hope, or for a moment giving up on miracles, have matured with experience and come to terms with the fact that God's end timetable is determined by his sovereignty and not the latest Christian paperback predictions.

Settling down creates an organisational paradox. On the one hand, the act of settling in seems the betrayal of things hoped for; a denial of charismatic gifts and a turning away from revival. On the other hand, institutionalisation can be not merely a settling-in but a digging-in – laying a sure foundation for long term flourishing. This institutionalism, what Weber meant by the 'routinisation of charisma', allows a 'precious heritage' to be passed on to future generations. Church history is littered with dead sects that fizzed and burnt out without long term impact because they failed to put sufficient input into training and congregational consolidation.

What William Kay has superbly captured in this book is a movement that has not only survived almost a century of existence, but one that is very much alive. Dr Kay's approach is partly historiographical but mainly empirical. His survey of nearly a thousand Pentecostal leaders is the backbone of this study and what it partly reveals is that many pastors have adapted to the pressures of modernity, and in the process have changed their minds on some social practices that would have once been thought of as 'worldly' (from watching television to drinking alcohol). What is more surprising, however, is that the survey shows, even more convincingly, just how much of the early Pentecostal vision still remains.

This to me is a crucial factor for both the survival and future growth of the classical Pentecostal denominations. Without the maintenance of Pentecostal distinctiveness they will dribble back to the mainstream where they will be absorbed into bland evangelicalism.

The reality, as Dr Kay shows us, is that Pentecostals are sufficiently earthed into British religious culture for them to be ready for the long haul that sustained mission demands. I am not sure that the same could be said of neo-Pentecostals, i.e. the mainline charismatics and independent new churches. Here we are at the end of the twentieth century and the memories of the 1970s' heydays of the charismatic renewal are already fading. Whither the Catholic charismatics? Where would the Anglican Renewal be without Holy Trinity Brompton and Chorley Wood? And what happened to 'the fastest growing churches' in Britain of the 1980s – the 'new churches' of Restoration? The answer is that many have been deflected from 'stream' to 'stream'; some streams have dried-up and died. Others have survived as event churches moving from happening to celebration but without (unlike the classical Pentecostals) digging-in, putting down roots, nurturing the next generation of revivalists, looking for the fruits as well as the gifts of the Spirit.

If I was a betting man – and as Dr Kay shows us, gambling is still universally eschewed by Pentecostals – I would put my money on the old Pentecostal denominations still to be with us, and thriving, at the end of the next century. I'm not prepared to put my shirt on the new churches, and don't relish the long-odds on the Renewal.

Professor Andrew Walker,
King's College, London.

Acknowledgements

The writing of this book has only been possible because of the implicit support of the Principal and Governors of Trinity College, Carmarthen. To them I am genuinely grateful for the opportunity given to me by the research post to which I was appointed in January 1994. Freedom to think and write flowed from my generous job description.

I also place on record my gratitude to the 930 Pentecostal ministers drawn from the Apostolic Church, Assemblies of God in Great Britain and Ireland, the Church of God and the Elim Pentecostal Church who responded to the bulky questionnaire I sent them. They are busy people and many of them had previously answered other questionnaires on other topics. That they found the time to answer this one must be partly due to the support I received from the Executive Councils or Overseers within these four denominations.

Pastor David Miles, of the Apostolic Church, was involved at an early stage of this research, as were members of the Centre for Theology and Education, especially Mandy Robbins and Anne Rees, whose cheerfulness and care were invaluable.

I also received help from my younger son, Samuel, who undertook the tedious but necessary process of coding questionnaires though he was paid for undertaking this task, it was hard-earned money! Meanwhile my elder son, Matthew, encouraged me from a distance!

I am grateful too to the Donald Gee Centre for Pentecostal and Charismatic Research, housed at Mattersey Hall, whose rich troves of material were invaluable for the more historical sections of this book.

I am also grateful to Professor Margaret Poloma who kindly gave me permission to use several items originally devised for use in her study of Assemblies of God in the United States.

My thanks also go to my friend and colleague, Revd Professor L.J. Francis, whose truly prodigious endeavours in the field of practical theology and empirical research have been an instructive inspiration. He has been generous in offering his advice, especially in the early stages of this project and in providing departmental funds to allow it to proceed. Without this help, I doubt whether the research would have been started.

During the course of writing I have been glad for access to the advice of Revd Desmond Cartwright of Elim, Revd Dr Douglas LeRoy of the Church of God, Revd Gordon Weeks of the Apostolic Church and Revd Paul Weaver of the Assemblies of God in Great Britain and Ireland. They have saved me from numerous errors of fact and interpretation though naturally I take responsibility for any that remain.

Lastly, my wife, Anthea, has been consistently supportive throughout the course of the writing of this book and without her encouragement I doubt whether it would have been completed.

William K. Kay
Easter 2000

Introduction

The Pentecostal and charismatic movement is one of the wonders of the twentieth century. Often unnoticed by academic analysts, particularly in the West, it is a vast, sprawling network of churches and denominations straddling the globe. It is strongest in Asia and Latin America but also present in most of the European countries. It includes free-standing Pentecostal denominations as well as charismatic fringes to the older churches. Its style of worship and its experimentation with church structure has enabled it to adapt to the rapid social and economic changes within the countries where it exists. It is predicted that by 2020 approximately 8 per cent of the world's population, or 502 million people, will either be members of, or worship in, Pentecostal and charismatic churches.[1]

This book fastens attention on Pentecostal churches within Britain, particularly in England and Wales. These churches represent the first wave of Pentecostalism within Britain and they date back to the period before the 1914–18 war. I have written about them in a way that is intended to appeal to as wide a diversity of people as possible. There is an account here, more detailed than in previous attempts, of their common history – while explaining where their own momentum took them along unique paths. In this sense I am writing for church historians. There is also an account here of the development of Pentecostal theology and its application to contemporary issues. In this sense I am writing for theologians. Yet, at the heart of this book and driving its concerns, is a database containing responses of Pentecostal ministers to a specially designed questionnaire intended to reveal a range of hitherto unknown

[1] Barrett and Johnson, 1998.

information. The analysis of this data ought to appeal to sociologists and psychologists. But beyond this, I want to communicate with ministers and lay people whose practical knowledge of Pentecostal churches arises from their participation in the life of Pentecostal congregations.

Academic disciplines can be defined by their characteristic concepts and methods. History tells the story of events making use, if possible, of documents originating with the eye witnesses of those events. History is a story, a connected narrative that puts people and events together into a coherent sequence but, of course, the historian must select the events that are pieced together[2] – there is no such thing as objective history. With any account that includes reference to miracles there are bound to be special problems since some historians, on principle, will refuse to credit any action to divine intervention. This makes the telling of history very difficult if it concerns people who believe that God did indeed answer their prayers or endow them with gifts of the Holy Spirit. To overcome this problem I have made a deliberate decision to accept the primacy of an account given by eyewitnesses, even if these accounts include reference to miraculous occurrences, over an account resting on secular and agnostic presuppositions.[3]

Yet, at the same time, I have made use of the methods of the social sciences which have sometimes been accused of 'methodological atheism'. I am happy to measure social factors like the percentage of a congregation exercising spiritual gifts, or psychological factors like attitudes and to report how these relate to other factors and, by this means, to attempt to construct a model explaining events in Pentecostal churches. To take one example here: there is a correlation between the personality of minister and church growth. Extraverted ministers are far more likely to enjoy growing churches than introverted ministers. This finding is discussed later and illustrates the kind of associations that can be discovered. Extraversion belongs to psychology whereas measurements of congregations belong to sociology, to social facts. The connection between the two is made by well-established social science methods explained in more detail below.

---

[2] Carr, 1986.

[3] Kay, 1992.

Theology, perhaps more than anything else, is characterised by talking about God in a logical way. To talk about God like this may begin from the documents of faith, the Bible and the creeds, and build up an account of the God described there. Yet theology can with equal validity begin with the experience of today's individuals and, making use of a questionnaire addressing individuals who have had distinctive experiences of God, a contemporary theology can be assembled. In the case of Pentecostal Christians there is a recognised mirrored relationship between the Bible, describing God and the religious life of the people of God over centuries, and the personal experience of God in the life history of the believer.[4] The believer understands his or her contemporary religious experience by reference to what is described in the scriptures. 'The experience of those who walk the pages of scripture, and their understanding of experiences, helps me to understand mine.' That is what the Pentecostal Christian would claim.

Nevertheless, in a more academic vein Pentecostal theologians would tease out the connections between theology as a 'second order activity', a thoroughly cognitive reflection on experience, and theology as stemming from a pretheoretical faith which, though pretheoretical, is still within the sphere of thought. 'Human beings are never only "pretheoretical" . . . is not faith a much more complex integration of imagination, interpretation, theory and the pursuit of responsibility in the experiential process?'[5] To place theology entirely in the sphere of thought is to make theology a matter of the mind and to leave the emotions well out of sight, confined to the margins, and irrelevant to the great issue of truth. To place theology in the sphere of the whole person is to make it a matter of every human capacity, of the mind *and* the emotions, and to understand the two as belonging together and bearing witness to each other. Such a theology still engages with truth but it does so from a broader basis and using a wider spectrum of evidence.

---

4 Others have drawn a distinction between 'kneeling theology', the theology of devotion, 'sitting theology', the theology of reflection, and 'holding-at-arms-length theology', the theology that emerges from critical examination. I am indebted to Professor Jeff Astley for this distinction.

5 Yong, 1998.

I take the view that the gulf which separates the academic world from the everyday world and the still relevant gulf which separates the arts from the sciences both need to be bridged. The notion that an expert is someone who 'knows more and more about less and less' seems to me to be not only untrue but also depressing; it implies that experts know a great deal about what counts, to outsiders, as virtually nothing. Yet whether it is nothing or not, the expert is still the expert, there to be consulted by the chatshow host and given three minutes to explain a complicated answer to a question that starts from blank ignorance. In this connection I was once interviewed about speaking in tongues by a television researcher who knew next to nothing about religion, even less about Christianity and whose acquaintance with the Pentecostal and charismatic movements was breathtakingly naïve. Where do you begin with someone whose idea of everyday life is so different from your own? And how can you explain a social science research project to someone whose idea of probability seems detached entirely from any mathematical study of chance and outcomes?

In writing for several audiences I am aware of the danger of pleasing none of them. But these audiences live side by side, watch the same television shows, vote in the same elections and talk in that marvellously rich and absorbent system of signs and sounds called the English language. Surely, if a rounded account of the four main Pentecostal denominations within Britain is going to be given, it must make use of several academic disciplines and techniques. For this reason, each chapter of this book begins with an introductory perspective, whether historical, theological or theoretical, before turning to the new data specially collected for analysis here.

All this is a daunting undertaking, not least because words that mean one thing in one discipline may mean something else in another. The word 'charismatic' is a case in point. To the secular intellectual, 'charismatic' is the adjective to describe someone gifted and glitzy. To the secular non-intellectual 'charismatic' is even wider than this. Boris Becker, the tennis star, described the Wimbledon centre court as 'charismatic'. To the sociologist, remembering Max Weber, the term means something closer to that used by the secular intellectual. To the Christian theologian the meaning must start from the text of the New Testament where the word, which is a Greek one, is extensively used.[6] It must also be placed alongside other New Testament words like *charis* which means 'grace', a term loaded with meaning that comes out of the very gospel itself. 'Charismatic' in this context therefore refers to the grace gifts conveyed by the Holy Spirit to individuals and congregations. It certainly does not apply to *any* gift possessed by *any* individual, whether showy or natural, and by no stretch of the imagination would it be a suitable description of a tennis court!

In a post-modern world, where personal narratives determine meaning, it is also reasonable to introduce the author. I write as a Pentecostal minister with two doctorates, one in education/psychology and the other in theology. In this respect, I have tried to bridge the arts-science gulf in my own mind, but I do so with awareness that academic disciplines are meant to be places where public knowledge exists. To employ these disciplines in writing about Pentecostals who, as we shall see, have a distinct worldview, is an important way of helping Pentecostal Christians see themselves, and see themselves often bathed in the sort of light which non-believers might use.

Another way of putting this is to say that the book is intended to be a scientifically derived factual account of Pentecostal churches and also to contain something of the feelings and emotions only derived from subjectivity. So here you have what is intended to be an inside *and* an outside view of the Pentecostal churches. Perhaps this is an impossible task. But perhaps it *is* possible to slip between two modes of description in ways that seem natural and unforced. The outer description of Pentecostal churches is carried through with numbers and tables which give a countable and verifiable set of reference points; the inner description is more subtly produced and comes with the commentary on the figures – it picks up matters which might be of interest not only to sociologists and theologians but also to church leaders.

Research study

The central information in this book was gained during 1996–7. Whilst working as Senior Research Fellow at the Centre for

---

[6] The word is used as a noun, *charisma* (singular) and *charismata* (plural).

Theology and Education at Trinity College, Carmarthen, I supervised a postal survey by questionnaire of all the Pentecostal ministers in Britain belonging to the four 'classical' Pentecostal denominations: Assemblies of God, the Elim Pentecostal Church, the Apostolic Church and the Church of God.

I apply the word 'denomination' to these Pentecostal groups with an awareness of its sociological connotations. Andrew Walker's fourth edition of *Restoring the Kingdom* (Guildford, Eagle, 1997) discusses the contrast between sects and denominations with care and takes the view that the language is hard to pin onto the 'new churches' in the sense that they manifest both denominational and sectarian features. Either way, sects should not be thought of as being all bad and denominations as all good. Nevertheless classical Pentecostals are easier to categorise because, although they were in their beginnings world-denying, unwilling or unable to co-operate with other Christian bodies and occasionally spiritually elitist – all marks of sectarianism – they are now much more inclined to adapt to their surrounding secular culture, to co-operate with other Christians and to admit that their spirituality fails to reach the standards to which they aspire. Decisively, Pentecostal groups are willing to admit that the validity of other Christian groups, especially charismatic ones, is equal to their own. In this sense, then, they are denominations and, in my view, they should not be afraid of the term. It is one that presumes continuity and settled protocols for the transferring of leadership from one generation to the next.

Sample

Each of these Pentecostal denominations publishes an annual yearbook listing its ordained clergy. Each distinguishes between ministers who work in the UK and missionaries who work overseas. For the purposes of this study, overseas workers were excluded. All other workers, active, retired, itinerant and pastoral, were included.

Although each denomination makes use of a different governmental structure, there are broad similarities between their operations. Assemblies of God and Elim each elect an Executive Council which has national authority. Both these Executive

Councils were approached and asked to give written support to the survey. This they did and a letter endorsing the project, and signed by the Chairman of each Council, was mailed with the questionnaire along with a freepost return envelope. Each questionnaire was completed anonymously but was identifiable by means of a numerical code. This allowed follow up letters to be sent to ministers who failed to respond. A second follow up letter was sent out to those who did not respond to the first and replacement questionnaires were offered to those who had mislaid them. Finally, a telephone follow up was used to selected ministers who had still not replied. This procedure led to 401 usable questionnaires from Assemblies of God ministers, a response rate of 57 per cent, and 367 usable questionnaires from Elim ministers, a response rate of 64 per cent.

The procedure adopted with the Apostolic Church was similar except that the endorsing letter was signed by the President of its Executive Council. This led to 100 usable replies, a response rate of 84 per cent. The Church of God letter was signed by the Field Director: Western Europe/Mediterranean/Middle East. Altogether 48 usable replies were received, a response rate of 21 per cent.

One independent evangelical church was included in the sample because its minister was ordained within Assemblies of God. Consequently the total sample, because of a further 13 cases where no denomination was filled in, amounted to 930 ministers. Altogether there were 907 (97.5 per cent) males and 23 (2.5 per cent) females. There were 242 (26 per cent) respondents aged under 39, 586 (63 per cent) aged between 40 and 64, 86 (9 per cent) over 65 years, and 16 of undeclared age. The sample, then, was predominantly male and middle aged.

Statistics

Because this book presents a comparison between different Pentecostal denominations as well as an account of Pentecostalism in general, the tables of figures shown here sometimes display statistics subdivided by denomination and at other times present figures drawn from the whole sample put together as one entity. However, the whole sample is only presented when analysis of variance (see below) showed that there were no differences between the denominations on the issue or item being presented. I have not given the analysis of variance figures for each occasion since it would be tedious to do so, but the principle of the presentations adopted here is a consistent one: where denominations are presented separately this is because there are significant differences between them; where denominations are presented together this is because there are no significant differences between them. The numbering of the tables points to the kind of statistics in them. Where the table has only two numbers, for example 6.1, this indicates that the table is the first in chapter six. Where the table has three numbers as in 6.1.1 this indicates that the table is the first at that point in chapter six to subdivide the figures between denominations.

I have attempted to reduce technical terms and statistics to a minimum, usually relegating them to footnotes, but on occasions it has been necessary to bring technical terms into the main text, particularly in chapter nine where the analysis deliberately replicates a study carried out in the United States. So a brief discussion of technical terms will be given here. I can only plead with non-statistically minded readers to persevere even if they do not understand fully what all the numbers mean or, indeed, if an approach involving quantification raises questions in their minds. Well before the end of the book, I hope everything will fall into place.

The most common means of associating two sets of numbers is by means of a *correlation coefficient*. The correlation coefficient ranges from −1 through 0 to + 1. A correlation coefficient of −1 would indicate that, when two sets of figures were compared, the top score in the first set was related to the bottom score in the second set and the second top score in the first set was related to the second bottom score in the second set, and so on. For example, negative correlations can be found between the consumption of certain fatty foods and life expectancy. On average, as consumption of these foods goes up life expectancy goes down. Positive correlations relate high scores in one set of numbers with high scores in the other. For example, positive correlations are found between height and weight. On average, taller people are heavier. But in practice it is rare to find correlations that get near the perfect 1. Although taller people are generally heavier, there are a number of short heavy people within the population. The correlation between height and weight is high but not perfect. If there is no relationship, either positive or negative, between two sets of figures, the correlation coefficient dwindles to zero.

Most correlation coefficients, and most statistics, have associated with them a p, or probability, value. This p value indicates the extent to which the correlation would have occurred by chance. Thus a p value of .05 indicates that the correlation would have occurred randomly five times in a hundred. By convention p values of .05 are worthy of comment. In other words, a relationship that would have come about less than five times in a hundred by chance is likely to indicate a real association (like the one between height and weight or fatty food intake and life expectancy).

There is always the possibility that high positive correlations indicate causation but the interpretation of the statistics requires care since two variables that correlate may only do so because they are both caused by a third. The pupil who can play the piano may also be able to play the guitar. There is a correlation between piano playing and guitar playing. But playing the piano does not cause someone to be able to play the guitar. It is more likely that the ability to play both instruments is itself caused by general musical competence. The implication of a third variable in the relationship between two others can be statistically removed by *partial correlation*, a technique employed in chapter ten.

Some variables cannot be correlated with each other because they are of the wrong type. You cannot correlate membership of political parties with religious affiliation because, unlike height and weight, the variables are not continuous. To meet this difficulty, these kinds of variables are broken down by *crosstabulation* and, once this is done, statistical measures of association can be calculated, the most common of which is chi square that functions very similarly to a correlation coefficient.

In addition to correlation, it is common to test for differences between groups. Does the mean or average score of group A differ from the mean or average score of group B? Again statistical tests and probability values can be computed and the most usual test applied to the data within this book is an *analysis of variance* to distinguish between the four Pentecostal denominations represented here. The statistic associated with the analysis of variance is the F ratio. A high F ratio indicates the likelihood of differences between groups and, where analysis of variance results have been reported, then the F ratio and the p value are given together. When the p value is significant then the F ratio points to significantly different group means.

Two other statistics are calculated later in this book. The first is the *alpha coefficient* which is used to test for the reliability of scales. Scales are composed of a series of similar items whose scores are added together. Scales, because they are composed of several items, are more stable than individual items and they can be used to point to an underlying psychological or theological construct. For example, if we were interested in someone's attitude to food, it would be useful to construct a scale that contained items relating to different kinds of food. It would be far better to ask: 'Do you like ice cream?', 'Do you like spinach?', 'Do you like lasagne?', and so on, rather than to rely on the single question, 'Do you like food?' But we need to have some means of checking that the different items related to food do themselves hang together coherently. This is what the alpha coefficient provides for us. It is actually based on a series of internal correlation coefficients calculated on the items that compose the scale.

It is usual to refer to the alpha coefficient as being a measure of the scale's reliability. A reliable scale is one that will give similar results on different occasions and, ideally, the same scale items would be given to the sample twice to ensure that all the results remained consistent. In practice this is usually impossible and so the alpha coefficient, by representing the correlations between every permutation of items within the scale, produces the effect of repeated testing: it is as if many shorter versions of the scale were tested on the same population. High alpha coefficients are easier to achieve with longer scales.

Second, statistics connected with *multiple regression* are given in chapter nine. Ordinary regression (or correlation – the terms are almost interchangeable in this context) involves just two variables. Multiple regression can in theory involve any number. In each instance one variable (called the dependent variable) is correlated with one or more others (called the independent variables). The technique permits the researcher to see how or if several independent variables are related to the dependent variable. For example, are the age of a minister, the minister's training and the minister's gender related to church growth? By using multiple regression we can relate age, training and gender to church growth simultaneously to detect which of the three variables is most significant. It is also possible to adjust the way the equation is calculated by entering one of the variables first and the other two later. By this means we can equalise any effects of imbalances in the first variable on the other two. For instance, using an example not based on real data, if we were using the three variables age, gender and training in relation to church growth, we might know that female ministers tended to be younger and better trained than male ministers. So, we would enter gender to the equation first and remove the effects of this variable before entering age and training. We could then examine the effects of age and training without worrying about the larger number of females in this example who were younger and better trained. If we did not do this then we might draw conclusions about age and training which really ought to be drawn about gender.

References

I have used footnotes and adopted a system of giving the name of the author of a particular text and the date of first publication since these are the two most important pieces of information about an historical document. The advantage of footnotes is that the reader may glance quickly down to check a reference without interrupting his or her flow of thought while engaging with the main text. To simplify the process further I have ensured that full bibliographical details are given at the end of the whole book rather than at the end of each chapter since finding a chapter end only slows down the process of hunting for information during the process of reading.

I have not used the Latin abbreviations common in some publications simply because they seem to me to have the disadvantage of causing readers to search back through footnotes, sometimes over many pages, to the original citation of a reference. That seems to destroy the advantages footnotes have over endnotes. Similarly I have avoided the short title convention since this excludes information about date of publication and assumes that each reader can retain in memory the full title of a text and is not interested in the date of publication, both questionable assumptions.

And finally . . .

Each chapter follows a similar pattern. It begins with an overview, is followed by an historical or theological introduction often divided up into denominational subsections, and then asks what the original data collected for this study have to say before coming to a conclusion. Where the denominations are historically or theologically similar they are dealt with together.

This book, like many others, is published at the start of a new millennium. It looks back to the last century and forward to the next. Particularly in the last chapter I have begun to think about what might have happened in the past and what might happen in the future. That double orientation is another facet of this important and fascinating subject.

1

Pentecostal Denominations Emerge

Overview

This chapter outlines the historical development of the four Pentecostal denominations covered in this book. Beginning from common sources that can be traced back to the evangelical theology of holiness and to its expression in the Welsh Revival and running through the common filter of the Sunderland Conventions, the three British-based denominations, Assemblies of God, the Apostolic Church and the Elim Pentecostal church, run together in rough parallel. The Church of God's beginnings are traceable to the work of the Holy Spirit in Tennessee from 1886 onwards. Only in 1953 did the church begin to form congregations in Britain.[1]

Historical background

The social and economic background of Britain has undergone vast and seismic changes in the period during which Pentecostal churches have become established. In 1875, when the important Keswick conferences began in the pre-Pentecostal epoch, Britain was the proud possessor of an empire stretching across the world. Queen Victoria was Empress of India as well as Queen of the unified United Kingdom. Britain had been more or less continuously at peace since Napoleon's defeat in 1815 and the advances of modern science and technology had only just begun to influence

---

[1] Arnold, 1992, 25.

the lives of ordinary people.[2] Ships were still largely built of wood. Air flight had not been discovered (only in 1909 did the Wright brothers fly and only in 1919 did commercial airlines set up shop). The telephone was unheard of (only patented in 1876, though by 1900 there were 210,000 telephones in Britain). Travel took place by horse. There was no television (the BBC was formed in 1922 and radio broadcasts began). The currency of sterling was the strongest in the world and London the leading economic centre in existence. Membership of the trade union movement in 1888 only amounted to 800,000 and no Labour government had ever been in power. Indeed, the Labour Party was not fully formed until 1906. Admittedly, health and sanitation had improved in the Victorian era and local government had begun to administer a national education system after the 1870 and 1902 Education Acts. In a series of Factory Acts culminating in 1891 national government prevented the exploitation of children and improved health and safety at work. But women could not vote until 1928 and only a tiny élite (of Anglican men) received university education.

During the next hundred years all the apparently immovable social and economic certainties would be challenged or overthrown. It is almost impossible to overestimate the impact of the Great War of 1914–18. Seen from a narrowly British point of view it was a catastrophe. Not only did it undermine and break up the old social order, including the empire, but it also dealt an enormous blow against orthodox Christian belief and the place of the churches within the life of the nation.[3] The changes that took place in the 1920s and 1930s reflected these convulsions. Those who survived the war, particularly the opinion formers in the artistic and intellectual élite, pursued a modernist agenda that could lead to a sense that life was random and absurd. From 1924 in the world of pictorial art surrealism emerged; in poetry *The Waste Land* (1922) of T.S. Eliot expressed the sense of a decaying civilisation; in literature the disintegration of realism was epitomised by the verbal conjuring of Joyce's *Finnegans Wake* (1939). If one word summarised what was happening it was the word 'secularisation'. A process felt through

---

[2] The Crimean War 1853–56 had remarkably little impact on the lives of most people in Britain.

[3] Inge, 1926.

the preoccupations of high culture but also in popular culture, in films and musical entertainment, in leisure activities and sport.

Britain was still, even in the 1920s and 1930s, a deferential and stratified society. It was not as deferential and stratified as it had been in the period immediately before the Great War when an 'upstairs' and 'downstairs' culture existed, but was socially demarcated nevertheless: servants lived downstairs and were graded according to a complicated hierarchy of domestic jobs and skills; the middle class enjoyed life upstairs ranked according to a pecking order based upon closeness to the old aristocracy.[4] Early photographs of crowds at football matches show the smartly dressed working-class in their cloth caps standing on the terraces at Arsenal or Liverpool, drunk perhaps, but largely well behaved and non-violent. It is these working men who had marched in their thousands to the trenches of the Somme and though some returned determined to see a better future for themselves, the general strike of 1926 was largely a failure.

Moreover, what had begun in the Victorian era with immigration to Britain from Ireland and a gradual expansion of the birth rate, continued in the twentieth century. People moved from farms and villages into the cities where there was work. Industrialisation and urbanisation continued and, with the process of uprooting from village communities, religious life became more easily forgotten or disjointed. This was another strand in the tapestry of secularisation. Church attendance among Protestants failed to keep pace with the general population and the influence of organised religion declined. For instance, whereas 65 per cent of live births were baptised in the Church of England in 1902, this figure had dropped to a mere 27 per cent by 1993.[5] Only the Roman Catholic Church managed to keep a semblance of numerical strength in Britain during the twentieth century, though recruitment to the priesthood and religious orders dropped sharply.[6] In the period after 1945, the percentage of the adult population believing in a personal God fell while the percentage of atheists rose.[7] Meanwhile,

---

[4] The film *Titanic* illustrates this: upstairs is the ballroom, downstairs is steerage.

[5] Bruce, 1995, 59.

[6] Louden, 1998.

[7] Kay, 1997.

Liverpool, Manchester, Birmingham and the other big industrial cities continued to grow and the population of England and Wales, which had jumped from 22 million in 1871 to 35 million in 1891, moved upwards again to 43 million in 1951 and then to 49 million in 1991. As a presence within British society the church became weaker and sometimes invisible.

In all these changes the family at first largely remained a stable and treasured unit. Divorce was infrequent and travel the privilege of the rich few. Yet, particularly after 1945, the family underwent a metamorphosis.[8] Wives began to go out to work; divorce became more common; travel increased; single parent families became more prevalent.[9] Some of these changes were brought about as a growing population swamped the old social structures and so altered social attitudes, but others could be accounted for by economic transformations and a corresponding expansion of the education system. Access to primary education at the start of the twentieth century resulted in almost universal literacy and therefore high circulation newspapers that usually reflected the political stances of their influential proprietors.[10] By the end of the nineteenth century, aided by the growing railway network, daily circulations of 1 million were possible.

And this trend continued. After 1944 the British electorate determined that every child should have a free secondary education and, as the 1980s progressed, free *secondary* education was extended to become a system of mass *higher* education. Access to higher education initially disseminated the opinions of the previous generation's cultured but irreligious élite more widely but, as it expanded further in the 1990s, the institutions of higher education tended to become more technical or vocational. They prepared young men and women for the job market without inculcating any moral or spiritual values. These institutions were irreligious and felt that, in

---

[8] Young and Willmott, 1975.

[9] The *Sunday Times* of 15th August 1999 reported that 37 per cent of live births in Britain were outside wedlock.

[10] The *Daily Express* faithfully supported Edward VIII in the abdication crisis and then opposed Indian independence after 1945. The Murdoch press, powerful in England at the end of the twentieth century, rarely supported the monarchy; Murdoch showed sympathy with Australian republicanism.

the name of academic freedom, this was what they ought to be. Furthermore, the influence of the popular media upon an educated populace was to make popular culture more widely acceptable rather than to increase appreciation of high culture.[11]

In essence, the period 1875 to 1995 is an era of increasing prosperity and education but, at the same time, a period of increasing diversity, fragmentation, pluralisation and equalisation. Society, which had been highly stratified, became much more egalitarian, a change reflected in a switch from a selective system of education to one that was comprehensive. The privileges of a few – foreign travel, cars, home ownership, television, foreign food, personal autonomy – became the right of all. Deference disappeared or, if it appeared at all, was directed towards sporting and musical icons, to 'celebrities', whose fame and wealth conferred on them a kind of secular 'holiness' and to whom daughters of the royal families of Europe might appropriately consider marriage. As a further symbol of these changes, Queen Elizabeth II was never Empress of India and the United Kingdom began to devolve itself into smaller, potentially disunited regions. Domestic servants vanished from middle-class homes and were replaced by electrical appliances of amazing ingenuity and utility. The upstairs-downstairs culture had disappeared.

In telling the story of the Pentecostal churches in Britain against the backdrop of a century of unprecedented social change, what is at first noticeable is a stir in the evangelical churches at the end of the nineteenth century.

Holiness

The Keswick Convention began in 1875. An authorised history traces the influence of American holiness preachers on the Convention's founding.[12] Robert and Hannah Pearsall Smith arrived in England in 1874 and, at a conference in Oxford, spoke about the 'promotion of scriptural holiness'. The message of the preachers was that:

---

[11] Football became a topic of middle-class conversation in England after the European and World Cups at the end of the 1990s. Nick Hornby's *Fever Pitch* (1996) led the literary way.

[12] Pollock, 1964.

> You could have intimate companionship with Christ all day long, that God's will and your happiness were one, that the Holy Spirit and not yourself overcame your temptations; but you had to make a deliberate act of full surrender and enter a 'rest of faith' – there would be a crisis leading to a process.[13]

The impact of their preaching was sufficient to lead Canon Harford-Battersby and Robert Wilson to arrange for a week of Bible teaching under canvas in the summer of 1875. They had hoped Pearsall Smith would be their main preacher. He had preached at a conference with some 8,000 delegates at Brighton that summer but the admission that he had whispered an 'ancient heresy or delusion to a young woman in emotional and spiritual distress' was sufficient to bring his public ministry to an abrupt end.[14] He returned to America and Keswick started without him. Its distinctive message was summarised by Handley Moule, once Principal of Ridley Hall Theological College at Cambridge and subsequently Bishop of Durham, as 'holiness by faith'.[15] Moule's earlier encounter with holiness preachers had been mixed. He had been impressed by the gravity and balance of Evan Hopkins during a Cambridge mission in 1883, but the following year had been alarmed by two extremists, Oliphant and Smyth-Pigott, both then Anglican curates, who held a further mission that encouraged 'wildish hymns' and made the unashamed claim that sin could be eradicated from the believer for ever. But Moule's worries about holiness teaching were dispelled later that year and he was to become one of its strongest supporters and best advocates.

His explanation of 'holiness by faith' rested on a biblical understanding. Holiness is surrender to the will of God and results in practical changes to character and lifestyle. Faith is simple trust and reliance in God. Holiness by faith is 'no substitute for justification by faith. Rather it presupposes it; it is itself the sequel truth which

---

13 Pollock, 1964, 26.

14 Pollock, 1964, 35. Heslam, 1998, 42, states that Smith had been involved in 'an adulterous relationship'. Even if this is not true, the effect was to remove Smith from ministry and to reduce the esteem in which the holiness movement was held.

15 Moule, 1907.

justification takes for granted as its complement and crown' and the process by which holiness is gained is 'precisely the same faculty as that exercised in receiving remission [from sin]'.[16]

Moule's exegesis was careful to state that the doctrine of holiness needed to be taken in conjunction with other doctrines. Holiness did not replace justification or remove the possibility of guilt. The balanced Keswick message had to guard against eradicationism or 'sinless perfection' and any prescriptiveness about the nature of the crisis that led to the process of sanctification. Balanced or not though, Keswick was distinct in its insistence that there *was* an experience subsequent to conversion by which the believer might gain holiness, and Keswick had to defend its position from the criticism of those like the Brethren who argued that 'the crucial stage of sanctification' took place at conversion – there was no special experience beyond the new birth.[17]

This balance was largely maintained. The Anglican ethos of Keswick ensured that it served the church interdenominationally. It did not veer into world-denying or sectarian forms of Christianity. Yet, alongside the Keswick influence and stemming from the long tradition of Wesleyan spirituality, holiness ideas leading to more radical forms of expression also circulated.[18] Here the emphasis was on 'entire sanctification' or 'full salvation' attained through a crisis experience of 'perfect love'. The terminology and the experiences they described could be made compatible with Keswick teaching, but there was always the possibility that they might peel off in different directions and produce another set of norms. After all, what exactly was the crisis and why should a process follow it? Why shouldn't a process lead to a crisis and what would happen if a search for holiness led to the discovery of divine power? It was this sort of logic that was ultimately to lead to Pentecostalism. Once Pentecostalism was established, however, Keswick was hardly favourable to it. Scroggie, one of its most prominent preachers, argued in 1912 in his church magazine against speaking in tongues as a sign of the Holy Spirit, and he repeated this in 1921 from the prominence of a Keswick platform.[19] Chadwick, in a position more friendly to

16 Moule, 1907, 69, 71.

17 Bebbington, 1989, 158.

18 Bebbington, 1989.

19 Randall, 1995.

Pentecostalism, accepted the validity of spiritual gifts, though this did not mean that he meant what Pentecostals meant by baptism in the Spirit.[20]

Welsh Revival

Pollock and others made the connection between Keswick and the Welsh revival.[21] A 'Welsh Keswick' was held in Llandrindod Wells in the summer of 1903 and among the speakers were Evan Hopkins and Jessie Penn-Lewis. As a result, a group of six young ministers from north Wales met together monthly to pray. A year later a second convention was held and shortly afterwards the revival sprang to life.[22] Evan Roberts (1878–1951), a young man training for the ministry, became its leader – insofar as it had a leader.

One interpretation of events is that the Welsh revival was the spread of an intensified Keswick experience through the Welsh churches and chapels. Certainly Evan Roberts visited Keswick in 1906 and there were then attempts by Welsh preachers and visitors to replicate in the Keswick tents the meetings they had held in Wales.[23] When Evan Roberts retired from preaching soon afterwards, he went to stay at Jessie Penn-Lewis' house in Leicestershire. Another interpretation is less friendly to Keswick. It argues that Keswick's concern for decorum had the effect of preventing revival from being carried from Wales to England. Mrs Penn-Lewis, too, has been implicitly criticised for her 'special teachings' about the 'cross experience' and the 'throne experience' and for her 'interference' with the Free Church Council mission in 1906 when Roberts was asked to preach.[24] It is not clear what this 'cross experience' was,

---

[20] Randall, 1995.

[21] Pollock, 1964, 119f. Also Garrard, 1930.

[22] In September, 1904.

[23] 'A large contingent from Wales had brought something of the glow and fervour of the Welsh Revival and it seemed that the Convention was on the brink of a like "visitation form on high". Opinions are still divided as to what truly transpired that memorable year [1905]. Some feared that emotionalism would run riot; others affirmed that the Convention leaders "quenched the Spirit" and checked what might have been a nation-wide Revival', Stevenson, 1959, 406. Emotionalism, it seems, was the great fear.

[24] Jones, 1995, 161.

but it appears to have been an extreme form of identification with Christ that claimed that the human ego or self was abolished. Once abolished, human behaviour became selfless and presumably sinless.

The most dramatic results of the revival were seen in the non-conformist chapels rather than the Anglican Church. Yet there is evidence that the Anglican community benefited from what was happening among its less socially exalted neighbours. At Pembrey the vicar noted that, though the revival only affected his Welsh-speaking communion, attendance increased by about one hundred people and elsewhere numbers of confirmation candidates increased and spiritual life deepened. It is arguable that there were really 'two revivals', an emotional one in the chapels and a teaching one in the church, and that it was the church that gained in the long term.[25]

It is likely that an awakening preceded the revival itself.[26] In 1899 W.S. Jones was affected by Moody's evangelistic team and persuaded that he should pray for a new experience of consecration to God. This he did, and there was an impact on Carmarthen and southwest Wales. In 1903, after the convention at Llandrindod, hesitations about 'receiving the Holy Spirit in a new way were laid to rest' and congregations were affected in Glamorganshire, Clwyd and Dyfed.[27] Roberts began his ministry holding missions with other students near Newcastle Emlyn before he felt constrained to return home to Loughor and preach in its Calvinist Methodist chapels. His approach was friendly and he would often wander up and down the aisles asking people about their spiritual state. Prayer groups were organised and Roberts told them to pray for the Spirit. Baptists and Independents heard what was happening and came to see. Roberts himself continually stressed the need to obey the Spirit. When he was asked to preach in Pontypridd he took two young women as singers and a small congregation gathered. One of the girls sang and then began to weep and the other girl did the same. When the preacher remained silent, the congregation were perplexed until they saw him weeping too. A chapel member fell to her knees and began to confess her sins and others followed. No sermon

---

25 Brown, 1986, 155.

26 Jones, 1995.

27 Jones, 1995, xvii.

had been given and the service continued beyond lunchtime and became an evening prayer meeting. Roberts was asked to remain overnight and he preached for an hour on the Monday evening.

This pattern continued as the revival spread. Roberts would be invited to preach and would sometimes do so but also often pray, or pray and weep, and, when members of the congregation would fall down, he would walk over to them and tend to them like a doctor visiting a patient. As the months of that extraordinary year passed, Roberts travelled more widely afield, particularly to north Wales. There was always criticism of various kinds and towards the end of the year Roberts was clearly becoming exhausted. When a congregation refused to respond to his pleading or his prayers, he would sometimes walk away and at others pronounce judgement on the hidden sins of his listeners. He upset church leaders by becoming unpredictable in other ways, sometimes refusing to preach at places where he had previously accepted an invitation and invoking the Spirit as his reason for changing his plans. When congregations became resistant, Roberts conveyed his overwhelming sense of the fear of God. The revival was therefore not marked by its passionate evangelistic preaching. Instead the emphasis was on the free moving of the Spirit and this was expected to lead to the public confession of sin and the proclamation of Jesus. Roberts gave little or no systematic Bible teaching although, in his preaching, he could on occasions appeal to his hearers to be 'baptised with the Spirit'.[28] What he meant by this phrase would not have satisfied Pentecostal denominations.

Azusa Street

Across the world, on the west coast of the United States, news of the Welsh revival was received with excitement. Roberts wrote three letters in 1905 in response to Frank Bartleman's (1871–1936) enquiries and in them all urged intense prayer for California. When, in 1906, revival broke out in Azusa Street (even today a poor area of Los Angeles), there were similarities with what happened in Wales. The meetings were spontaneous, unstructured and had little formal ministerial leadership. They grew out of intercessory prayer rather

[28] Jones, 1995, 134.

than from preaching. Yet there were significant differences too. W.J. Seymour (1870–1922), who led the Azusa Street mission, believed that speaking with tongues evidenced the baptism in the Holy Spirit.[29] The prayer meetings, though they focused on Christ, began to expect speaking with tongues, and such speaking with tongues, when it was reported in the *Los Angeles Times*, drew further crowds of enquirers, both sceptical and pious.[30]

In 1905 T.B. Barratt (1862–1940), a Methodist pastor of English extraction who worked in Norway, visited the east coast of the United States to raise money for his evangelistic projects. After the Azusa Street revival began he received the first issue of *The Apostolic Faith* (dated September 1906) and, on the basis of what he read, he wrote to Los Angeles and received a letter encouraging him to pray and to believe that he would be able to speak in tongues. This he did on 15 November that year, and he returned to Norway to propagate the Pentecostal message.[31]

A.A. Boddy

One of the most significant visitors to the Welsh revival was the Revd Alexander A. Boddy (1854–1930), the Anglican vicar of Sunderland. He had a longing to see a revival break out in his own parish. He invited Evan Roberts to Sunderland but Roberts stayed in Wales and so Boddy visited Wales for himself. What he saw impressed him but it may also have showed him how little impact revival phenomena had on denominational structures. The Welsh churches continued much as before when the revival waves had passed, although all of them had enjoyed increased attendance. There is disagreement about whether speaking in tongues occurred but, whether it did or not, this was not central to what happened.[32]

Three years later under T.B. Barratt a religious awakening occurred in Oslo, Norway, and Boddy went there also. In comparing the two he wrote:

---

[29] Bloch-Hoell, 1964, 35; Barratt, 1927, 105.

[30] Robeck, 1988, 32.

[31] Bloch-Hoell, 1964, 67.

[32] Turnbull, 1959, 18; Kay, 1989, 90; Williams, 1981, 55.

> My four days in Christiania (Oslo) can never be forgotten. I stood with Evan Roberts in Tonypandy, but have never witnessed such scenes as those in Norway.[33]

Boddy's description of his trip to Norway was published in the *Latter Rain Evangel* (February 1909) and shows that the underlying theology in each place was different. After preaching about healing:

> I asked those who had received the holy Spirit with the sign of Tongues to lay hands on me for a Baptism of the Holy Ghost. The blessed Holy Spirit came on me just then, filling me with joy, love and peace.
>
> The inflow of the blessed Holy Spirit occurred March 5, 1907, but not until Dec 2nd, nine months later, did the Lord give me the sign of the tongues. (Original capitalisation.)

Boddy's theology here is of a filling or inflowing of the Holy Spirit and of a *sign* of tongues.[34] The phrases 'holy spirit with the sign of tongues' and 'Baptism of the Holy Ghost' appear to be synonymous. In Wales, the stress was on repentance, judgement, recommitment to Christ and holiness. In Norway, although there was impassioned gospel preaching, there was also opportunity for the laying on of hands for the reception of the Holy Spirit and the gift of tongues. The theology of Norway was that the fire of the Holy Spirit would drive the church forward.[35] And, though there was no insistence that speaking with tongues always accompanied the arrival of the Holy Spirit, there was an expectation that *some* sort of manifestation would occur.

In the summer of 1907 Boddy 'had a unique opportunity to distribute thousands of copies of the pamphlet *Pentecost for England*' at Keswick.[36] Presumably the visitors to Keswick were not

---

[33] Quoted in Gee, 1967, 20.

[34] The notion of tongues as a 'sign' is found in *The Apostolic Faith* (September, 1906), 2. The author of this unsigned article was probably W.J. Seymour, in which case he was probably using either his own terminology or that of C.F. Parham, whose Bible School he had attended.

[35] Barratt, 1909, 34.

[36] Bloch-Hoell, 1964, 83.

impressed but the incident shows Boddy's determination and leadership qualities. Indeed, other influential Christian personalities attempted to dissuade Boddy from championing the Pentecostal cause. Jessie Penn-Lewis wrote a letter to him in October 1907 in which she said she could not 'be true to God without writing you in His name to say how pained and grieved' she was 'to hear of such "manifestation" being attributed to the Holy Ghost'. She went on to warn Boddy against T.B. Barratt whom she thought was likely to become paralysed. 'From all that I have heard of Pastor Barratt's physical condition, I am confirmed in my conviction. Paralysis is the only result eventually.'[37] But Boddy ignored such baleful predictions and continued to value Barratt's ministry. Barratt died in 1940 having worked indefatigably in the Pentecostal cause for the second part of his life. Moreover, Boddy visited Keswick again in 1908 to press on other visitors the claims of knowing 'experimentally the secret of victory and power'.

Sunderland Conventions (1908–14)

According to Donald Gee, the best historian of the Pentecostal movement in Britain in the first half of the twentieth century, the Whitsun Sunderland Conventions 'must occupy the supreme place in importance' in the early life of the Pentecostal movement in the British Isles.[38] These conventions were instigated, organised and publicised by Boddy and he must be given credit for shaping the British Pentecostal movement in its infancy. Sermons and discussions, published in remarkable detail in the pages of *Confidence*, showed the developing thinking of the delegates. The conventions were held in Boddy's parish and he was their dignified and respected chairman.[39] To Sunderland came many of those who were later instrumental in the founding of the Pentecostal denominations studied in this book.

[37] Penn-Lewis, letter written to Mr Boddy, October 28, 1907. The letter is kept in the Donald Gee Centre.

[38] Gee, 1967, 37.

[39] Boddy was also a good example of how to cope with opposition to Pentecostalism. Boddy wrote, 'We were spoken against, written against, shut out and banned, but we have continued to this day, and do not intend to go back' (*Confidence*, May, 1910, 104).

The ready take up of *Confidence* and the consistent support for the conventions shows that there was already a pool of Christians – perhaps numbering many thousands – who were prepared to follow holiness doctrine where they felt the Spirit was leading them. Although Boddy was a propagator of Pentecostalism through his writing and by his conventions, he did not travel round the country holding meetings. The holiness preachers a decade or two before had pursued this sort of activity.[40] Instead he demonstrated how Christians with an experience of tongues-speaking could meet together amicably to work out the implications of their new-found ability. Given the explosiveness of the American holiness scene, this was an invaluable contribution.

The best indication of the original basis for the Sunderland Convention is found in the words carried on the admission ticket to the 1908 services:

> I declare that I am in full sympathy with those who are seeking 'Pentecost' with the sign of tongues. I also undertake to accept the ruling of the Chairman.

The term '"Pentecost" with the sign of tongues' was Boddy's and shows that, at that stage, speaking in tongues was interpreted as having an evidential value. But Boddy's thinking about 'Pentecost' seems to have been modified after about 1912. In 1909 his wife wrote an article in his magazine, *Confidence*, in which she argued that tongues are 'not necessarily a convincing sign' of the baptism of the Holy Spirit. She wished instead to stress the importance of divine love. Boddy appeared to accept this position in the sense that his vision was always for a revived and renewed church rather than for new and separate Pentecostal denominations.[41] As early as 1908 he had pointed out that:

---

[40] Reader Harris is an obvious example. His Pentecostal League, though it bitterly criticised Pentecostalism for its advocacy of tongues, unintentionally prepared the way for the Pentecostal movement. 'Meetings were held regularly in many places, such as Bristol, East Croydon, Folkstone, Plymouth, Chelsea, Brixton, Sunderland, Birmingham and Leicester' (Bloch-Hoell, 1964, 82).

[41] I have argued in Kay (1998) that Boddy's eventual position was a nuanced one expressed in the title of an article 'Tongues: the Pentecostal

> One of the proofs, to this writer's mind, that the Lord is in this, His work, is that He had brought together at Sunderland Friends, Brethren, Methodists, Salvationists, Baptists, Congregationalists, and Church-folk, and they have all been one in spirit and one in trusting the precious blood. Denominationalism has melted away and the barriers disappeared as the Holy Spirit came in full possession.[42]

The programme shows such a conclusion for the 1913 Convention. It was addressed to 'the task of the Pentecostal movement' and the 'conditions of Apostolic revival'[43] which it saw as being to 'stir up the people of God' and 'restore the apostolic gifts' and preach the gospel 'as a last call of the Lord'. There was no hint here about the formation of a Pentecostal denomination. Rather the emphasis was the opposite. 'We cannot move on in this Pentecostal Movement', it was stated, 'without unity in the Body of Christ'.[44] In an editorial in 1911 Boddy had confirmed his position unambiguously: 'The Editor . . . does not feel that the Lord's leading . . . is to set up a new Church.'

W.O. Hutchinson

William Hutchinson (1864–1928), born of Primitive Methodist parents, was converted in 1881, during the preaching of C.H. Spurgeon. His faith was revived and he later became a Methodist lay preacher. Some time after 1903 he accepted water baptism by immersion as the biblical mode and transferred to the Baptist church. A little later he heard Reader Harris (1847–1909)[45] preaching a holiness message that identified the 'baptism in the Holy Spirit' with an experience of a 'clean heart' before God.

---

41 (*continued*) sign; Love: the evidence of continuance', *Confidence*, Nov 1910, 260. Whatever his position on the sign or evidential value of tongues, Boddy remained within the Anglican Church after Pentecostal denominations were formed.

42 *Confidence*, September, 1908, 5.

43 *Confidence*, April 1913, 74.

44 *Confidence*, September 1913, 183.

45 Harris was a staunch believer in British-Israelism so that it is no surprise that Hutchinson, at the end of his life, embraced the doctrine.

Essentially, Harris used 'baptism in the Spirit' to describe an experience of sanctification subsequent to conversion but without the accompaniment of speaking in tongues. Bebbington classifies Harris as an 'eradicationist' in that he appeared to believe that the crisis experience he proclaimed removed even the tendency to sin.[46] Whatever the influence of Harris on him, in 1906 Hutchinson visited the revival in south Wales and had a vision of three balls of fire above his head, the first of which he believed symbolised the gift of tongues. In 1908 he attended the Sunderland Convention and was one of those who spoke in tongues there and then, an event reported in the supplement to *Confidence*.[47] On returning to Bournemouth Hutchinson began a prayer meeting in his own home at which he laid hands on someone who immediately spoke in tongues. Hutchinson left the Baptist church, bought a piece of land and erected a hall that was opened in November 1908 as the first purpose-built Pentecostal church in Britain. It was called Emmanuel Mission Hall but changed in 1911 to become Apostolic Faith Church.[48] The new name copied the one adopted by the journal issued from Azusa Street. Presumably Hutchinson hoped that his church would do for England what Azusa Street had done for the States.

In addition to evangelism and speaking in tongues Hutchinson's early ministry featured healing and prophecy.[49] At this point Hutchinson's teachings were very similar to those of other proto-Pentecostals. He believed in a three-stage process of conversion, crisis sanctification and baptism in the Spirit with speaking in tongues. In 1910 he founded the periodical *Showers of Blessing* that broadcast his teachings, widened his circle of influence and began to show how a network of new Pentecostal churches were coming into existence. As well as news items of this kind the magazine carried transcriptions of prophecies that had been given in Hutchinson's congregation. This set a dangerous precedent and had the result of lifting these utterances to a position where they could not be properly evaluated.

---

46 Bebbington, 1989, 173.
47 *Confidence Supplement*, June 1908, 2.
48 Hathaway, 1996.
49 Worsfold, 1991, 36.

Missions

The Pentecostal Missionary Union (PMU) was formed in 1909 under Cecil Polhill's leadership. Missionaries who had been expelled from other missionary societies for speaking in tongues were glad of its support and Polhill, who had been one of the original 'Cambridge Seven' who went to China, wanted to see missionary work Pentecostalised. A council of between ten and fourteen members administered the PMU though Polhill, because of his social standing and his wealth, was always its most influential figure. Reference to the PMU occurred regularly in *Confidence*.

The Pentecostal outpouring at Azusa Street, in Sunderland and elsewhere across Europe and the world, was understood by the early Pentecostals as a sign that the end of the age was near. They believed that the outpouring of the Spirit should be seen as a stimulus to a huge evangelistic harvest. For this reason there was always a strong expectation that Pentecostal congregations, when they were established, would support missions and within the Pentecostal denominations from the earliest days missionaries were treated as men and women of high status. Once, however, it became apparent that speaking in tongues was unrelated to the speaking of foreign languages on the mission field, it was obviously necessary that missionary candidates should be trained and prepared for their work. In Britain two training schools, one for men founded in 1909[50] and then re-established in 1913,[51] and the other for women founded in 1910,[52] were established in London.

Despite Polhill's attempts to secure the financial viability of the PMU, he came to realise after the 1914–18 war that it would only function successfully if it were attached to denominational church structures.

---

[50] Gee, 1967, 61, explains how the first training school for men began under A. Moncur Niblock in Paddington in West London. In 1913 it was re-opened by Mr Polhill.

[51] According to *Confidence*, October 1913, front page, the number of students in attendance was small and so the men were housed in a private property in Hackney. In this sense the schools were informal.

[52] See *Confidence*, February 1910, 32, for a reference to the opening of the women's Bible School under the principalship of Mrs Crisp on 30 January, 1910.

Apostolic Church

D.P. Williams (1882–1947) went to Loughor to hear Evan Roberts preach on Christmas Day, 1904. A little later Roberts came to pray for him and he fell to the floor for two hours and had a vision of Christ.[53] In 1909 Williams spoke in tongues for the first time.[54] Though a Congregationalist, he continued to meet other converts of the revival at informal prayer and house meetings, some of which became independent chapels. In 1910 Hutchinson visited Penygroes and ordained Williams as the overseer of the Penygroes assembly.[55] In 1914 at an Apostolic Faith Convention in London Williams was called to be an apostle.[56]

The influence of Hutchinson on Williams and the young Apostolic Faith Church was considerable. Hutchinson's views on the value of prophecy as a method of guiding and governing the church were largely, if not completely, accepted and his view of the role of the present-day ordination of apostles, prophets, pastors, evangelists and teachers became foundational to the Apostolic Faith Church's understanding of itself. Men would be called to particular ministries and apostles and prophets might function together in pairs. Prophetic utterances were written down, often for publication, and had a profound effect on the way people or congregations made major decisions.

However, a defection from Hutchinson's authority appears to have been prompted by basic disagreements of another kind: the contentious issues of church government, property and accountability. In January 1916 the majority of the Welsh assemblies formally severed their relationship with the Bournemouth parent body to form the nucleus of the Apostolic Church. From April 1916 the Apostolic Church published its magazine *Riches of Grace* and the first edition named 19 assemblies in Wales. In August of that year the first of the annual conventions at Penygroes in Carmarthenshire, Wales, was held. After the Apostolics in Wales had broken free of Hutchinson, his theological views became

[53] Worsfold, 1991, 12.

[54] Turnbull, 1963, 33, 34.

[55] Worsfold, 1991, 22.

[56] Worsfold, 1991, 56.

increasingly divergent from those of the majority of Pentecostals and evangelicals and the denomination he had founded shrunk to a tiny remnant.

Meanwhile the Apostolic Church went from strength to strength, often by accepting existing congregations which had become Pentecostal in experience and doctrine. In 1919 the Burning Bush Assembly, Glasgow, led by Andrew Turnbull (1872–1937) and the Apostolic Church, Hereford, led by Edgar Frank Hodges (1872–1949) also joined. Growth took place as existing churches banded together under Apostolic leadership and teaching. In 1920 an assembly in Belfast led by Pastor B. Fisher joined the Church. In 1922 at the Easter convention in Bradford the Apostolic Church of God led by Pastor H.V. Chanter (1890–1966) also joined the Church. This church had been formed in 1917 by a group that left Mr Smith Wigglesworth's Bowland Street Mission over the issue of directive prophecy. They had eight assemblies by 1922.

It made sense for the exact doctrines of the Apostolic Church to be clarified and so, in 1920, its eleven tenets of faith were published in English (previously they had been in Welsh). These tenets show that, in addition to evangelical belief in the inspiration and authority of scripture, in the Trinity and the atonement, church government is 'by apostles, prophets, evangelists, pastors, teachers, elders and deacons'. Belief is also expressed in the baptism of the Holy Spirit 'with signs following' and the 'nine gifts of the Holy Spirit', the possibility of falling from grace and the obligatory nature of tithes and offerings.

Organisationally the Church dealt with growth by dividing itself into sections, each under an apostle. In 1922 representatives agreed that the Apostolic Missionary Movement should be formed and that this would function as a visible unity in four sections (around Glasgow, Bradford, Hereford and Penygroes). The missionary headquarters would be in Bradford. D.P. Williams was appointed president of the Missionary Council. The first (of many) missionaries were sent in 1922 to Argentina and one of the first converts was Mr Luis Palau (senior) who was later the father of the internationally known evangelist. By 1934 these four sections had become seven and in 1937, at a meeting in Bradford, a new constitution was adopted which brought the churches into one framework under a General

Council of Apostles and Prophets who were to meet twice a year. Within the UK the Church was divided into twelve areas and an Overseas Constitution was included for the benefit of the expanding Church abroad. The Bible College at Penygroes was started in 1933 and continues to train students for Apostolic ministry. Recent changes have brought degree courses onto the college's curriculum.

Once the 1937 constitution had been agreed, committees and procedures tended to multiply and spiritual and numerical growth slowed down. When the Latter Rain revival broke out in Canada in 1948, its effects were felt in the UK. The revivalists emphasised decentralisation of finance and property and insisted upon the autonomy of each local assembly.[57] Though the Apostolic leadership in the UK reaffirmed its acceptance of Apostolic beliefs and principles, various ministers left to join the new movement. Subsequently, the constitution was revised by simplification in 1961 and again in 1985 and 1987 and the administrative offices combined and moved to Swansea. According to 1995 figures there are 116 Apostolic churches and 5,500 attenders in the UK.[58]

Elim

George Jeffreys (1889–1962) was converted in November 1904 during the early days of the Welsh revival and, after being baptised in the Holy Spirit with speaking in tongues, probably in 1911, and training under Thomas Myerscough in Preston, was 'set apart for ministry' at an Independent Apostolic Church at Maesteg in 1912.[59] Hathaway suggests that Jeffreys may have been baptised in the Spirit in Bournemouth under Hutchinson's ministry and that he later was at pains to conceal this because of Hutchinson's eccentric doctrinal

---

[57] Riss, 1988, 112f.

[58] Brierley, 1998, table 9.12.2.

[59] Jeffreys' ordination certification, dated 18 July 1917, says he was 'set apart for the regular work of the ministry by the Independent Apostolic Church known as Emmanuel Christ Church in the town of Maesteg . . . on the thirteenth day of November in the year of our Lord one thousand nine hundred and twelve'. Jeffreys' second or formal ordination, and the one to which he later referred, took place at the hands of Moelfryn Morgan, a Welsh Congregational minister.

position and the hostility evoked by it among other Pentecostals.[60] Whether or not this was so, it is clear that Jeffreys' gifts as an evangelist were soon recognised. After attending the Thomas Myerscough's Bible School in Preston (where his fellow students included E.J. Phillips and W.F.P. Burton), he was invited by A.A. Boddy to speak at the Sunderland Convention in 1913 and stayed on to preach in the parish. This led to an invitation to preach in Ireland and, by 1915, Jeffreys had formed the Elim Evangelistic Band, a group of preachers who campaigned in Ulster during the 1914–18 war. The first Elim church was established in Belfast in 1916. In 1918 the Elim Evangelistic Band was combined with Elim Churches and Elim Missions to form the Elim Pentecostal Alliance.[61] The first church in England was formed in 1921.

From 1925 to 1934 Jeffreys preached up and down mainland Britain and everywhere he went there were huge crowds, records of healings, conversions, baptisms in the Spirit and the establishment of new churches. In 1927 on Easter Monday, and for several successive years, Jeffreys hired the Royal Albert Hall in London and held a massed rally, baptising 1000 people in 1928 and drawing members of Elim churches into a sense of community and unity.[62] Initially Elim was set up as a revivalist agency with ecumenical intentions towards other free churches and evangelicals.[63] As the campaigns continued, new converts began to look for places to worship that fostered the revival atmosphere and it was inevitable that new Elim churches would become their natural home. The revivalist agency began to turn into a denomination. In the view of E.C.W. Boulton, then an Elim minister and writing around 1928, the need for stability within the burgeoning Pentecostal movement in Britain was imperative: many people who had left one form of Christianity to welcome Pentecostalism were inclined to 'go from luke-warmness to lawlessness' in one radical step. By setting up denominational discipline and structures Christian liberty could be harnessed for evangelistic ends.[64] In Wilson's more sociologically

---

[60] Hathaway, 1998, 10.

[61] Boulton, 1928, 41.

[62] Cartwright, 1999.

[63] Wilson, 1961, 35.

[64] Boulton, 1928 (revised by Cartwright, 1999, 21).

attuned view, the process of bureaucratic organisation was a behind the scenes activity of which Jeffreys was at first largely unaware. He knew that the *Elim Evangel* (started in 1919) reported on his stream of campaigns and was sold in the churches. He was aware of the work of the publishing house and the administration at the headquarters building at Clapham in south London, but he probably did not realise just how fundamental the office work was. A council to hold trust property had been formed and its members included Jeffreys and his colleague E.J. Phillips (1893–1973), across whose desk ran most of the important lines of communication within the young denomination.

When the prospect of joining with the Assemblies of God (see below) came to nothing, denominational rivalry was bound to arise even if Pentecostal leaders were friends with each other and agreed on most points of doctrine. Elim's distinctive form of church government was never going to appeal to the churches of Assemblies of God. As Donald Gee pointed out:

> The majority of Elim assemblies came into existence through the instrumentality of one man's spiritual gifts and looked to one personality as their founder. To them, therefore, a unified form of central government was natural, logical, acceptable and successful . . . the Assemblies of God . . . originated with scores[65] of entirely independent assemblies agreeing to co-operate, that had grown up through long years under the utmost variety of individual leadership and expressed many sincere but diverse views in church government.[66]

The centralisation of the movement could be seen at one level in the huge Easter conventions at the Royal Albert Hall and in the Christmas addresses published in the *Evangel* each year. George Jeffreys was in charge of both. At another level the centralisation was legal and constitutional. A national conference of ministers met annually from 1933 onwards and discussed Elim organisation without having any right to inaugurate changes. Power lay with Jeffreys and Phillips.[67] In 1934 Jeffreys drew up a constitution that circumscribed his authority

---

[65] Boddy estimated that there were at least fifty Pentecostal centres as early as 1908. *Confidence*, November 1908, 9.

[66] Gee, 1967, 130.

[67] Hathaway, 1998, 19.

while protecting his leadership of the work. He became President of the Executive Council for life and was allowed to nominate three of its other eight members. In other words, he and his nominees amounted to just under half the Executive Council and, since the Council controlled the *Evangel*, set the salaries of ministers, appointed and dismissed ministers and was able to make binding rules for the whole movement, Jeffreys appeared to have set down formally and in writing the extent of his enormous influence.

Yet, in another sense he was restricted. He could not command the majority of the Executive Council and this became crucial in the following years. Jeffreys had accepted the British Israelism (BI) theory from about 1920 onwards. The theory explained the power and prominence of the British Empire and the British peoples by identifying them with the ten lost tribes of Israel. The Old Testament blessing on Israel was, it was believed, to be found on Britain and its peoples and on many Americans, since they were descended from British colonists. By accepting the theory, Jeffreys altered his perception of the role of biblical prophecy and endangered his relationships with other evangelical Christians and Pentecostals.[68] The 1933 ministerial conference discussed the issue, but after a lengthy debate only 13 ministers out of 78 supported the view and a decision was taken to ban any BI preaching in centrally-governed Elim churches. Hathaway interprets Jeffreys' subsequent behaviour as being motivated by attempts to get round the ban.[69] When the Executive Council failed to stand against the conference decision, Jeffreys spent time preaching in locally-governed churches where the ban did not apply.

Jeffreys' character is difficult to fathom. He was a shy man and during the busiest and most successful period of his ministry he was protected by the Revival Party who prevented anyone else drawing close to him.[70] The evidence that he could become involved in

---

[68] Numerous refutations of the theory have been written (e.g. C Palmer, *British-Israelism*, London, Victory Press, 1942), but the *Elim Evangel* did not mention the matter till Palmer's book was published. Since the dissolution of the British Empire BI's attractiveness has practically vanished.

[69] Hathaway, 1998, 23.

[70] The Revival Party included Albert Edsor, his pianist, driver and later secretary, Robert Darragh, his song leader and James McWhirter.

protracted personal arguments, however, is indisputable. From 1925 onwards Jeffreys found contact with his brother, Stephen, painful and the two parted company shortly afterwards. Stephen worked as an evangelist in the Assemblies of God while George continued building up Elim.[71] George's most prolonged personal clash came, according to Hudson's detailed analysis, with E.J. Phillips, a brilliant debater and dedicated administrator. Their disagreement included the issue of church government, and the churches especially implicated in their dispute were those in Ireland, where Elim had begun but where the need for reform seemed greatest. But the dispute also focused on BI. Hudson suggests that Jeffreys and Phillips reacted in similar ways to both issues. Phillips wanted to leave the Irish churches unreformed; Jeffreys believed that he knew what the churches really wanted and that reform was a necessity. Phillips wanted to leave Pentecostal doctrine where it was; Jeffreys wanted to move in the direction of BI, even at the cost of estranging other Pentecostals.

In a letter to Phillips after a rare meeting between the two men in January 1939, Jeffreys had written:

> I am not conscious of the failure you believe I am suffering from, viz. my unwillingness to give up my power . . . if my memory serves me right, you are the first friend in twenty-five years to acquaint me of that failure . . . I honestly believed that you considered the BI question to be the real cause of the trouble between us. It was said that my Local Government[72] scheme was formed to propagate BI; my proposal at the last Ministerial Conference was a back door through which I intended to bring BI into the Movement, and most unfair of all, my offer to give up Sole Trusteeship was a bribe to bring in BI through lay representation.[73]

---

[71] Hudson, 1999, *passim*.

[72] This was the scheme Jeffreys formed to democratise the churches by removing a measure of control from the central Elim authorities and passing it over to local congregations.

[73] Letter, Jeffreys to Phillips, 18 January 1939; cited by Hudson, 1999. Wilson, 1961, 47 makes essentially the same point. 'The veto on British-Israelism may in itself have been sufficient to prompt Jeffreys to seek a rather looser framework and free himself from the administrative clique.'

The letter reveals that Phillips had told Jeffreys that the real issue between the two men was not the doctrinal one of BI, though that was the apparent cause of friction, but it stemmed from Phillips' perception that Jeffreys needed a power base in Elim and would refuse to relinquish it.

Tension and disagreement between Jeffreys and the Executive Council surfaced in the next few years. Ostensibly this was caused by the undemocratic government that prevailed in most churches. While many congregations had bought the buildings where they worshipped by sacrificial giving, the Executive held the title to these properties centrally. Moreover, when the annual conference met, lay members were excluded. Deacons and elders, who contributed to the success of local churches, had no national voice in the direction and running of the whole movement. Jeffreys attempted to democratise the ownership of buildings so that the people who paid for them controlled them and he also tried to widen the basis for conference membership. These aims, praiseworthy though they were, would have also served the cause of BI, since the tight control on what went on in churches would have been relaxed by the devolution of decisive powers to local congregations.[74]

Matters came to a head in 1939 when Jeffreys wrote to ministers before their annual conference repeating his intention of relinquishing the Presidency and urging further reforms, including the establishment of district presbyteries and model trust deeds for each church. Though the conference made concessions, these were insufficient to prevent Jeffreys' resignation. Later the conference offered Jeffreys the post of Moderator and of Principal of the Bible College, but these were insufficient to retain his services. He had formed the World Revival Crusade as a vehicle for his continuing ministry and left Elim forever.[75] Hudson summarises the issue like this:

> The split was ostensibly about Jeffreys' desire to allow greater autonomy for the local churches but it was fuelled by the whole British Israel

[74] Edsor, 1989, lists and describes Jeffreys' continuing crusade ministry in the 1950s. Jeffreys formed the Bible Pattern Church Fellowship in 1940. It never grew large and was later dissolved.

[75] Hudson, 1999, section 3.3.

question and the formation of the World Revival Crusade in 1936[76] which was seen to be an alternative to the Movement. It was aggravated by the absence of Phillips from the work through sickness when Jeffreys discovered the financial situation of the Movement, but ultimately it was about a lack of trust between the charismatic leader of an evangelistic Movement and the administrative and pastoral staff who were attempting to sustain a large number of new churches.[77]

After Jeffreys' departure the whole Executive Council was elected annually by the general conference, a body that included some lay representatives. The three nominees chosen by Jeffreys were dropped. Despite the loss of its gifted leader Elim continued to grow, though only gradually in the 1940s and 1950s. New churches that were added in the period immediately after 1935 were often small and unable to contribute a surplus, as the big campaign-founded churches could do, to general funds. The rapid expansion in the heyday of Jeffreys' crusading zeal was never recaptured.[78] Constitutional changes in the late 1930s and 1940s had had little effect on the Executive's power. According to Wilson there were thirteen official committees in Elim in 1954 and the Executive had a majority on ten of them. E.J. Phillips who represented continuity through all these changes eventually retired in 1957, though he lived on till 1973.

In the 1960s Elim, like other Pentecostal denominations, was affected by the charismatic movement. Worship styles became freer and ethical rigorism tended to relax. In the 1970s when the new churches appeared, Elim was affected again.[79] After an important annual conference in 1981 (that was reconvened to continue unfinished business at Southport) a prophecy was given about the

---

[76] Cartwright, personal communication, gives the date of its formation as 1935. By June of that year funds totalling £3,818 were available for the new Crusade movement.

[77] Hudson, 1999, section 3.3.

[78] Jeffreys himself continued to work evangelistically and founded the Bible Pattern Church Fellowship in Nottingham at the end of 1940.

[79] Jackson, 1999. The term is used to refer to restorationist churches that had previously been called house churches. Since these groups have outgrown houses, new churches is a better designation.

need to repent over money, morals and party spirit. From 1982 onwards the notion of every member ministry was expanded and personal relationships were strengthened. After a trial in Scotland, Region Superintendents were introduced in England in 1987. At this Conference, too, the General Secretary became the General Superintendent, and the change in title spoke of a new, spiritual function. But, despite Conference decisions, changes at grass roots level did not always take place.[80] Nevertheless, increasingly an emphasis on the role of ministry gifts rather than constitutional office was accepted as the means by which congregational life and growth might be secured. However, ministers continued to be sent by headquarters to churches and there is still a tension, perhaps a creative tension, between constitution and charisma. Modernisation in the 1990s has resulted in a revision of the Fundamental Truths and in the introduction of a non-residential Church Training Programme (1990) and of graduate and post-graduate courses at Regents Theological College, Nantwich. At present there are 577 Elim assemblies in the UK with a membership of 62,000.[81]

Assemblies of God

Evidence from the autobiographies of Nelson Parr (1886–1976) and John Carter (1893–1981) confirms that, before the formation of Pentecostal denominations, there was considerably fluidity in the terminology applied to experiences of the Holy Spirit. Parr, for instance, speaks of a 'cleansing baptism' and a 'baptism of fire' that he had heard about after he began attending prayer meetings in 1908. During a visit to Keswick he went forward to receive 'the gift of the Holy Spirit' but the experience left him unsatisfied. After hearing about speaking in tongues in North America, he attended the Sunderland Convention, probably in 1910 and certainly in 1911.[82] His search for spiritual experience intensified. On Christmas Day 1910 he found what he was looking for and spoke in tongues

---

[80] Jackson, 1999.

[81] Brierley, 1998, table 9.12.5.

[82] Carter mentioned this in a sermon preached at the Assemblies of God General Conference in 1979.

for several hours during and after the morning service. Carter, with his brother Howard (1891–1971), attended the Convention a little later in 1912, though he did not speak in tongues himself till about 1914.[83] In 1919 Carter went for two years to Belfast to join the Jeffreys' Evangelistic Band.

While the Sunderland Convention largely resisted the idea of separate Pentecostal denominations and too sharp demarcations of the baptism of the Holy Spirit, Parr, by contrast, moved in a direction of greater rigour. He was almost certainly influenced by the debates taking place in the United States after the formation there of Assemblies of God in 1914,[84] and was also, probably, conscious of the pressure for a new denomination that came either from Hutchinson's *Showers of Blessing* or from the proselytising of the Apostolics.

Apart from his natural tendency for rigour, Parr would have been aware of the financial needs of Pentecostal missionaries. On his first furlough from the Congo in 1922, W.F.P. Burton (1886–1971) attempted to bring together many of the scattered assemblies into a loose federation, partly for the purpose of providing support for missionaries. This gave rise to the Sheffield Conference and the setting up of a Provisional Council 'for the advice and assistance' of congregations in the UK and Ireland. Parr sent out a circular letter in November 1923 inviting leaders to 'establish a union of Assemblies' and giving his reasons for association. These were to: '(1) persevere the testimony to the full gospel, including the baptism of the Spirit and to save the work from false teaching; (2) strengthen bonds and create a fuller degree of cooperation; (3) cooperate in evangelistic and missionary work; (4) present a united witness to outsiders; (5) exercise discipline over the disorderly; (6) save the assemblies from falling into unscriptural organisations'. Parr also knew that some Pentecostal ministers had suffered imprisonment for conscientious objection in the 1914–18 war. By writing pacifism into the rationale of the new body, he was able to articulate the predominant Pentecostal attitude towards war and, at the same

---

[83] Carter, 1979.

[84] I deduce this from the similarity between the wording of the eventual Fundamental Truths of British Assemblies of God and of those adopted by American Assemblies of God some ten years earlier.

time, prepare the ground for exemption from military service for participant ministers in any future conflict.[85]

The letter resulted in a gathering at Aston, Birmingham, in February 1924. Fourteen people met and a number of others were unable to be present owing to a railway strike. Parr was elected Chairman that day and assured those present that 'the autonomy of the local assembly would be strictly observed'. The union of assemblies that was envisaged would operate at three levels. First, assemblies would adhere to the same Fundamental Truths. Second, assemblies should maintain fellowship through District Presbyteries. Third, a General Presbytery would be set up composed of all local pastors or elders.

The Fundamental Truths included reference to 'the Baptism in the Holy Spirit, the initial evidence of which is speaking with other tongues' and 'the gifts of the Holy Spirit and the offices as recorded in the New Testament'.[86] 'Pentecost with the sign of tongues' was therefore written into the foundation documents of British Assemblies of God, thereby effectively adopting the early position of Boddy.

A second meeting was held in Highbury, London, in May 1924 with eighty people present. During the first day a letter was received from the Elim leaders who had been excluded because their centralisation was greater than the Assemblies of God leaders had in mind. When the Elim representatives arrived on the second day, E.J. Phillips suggested that all the Pentecostals represented at the meeting should work together and that Elim, whose crusading success under George Jeffreys was already evident, should provide the evangelistic arm of the combined work. The idea would have brought powerful personalities into close proximity and friction would have been inevitable. It was probably Howard Carter who expressed the view that two independent groups of churches would

---

[85] Parr, 1972, 26–27.

[86] The statement of Fundamental Truths as originally proposed at Sheffield were virtually identical to those of the Elim Evangelistic Band. These were taken over and used as the main basis for Assemblies of God. The only change of substance was the introduction of wording taken from American Assemblies of God on the 'initial evidence'. I am grateful to Desmond Cartwright for this information.

better safeguard the survival of Pentecostalism than one larger one. Thirty-seven assemblies in England and one in Belfast joined immediately and thirty-eight from Wales and Monmouth joined in August, accepting the pattern that had been worked out at the Aston meeting. The Assemblies of God became established. The Elim ministers continued on their own, though they did not make the final decision till later in the year after Jeffreys had been to the USA and had been unimpressed with the condition of the Assemblies of God congregations he had seen over there.[87]

At the end of 1925 several senior members of the Pentecostal Missionary Union (PMU) resigned. The remaining members, who were by now representatives of Assemblies of God, took responsibility for the whole enterprise, and the two bodies merged. This provided Assemblies of God with a ready-made missionary work. Howard Carter, who had been in charge of the PMU Bible School at Hampstead, London since February 1921, was joined there by his brother John, C.L. Parker (sometime Fellow of University College, Oxford), T.J. Jones and Harold Horton. Though the school maintained its independence, it served the assemblies and taught the distinctive doctrines of Assemblies of God. After 1950 the school became the official Assemblies of God college (owned by the denomination) and Donald Gee became its first Principal. From about the 1980s the college began to enter its students for public examinations and in the 1990s honours degrees were offered. Although the college was interdenominational in outlook, it provided an acceptable place where future Assemblies of God pastors could receive academic and pastoral training.

The number of assemblies increased from 140 in 1927 to 200 in 1929. By 1933 there were 250; in 1939, 350. In 1946 there were 403 assemblies and in 1957 there were 506.

The 1930s and 1950s were periods of steady growth. The war years put a stop to campaigning but were rewarded by a more than usual sense of unity among ministers. By the 1960s, when the charismatic movement burst on the scene, Assemblies of God was in

---

87 Hathaway, 1998, 16. American Assemblies of God had only just escaped a major religious division over 'the new issue' and were, in any case, unimpressive compared with the work of Aimee Semple McPherson's in Los Angeles, which Jeffreys knew.

need of 'Another Springtime' (the title of a sermon preached at the General Conference by Donald Gee in 1960), and many attempts were made to secure this, mainly by reforming the intricate and increasingly complex constitution.

In the 1970s tensions between reformers and conservatives led, at the end of the 1980s, to a simplified constitution, which also appeared to encroach on local church autonomy since it gave authority to Regional and National Superintendents. A policy of regionalisation grouped congregations together into larger blocks and also allowed for the delegation of business matters to smaller subgroups of ministers. The result of these moves was to centralise aspects of the spiritual leadership of the Assemblies of God, and some ministers, particular older ones, objected to this. To add to these uncertainties, several large assemblies left the denomination and joined forces with the new churches in the charismatic movement.

In the 1990s efforts to combine reforms with an emphasis on church planting were partly successful but it was difficult to accelerate growth at home while maintaining overseas efforts. Shortages of money were both a symptom and a cause of these strains.

In the late 1990s attempts were made to ensure that efforts and departmental structures, particularly in education, training and church planting, were co-ordinated, and ambitious targets for growth were set. At the same time, expansion of facilities at the college at Mattersey permitted a full range of degree courses to be offered for ministers in training and for postgraduate courses to be inaugurated. The General Superintendency combined with a National Leadership Team, a body comprising Regional Superintendents and heads of departments, has the potential to provide both spiritual and practical leadership while allowing individual ministries to operate productively at local level. At present there are 646 assemblies with 818 ministers and a membership of 54,000.[88]

The Church of God

Both Conn and Synan tell the story of the Church of God's formation and growth, the first from the viewpoint of an adherent and the

[88] Brierley, 1998, table 9.12.3.

second from that of a friendly, but more critical, observer.[89] The origins of the church are found in the holiness movements that made an impact on the American religious scene at the end of the nineteenth century. When holiness preaching was amalgamated with Methodist doctrine, there was a ready-made framework for belief in a 'second work of grace', a crisis of sanctification that ushered the believer into a new realm of life. Indeed, without much difficulty a 'third work of grace' could be added to the second so that, in addition to sanctification, believers could be directed to look for a spiritual baptism. The 'fire baptised' way propagated by proto-Pentecostal preachers resulted in emotional revivalist scenes in the American Mid-West, and there were scattered reports of speaking in tongues. Such preaching provoked controversy and sometimes violence, both because of the undignified behaviour often accompanying it and because Christians who had not passed through such experiences were made to feel deficient in their faith.

With hindsight it is possible to see that what holiness preachers had done was enough to prepare the ground for more stable and biblically based churches to be established. In 1907 the Church of God (Cleveland, Tennessee) was officially formed, though its name had been in use since 1886.[90] After early troubles it grew rapidly through good organisation and steady leadership from the 1920s onward, first in the USA and then by missionary work in over 155 countries of the world, including the Caribbean. It currently has a membership of 5.7 million, served by 29,500 ministers in 29,141 congregations.

It was from the Caribbean that the Church of God was carried to Britain.[91] Among the first West Indian immigrants in the 1950s were Church of God members, some of whom came to London for the third World Pentecostal Conference which was held in 1952. These black Pentecostals received a cold reception from

---

[89] Conn, 1977, and Synan 1997. Dupree, 1996, provides extensive information on African-American holiness and is a valuable source relating early Pentecostal and pre-Pentecostal movements to their eventual denominational manifestations.

[90] Conn, 1988, 198.

[91] I am grateful to Revd Dr Douglas LeRoy of the Church of God for much of the information in this and the following paragraphs.

British churches. Among them was Oliver Lyseight (b. 1919), who grew up in the rural poverty of Jamaica tending animals and cultivating banana and sugar cane plantations. On Sundays he attended the Methodist church. In 1939 he made a commitment to Christ and, after a brief spell working in the USA, returned to pastor his first congregation within the Church of God in 1942. After an economically disastrous hurricane hit Jamaica in 1951, he sailed to Britain in the autumn of that year. He experienced racial discrimination as he looked for accommodation and a job. Whenever he could he preached at weekends, and at an Assemblies of God congregation in 1952 he heard an interpretation of tongues promising that God was going to work among the West Indians.

In his own account Lyseight remembered:

> We ministered to thousands of people . . . we still were not satisfied to be ministering only to the native population, while some of our own people were drifting away and backsliding as they poured into the country as strangers, unaccustomed to the ways of Britain . . . we saw their plight, and then decided to start up the work – just to have fellowship and somewhere to worship – where our people from the Caribbean could attend freely and feel welcome; we suffered many adversities.[92]

In 1953 A.D. Brown and G.S. Peddie joined Lyseight and they conducted a campaign based at the YMCA hall in Wolverhampton which led to the founding of their first congregation. By 1955 they had contacted the Church of God and been visited by its Foreign Missions Secretary, Paul Walker. By 1957 there were, according to a report in the *Church of God Evangel* (October 1957), 150 members in five churches, with Handsworth being the largest.[93] A year earlier Elim had given serious consideration to formal affiliation with the Church of God in the United States, but the necessary 75 per cent vote in favour had not quite been attained at the Conference in October. Similar consideration was given at the British Pentecostal Fellowship in 1956 where there were hopes – eventually frustrated –

---

[92] Lyseight, 1995, 35, 36.

[93] I am grateful to Desmond Cartwright for this information.

that black congregations might be incorporated within the existing British Pentecostal denominations.[94]

Once these attempts at formal assimilation had come to nothing, it was evident that the Church of God would continue its separate development. Although there were early internal rivalries and disputes over ownership of buildings, by 1978 they had bought or erected 35 church buildings and six manses, divided the country up into several districts with churches in each, set up committees for overseeing separate aspects of the work and established a foundation of ministry and organisation that could support further growth.

Yet, having started these new congregations, Lyseight and his fellow workers were unable to register under their own church name because the name had been previously registered by a 'Jesus only' group. Consequently the Church of God in Britain is called the New Testament Church of God but this name does not indicate separateness of practice or doctrine. The same fundamental truths are adopted throughout the world by all Church of God congregations and its members all have the right to attend the Church's General Assembly every two years. Moreover, all ministers receive basically the same training wherever in the world they work. Commonality is further supported by asking all ministers throughout the world to make use of the same credential-giving council. By this means Church of God doctrine and polity remain recognisably uniform, although minor differences sensitive to cultural contexts are acceptable.

According to Hollenweger the Church of God, once notable for its ethical rigorism, is now more relaxed in its stance towards fashion and leisure pursuits but this change, as we have seen, is a logical outcome of vast geographical expansion.[95] The Church of God's pacifism has also been modified, though not its fundamentalist position on the Bible or evolution. Its acceptance of speaking with tongues as the initial evidence of the baptism of the Holy Spirit and the premillennial return of Christ are held in common with other Pentecostals, though the Church of God also believes that the baptism of the Holy Ghost is 'subsequent to a clean heart' and that

---

[94] Unpublished paper, 'Side Streams', by Desmond Cartwright.

[95] Hollenweger, 1972, 50.

feet washing is an ordinance to be observed at the pastor's discretion in a service separate to Holy Communion.

Unlike other Pentecostal groups, the Church of God places its ministers into one of three ranks of ministry. The lowest is that of an *exhorter* who is given the right to preach; above this is the *licensed minister* who has the right to pastor, marry, serve Communion and baptise; above this, and after at least five years of service as a licensed minister, is an *ordained minister* who functions more like a traditional bishop. Women may be licensed but not ordained and this means that women can oversee local churches although they cannot become the national or local overseers. The UK has about 19 female licensed ministers.

Recognition of all three ranks of ministry occurs within a local church setting although credentials are often presented at national gatherings. The point of this procedure is to stress the relationship between a minister and a congregation. Only if a congregation recognises a person's ministry can he or she proceed to wider levels of denominational recognition. So, in order to become an exhorter it is necessary for the licensed minister to recognise the faithfulness and lifestyle of the possible candidate and also for this candidate to be accepted by the congregation. After recognition there is a period of training that usually takes place on a part-time basis and culminates in a written examination that is followed by an interview to probe matters raised by the examination. Each level of ministry is entered in the same way and with a similar training and examination system.

Each congregation is expected to take financial care of its minister and its facilities and then to contribute 10 per cent of tithes (not offerings) to the National Office. The National Office then contributes 10 per cent of its finances to the European Office. The European Office then contributes 10 per cent of its money to the International Office and, in this way, there is a sense of belonging and different levels of the Church of God are made interdependent.

At a national level, the Church of God ensures coherence by arranging an annual National Convention for preaching and teaching and this is complemented by a National Ministers Meeting where business is conducted, and by a Ministers and Workers Seminar. As a result of these arrangements ministers throughout Britain meet together at least three times a year. Planning and strategy are the responsibility of the National Overseers and in England and Wales the National Overseer is voted into office every four years. He is supported by an Executive Council of ten men to plan strategy, set the budget, purchase properties and ensure spiritual progress.

On alternate years the National Overseer and Executive go to the General Assembly in the USA or to the European Assembly. Because ordinary church members are entitled to vote at it the General Assembly is the largest deliberative body in the world. At San Antonio in 1998, for instance, 30–40,000 people were present and took part in debate and voted on agenda items using an electronic voting system. Prior to the Assembly itself, 6,500 ordained ministers met for several days to arrange the agenda.

The European Assembly has about 3,000 churches and 592,000 members and the Assembly itself runs to about 1000–1500 people who are delegates rather than representatives. This means attendance is not a right and that the people who attend are selected by the national churches. The European Assembly can and does make recommendations to the National Assembly. For example the wearing of jewellery was not acceptable to the original holiness tradition within the USA but is much more acceptable in Europe and Africa. As a consequence the wearing of jewellery in African and European Church of God congregations is permitted and the traditional ban became a 'guideline' rather than a 'teaching'. Guidelines are optionally observed by members while teachings are compulsory. A similar distinction might occur over the wearing of head coverings that are not acceptable in the United States but are seen as necessary within an Afro-Caribbean context or cultural setting. In Britain the church has about 20,000 members in England and Wales and 122 congregations in England. While it is predominantly a black church in England and Wales, this is not the case worldwide.

Moreover, despite its holiness guidelines, the church is clear that it is not legalistic. The church intends that individuals should be free to 'work out their own salvation' under scriptural principles. A parallel variety is seen in the openness of the church to all styles of worship, whether these are traditional, contemporary or charismatic. Worship is seen as defining a relationship with God and, because a communal experience of a group of people depends on their culture and the mix of personalities within the group, different styles emerge.

2

Denominational Problems

Overview

This chapter outlines problems that face Pentecostal ministers and their congregations. It shows that within the UK the growth and impact of Pentecostal churches has a downside. Some Pentecostal churches are in decline and some ministers face financial hardship. Many are worried about the future of their denomination. In general the Elim ministers present the healthiest evaluation of their denomination and the Apostolic ministers the least healthy. By introducing the themes of decline and concern here, and by referring to them later when the issues of burnout are addressed, the sacrifices of Pentecostal ministers will become apparent and the tendency to triumphalism be put in perspective.

Historical perspective

The rapid growth of Pentecostal churches has been associated with a variety of problems. In some instances these problems, paradoxically, have fostered growth and in others they have been as a consequence of growth. Where a congregation has *split*, for instance, though this has been painful for the members involved, two healthy congregations have sometimes emerged where previously there was only one. In other instances, congregations have mushroomed rapidly and controversy has erupted over points of doctrine or behaviour. If young people in large numbers become members of an established congregation there are likely to be disagreements over apparently trivial matters like the wearing of modern fashion accessories or the style of music used in worship. Young people tend to dress more provocatively than older people and to prefer more expressive music closer to the norms of the secular music industry. Dissension over *moral norms* also occurs when there are generational differences. *Doctrinal dissension* can likewise be found in Pentecostal churches, either between a minister and congregation or between congregational members. There must be a source of teaching which is supporting or propagating the doctrines which are at variance with each other. The arrival of tape and video ministry can be one way this happens. Well-funded parachurch evangelists or preachers are able to distribute materials at low cost and these have historically been attractive to church members who feel that the famous preachers must be closer to God than their own pastor. Alternatively, conferences and conventions can produce similar effects. Where bad feeling arises for these reasons, the life of a congregation will diminish and stagnation may occur. One reaction to such friction is an attempt to induce uniformity through constitutional change or the enforcement of a denomination's constitutional requirements. The process of *centralisation* may, negatively, be seen in this light though, positively, it may also be seen as an opportunity for visionary leadership and better collaboration, within the denomination and interdenominationally.

These problems, though they are to be found in congregations, are also reflected among ministers. Splits within congregations affect ministers deeply and examples are to be found of this in all the denominations featured here. Assemblies of God and Elim have both suffered in this way, though better supervision through local superintendence is reducing the worst aspects of such breakages. In the statistics given later in this chapter, splits represent a numerical disaster for a congregation which, within a few days, can be halved after many years have been taken to build it up. A similar effect is caused by the mass migration of congregational members from one church to a new one that opens up nearby. This is double-edged 'transfer growth': one minister's 'transfer growth' is another minister's 'transfer decline'.

Historically, there has been some interchange of members or ministers between Elim and Assemblies of God in this way.[1]

[1] Kay, 1989.

Assemblies of God and Elim solved their problems at the level of their Executive Councils which met to prevent competition of this kind. There has also been interchange between the established Pentecostal denominations and the new churches, most notably in the 1980s when the new churches were beginning to make their mark.[2] At the local level formally organised ministerial fraternal meetings can help to prevent a breakdown of relationships between congregations and some new churches and Pentecostal churches were able to ensure that transfer did not take place at least without the tacit approval of the minister whose members were leaving.[3]

Moral norms within congregations are inevitably influenced by changing moral norms within society as a whole. Two scenarios are normally played out: the moral norms of the younger generation are more lax than those of the older generation. This is observable on a Europe-wide basis where the generation born in the 1940s, having been disciplined by war and unemployment, is inclined to value duty and self-control while the post-war generation values self-expression, consumerism and freedom.[4] Alternatively, sub-groups within society clash with each other, northerners with southerners, or middle with working class. The size of most Pentecostal churches (less than 100 members) tends to produce relatively homogeneous groups of people. In ministerial terms, however, clashes over moral values are noticeable when national conferences are convened. Attempts to control moral expectations have formed the basis of debates over the use of alcohol, over clean-up television campaigns and over women's clothing, though since the late 1980s a liberal position is increasingly accepted, if not actively propagated.[5]

Doctrinal dissension within Pentecostal churches was famously illustrated by George Jeffreys' dispute with Elim.[6] The dispute

---

2 Walker, 1985.

3 This was certainly the case in Basingstoke in the 1970s where the large Community Church took a lot of members from elsewhere but relationships between ministers remained generally good because of attempts to act in the best interests of all concerned.

4 Barker, Halman and Vloet, 1992.

5 Thompson, 1997; Kay, 1989.

6 Cartwright, 1986; Wilson, 1961; Hudson, 1999.

concerned church governance and led to a painful parting of the ways after debates at the Elim conference in 1939. Similar disputes took place in the Assemblies of God when C.L. Parker argued against the accepted interpretation of judgement after death (in 1954) and when there was controversy over the best methods of evangelism, especially when it touched on the issues of free will and predestination (in 1955). Such debates involved ministers and brought into the open matters that the shared statements of fundamental beliefs could not avert. Generally speaking, statements of fundamental beliefs act like creeds, defining who is allowed in and who should be kept out, and maintaining a basis for common action and worship.[7] Consequently these statements can become more or less inclusive, more or less liberal. Statements about speaking with other tongues as the initial evidence of baptism in the Spirit are bound to be exclusive, and were designed to be so by the early Pentecostals who drew them up. Within a mobile and communicative society like modern Britain the tendency must always be to relax this exclusivity and, as the figures given below show, younger ministers are less rigorous than their older colleagues.

What do the data show?

Congregational decline

Although, historically, both the numbers of Pentecostal congregations and ministers have increased, there is evidence in table 2.1 that about 30 per cent of congregations decline in a typical year. Of

Table 2.1 *Annual congregational decline*

Number	Apostolic %	Assemblies of God %	Elim %	Church of God %	All %
none that I know of	81.8	70.9	67.4	69.8	70.5
1 to 5	16.9	22.2	21.9	25.6	21.7
6 to 10		3.2	5.6	4.7	4.0
11 to 20		2.8	3.4		2.6
21 to 30	1.3	.6	.9		.8
more than 30		.3	.6		.4

[7] Kay, 1993.

Table 2.2 *How many funeral services did you conduct last year?*

Number	AC %	AG %	Elim %	CG %	All %
less than 5	91.7	89.5	79.4	87.0	85.5
5 to 9	7.3	8.2	16.7	10.9	11.7
10 to 19	1.0	1.3	2.5	2.2	1.8
20 to 29		.8	1.4		.9
30 to 39		.3			.1

course, as we shall see, these figures are off-set by growth in other congregations, but the general picture is one of growth *and* decline, of new converts coming in at the front door and others leaving by the back door. In the majority of cases decline is fairly small, between 1 and 5 per cent, but in nearly one in ten congregations losses are higher.

Congregational decline may be as a result of the death of church members, but the figures on funerals do not suggest this. Table 2.2 shows that a small number of ministers (14.5 per cent) conducted five or more funerals in the course of a year whereas table 2.1 shows 29.5 per cent saw a decline of some kind. Clearly, though funerals may contribute to the decline of some churches, there are other factors at work as well.

Another way of looking at congregational stability is to see what the balance between baptisms and funerals is. If there are more baptisms than funerals, then, if no one leaves for other reasons, the churches should grow and here a comparison of tables 2.2 and 2.3 shows that while 14.5 per cent of ministers conducted more than five funerals, a much larger percentage (46.7 per cent) carried out more than five baptisms.

Table 2.3 *How many people did you baptise last year?*

Number	AC %	AG %	Elim %	CG %	All %
less than 5	80.0	50.0	48.1	66.7	53.3
5 to 9	11.6	19.7	21.9	15.6	19.5
10 to 19	4.2	18.1	15.3	13.3	15.2
20 to 29	4.2	6.5	8.9	4.4	7.1
30 to 39		2.8	1.9		2.0
40 to 49		1.6	.8		1.1
50 or more		1.3	3.1		1.8

Table 2.4 *How many marriage services did you conduct last year?*

Number	AC %	AG %	Elim %	CG %	All %
less than 5	97.9	92.5	88.1	95.7	91.5
5 to 9	2.1	5.9	10.8	2.2	7.3
10 to 19		1.0	.8	2.2	.9
20 to 29		.5			.2
30 to 39			.3		.1

On the other hand, nearly half of Pentecostal ministers carried out no more than five baptisms in the course of a year. Since Pentecostals baptise adults, and baptise them on confession of their faith, the number of baptisms in a year equals the number of conversions plus the number of young people who have grown up in the church and come to faith. It is an index of the vitality of a congregation. About half the congregations are unimpressive.

Marriage services are also an indication of church life (table 2.4). The figures cannot be translated into an index of church growth but they do give a general indication of the number of young people of marriageable age in churches.

When funerals, baptisms and weddings are taken together though, they show that this is not the major part of the Pentecostal minister's function. This is because Pentecostal churches are made up of a believing community and weddings and funerals are normally only carried out on behalf of regularly attending members.

Finance

During the period when these data were collected, average male earnings in the UK were approximately £260 per week take-home pay. Although the comparison is inexact because of the allowances ministers often receive, the indication is that the majority were paid significantly less than secular employees. Over two-thirds were paid below the UK average and a significant proportion (15.3 per cent) were paid roughly at the level of those receiving the state old-age pension. The financial remuneration of Pentecostal ministers is generally in the hands of their congregations rather than at a level set by a central body, and there are not usually sufficient denominational funds even to alleviate hardship. Ministers of small churches must either energetically engage in evangelism or rely on wives or families for additional finance if they are to prosper.

Personal financial stringency is also a problem for Pentecostal denominations, and it is reflected in the pay provided for Pentecostal ministers. As we shall see (in chapter 7) there is considerable variation in the level of pay afforded to Pentecostal ministers, and there are differences between denominations, but in response to the questionnaire item 'Christian ministers are usually underpaid', the agreement of ministers with this proposition ranged from 77 per cent (Assemblies of God), through 70 per cent (Apostolic) and 68 per cent (Elim) to 63 per cent (Church of God).[8] Between two-thirds and three-quarters of ministers, therefore, agreed with the statement. An indication of their general feeling of being undervalued. When the figures are looked at the other way round, almost exactly 11 per cent of Apostolic, Elim and Church of God ministers disagreed with the statement while only 5.3 per cent of Assemblies of God ministers disagreed. Clearly, Assemblies of God ministers seem to be those who feel the financial pinch most tightly. Moreover (as chapter 7 also shows), there is a relationship between levels of pay and pension provision.

Denomination

Table 2.5 shows that nearly two-fifths of Pentecostal ministers are worried about the future of their denomination. Or, putting this another way, less than half are *not* worried about this. But why should they worry? Table 2.6 gives one possible reason for this.

Centralisation can stifle local initiatives and rob ministers of the opportunity for flexible working patterns. Denominational differences are evident here but even in the best case (Assemblies of God) a meaningful proportion of ministers are concerned. Decentralisation, then, would not remove ministerial worries entirely.

Analysis of variance showed that worries about the future of one's denomination and the judgement that the denomination is too centralised are significantly different in different denominations. Elim ministers and Church of God ministers are least worried

---

8 Analysis of variance shows that the differences between denominations are significant ($F = 5.984$, $p < .000$).

Table 2.5 *I am worried about the future of my denomination*

	AC %	AG %	Elim %	CG %
Disagree	33.7	38.5	55.7	55.1
Not certain	7.6	15.2	17.0	8.2
Agree	58.7	46.3	27.3	36.7

F = 14.158, p < .000

and their level of worry is not significantly different from each other but, in the case of Elim ministers, *is* significantly different from the level found in Apostolic and Assemblies of God ministers.[9] Similarly, Assemblies of God as the least centralised of the denominations, is perceived to be such by its ministers. Their fears over centralisation are significantly lower than those of the ministers in the other three denominations.

Moral and doctrinal disagreements

Substantial minorities exist within Pentecostal denominations. This is not surprising since all the denominations have grown beyond the point where strict uniformity might be expected. Within the Anglican Church there are three quite distinct streams within each province, conservative, middle-of-the-road and liberal. Pentecostal denominations have not reached this position of diversity yet but the figures given below show that within a generation distinct conservative and liberal churchmanships could easily begin to appear.

Tables 2.7 and 2.8 show the areas where doctrinal or moral disagreements are found. A tick (✔) is placed in the column of a denomination if a fifth or more of ministers holds different views from their colleagues. These comparisons are made within, rather

Table 2.6 *I think my denomination is too centralised*

	AC %	AG %	Elim %	CG %
Disagree	38.0	68.2	56.1	50.0
Not certain	12.0	18.1	24.1	22.0
Agree	50.0	13.7	19.8	28.0

F = 19.354, p < .000

9 Showed by post-hoc contrasts (bonferroni method) not detailed here.

Table 2.7 *Doctrinal items where 20 per cent+ of ministers hold opposite viewpoints*

	Apostolic	**Assemblies of God**	**Elim**	**Church of God**
Speaking with tongues is necessary as initial evidence of the baptism in the Holy Spirit			✔	
Baptism in the Spirit can occur without speaking with tongues	✔	✔		✔
I do not believe the Bible makes the exact order of end-time events clear	✔	✔	✔	✔
I believe Christians are in daily conflict with demons	✔	✔	✔	✔
I do not believe Christians can be possessed by demons	✔	✔	✔	✔
I believe Christians will suffer during the 'great tribulation'		✔	✔	✔
Singing traditional hymns is a vital part of Christian worship		✔	✔	
All Christians should experience material prosperity		✔		✔

than between, denominations because that is where they are most relevant. So, for example, more than 20 per cent of ministers within the Elim church think that speaking with tongues is necessary as initial evidence of the baptism in the Holy Spirit or that this is not so.

Identity of belief and practice is much easier to achieve in small denominations. As they grow, there is almost bound to be a diversity of views among ministers. Yet, though it is true that there are more areas of disagreement among the two larger Pentecostal denominations, Assemblies of God and Elim, the disagreements among the other two are not far behind. Diversity is present even among relatively small groups of ministers.

The two tables show how, despite the doctrinal statements that all these denominations hold, and which they expect their ministers to uphold, there is considerable disagreement. Even on the issue of speaking with tongues, which is fundamental to Pentecostal

Table 2.8 *Social and moral items where 20 per cent+ of ministers hold opposite viewpoints*

	Apostolic	**Assemblies of God**	**Elim**	**Church of God**
Christians should not drink alcoholic beverages	✔	✔	✔	✔
Christians should not buy and sell on Sundays unless absolutely necessary		✔	✔	
Christians should not take part in social dancing	✔	✔	✔	
Christians should not take part in sporting activities on Sundays	✔	✔	✔	✔
A minister who, after ordination, divorces and remarries should not continue to serve as a minister	✔	✔	✔	✔
A minister who divorces before ordination and remarries after ordination should not continue to serve as a minister	✔	✔		✔
Women should have exactly the same opportunities for ministry as men	✔		✔	
Women should not baptise			✔	✔
Women should not be in charge of congregations	✔		✔	

churches, there is disagreement in a negative sense: three denominations have substantial minorities who believe that the baptism in the Spirit can occur without speaking with tongues. The majority of the ministers in these denominations, as the first row of table 2.7 shows, accept that speaking with tongues is the necessary initial evidence of the baptism in the Spirit. But the acceptance by large minorities that the baptism in the Spirit is possible without tongues might be thought to remove the distinctive doctrine which initially justified the separate existence of Pentecostalism. The Elim Church has never held this view in its fundamental beliefs but, nevertheless, has a substantial minority which goes *against* its *less* rigorous position.

The other issues over which there is disagreement are, for the most part, not tied into constitutional or fundamental statements.

The whole matter of demonology is fraught with potential for dissent because, by and large, the relationship between experience and doctrine is such that the evidence can be interpreted both ways. If someone has a personal problem and it improves after exorcism, then demonisation must have been the cause; and, if the problem recurs, then the demon must have returned. Yet if there was no demon, but the person being ministered to *believed* there was a demon, then improvement is an equally probable outcome. There is no obvious criterion for deciding whether a demon is present or absent. The two statements about demons produce dissent in all the denominations (see also chapter five).

Eschatological beliefs are also problematic – again because it is difficult to validate them. Where biblical texts are open to variant interpretations, and this is certainly the case with eschatology, there is bound to be disagreement. We observe the paradox that there is a diversity of views about whether the Bible makes the exact order of end-time events clear: disagreement about whether it is clear or not suggests that it is unclear! In the case of the Assemblies of God and Church of God doctrinal statements a particular interpretation was seen to be correct at the point when the denominations began and it is this which produces the degree of consensus that exists. The Elim Church has simplified its eschatology to assert only belief in the physical and visible return of Christ in glory to reign. Yet, even here, there is a 20 per cent plus proportion of dissenters. All of these denominations show a range of views on the possible suffering of Christians in a 'great tribulation' (see also chapter five). Only the Apostolics manage unity on this point.

Hymn singing concerns style of worship. The two larger denominations, Elim and Assemblies of God, contain divergent views about the value of hymns. These two groups of churches use worship songs on overhead projector slides and it is these that have largely replaced hymns. Consequently hymns have fallen out of fashion, especially among younger worshippers. In the Apostolic Church and the Church of God, there is no dissent about the value of hymns, but this suggests less variation in the style of worship in these congregations and this, in turn, may be damaging to their ability to attract youth.

The issue of prosperity will be discussed in connection with healing in chapter three. It is sufficient to point out that dogmatic views about prosperity have been advanced by ministers, especially those who are fighting against financial hardship. The potential for disagreement about this matter exists strongly in two of these denominations, Assemblies of God and the Church of God.

The four moral issues concerning alcohol, buying and selling on Sundays, social dancing and sport on Sundays have various degrees of support among these Pentecostal ministers. Alcohol is the most contentious of these issues and the surprise must be that in each denomination at least a fifth of ministers is unwilling to condone total abstention. The Assemblies of God specifically disapproves of alcohol in its constitution, though there is implicit recognition that the case for teetotalism cannot be made from the text of the New Testament. The other groups have similar anti-alcohol traditions, but these clearly do not command overwhelming support.

Evidence for traditional Sunday observance and disapproval of social dancing is also apparent but, again, substantial minorities fail to accept these views. It remains to be seen whether minorities will become majorities in the next few years and, if this is so, traditional holiness norms will be revised.

Opinions about the divorce and remarriage of ministers are similarly varied. The traditional position has been strict: no one who divorced after conversion should be allowed to hold ministerial status. Yet, in recent years, this view has been relaxed. The Apostolic Church has argued in *When the Vow Breaks* (1986) for the permissibility of the remarriage of the innocent party in any divorce case, and this has the obvious implication that a minister who is an innocent party attracts no guilt, and therefore no forfeit of ministerial status, if he or she remarries. A similar position would be likely to occur within the Assemblies of God where a Marital Status Committee has been set up to investigate and rule on tangled cases involving ministers (see chapter six for a fuller discussion).

The three items on women's ministry all show some degree of dissent, apart from within the Assemblies of God which has had a general acceptance of women preachers and pastors from its beginnings.

Tables 2.9 and 2.10 show the same data as tables 2.7 and 2.8 but, instead of using the full age range, they limit comparisons to ministers under the age of 40 to discover whether the upcoming

Table 2.9 *Doctrinal items where 20 per cent+ of ministers under 40 years hold opposite viewpoints and young/old comparisons*

	AC	AG	Elim	CG	$X^2/P<$
Speaking with tongues is necessary as initial evidence of the baptism in the Holy Spirit	✔		✔		30.00 .000
Baptism in the Spirit can occur without speaking with tongues	✔	✔		✔	32.83 .000
I do not believe the Bible makes the exact order of end-time events clear	✔	✔	✔	✔	11.02 .004
I believe Christians are in daily conflict with demons	✔	✔	✔	✔	NS
I do not believe Christians can be possessed by demons	✔	✔	✔	✔	NS
I believe Christians will suffer during the 'great tribulation'			✔	✔	33.02 .000
Singing traditional hymns is a vital part of Christian worship	✔	✔	✔		35.03 .000
All Christians should experience material prosperity	✔	✔	✔	✔	NS

generation of ministers is divided about the same sorts of issues as the denomination as a whole. The last column in tables 2.9 and 2.10 record the result of a comparison using chi squared between ministers over and under 40.

Comparison between denominations

The Apostolic Church stands out from the other three. It has the highest percentage of ministers whose congregations have not declined, but it also contains the highest percentage of ministers who have held fewer than five funerals, baptised fewer than five people and held fewer than five weddings in the course of a year. The Apostolic Church presents a picture of stability and lower levels of activity than the others.

By contrast the Elim Church has the lowest percentage of ministers whose congregations have not declined, and the lowest percentage of ministers who have carried out fewer than five funerals, fewer than five baptisms and five weddings in a year. The Elim Pentecostal Church presents a picture of the greatest activity. True, it has more churches that register decline, but it has more

Table 2.10 *Social and moral items where 20 per cent+ of ministers under 40 years hold opposite viewpoints and young/old comparisons*

	AC	AG	Elim	CG	$X^2/P<$
Christians should not drink alcoholic beverages	✔	✔	✔	✔	64.81 .000
Christians should not buy and sell on Sundays unless absolutely necessary		✔	✔	✔	61.35 .000
Christians should not take part in social dancing	✔			✔	105.00 .000
Christians should not take part in sporting activities on Sundays	✔	✔		✔	101.09 .000
A minister who, after ordination, divorces and remarries should not continue to serve as a minister	✔		✔		14.19 .001
A minister who divorces before ordination and remarries after ordination should not continue to serve as a minister	✔	✔		✔	35.26 .000
Women should have exactly the same opportunities for ministry as men	✔		✔	✔	NS
Women should not baptise	✔				31.48 .000
Women should not be in charge of congregations	✔	✔	✔		NS

baptisms and weddings also; it has more people coming in through baptism and leaving through funerals. The Assemblies of God and the Church of God are intermediate between these two ends of the spectrum. In terms of growth, as shown by baptisms, and life as shown by weddings, Assemblies of God is similar to Elim.

Denominational worries were highest in the Apostolic Church, where well over 50 per cent of ministers confessed to concern and exactly 50 per cent thought that centralisation was a major problem. Conversely, the Elim ministers were least likely to be worried about their denomination's future. Assemblies of God ministers showed relatively high levels of worry, though this may be explicable in the light of recent changes to the organisational structure locally. Not surprisingly Assemblies of God ministers, who come from a tradition of local church autonomy, were also least likely to think their denomination too centralised.

When the *doctrinal* items are compared, the Assemblies of God shows itself to have marginally more topics of dissent among its ministers than the other denominations. The Apostolics show only four topics of dissent, but little can be read into these comparisons because they do not convey the strength of feeling behind dissension. The *social and moral* items provoke dissent fairly evenly across all four denominations and this suggests that all Pentecostal churches feel similar pressure from the secular world.

It might be thought that these disagreements occur between the generations and that what tables 2.7 and 2.8 show is a more liberal set of opinions being held by younger ministers and a more conservative set by older ministers. Tables 2.9 and 2.10, using the same criterion of 20 per cent plus at either end of the scale show, contrary to expectation, that ministers under 40 had *more* topics of disagreement than older ministers. For the Assemblies of God and Elim ministers these disagreements, however, were concentrated in the areas of doctrine, whereas for the Apostolic and Church of God ministers the disagreements lay in the social and moral areas. Yet the final column of these tables also shows that there are *also* disagreements between younger and older ministers. In each instance where the chi squared is significant the younger ministers hold a more liberal position. They are less likely to adopt both doctrinal distinctives and moral and social distinctives. This also applies to their willingness to endorse the belief that Christians will go through the 'great tribulation' which is more widely held in non-Pentecostal circles. The implication of this comparison is twofold: as younger ministers grow older the denominations will gradually lose their doctrinal, social and moral distinctiveness; and dissension between ministers over these distinctives may increase.

Conclusion

What are the problems facing Pentecostal churches? Are they likely to overcome them? What problems are systemic and what problems are the consequence of social and cultural change?

The problems facing Pentecostal churches are in many respects the problems facing all churches. Churches are voluntary bodies.

People come and go as they will. In a free society Pentecostal ministers cannot insist that people do as they are told. Yet Pentecostal ministers have to retain their existing congregations and then to attract new people and, when they have done this, to integrate the new people among the old ones. Even when they are successful in attracting new people, ministers may still lose members who find themselves drawn to the church down the road or forced to move by changes of job or personal circumstance.[10] The figures presented here show that some churches are characterised by activity in the form of baptisms, weddings and funerals while others, as it happens generally smaller and less vibrant churches, are more likely to be static. But the static churches in the end suffer from natural decline, from the death of old members, so that they are not really static after all.

At congregational level the problems of Pentecostal churches come from a failure to recruit new people and to retain the young people who have grown up in the church. But at a denominational level the problems are caused by quite separate factors. The first arises from demoralised and worried ministers. These are ministers who, because they are concerned about the future of their denomination, and perhaps because they feel the denomination is too centralised and therefore too restrictive, worry about the whole endeavour to which they are attached. Here are ministers who may have served for many years in one or other of the Pentecostal denominations but who feel that their denominations are in the doldrums. We cannot identify all possibilities from the statistics given here, but these ministers may be worried about their national leadership or about recent constitutional changes or about flirtation with new doctrines or administrative structures. Whatever their worries, they fear for the future.

The second category of problem arises from a different quarter altogether. This is the difficulty brought about by growth and diversification. The figures presented here show that, even within relatively small denominations, a diversity of doctrinal, social and moral views is held by the ministers. Moreover, this diversity is present in the younger age band of ministers and is not simply a function of disagreements between younger and older ministers.

---

[10] Richter and Francis, 1998.

This suggests that this problem will not go away with the passing of time but that, as the younger ministers move into middle age, contrasting viewpoints will continue to be held. In other words, there are problems of pluralisation within denominations. Consequently, the potential here for secession cannot be ignored. Nor will it become simpler to obtain unanimity at annual conferences and, if this is the case, leadership of Pentecostal denominations may become more complex, more a matter of compromise and half measures.

The overcoming of these problems is tied into the centralisation/decentralisation options. Centralisation is likely to produce greater uniformity but this may be at the price of severe disagreements on the floor of the annual conference. Decentralisation may encourage local initiatives and prevent confrontations with denominational officials but this may be at the price of greater eventual diversity. The puzzle to be solved by the Pentecostal denominations is that of retaining enough centralisation to allow unanimity to emerge while, at the same time, encouraging sufficient diversity to allow creativity and the freedom which the more adventurous Pentecostal ministers value.

Can Pentecostal denominations overcome their problems? The answer must be affirmative. Pentecostal denominations are capable of arriving at a powerful sense of spiritual and emotional unity within their annual conference sessions, and over the past 20 years they have demonstrated an ability to reform themselves without alienating either the old-timers or the young radicals. Given their twin commitments to the leadership of the Holy Spirit and the Scripture, it is perfectly possible for Pentecostal ministers to respond flexibly to contemporary challenges.

Some of the problems, particularly the doctrinal ones, may be systemic in the sense that they can probably be eliminated by an emphasis on the training of ministers. Particularly within the Assemblies of God, where training has until recently not been a requirement for all ministers, it has been easy for ministerial candidates to pick up idiosyncratic doctrinal packages. Consistent training ought to produce greater doctrinal harmony, at least on fundamental issues. The real difficulty arises with matters which cannot be seen as fundamental and about which there is legitimate individuality. Questions to do with demons and material prosperity come into this category and are capable of generating fierce argument. Currently within Britain the lack of television evangelism has reduced the profile of ministers who defend demonisation and prosperity teaching but, if religious television becomes more open with the arrival of cable and digital technology, the possibility of disharmony becomes greater. Pentecostals have a weakness for 'big' well-funded ministries.

The social variation seen among ministers is less problematic than it at first appears. Many Pentecostals are remarkably pragmatic and have been able to adapt to new moral and social norms, particularly if they have young families who refuse to be old-fashioned. As Pentecostal ministers are able to exercise enormous influence in their own congregations, clashes over moral and social norms tend to occur between the minister and his or her congregation rather than between ministers themselves. In addition, Pentecostals are part of a larger and wider evangelical culture which sets a generally agreed range of standards within which most of this kind of diversity is held. So the social and cultural disagreements between Pentecostal ministers may, in the end, be easier to resolve than those which are systemic and, in principle, correctable by simply adjusting the system.

3

Vocal Spiritual Gifts

Overview

This chapter begins a discussion of spiritual gifts, or *charismata*, which will run as a theme through this book. In chapter seven the charismatic activity of a minister and his or her congregation are correlated. In chapter nine charismatic activity is examined in relation to church growth. In this chapter the concern is with the meaning and function of the verbal charismata (tongues, interpretation and prophecy) and the frequency of their occurrence.

Sunderland: tongues

In relation to the charismatic gifts, and particularly the vocal ones, the Sunderland Conventions were an important and formative forum of debate. What was discussed there, and in many respects the line that was taken by its speakers, was adopted by the Pentecostal denominations that later emerged. The most obvious example concerns speaking with tongues. Boddy wrote in the first issue of *Confidence* (April 1908) that 'tongues is the Seal of Pentecost'. He put it this way:

> One is often asked, 'Do you think anyone can have had the Baptism of the Holy Ghost and not have had the Sign of Tongues?' I cannot judge another, but for me, 'Pentecost means the Baptism of the Holy Ghost with the evidence of the Tongues'. (Original capitalisation.)

In the same article he distinguished between 'the Seal of the Tongues as a sign of the indwelling of the Holy Ghost (given very specially at one point in the Spiritual experience)' and a '*continuous* Gift of Tongues' (original emphasis). For this distinction Boddy refers to 1 Corinthians 12:29 where it is made clear that not everyone spoke in tongues. Boddy understands this to mean that not everyone *continued* to speak in tongues 'though St Paul wishes that all did'.

Pastor J. Paul of Berlin also taught the doctrine of tongues as 'the seal' of the baptism in the Holy Ghost at a conference in Germany in December 1908. The words 'seal' and 'sign' seem to be used interchangeably and though later Boddy spoke about tongues as the 'Pentecostal sign; Love the sign of continuance', he did not drop the notion that tongues served an evidential purpose.[1] They were a sign, an indication, a mark that something spiritual had happened to the receiver. By 1910, when presumably Boddy had met people who had spoken in tongues but whose outlook and lives were far from those of fervent Christians, he may have changed his view slightly. The point to notice, however, is that in talking about tongues as a sign Boddy is close to those who later spoke about tongues as 'initial evidence'. By putting a stress on the word 'initial' rather than the word 'evidence' it becomes clear that the later Pentecostal denominational position implies that other evidences, non-initial ones, will be forthcoming. For Boddy the Spirit-filled Christian should have spoken in tongues, and before manifesting divine love. For most Pentecostal denominations the Spirit-filled Christian should speak in tongues and then go on to Christian service in the context of the church. In the case of ministers there should be 'fruit' from ministry, but the general idea of tangible consequences following religious experience is the same.

By 1911 Boddy was able to deal with vocal spiritual gifts as they applied in congregational settings and many of the conclusions he reached could easily have been repeated in most ministerial gatherings fifty years later.[2] Utterances in tongues should be limited to two or three people in any one meeting and prophetic messages should not be used for daily guidance and, in all circumstances, they should be tested against Scripture. Frequent expressions like, 'The Lord says . . .' only weaken the power of what is said and 'there is

[1] *Confidence*, November, 1910.
[2] *Confidence*, January, 5f.

constantly a danger of self-willed persons' trying to get their own way by attributing their wishes to divine impulses. Believers are always right to ask that whatever is said be confirmed in other ways since we can 'never fear the real leadings of the Holy Spirit'.

Denominational positions on tongues

In describing the doctrinal position of four Pentecostal denominations, what is remarkable is the similarity between them.

The Apostolic Church in its tenets simply says that 'the Baptism of the Holy Ghost for believers, with signs following' is 'an essential basis of the fellowship and union of the members of the church'. Turnbull, in an authoritative account of Apostolic history and practice, elaborates on this by saying 'so when we receive the baptism of the Holy Spirit we shall also speak with tongues'.[3] Similarly Rowe, in an account of Apostolic doctrine, writes

> We steadfastly maintain that no one can testify with Scriptural certainty that they have received the Spirit in this manner unless they can say they have spoken with 'other tongues'.[4]

Elim and Assemblies of God can be taken together as their dialogue on the place of speaking with tongues is best seen in an historical perspective.

From their respective beginnings in 1915 and 1924 Elim and British Assemblies of God have hesitated on the brink of combination: an idea mooted as early as 1924. Subsequent suggestions that the two denominations work together more closely were also made after a Unity Conference 'to seek to find a basis for unity without compromising any vital truths' was held in London in 1939. In 1948 fourteen leaders from five British Pentecostal groups met for two days in London and issued a joint statement.[5] The two largest of the groups were Elim and Assemblies of God and they helped to form the British Pentecostal Fellowship whose doctrinal statement included the rubric 'we believe in the baptism in the Holy Spirit with

---

[3] Turnbull, 1959, 157.
[4] Rowe, 1988, 135.
[5] Kay, 1989, 205.

supernatural evidence and in the gifts of the Spirit'. The lack of specificity was deliberate. It allowed the Elim and Assemblies of God positions to be subsumed within the same form of words.

In 1922 the Elim constitutional position was that 'the Holy Ghost, which is the promise of God, is accompanied by speaking in other tongues as the Spirit gives utterance'. Jeffreys himself, writing in 1929, did not insist on tongues as the initial evidence, though he disparaged the 'receive-it-by-faith' school and cited Acts 2:4 as the biblical pattern of what ought to be expected. In 1934 the Elim position was changed to reflect the Foursquare Gospel and the relevant words were, 'we believe that our Lord Jesus Christ is the Baptiser in the Holy Ghost, and that this Baptism with signs following is promised to every believer'. In 1993 the position was altered to place more emphasis on enduement with power for service. This position remains in current force. It asserts a baptism in the Holy Spirit given by Christ and evidenced by 'signs following', that is, some form of physical manifestation – usually but not necessarily tongues.

The British Assemblies of God position was built into the Statement of Fundamental Truths it had adopted in 1924 and which appears from its phraseology and the order of its subject matter to have been strongly influenced by the similar doctrinal statement adopted by Assemblies of God in the United States in 1916. It has remained almost entirely unchanged since that time. The current British Assemblies of God Statement of Fundamental Truths says 'We believe in the baptism in the Holy Spirit, the initial evidence of which is the speaking with other tongues as the Spirit gives utterance. Acts 2:4; 10:44–46; 11:14–16; 19:6; Isa 8:18.'

In October 1963 a joint meeting took place between representatives of Elim and Assemblies of God with a view to a possible merger. The discussion broke down over the single word 'initial'. As Alex Tee, one of the participants in the discussion, explained to me 'speaking with tongues was, for Elim, the "invincible evidence" because someone filled with the Spirit *might* prophesy rather than speak in tongues, or prophesy *before* speaking in tongues'.[6] Yet, despite the failure of the discussions to produce any concrete results, Elim and British Assemblies of God continued to work together both by instituting regular joint meetings between their Executive

---

6 Kay, 1989, 285, original emphasis.

Councils and through shared General Conferences, most recently at Bognor in 1996 and again in 1997. These Conferences retained separate business sessions but in other respects were unified.

As far as the theology of the baptism in the Spirit was concerned, the British Assemblies of God position was defended and expounded consistently by its leading ministers, notably Donald Gee and Harold Horton.[7] Elim writers often accepted the same position without difficulty, though others entertained reservations.[8] Canty argued that 'I do not think it logical to say that tongues are the initial evidence of the Baptism, because some tongues are unreal' but he went on to add, 'nevertheless I do not accept that in normal experience there is a true Baptism *without* speaking in tongues'.[9]

As a practical matter concerning the beliefs of ministers it needs to be noted that British Assemblies of God ministers are only required to give formal assent to fundamental denominational doctrinal truths once. That is at the point when they first apply for accreditation.[10] The same is true of Elim ministers. Despite what appears to be the looseness of this system for ensuring doctrinal conformity, the annual General Conferences of both fellowships are rarely occasions for deep-seated doctrinal disagreement. Where there is a threat of this, it is normally sufficient for the position incorporated within the fundamental truths to be restated through a seminar or public presentation for disquiet to be removed.

The Church of God's Declaration of Faith states that 'we believe . . . in speaking with other tongues as the Spirit gives utterance, and that is the initial evidence of the baptism of the Holy Ghost'.[11] Nevertheless, Conn quotes a survey carried out in 1967 showing

---

[7] McGee, 1991, 119–130.

[8] E.g. Walker, 1976, 34.

[9] Canty, 1987, 84, original emphasis.

[10] The position with Assemblies of God in the United States is different. Ministers there are required to renew their credentials annually and to fill in a detailed questionnaire about doctrinal distinctives. Where they disagree with these distinctives, a written explanation is required. Ministers are required to agree that 'speaking with tongues is the initial physical evidence of the baptism in the Holy Spirit'.

[11] Quoted in Hollenweger, 1972, 517.

that only 61 per cent of Church of God members were baptised in the Spirit.[12] It is not clear how this figure was arrived at – probably the survey found that only 61 per cent of members spoke in tongues. Such a finding does not reflect on the experience of ministers but it does show that the means for transmitting the experience of the Holy Spirit from ministers to members is inefficient. A measure of subsequent debate about tongues or tongues-and-interpretation in the Church of God has taken place within the open and academic forum of the *Journal of Pentecostal Theology*. For example Thomas, Professor of New Testament at the Church of God Theological Seminary, has defended the traditional Pentecostal position on tongues while appreciating scholarly variants that wish to see Christian initiation as a one-stage process. Thomas points out that:

> Pentecostals are not opposed to a one-stage process so long as the Pentecostal/charismatic experience is an integral part of reception of the Spirit.[13]

In other words, provided room is made for the tongues-speaking experience in Christian initiation, it matters very little whether there are two stages, new birth and then baptism in the Spirit, or one multi-component experience that includes several aspects, among which is baptism in the Spirit accompanied by speaking with tongues.[14]

Sunderland: interpretation of tongues

Interpretation of tongues is the least contentious of the charismatic gifts. Once it is granted that interpretation operates in conjunction with speaking with tongues, then it becomes easy to make a coherent case for public interpretation to follow public utterances in tongues. This case presumes and strengthens the view that tongues has two functions: one as marking the baptism in the Holy Spirit and the other as a means of edifying the individual or the church.

---

[12] Conn, 1977, 357.

[13] Thomas, 1998, 21.

[14] This is essentially the position put forward by Pawson, 1997.

Private speaking with tongues builds up the individual, public speaking with tongues, so long as it is interpreted, builds up the church.

Without this set of understandings, it is only possible to see interpretation of tongues as operating in relation to natural languages or the sign function of tongues. Neither of these views was ever considered at Sunderland, presumably because the first would have made interpretation a companion of xenoglossia (that is, speaking human foreign languages without learning them) and the second would have placed peculiar restrictions on the baptism in the Holy Spirit which could only have legitimately taken place when someone else was present to interpret the sign utterance.

The discussion of interpretation at Sunderland, and the practice that was observed there, is very similar to that found in most Pentecostal churches today. During a period of open worship someone will speak in tongues loudly enough for the congregation to fall silent and listen. After a few moments someone else (usually) will interpret the utterance in the congregation's main language. The interpretation will normally be spoken, though it can be sung, and it will usually sound like a prophecy in the sense that what is said will be directed as from God to the congregation. Phrases like, 'The Lord says to you this morning . . .' or 'Your God would remind you . . .' show that the words which follow are intended to have a divine force. Less commonly interpretation will be given in the first person, as if spoken directly by God, and take a form like, 'I, the Lord, say . . .'. More recently, Pentecostal congregations have adopted interpretations that are given as if spoken by the utterer in tongues to God. The 'I' of the interpretation is a human one. 'My heart is lifted up in praise to you and I worship you . . .'. The interpretation is as from the congregation to God and, when spoken in this way, is not directive but simply expressive of praise or thanksgiving or worship generally.

A lengthy discussion about the place of tongues and tongues-and-interpretation in congregational life was reported in *Confidence*, December 1914. One speaker asked why utterances in tongues might contain the repetition of sounds over and over again although the interpretation might be shorter and without repetition. In his view there was no place for public speaking with tongues during congregational meetings, and especially so when utterances in tongues interrupted sermons. The general view of other delegates was more favourable to tongues. American visitors (who presumably had longer experience than the British) took the view that tongues and interpretation were equivalent to prophecy and, if prophecy was permissible and edifying, then tongues and interpretation should be also. Others pointed out that languages required different amounts of words to say the same things and so it should be no surprise that discrepancies in lengths between tongues and interpretations occurred. Others, again, suggested that prophecies could be given in tongues and offered examples where they felt this had occurred.

An article specifically on the gift of interpretation was carried in the November 1910 issue of *Confidence*. The author, in an unpolemical way, insisted that interpretation should not be used as a method of guiding Christians. 'There are no examples of Timothy or Titus or other elders going to an interpreter to get their directions from the Lord. In the entire absence of such examples, I think the brethren err to set such an example in the work now.' Rather the purpose of interpretation is 'primarily devotional' because, though the Holy Spirit, enables utterance in an unknown language, it is not the Holy Spirit who speaks but the person him or herself; the utterance is simply a human one in a language beyond the speaker's comprehension.

Denominational positions on interpretation

There is little difference between Pentecostal denominations in their understanding of interpretation of tongues. Rowe, speaking for the Apostolics, wrote:

> The one and only purpose for this Gift of Interpretation is that messages given in unknown tongues may be conveyed to the hearers in the language which they understand. The Gift is purely supernatural.[15]

Rowe further makes the point that the gift is one of *interpretation* rather than translation. In other words, it is not necessary to believe that what is said in a known language corresponds exactly in a word

---

15 Rowe, 1988, p 185.

for word sense with the utterance in tongues. This point was made by Horton in his 1934 book, *The Gifts of the Spirit*, and has been accepted by Pentecostals ever since. With respect to the direction of interpretation – from congregation to God or God to congregation – Horton was of the opinion that the two things shaded into each other. A prayer to God about his qualities and requirements may be interpreted by a hearer as a message from God about these same qualities and requirements. Despite the apparent opposition between the first and the third person in a sentence, there is in practice an overlap between them. The visitors to Jerusalem heard the disciples speaking with tongues on the Day of Pentecost. 'Was not', asks Horton rhetorically, 'the recital to God of his "marvellous works", a recital to men of the same works?'[16]

Sunderland: prophecy

The first convention discussed prophecy and a report of the discussion was given in volume three (June, 1908) of *Confidence*. Boddy opened the proceedings by suggesting that letters of commendation should be made available from 'well known leaders' so that 'unsuitable persons' could not lead others astray. He also argued that prophecy was as much 'speaking out in the power of God' as foretelling. The notion that New Testament prophecy was a recital of future events, either national or personal, was one that he wished to quash and he backed this up by asserting that there was no precedent for treating tongues and interpretation (which he clearly took to be equivalent to prophecy) as an oracle for guidance over the details of daily life. Boddy was happy to argue that God gives guidance through 'common sense' which, for those who have faith, is under God's control.

Similarly other contributors struck cautious notes. Miss Schofield believed that some prophecies emanated from the unconscious mind rather than from the Holy Spirit and a Miss Scott believed that prophetic messages could be begun in the Spirit and ended 'in the flesh'. Miss Sisson surveyed the fate of missionaries who had been sent out by the Apostolic Faith Mission (presumably under the guidance of prophecy), some of whom had died, others

---

[16] Horton, 1946, 170.

of whom had returned under their own volition and yet others of whom had not been allowed to remain in the country where they had gone to work. Whatever the truth of the guidance these people had received, it was still important to support missionaries financially.

A rather different complexion was put on prophecy by reports from America of the man who had predicted a tidal wave and earthquake on the Pacific coast and who had been confined to a mental asylum. Another person had predicted an earthquake and a report had been given in the local paper about a fortnight before the San Francisco earthquake took place. The two cases implied that people should be treated gently even when their predictions were alarming.

The mixed message that emerged from these considerations was that prophecy, while an important gift of the Spirit for the New Testament church, should be treated with caution and certainly not used as a method of daily instruction.[17] Barratt who, in a later edition, revealed that in none of his travels had he been guided by prophecy, supported this robust position.[18] By 1911 the Sunderland speakers focused on the function of prophecy as simply to exhort, edify and comfort and seemed to have left behind the more apocalyptic possibilities that had been aired three years previously.[19] A later discussion at the 1914 convention returned to prophecy in the context of the ministry of women.[20] It made a distinction between prophecy 'in the wider sense and prophecy in the proper sense' by which it appeared to mean prophecy within the local assembly and prophecy as a ministry exercised by recognised individuals like Silas in the book of Acts.[21]

---

[17] This point was also made by Mary Boddy in her article, 'Messages and manifestations', *Confidence*, December 1908, 14. 'Nowhere can we find in the Word of God, in this dispensation, any suggestion, that guidance in the affairs of daily life for ourselves, and especially for others is to be given thus' (original italics). *Confidence*, August 1908, 14, carried a warning against 'travelling false prophets'.

[18] Supplement to *Confidence*, December 1908, 3.

[19] *Confidence*, November 1911, 249.

[20] *Confidence*, November 1914, 209f.

[21] There was a need to be cautious. Pentecostalism was being attacked in various ways, not least by Mrs Penn-Lewis who saw the whole thing as

Denominational positions on prophecy

There is a sharp distinction between the position of prophecy taken by Hutchinson's Apostolic Faith Church and by the other Pentecostal denominations. The Apostolic Faith Church taught vigorously that prophecies given by its ministers were exactly equivalent to the words of Scripture.

> Now to deal with the difference, if any, between the Written and the Spoken Word. Going straight to the root of the matter, there is *no difference at all*, because if it is the WORD OF God, whether it be WRITTEN OR SPOKEN it cannot be anything else but God's Word, and therefore in that sense it is the same identically . . . we also declare that the Spoken Word of God given through the Gifts of the Holy Ghost, and which He has imparted for that very purpose is infallible.[22]

The consequence of this teaching was that there was very little by which prophetic utterances could be judged. Once someone had given a prophecy, and especially if this prophecy was given by a recognised prophet within the congregation, it was bound to be correct, authoritative and beyond contradiction.

It was this sort of teaching that the Sunderland conventions repudiated. But, when Hutchinson began to teach that the man-child of Revelation 12 was a new incarnation of Christ, and to associate this position with himself, and when he amalgamated this

---

[21] (*continued*) being demonically inspired. *Confidence* (July 1913, 136) deals with her book, *War on the Saints*. The book says that Peter was led by evil spirits when he tried to impose Mosaic law on Gentiles (Galatians 2:11–14). Boddy and others who had formed themselves into the International Advisory Pentecostal Council refuted this view by pointing out that Peter was motivated by fear, as the text in Galatians explains. But, if the apostle Peter was seriously thought by a Keswick speaker to be inspired by demons, it was easy enough for others to attribute demons to twentieth-century Pentecostals.

[22] Hutchinson-Dennis in *Showers of Blessing*, April 1915, 14, (original emphasis). This teaching was reiterated as item 11 in a statement of 'what we believe . . .' and published in 1922 under the title *Doctrine and Articles of the Belief of the Apostolic Faith Church.*

teaching with British Israelism and announced that George V was the King of Israel, other Pentecostals felt their worst fears were being realised.[23] The majority of Pentecostals thought that Hutchinson's views on prophecy had led him to adopt an overall eschatological position that was disastrously unscriptural. The man-child teaching, in this sense, confirmed that modern prophetic utterances were not, and could not be, in any way on a level with the canonical text of Scripture.

Hutchinson influenced the Apostolic Church though its position on prophecy deviated from his. The Apostolic view is that prophecy is 'a direct message from the Lord to the local church' but this means that prophecy should only be given when the local church is assembled with its presbytery in charge. Youth meetings or other meetings involving subgroups of the church are not the place for prophecy. 'The Apostolic Church does not believe or teach that prophecy is infallible.' On the contrary, prophecy should be judged according to scriptural principles and the resulting utterance must help to edify, exhort and comfort the church (1 Corinthians 14:3). The gift of prophecy is therefore not intended to contribute to the government of the church.[24]

By contrast the office of prophet *is* intended to take part in church government. Here the minister who has been recognised as a prophet is seen as working alongside apostles to confirm their decisions, give direction for ministry, indicate the presence of ministers and give revelation concerning spiritual gifts. The prophet exercises the gift of prophecy but his authority within the church comes from his office rather than his gift.[25] This present position of the Apostolic Church is, according to Worsfold, not the one that was prevalent in the first few decades of its existence.

> Since the 1940s the use of prophecy by the AC for nominating local offices was gradually abandoned and these appointments were made by

[23] Hathaway, 1996.

[24] Quotations in this paragraph are from *Introducing The Apostolic Church: a manual of belief and practice*, Penygroes, The Apostolic Church, 1988, 156, 157.

[25] See *Introducing The Apostolic Church: a manual of belief and practice*, Penygroes, The Apostolic Church, 1988, 179, 180.

> the apostleship. Now the local appointment is usually activated by the local minister in conjunction with the regional superintendent. This writer believes that the occasional use of prophecy in this manner should find a place in the current renewal of practices which the church is experiencing. It is doubtful if it will ever become a routine practice in the AC again.[26]

Rowe's account of Apostolic Church doctrine appears to take a position similar to Worsfold. He accepts that there may be a basis for *direction* by prophecy, and he cites here Acts 13:1–4, but he does not make great play of this. In the same way, he thinks that 'there is value in inspired, Apostolic exposition upon the Spoken Word' without being insistent upon its place in church life.[27] Turnbull's account shows how co-functioning of apostles and prophets operated in the period before 1959, when his book was written:

> A large number of the decisions in our Councils and Executives are also made by the apostles. In all such meetings prophets as well as apostles are present, as we are always willing to hear what God has to say to us through his ordained channels. Many calls and changes have been made through the word received through the prophets, but it is not acted upon until it is first of all confirmed by the apostleship, who bear the final and first responsibility.[28]

A more recent account of Apostolic beliefs is given in an unpublished manual used at the Penygroes training school. The manual stresses that it is not necessary to believe in the infallibility of prophets while quoting with approval the comment from an Apostolic leader that 'rarely do true prophets make a mistake'.[29]

The position of the Assemblies of God, Elim and the Church of God follows the lines first drawn by the Sunderland discussions. Prophecy is important, but should not be taken as a decisive means of guidance for individuals and, in any event, should be treated with

---

26 Worsfold, 1991, 60 note 2.
27 Rowe, 1988, 270.
28 Turnbull, 1959, 178.
29 Massey, 1998, 77.

care since it might contain merely human components. The earlier Pentecostal writers reacted against the earlier Apostolic view and were careful to distance themselves from it. For instance, Gee included a passage in *Wind and Flame* that drew a distinction between the name given to a particular church office or ministry and the reality and power of that office or ministry. So far as he was concerned, the name or label attached to people was of far less importance than what they did and how they did it. Some people might be called pastors but might really be evangelists. Others might be called missionaries but might be apostles. The designation caused controversy, especially when different degrees of authority were attached to it.[30]

Horton was more precise in his opposition to the Apostolic Church's position. There was no disagreement about the role of prophecy in the congregation. Horton understood prophecy as the 'simplest form' of 'divinely inspired and anointed utterance' which was 'entirely supernatural'. Moreover, New Testament prophecy was as different from Old Testament prophecy as New Testament priesthood was different from Old Testament priesthood. Horton enthusiastically accepted the 'priesthood of all believers' and argued that, just as all New Testament believers had access to God as priests, so all New Testament believers could prophesy as the Holy Spirit within them gave them the ability to do so. But the ability to prophesy, widespread though it might be, did not correspond with the possession of prophetic office. This office only emerges gradually when the 'simple gift' begins to include revelatory aspects. In this respect Horton's distinction is almost universally accepted by Pentecostals. The difference between other Pentecostals and the (earlier) Apostolic position lay in the extent to which prophecy, or prophetic ministry, might be involved in the *government* of the church, that is, in making decisions about congregations and the lives of individual Christians. 'Guidance', says Horton, 'is not indicated as one of its [prophecy's] uses in the comprehensive definition in 1 Corinthians 14:3. It is not – indeed no spiritual gift is – intended to take the place of common sense and natural judgement'.[31]

---

[30] Gee, 1969, 74.

[31] Horton, 1934, 181.

Whatever their views in the 1920s and early 1930s, however, by the time of the Pentecostal Unity Conference of 1939 the three main Pentecostal denominations – Elim, Assemblies of God and Apostolic – had come to remarkable unanimity and were able to minute that 'all prophetic utterances, especially those for guidance, are judged by a responsible body of believers'.[32]

Sunderland: words of wisdom or knowledge

Little was said at the Sunderland conventions about the words of wisdom and knowledge. There were sporadic comments about the 'nine' manifestations of the Spirit (listed in 1 Cor. 12)[33] but no systematic teaching or discussion of wisdom or knowledge. Boddy, for instance, looked back on the year 1907–08 and thought that he had seen 'in some measure all the nine gifts of 1 Corinthians 12',[34] but he gave no examples of wisdom and knowledge and it must be assumed that he thought these had been manifested in the ordinary course of life without being worth special attention in the pages of *Confidence*. Certainly such gifts were less controversial and dramatic than those like tongues, prophecy and healing and so it is no surprise that the young Pentecostal/charismatic movement was less taken up with them.

Denominational positions on words of wisdom and knowledge

Within British Assemblies of God the oral tradition states that during Howard Carter's imprisonment for conscientious objection during the 1914–18 war, he meditated on 1 Corinthians 12–14 and believed that he had been given the revelation by God that these gifts were entirely supernatural in nature and operation.[35] When

---

[32] Quote in Randall, 1999, 223, from the minutes of the Apostolic Church General Executive Meeting held at Workington, 6 to 13 June 1939.

[33] E.g. *Confidence*, May 1913, 93.

[34] *Confidence*, September, 1908, 4.

[35] Some hint of this is given in the introduction to Carter 1946, 1, where he writes, 'it was during the First World War that this study had its origin'.

Carter became Principal of the Hampstead Bible School, he ensured that his teaching on spiritual gifts was given to the students and also became known by the faculty, among whom was Harold Horton. Horton was eloquent and literate and a far better writer than Carter who, though he did throughout his life write articles, never made the impact on the printed page that he made face to face or in preaching. Horton, in the introduction to *The Gifts of the Spirit*, gives Carter the credit for the approach he took. He wrote

> The studies have really arisen out of the most happy acquaintance I made many years ago with Mr Howard Carter of the Bible School and Missionary Association . . . I have, moreover, recently been favoured with the loan of Mr Carter's schedule of private notes on the subject.[36]

Carter argued that the gifts of the Spirit must be unrelated to human abilities. He pointed out that the gift of tongues was not thought by any commentators to be related to the linguistic abilities of the disciples. Nor were the healing miracles of the Bible anything to do with medicine. If these two gifts were supernatural in origin, then it was logical to suppose that the word of wisdom and the word of knowledge were similar. A word of wisdom, to be worth the name, must be more than sanctified good sense: in his view a word of wisdom was essentially, 'a supernatural revelation of the mind and purpose of God communicated by the Holy Spirit'.[37] In the Old Testament Moses received a word of wisdom on the top of Mount Sinai when he received the law that was given to Israel. In the New Testament, a word of wisdom was received by Agabus when he predicted a famine (Acts 11), and this shows how there is a prophetic element within the wisdom that is given.

Gee took a similar view except that he was more inclined to see a word of wisdom as being manifested in the solution to practical problems.[38] The appointment of deacons in Acts 6 was, to Gee's mind, a wonderful example of a word of wisdom that prevented unrest in the church and, at the same time, enabled the apostles to redouble their efforts in preaching and teaching. Even in the

---

[36] Horton, 1934, 7.

[37] Carter, 1946, 17.

[38] Gee, 1937.

ministry of Christ a word of wisdom might be found in the answer given to those who asked whether tribute should be paid to Caesar (Matt. 22:21).

In their description of a word of knowledge, however, Carter and Gee disagreed. Both accepted the supernatural nature of the gift but Carter argued that it should be defined as 'the supernatural revelation of the existence, or nature, of a person or a thing, or the knowledge of some event, given to us by the Holy Spirit for a specific purpose'.[39] Numerous examples of this were to be found in the Old Testament (e.g. Elisha has a revelation of the plans of the Syrians, 2 Kings 6:12) and in the New Testament (Jesus' conversation with the Samaritan woman). Essentially, the word of wisdom is a participation in divine omniscience. Gee believed that the word of knowledge was coupled with the teaching ministry within the church and that Carter's emphasis confused the word of knowledge with prophecy. To Gee it was inconceivable that the teaching ministry within the church should be unsupported by any supernatural gift of the Spirit. The teaching ministry needed to bring the voice of Christ into the church through the lively exposition of Scripture and, unless a word of wisdom was in evidence here, this ministry simply became a routine or non-Pentecostal function.[40]

Both the Apostolic Church[41] and the Church of God[42] accept the line on the word of wisdom and the word of knowledge developed by Carter. The Elim position is broadly similar, though its recent updating omits any reference to the number of gifts of the Spirit specified in Scripture,[43] and this may have the effect of removing the clarity with which earlier Pentecostal expositors concentrated on wisdom and knowledge.

---

[39] Carter, 1946, 30.

[40] Carter, 1946, 30, may have been referring to Gee's (1937) view when he maintained that 'a word of knowledge is not knowledge of the word' that is, it is not proficiency in the biblical text. If this is so, Carter misunderstood Gee's view.

[41] *Introducing The Apostolic Church: a manual of belief, practice and history*, 1988, 154.

[42] Conn, 1966, 56, 57.

[43] Schatzmann, 1998, 89.

A more recent exposition of a word of knowledge places it in conjunction with gifts of healing. The preacher will address a congregation and, on the strength of a word of knowledge, detect the presence of various illnesses that may be healed. In other words the word of knowledge is a prelude to, and incentive for, faith by those who have illnesses. People think that if the preacher knows their physical condition in such detail God can heal them. This idea of a word of knowledge is partly present in the ministry of Smith Wigglesworth (1859–1947) whose legendary ministry exemplified Pentecostalism in the 1920s and 1930s. Wigglesworth was brusque and uneducated but he travelled the world preaching and appeared to have confidence that every illness he encountered could and would be healed by God. He was an unconventional and unpredictable character but his ministry is still remembered and people continue to recall remarkable healings associated with it.[44] The word of knowledge as an adjunct to healing has been popularised from the 1960s onwards by healing evangelists and by tapes and videos that circulate conferences and congregations. Younger Pentecostal ministers, across the denominations of British Pentecostalism, are likely to be more influenced by these than by the debates between Carter and Gee.[45]

What do the data show?

Baptism in the Spirit

Table 3.1 shows that almost every single Pentecostal minister considers him or herself to be baptised in the Holy Spirit. This is hardly surprising given the insistence on the reality and importance of this experience in the fundamental truths of Pentecostal denominations.

Initial evidence

Table 3.2 shows the agreement of ministers with items connected with baptism in the Spirit. Not surprisingly the great majority of

---

[44] Wigglesworth, 1924, 140.
[45] Chapell, 1987.

Table 3.1 *Frequency of baptism in the Holy Spirit (ministers)*

Denomination	No %	Yes %	Don't Know %
Apostolic Church		100.0	
Assemblies of God	.2	99.8	
Elim		99.7	.3
Church of God		100.0	

these ministers in all four denominations believe that there is a distinct experience that might be called 'baptism in the Spirit'. The ministers differ on whether speaking with tongues is the initial evidence of this baptism. The Assemblies of God is by far the strongest in its adherence to this position and even the Elim Church, which has deliberately avoided making tongues the sole sign gift and which has modified its position most recently, gives great emphasis to tongues as an initial evidence. The surprise occurs with the Church of God which, despite its official acceptance of this tenet, gathers remarkably weak support from this sample of ministers. The figure does not come to nearly half.

The position of Elim ministers is logical and comes close to their reaffirmed fundamental truths. Over 70 per cent believe that baptism in the Spirit can occur without speaking with tongues but over 90 per cent believe that some evidence, the evidence of 'signs following', will be found. Interpretation of the responses of the other three denominations is problematical. In the case of Assemblies of God ministers, since most believe that the initial evidence is speaking with tongues, they probably equate tongues with a 'sign following'. The other denominations may substitute some other sign for tongues and come close to the Elim position, that is, they may believe that *some* sort of sign should follow the baptism in the Spirit but they are not able or prepared to specify precisely what this sign should be.[46]

There are both positive and negative implications for the denominations from these figures. For those denominations that

---

[46] Analysis of variance (not reproduced here) shows that there are no significant differences between the four denominations in their responses to the last item in the table. All four denominations believe some sort of sign follows baptism in the Spirit.

Table 3.2 *Agreement with baptism in Spirit items by denomination*

Items	AC %	AG %	Elim %	CG %
I believe there is a distinct Christian experience which might be called 'the baptism in the Spirit'	96	98	97	84
Speaking with tongues is necessary as initial evidence of the baptism in the Holy Spirit	68	81	42	29
Baptism in the Spirit can occur without speaking with tongues	37	30	72	30
The baptism in the Holy Spirit is evidenced by 'signs following'	94	88	91	90

spell out speaking with tongues as *the* initial evidence, it is clear that their ministers do not believe what they are meant to believe or what they originally believed when they were first ordained. This is a negative implication in the sense that it implies that Pentecostal denominations are losing their flagship doctrine. It implies that some Pentecostal congregations are Pentecostal in name only and have little connection with the early twentieth-century traditions that gave them birth. Positively, however, the acceptance of an experience of the baptism in the Spirit, even if the evidence for this is unclear, suggests that collaboration between Pentecostal denominations should not become stuck in the thickets of doctrinal minutiae.

Frequency of verbal charismata

Pentecostal theology of speaking in tongues distinguishes between the sign function of tongues as an indicator of the baptism in the Holy Spirit and the use of tongues as a form of private prayer. While it is possible for Pentecostal ministers to have spoken in tongues on the occasion of their baptism in the Spirit and then to have lapsed, it is much more likely that they will speak in tongues on that occasion and then regularly thereafter. Table 3.3 below shows that this is indeed the pattern. The great majority of Pentecostal ministers either speak in tongues nearly every day or at least once a week. Only a minority find speaking in tongues merely occasionally beneficial but, when this information is examined by denomination, it is clear that the Church of God ministers are unlike the rest. Although all Church of God ministers have spoken in tongues at some time or other, it is

Table 3.3 *Frequency of speaking in tongues (ministers)*

Denomination	**never**	**used to but not now**	**occasionaly**	**once a month+**	**once a week +**	**nearly every day**
AC			5.1		13.1	81.8
AG			2.0	.5	6.7	90.8
Elim	.5	.5	3.5	1.1	14.2	80.2
CG			37.5	12.5	29.2	20.8

reasonable to assume that they view tongues as being less useful for prayer than the other ministers.

Table 3.4 shows how often Pentecostal ministers operate verbal charismata. Ministers were asked to record 'how often in the past three months *you* have . . .' It is assumed that within three months a minister will have attended Sunday services, one in the morning and one in the evening, and a midweek service, making a total of 39 services in all. If a minister had operated a spiritual gift in half of these services, he or she would fall into the 19 plus category; if a minister had operated a spiritual gift at one service a fortnight, he or she would fall into the 1–6 category.

The mean in the final column of the table is obtained by assigning a value of 1 to none, a value of 2 to 1–6, and so on.

The right hand column in table 3.4 shows that the most frequent charismatic activity of Pentecostal ministers in Britain is singing in tongues. This would occur during worship and might take place privately or at any kind of service. This explains why nearly a third of ministers sing in tongues nineteen or more times in a three-month period. What is surprising, though, is that a relatively large minority (16 per cent) have not sung in tongues at all during the same period. There is obviously disagreement over the value of tongues among Pentecostal ministers, and table 3.5 shows that this is denominationally based.

Prophecy is the second most common spiritual gift exercised by Pentecostal ministers. The majority (nearly 80 per cent) prophesy at least once in a three month period and some prophesy much more frequently. Again, however, there is a minority for whom this spiritual gift is absent from their normal experience.

In practice there may be a connection between singing in tongues and prophecy in the sense that the worship expressed by

Table 3.4 *Frequency of verbal charismata in last three months (ministers)*

Verbal charismata	**None** %	**1 to 6** %	**7 to 12** %	**13 to 18** %	**19 plus** %	**Mean**
Given a public utterance in tongues	54.4	32.2	5.1	2.5	5.8	1.73
Interpreted tongues	40.1	45.2	9.0	3.1	2.6	1.83
Sung in tongues	16.0	29.9	14.1	10.9	29.1	3.07
Prophesied	20.5	53.2	15.4	4.7	6.2	2.23
Given a word of wisdom or knowledge	29.6	50.1	12.1	3.9	4.3	2.03
Given a prophecy privately to another person	48.3	39.3	6.7	3.0	2.6	1.72

singing in tongues might prepare a congregation for the reception of a prophetic utterance.

The majority of ministers (70 per cent) have given a word of wisdom or knowledge at least once in a three monthly period. This would usually occur during a service but could take place in a meeting or in private conversation. Interpreting tongues requires the context of a meeting because someone else must give the utterance in tongues that is to be interpreted. That a large number of ministers (40.1 per cent) have not interpreted tongues only suggests that someone else in their congregation has this role. And the same may be said for giving public utterances in tongues.

Table 3.5 shows how frequently *congregations* operate charismata. Ministers were asked 'how often in the past six months someone (apart from yourself) has done the following things in congregational meetings'. The questions were directed at a six-month period and so are not directly comparable with those in table 3.4. What they do show, however, is the relative frequency of charismata. Again singing in tongues is the most common phenomenon. Prophecy, utterance in tongues and interpretation of tongues occur at roughly the next level of frequency, and giving a word of wisdom or knowledge and private prophecy are the least common.

There are some congregations where very little charismatic life is seen. That there has not been a public utterance in tongues from the body of the congregation in six months in 9 per cent of cases, and no prophecy in 8 per cent of cases, would suggest that there are Pentecostal churches where Pentecostalism has become nominal, cold

Table 3.5 *Frequency of verbal charismata in last six months (congregations)*

Verbal charismata	**None** %	**1 to 6** %	**7 to 12** %	**13 to 18** %	**19 plus** %	**Mean**
Given a public utterance in tongues	9.1	39.4	22.8	10.6	18.1	2.8
Interpreted tongues	13.5	43.4	20.9	9.8	12.4	2.6
Sung in tongues	12.4	27.9	15.4	9.1	35.2	3.2
Prophesied	8.0	38.6	23.8	11.6	18.0	2.9
Given a word of wisdom or knowledge	23.5	46.0	16.8	6.1	7.6	2.2
Given a prophecy privately to another person	35.1	37.4	13.0	6.6	7.8	2.1

and weak. This is because the distinguishing mark of Pentecostal churches is their adherence to tongues speaking. If there are no public utterances in tongues, there are unlikely to be private utterances and, if there are no private utterances, the congregation has ceased to be Pentecostal in any living sense.

Table 3.6 helps the visitor to know what to expect in these Pentecostal denominations. Public utterance in tongues is most likely to be heard in an Elim congregation and least likely to be heard in an Apostolic congregation, but the differences between the congregations are not great. Congregational interpretation is most common in Assemblies of God though, again, the pattern between the denominations is similar. Singing in tongues, which occurs each week within the Apostolic, Assemblies of God and Elim congregations, is more of a rarity in the Church of God. Prophecy is least common in the Church of God but much the same in the other three. The visitor, then, to the three Pentecostal denominations that originated in Britain could expect to hear prophecy, singing in tongues and probably an utterance in tongues and an interpretation. A word of wisdom or knowledge would be rarer, particularly in Apostolic or Church of God congregations, but the practice would be quite acceptable in *some* Elim congregations (notice that almost as many Elim congregations have had thirteen plus occasions when a word of wisdom or knowledge is given as when none has been given).

Table 3.6 *Frequency of verbal charismata in last six months (congregations) by denomination*

Verbal charismata	Denom	None %	1 to 12 %	13 + %	Mean
Given a public utterance in tongues	AC	14	69.9	16.1	2.54
	AG	8.2	57.3	34.5	2.67
	Elim	8.5	65.2	26.3	2.83
	CG	10.9	65.2	23.9	2.67
Interpreted tongues	AC	22	69.2	8.8	2.21
	AG	11.6	59.8	28.6	3.06
	Elim	11.8	67.7	20.5	2.61
	CG	27.9	65.1	7	2.00
Sung in tongues	AC	21.7	54.3	23.9	2.60
	AG	10.8	39.1	50.1	3.44
	Elim	8.8	43.6	47.6	3.42
	CG	39.5	55.3	5.3	1.82
Prophesied	AC	6	59.1	34.9	3.01
	AG	7	59.3	33.7	3.09
	Elim	7.7	66.6	25.7	2.81
	CG	23.8	61.9	14.3	2.29
Given a word of wisdom or knowledge	AC	37.5	62.5		1.73
	AG	24.6	63	12.4	2.23
	Elim	19.7	61.8	18.5	2.46
	CG	17.4	69.6	13	2.43
Given a prophecy privately to another person	AC	63.4	34.1	2.4	1.45
	AG	34.5	53.1	12.4	2.13
	Elim	27.2	53.1	19.7	2.38
	CG	51.3	38.5	10.3	1.79

Function of interpretation

Table 3.7 shows that the majority of Pentecostal ministers think that tongues should not be interpreted from the congregation to God – in other words interpretations should function like prophecies rather than prayers. Yet, within Elim and Assemblies of God, the alternative position has gained considerable ground and about a third of ministers in these two denominations think it perfectly acceptable, perhaps even theologically preferable, that interpretations should be utterances of praise or prayer. Table 3.8 puts the

Table 3.7 *Tongues should be interpreted as from the congregation to God*

	Agree %	Not Certain %	Disagree %
AC	16	4	80
AG	31	14	55
Elim	36	14	50
CG	14	6	80

matter the other way round and a comparison of the two sets of figures shows that some ministers are happy with either direction. So, for instance, while 36 per cent of Elim ministers agree that interpretations should be in a Godward direction, 65 per cent think they should be in a congregational direction.

Other functions of tongues

An overwhelming majority of Pentecostal ministers evaluate speaking with tongues as an edifying and encouraging experience, and most think of it as being exciting, holy and calming as well (table 3.9). A great number of ministers consider speaking with tongues to be a form of private prayer and nearly all agree that tongues is a controllable, and therefore not an ecstatic or mystical, experience. It is not surprising, then, that speaking with tongues is thought of as beneficial to congregational life: it brings life and does not cause disorder.

Conclusion

The understanding of vocal charismatic gifts held by the Pentecostal denominations in Britain is similar to the one hammered out in discussion at the Sunderland conventions before the 1914–18 war. There are differences of course, but the main

Table 3.8 *Tongues should be interpreted as from God to the congregation*

	Agree %	Not Certain %	Disagree %
AC	92	5	3
AG	73	12	15
Elim	65	11	24
CG	92	2	6

Table 3.9 *Evaluation of experience of tongues*

Item	Agree %	Not Certain %	Disagree %
To speak with tongues is . . .			
An edifying experience	99		1
An encouraging experience	98	2	
An exciting experience	85	9	6
A holy experience	82	10	8
A form of private prayer	88	2	10
A calming experience	78	15	7
An uncontrollabe experience	2	2	96
Speaking with tongues causes congregational disorder	4	2	94
Speaking with tongues brings life to the church	87	7	6

outlines of understanding have remained largely intact. Speaking in tongues is seen to have three functions, one as a sign of the baptism of the Holy Spirit, another, in congregational worship, as a prelude to interpretation, and a third as a form of personal or collective prayer. All Pentecostal denominations accept the public operation of tongues within normal church services.

Early excitement about vocal charismatic gifts led to extreme positions that ignored the fallibility of charismata. The important text 'two or three prophets should speak, and the others should *weigh carefully what is said*' (1 Cor. 14:29) makes it plain that New Testament prophecy needs to be evaluated – in other words that charismatic gifts can err because they do not have the same weight as the canonical text. But these Pauline injunctions were ignored by W.O. Hutchinson, who after early promise rushed headlong to disaster. Fortunately, the majority of the Pentecostal movement stood clear and appreciated the role of charismatic gifts within the context of the checks and balances that the New Testament apostles carefully set in place. For this reason, after early disputes, the majority of Pentecostals had, by 1939, come to a place where, despite variations in emphasis, they shared a common mind. pan-Pentecostal gatherings could occur without friction.

Vocal charismatic gifts were largely seen to belong within congregations. Prophecy enlivened and illuminated local churches; singing in tongues, where congregations spontaneously broke into musical harmonies of glossalalic utterances, became a feature of worship; and utterances in tongues at which the whole congregation fell silent waiting for interpretation had an awesome effect on newcomers and visitors. The less common gifts, the word of wisdom and the word of knowledge, tended to be associated with healing but they were, perhaps inevitably, less easy to isolate and identify, and so less contentious.

Within these parameters of broad agreement there are denominational variations over the exact role of speaking with tongues in relation to the baptism in the Holy Spirit. British Assemblies of God emphasises the sign character of speaking with tongues more than other denominations but there is almost universal agreement that a specific spiritual experience called the 'baptism in the Spirit' should be seen as part of the teaching of the New Testament. The debatable issue is not whether there is such a baptism but whether there is more than one way of recognising its occurrence.

4

Healing and the Toronto blessing

Overview

Healing has always been vital to the progress and experience of Pentecostal churches and wherever Pentecostalism has taken root, healings have attracted newcomers, often in huge numbers, to its meetings. The theological basis for healing has been seen to lie in the atonement, in the work of Christ on the cross, and this has placed healing within the context of evangelism. Yet, as healing operates charismatically like other spiritual gifts, it has also been a feature of day-to-day congregational life. Against its historical background this chapter explores Pentecostal theology and the practice of healing today.

Some analysts connect the 'Toronto blessing', another example of the dramatic and well publicised occurrences familiar in Pentecostal churches, with earlier moves of the Spirit. The Toronto blessing, or laughing 'in the Spirit' and being 'slain in the Spirit', swept through many denominations, Pentecostal and non-Pentecostal, in the British Isles between about 1994 and 1997. This chapter explores how well the Toronto blessing was supported by Pentecostal ministers, what issues it raises, and what effects it has, or had, on the churches.

Sunderland: healing

Healing was extensively discussed at the Sunderland conventions and, as with the vocal *charismata*, the balanced view recommended there helped the young Pentecostal denominations avoid the errors of fanaticism and extremism. Boddy's wife, Mary, had been healed in 1899[1] and often wrote and spoke about the subject. The first issue of *Confidence* carried a report of a discussion held at Sunderland during the 1908 convention and at least one person said, 'since "Pentecost", I have found the Lord to be my Healer'. In the second issue, in an article entitled 'Health and Healing', Mary Boddy provided a general overview of the subject affirming that God healed in the Old Testament and that, 'on Calvary we can rejoice today that the Redeemer fulfilled the Scriptures and *bore away* not only our sin, but our sickness'. Theologically, then, she located the basis for divine healing within the atonement. Boddy, in the next issue of *Confidence*, also wrote about divine healing and drew attention to James 5 and the 'prayer of faith'. He made no mention of the atonement and assumed instead that the laying on of hands provided an opportunity for those with a 'gift of healing' to minister. Theologically, then, he assumed that the *charisma* of healing was a permanent possession of those who had received it and that they should exercise it in response to the faith of those who were sick. In *Confidence* (September 1908) Boddy looked back on the year and was able to say, 'sick ones have been healed, evil spirits discerned, rebuked and cast out, faith has been given, more than one miracle has been wrought'. In the November issue of *Confidence* for that year he carried a testimony of healing written by Carrie Judd Montgomery whose theological thrust was based on Romans 8 where the text asserts that the 'mortal' body of the Christian may be 'quickened' (that is, given life) by the Holy Spirit and, though one interpretation of this passage refers it to the resurrection of the Christian, Mrs Montgomery argued that it applied here and now and provided the basis for her healing.

These three strands within the theology of healing – in the atonement, through the Holy Spirit acting charismatically, and by the general power of the Holy Spirit – were never reconciled or systematised by either of the Boddys. They continued to stress the reality of healing and were wise enough to warn against the complete rejection of medicine, though their own personal preference appears to have been in this direction and they speak of 'taking the Lord as one's healer'. In *Confidence* (January 1910) Boddy

[1] Or 1900, the precise date is not known.

reproduced a paper he had written for the Durham Junior Clergy Society in which he had argued for healing using the three strands mentioned above but also accepting that 'only a few patients out of hundreds have faith enough to lean on the Lord. It must be Holy-Ghost-given Faith, and Spirit-given light'. In other words, while he saw healing as belonging to the present provision of God for some Christians, he recognised that doctors and nurses are a legitimate avenue for healing for most people. And, while warning against throwing medicine away, he also argued against the position of Christian Science which 'says that all pain and disease is unreal' and 'ignores the existence and power of Satan, and the work of the Atonement'.[2]

Throughout the next few years Boddy published testimonies of healing as well as accounts of Christians who had died, as in the case of Pastor Cantel, refusing medical treatment.[3] Boddy continued to stress that a Christian's stance on healing was an entirely individual matter but he must have been delighted to reprint an extract from the Bishop of Durham's address at the Church Congress that, however hesitantly, drew a connection between the health of the soul and the body.[4]

Denominational positions on healing

The Apostolic Church believes in the gifts of the Holy Spirit (tenet 6). The *Apostolic Church Manual of Belief and Practice* explains that healing is expected in response to the prayer of James 5 and the gifts of healing of 1 Corinthians 12:9. Gifts of healing are

> imparted to certain members of the church, and manifested through certain leaders . . . these gifts operate through the laying on of hands, anointing with oil . . . all healing is, of course, received through the atonement of Christ on the Cross, because of his stripes we are healed.[5]

---

[2] *Confidence*, August 1910, 176. A further dispute with Christian Science was reported in *Confidence*, July 1911, 163.

[3] *Confidence*, September 1919, 204. The same page that records Pastor Cantel's death mentions the healing of Pastor Jeffreys.

[4] *Confidence*, October 1910, 236.

[5] Turnbull, 1959, 164.

Rowe's Apostolic exposition does not link healing with the atonement in so many words. Instead he says

> Divine healing comes from the stream of the life of God in the Incarnate Christ which flows through the cross. The same power that raised Christ from the dead conquers the death process of disease in man. Mark that the cross is the *only* ground upon which we can appeal for *Divine* healing.[6]

The Elim Church, growing as it did out of the powerful healing ministry of George Jeffreys, is more reticent about divine healing than might be expected. George Jeffreys had a comprehensive doctrine of healing, most fully expounded in *Healing Rays* (1932). In essence he believed that whatever Adam had lost at the Fall was available as a future benefit because of Christ's death on the cross. Healing was an exception, though, since it was available as a present benefit. This is because there are only three dispensations in Jeffreys' dispensational scheme. The Old Testament was the dispensation of the Father, the New Testament period was the dispensation of the Son and the church age is the dispensation of the Holy Spirit. In each dispensation healing has taken place but in this current dispensation, when the Holy Spirit is constantly at work, Christian believers can expect to enjoy perpetual freedom from illness. All healing, however, is predicated on Christ's 'atoning and redeeming work' since in earlier dispensations people looked forward to it and in the present dispensation people may look back to it. Jeffreys is open to the possibility that healing might result from personal sin, but also notes that sickness may be attributable to natural causes and, in the latter part of his book, specifically rules out lack of faith as the only cause of a failure to be healed.

> We do not attribute all failures to lack of faith. There might be other reasons why people are not healed. Hindrances in the lives of seekers, and unwillingness to obey the commandments of the Lord, can hinder the work of healing. Again some are allowed to suffer for disciplinary and other purposes.[7]

---

[6] Rowe, 1988, p 347 (original italics).
[7] Jeffreys, 1932, p 165.

So far as doctors are concerned, Jeffreys quotes Paul's advice to Timothy to drink wine for his stomach's sake (1 Tim. 5:23) and deduces from this that co-operation with 'natural curative means' are endorsed by Scripture.

By 1934 the Elim fundamentals had softened their earlier position slightly. Now it was asserted that

> We believe that our Lord Jesus Christ is the healer of the body and that all who will walk in obedience to his will can claim Divine Healing for their bodies.[8]

Despite this, Elim evangelists like Alex Tee continued to preach that 'there is a sacred connection between the atoning work of Christ on the cross and divine healing' and drew a distinction between the general teaching of the Scripture and the so-called 'rhema' word of God that applies at a particular moment and to a particular situation and stimulates effective faith for healing.[9] Tee's use of this distinction does not stand up to examination in the Greek text of the New Testament but it was indicative of the influence on him of the healing evangelists in the Faith tradition for whose theology it was an important component.

In 1993 the Elim fundamentals were modified still further.

> We believe that the gospel embraces the needs of the whole man and that the church is therefore commissioned to preach the gospel to the world and to fulfil a ministry of healing and deliverance to the spiritual and physical needs of mankind.[10]

Such a change of wording allows a plurality of positions to co-exist comfortably within the denominational community. Healing is proclaimed – but its theological basis is left open; deliverance (the casting out of demons) is also given prominence – but its relationship with healing is undetermined.

The Assemblies of God fundamentals categorically states 'we believe that deliverance from sickness by Divine Healing is

---

8 Hathaway, 1998, 36, 37.

9 Tee, 1976, 203.

10 Hathaway, 1998, 36, 37.

provided for in the Atonement'. At face value this means that healing is available to Christians by faith in Christ in almost exactly the same way as forgiveness of sins. This kind of position could lead to an aversion to ordinary medicine. Nelson Parr, whose views would have helped to shape the fundamentals, explained his position on divine healing in a series of articles published as a booklet in 1955. Parr's distaste for 'drugs and the surgeon's knife' are evident in his account, but he is careful not to condemn medical practitioners because 'we do not find the Saviour ever condemned them'.[11] Parr's view, which was probably shared by many Pentecostals, was that extreme views of divine healing (e.g. when parents refuse to call in a doctor to attend to a dangerously sick child), should be avoided. Parr's reasons for shunning the extreme view stemmed from his concern to obey the laws of the land rather than because he thought doctors had an honoured place in the fight against human suffering.

The question of the extent to which healing is 'in' the atonement of Christ was sporadically discussed by Pentecostals. Gee confronted the issue in *Trophimus I Left Sick*, a title bound to show that healing was not so automatic in the early church as extremists might claim.[12] Gee wrote

> to assert that healing of our bodies rests upon an identical authority with healing for our souls in the atoning work of Christ our Saviour can involve serious problems of personal faith and confidence . . . where Divine Healing, though 'claimed', has not been received.[13]

While Gee did not directly oppose the notion that healing is in the atonement, Woodford, also a British Assemblies of God minister, effectively did so.[14] He argued that 'sickness and disease, as non-moral and non-spiritual manifestations' do not 'require atonement as a basis for any forgiveness or reconciliation'. This position was also supported in the same denomination by C.L. Parker.[15]

---

[11] Parr, 1955, 38, 61.

[12] The title comes from 2 Timothy 4:40.

[13] Gee, 1952, 21, 22.

[14] Woodford, 1956, 53.

[15] Parker, 1961.

The corollary of this view, which welcomed non-supernatural healing especially when illness was caused by improper diet or lack of rest or exercise, was enunciated by Linford, long-time editor of the British Assemblies of God periodical *Redemption Tidings*.[16]

Where all Pentecostals might agree that healing is a possibility dependent upon the grace that flows from Christ's atonement, the consolidation of this possibility into an appropriable right puts the entire matter on a completely different basis. If physical healing follows faith in the merits of Christ's death, then any disease, like any sin, can at any time be removed by proper belief. Thus the onus for healing, like the Arminian onus for salvation, falls firmly on the supplicant and God may be depersonalised and transformed into a mechanism by which human needs are met. This is the pastoral problem that Gee recognised.

Within the churches Pentecostal doctrine on healing might be interpreted and presented in quite different ways. Healing might be a Christian covenant 'right' that had to be asserted in the face of the devil's lies and thieving ways, or a gracious and divine provision that flowed from the love of God. Pentecostal doctrine was open to these two poles of opinion and was blown one way or the other by leading personalities. The American healing evangelists – Osborn,[17] Roberts and the less well-known Valdez – preached in Britain in the early post-war period and promoted the view that healing was a gospel right that faith could claim;[18] others like Gee, Woodford, Linford and Parker, offered a more nuanced view. The issues were aired within literature read by British Pentecostals[19] and in the relatively high circulation magazine, *Pentecost*, edited by Gee.[20] They received a further impetus through the ministries of Kenneth Hagin, Kenneth Copeland and Morris Cerullo[21] in the 1980s and

---

16 A. Linford, Editorial, *Redemption Tidings*, 18 May 1962.

17 Osborn, 1959, 99f speaks about 'faith in our own rights' among which is the right to be healed.

18 Kay, 1989, *passim*.

19 Harold Horton, while on a tour of the USA, wrote to *Redemption Tidings* (12 May 1950) and defended the authenticity and ministry of the healing evangelists.

20 Kay, 1989, 269.

21 It should be noted that Cerullo accepts the value of medicine. 'I thank

1990s when video and tape distribution could easily transcend national boundaries.

The problem for those who took the nuanced view was that they appeared to deny the texts in Isaiah 53 and 1 Peter 2:24 which coupled Christ's death with healing. If questions were asked about why everyone who was prayed for was not healed, or even why some people, after fervent prayer, got worse or died, answers were difficult to find. Perhaps the person who was ill lacked faith? But if this were so, what was to be made of people who were healed after they had relapsed into unconsciousness or of children who did not understand what it was they were meant to believe? Perhaps, then, the minister lacked faith? But most ministers would say that they neither felt more nor less faith when they prayed for people. They simply prayed and some were healed and some were not. An alternative position put the matter on a different plane. Healing, it was argued, was a spiritual gift given to a small number of fortunate individuals, most of whom were evangelists. The ordinary pastor could not expect to emulate the miracles of the Jeffreys brothers or the American evangelists. Consequently, it was best to wait till campaigns and crusades were held in the vicinity and then to gather a bus load of people and take them along to be prayed for.

This view, that healing was given permanently to certain gifted individuals, foundered on the biblical text. The gift of healing was given not for the person who was well but for the person who was ill. Thus to assume that a gift of healing was the permanent possession of the evangelists was absurd. Moreover, the context of gifts of healing in 1 Corinthians made it clear that this gift belonged within the life and activity of the congregation in the same way as tongues, interpretation and prophecy. How, too, were the elders of James 5 to be fitted into this account? They clearly were not evangelists. Furthermore, for those who thought about it, the percentage of people healed after prayer by the evangelist was not very different from the percentage healed when the local pastor prayed: it was simply that the evangelist prayed for more people and, out of the

---

[21] (*continued*) God for good doctors and for all the achievements of medical science which help alleviate the suffering and pains of humanity', Cerullo, 1979. 87.

hundreds who came forward, there would always be some dramatic manifestations.

Petts, writing as an Assemblies of God minister with academic credibility, examined all the instances in the New Testament where the traditional Pentecostal doctrine of healing in the atonement might be supported. He concluded, contra the views of some early Pentecostals and Osborn, Hagin and Copeland, that healing is only 'indirectly and ultimately' in the atonement. He accepted that the doctrine had been beneficial in asserting, even if the basis was incorrect, the continuing will of God to heal. And he applauded the focus on healing as part of the gospel and on salvation as being holistic in nature. But he criticised extreme forms of the doctrine for its destructive pastoral effects: it left the unhealed with a sense of guilt in addition to the physical problems that had prompted their search for healing[22]. In some cases, too, it had led to the unnecessary death of children whose medication had been withdrawn.[23]

The modified form of the doctrine that Petts wished to defend recognised that healing will take place at the parousia when corruptible and mortal bodies put on incorruptibility and immortality. Until that time, healing is to be understood as a gift of the Holy Spirit and a pledge and foretaste of the parousial consummation. To the extent that the resurrection of the dead at the parousia is a consequence of Christ's death, healing is *ultimately* located within the atonement. To the extent that the gift of the Holy Spirit is a consequence of Christ's death, healing is *indirectly* located within the atonement.

The care and scholarly way with which Petts examined the controversial texts indicated that Pentecostals had become capable of moving into the academic arena. Petts' views were gradually influential and it may be that in future Pentecostal ministers will draw more of their doctrine from an academic forum and less from the traditions that stemmed from prayer meetings and mass evangelism. Or it may be that there will be two Pentecostal theologies and churchmanships side by side, one academic, nuanced and complex and the other non-academic, simple and eminently preachable.

---

[22] Petts, 1993.

[23] Barron, 1987, 130.

The Church of God position is that 'divine healing is provided for in the atonement'[24] though, as with the doctoral studies of Petts, the re-examination of doctrine using academic apparatus is now taking place.[25] Thomas concluded, against his denomination's preponderant view, that Paul's thorn in the flesh indicated that illness could persist through the will of God. But the text also shows that, in normal circumstances, the Christian should pray and expect to be healed.

Theology and 'faith' teaching

The debate within Pentecostalism about healing that surfaced in the early post-war period revolved around the function of the atonement. Did Christ actually carry the sicknesses and pains of the believer on the cross in the same way as he carried sin? From about the 1970s onward this debate was mingled with another one. Did God intend Christians to be materially poor or should they, by faith, find a way to prosperity? Since material prosperity was reflected in the physical realm by health, the two themes often coincided. Health might be secured by faith as a Christian's right. Prosperity might also be secured in the same way and using the same faith. The evangelists who began by preaching healing often continued by preaching prosperity. Pentecostals who embraced healing found themselves following the preacher's logic and expecting prosperity. And, if prosperity was to be secured by giving, then giving might also release the faith that obtained healing.

The psychological appeal of prosperity teaching was considerable for ministers who often, especially at the start of their ministries, found themselves facing grinding poverty and huge financial commitments. The pastor who wanted to extend a church building was encouraged to believe that God would supply the necessary finance, even if he or she knew that directed congregational giving would reduce the sums that could be paid towards a stipend. Faith for a building project often made faith for personal finance necessary. The message that faith in God could produce prosperity was inevitably welcome and, though it could lead to

[24] Hollenweger, 1972, 517.

[25] Notably in the work of Thomas (e.g. Thomas, 1996).

amazing irresponsibility, often resulted in equally amazing and wonderfully successful projects.[26]

Faith as a means for obtaining healing or prosperity or, indeed, anything that was within the will of God was erected into a distinctive doctrine. It was associated with the healing evangelist Morris Cerullo (b. 1931) but it was also heard in the ministry of the earlier evangelists Kenneth Hagin (b. 1917), Oral Roberts (b. 1918) and T.L. Osborn (b. 1923). These men were often Pentecostal in background and invariably Pentecostal in experience. Their large crusades and high profile ministries were an apparent guarantee that they enjoyed the favour of God and that therefore their doctrine must be well-founded.

Faith became a matter of 'claiming promises' without a due regard for their context or any conditions that might attach to them. At its worst, faith meant taking more or less any verse in the Bible and treating it like a divine guarantee that certain things would happen. Even when common sense, Christian advice and other passages of Scripture argued in quite a different direction, Faith teaching insisted that such-and-such would happen and was the will of God. In relation to healing, this doctrine was often accompanied with 'positive confession' in which the believer could not consider that healing might not take place: to do so would be to lack faith, and to lack faith would prevent healing occurring. Positive confession often meant saying 'I have been healed' when no healing had taken place. Equally, positive confession meant saying, 'God is going to put a new building here' when God might be going to do no such thing. Once embarked upon, however, it was impossible to turn around. Faith must prevail against all negativity. Such teaching could produce marvellous powers of endurance and, if it was faith in a project that was genuinely within the will of God, everything worked out. The danger, sadly, was that the Almighty was thought to be susceptible to bullying by Christians who had taken a verse or two of Scripture to be the summit of divine wisdom.

---

[26] I can think of £1m church building projects that came to nothing and embarrassed both congregation and minister, other projects which incurred debts that took years to settle and yet others that were paid within months.

The Toronto blessing

The Toronto blessing spread to the UK in late May 1994.[27] It had begun in the Airport Vineyard Church in Toronto, Canada, some months earlier and was characterised by laughter 'in the Spirit' during church meetings and by falling down 'under the power' or 'being slain in the Spirit' and 'resting in the Lord'. The proverbially staid character of the British might be thought to have resisted these phenomena but, as the data presented below show, the main Pentecostal denominations in Britain were largely favourable to its arrival and, in many instances, to its practice.

Major and comprehensive studies, either theological or sociological, of the Toronto blessing are as yet unavailable. It has been linked historically with the Latter Rain movement that began in Canada in 1947 and which led indirectly to the rise of the healing evangelists in the early post-war period.[28] This historical perspective is less precisely adopted by Macchia who, in a cautious welcome, was nevertheless keen to emphasise the power of laughter to 'break us momentarily out of our secular and ecclesiastical routines' and to give us moments of transcendence.[29] Poloma, reporting on a sample of participant observers to the Toronto congregation where the phenomena were first seen, was more positive in her assessment of the effects of the blessing.[30] Over 80 per cent of her respondents were in favour of the experience. In a later and more detailed analysis Poloma considered the likely institutional trajectory of the Toronto Airport Christian Fellowship in the light of the life, power and spontaneity that characterised its beginnings.[31] In a still later publication, writing of the specific 'fruit' of the whole phenomenon, she differentiated between two broad categories of consequences: 'healing' and 'empowerment'. Healing is divided into 'spiritual healing' involving greater intimacy with God, 'inner healing' by which inner pains are relieved and other sorts of 'mental and spiritual healing'. Empowerment is similarly subdivided by

---

27 Roberts, 1994.
28 Faupel, 1995; Riss, 1982.
29 Macchia, 1996.
30 Poloma, 1996.
31 Poloma, 1997.

reference to charismatic gifts and an ability to pray for others. She was able to show a correlational link between spiritual healing and empowerment.[32]

An altogether less hospitable note was struck by Smail, Walker and Wright who commented on the theological paucity and manipulation they found in the blessing's main proponents.[33] Schatzmann, a New Testament scholar, was more forthright and thought the attempt to justify the phenomena by selective readings of church history and biblical proof texting reprehensible, although he avoided a final verdict by counselling a 'wait and see' approach.[34] These published opinions are also reflected in a multitude of website contributions both for and against what has happened. Similarly audio and video tapes contribute to the discussion.[35]

The issues raised by the Toronto blessing could be classified under three headings. First, there was the public perception of the Pentecostal charismatic movement. The secular press reported on what was happening in Britain. Articles appeared in *The Independent* (21 June 1994), in *The Times* (18 June 1994), the *Sunday Telegraph* (19 June 1994) and in the *Daily Mail* (22 June 1994). Similarly the religious press picked up what was happening. The *Church of England Newspaper* (17 June 1994) and the *Church Times* (24 June 1994) also reported and there was discussion in *Renewal* magazine, the *Baptist Times*, *Direction*, *Prophecy Today*, *City News* and the *Alpha* magazine.[36] Public perception of the churches affected by the Toronto blessing was shaped by journalists and, in the main, they were interested to discover that the churches were springing to life. Secular journalists were surprised to see people falling over in meetings and sometimes moved by the testimonies given by those who had been affected.[37] The churches became interesting because of the unusual occurrences that took place within their walls. But interest did not produce attendance and, indeed, embarrassing behaviour might in the end discourage those who were on the

[32] Poloma, 1998b.
[33] Smail, Walker and Wright, 1995.
[34] Schatzmann, 1995.
[35] Smail, Walker and Wright, 1995, 156.
[36] Roberts, 1994.
[37] Cotton, 1995.

fringe of the church, who were nominal believers. This public perception might damage the moral authority of the church – such as it was – and eventually, after a flurry of excitement, lead to further and rapid decline.

Second, the widespread effect of the Toronto blessing was often interpreted by its Pentecostal and charismatic supporters as the promise of revival on the verge of being fulfilled. For many years, certainly since the charismatic movement of the 1960s, Christians have prayed for a revival on an enormous scale, a revival similar to the one which swept Wales in 1904 or shook downtown Los Angeles in 1906.[38] Revival was thought to occur when miracles, signs and wonders spilled over into the streets in such a way that the power of God could no longer be denied by a sceptical world. Revival implied that many non-Christians, even many adherents of non-Christian religions, would simply, almost overnight, embrace the gospel and fill the churches with new converts, thus making a radical impact upon the moral life of the nation. Whether revival began in the churches and spread to the streets, and from the streets to the institutions of the nation, or whether it began in large public meetings in hired halls or arenas did not matter. The important thing was that the tide of revival, or the fire of revival, should sweep away spiritual deadness and opposition in the churches and transform the climate of the world outside. Revival only genuinely occurred if both church and world were affected. But it was bound to be turbulent and to contain within itself currents of spiritual phenomena as well as counter-currents of scepticism and hostility.

The understanding of revival on which these hopes were based was one derived from a study of church history as well as from the text of Scripture. The great revivals of the past had seized complete communities and transformed their corporate character. Along the way families were reconciled, pubs were emptied and churches were filled. Yet church history showed that revival was often associated with emotional phenomena. People cried, groaned, shrieked, fell over, fainted, trembled and laughed.[39] When these

---

[38] Hocken, 1984.

[39] Both the Methodist revival in Britain and the Great Awakening spear-headed by Jonathan Edwards in the eastern United States witnessed some of these emotional reactions. The respected Jonathan Edwards set out

phenomena were seen they were naturally criticised by the Christians outside the revival for whom such behaviour was indecorous and even ungodly.

Thirdly, the Toronto blessing raised theological issues. One of these was simply to do with the way the Holy Spirit operates. For many years healing evangelists had been accustomed to see those who were ill and who came forward for prayer falling over. As long ago as the 1920s Stephen Jeffreys used to ask those who were prayed for at the end of a meeting to sit down rather than stand in a line since there was the danger that they would hurt themselves if they fell over after prayer. There was even some press comment about the possibility that the chairs were wired up to electricity, such was the reaction of people once he laid hands on them. And similar occurrences can be found in the ministry of most of the healing evangelists in the decades that followed.[40] Being 'slain in the Spirit' is a term that can be traced back to the biblical account of the response of the young King Saul when confronted by the power of the Spirit of the Lord: he lay naked all night and prophesied (1 Sam. 19:23,24). In this respect there was nothing new or unusual about the Toronto blessing. Admittedly it took place on a larger scale and, particularly in the ministry of the televangelists, the pictures of large swathes of a congregation falling over as the evangelist stretched out his hands and prayed in a particular direction were jaw-droppingly extraordinary. Tapes of Benny Hinn also showed him blowing at people – where his breath was said to symbolise the power of the Spirit – who fell over.[41] It made for good television.

The theological issue arose from the question of whether the Holy Spirit could be expected to act in this way normally. This question was sharpened by the exegesis that was offered in defence of the Toronto blessing when people affected by it appeared to become completely incoherent, incapable of walking, staggering around the room and, so it was reported in some cases, barking like

---

39 (*continued*) 'Some Thoughts Concerning the Present Revival' in 1743 in which he defended authentic religious experience, but took enthusiasts to task.

40 Kay, 1989.

41 I saw a video of a meeting where this happened but cannot give details of the title of the tape or the date of the meeting.

dogs. The staggering and incoherence was explained as being the consequence of being 'drunk' in the Spirit and the text of the book of Acts was brought forward as a justification for this occurrence. When the Holy Spirit fell upon the waiting church on the day of Pentecost, Peter justified what happened by beginning his sermon with the words, 'these men are not drunk . . .' (Acts 2:15) and the implication that was drawn here was that the power of the Holy Spirit had overcome the early Christians to such an extent that they appeared to be drunk. Therefore the signs of drunkenness brought about by the Toronto experience were exactly what ought to be expected if the power of God present in the early church were to be revisited on the contemporary church.

But the classical Pentecostals had with great care, and after extensive study of Scripture, adopted the view that the sign of the Holy Spirit's presence was speaking with other tongues (or glossolalia). Indeed, studies of early Pentecostalism, before the emergence of Pentecostal denominations, had been troubled by the preaching of numerous criteria by which to discern the baptism with the Holy Spirit.[42] Only after the biblical criterion of speaking with other tongues, or slightly more broadly with 'signs following', did the confused theological scene settle down and allow for organisation and church growth. When the Toronto blessing began to have an impact upon the Pentecostal churches, such carefully laid theological foundations began to be threatened. It was variously said that the Holy Spirit could do what he liked; exceptions to rules ought to be expected during revival; dry doctrine should give way before living experience. Theologically the issue was to do with the source of Christian doctrine. Should doctrine be derived from Scripture or from experience? And if the answer to this question was that Christian doctrine should be derived from experience *and* Scripture, then what was the balance between these two factors? Classical Pentecostals, particularly older ones, privately expressed reservations about the Toronto experience.[43] Classical Pentecostals took the view that Scripture was ultimately normative and, consequently, since falling over, laughing and crying could not easily be found in the New Testament, one should treat the Toronto phenomena

---

[42] Trexler, 1990.

[43] Private communication.

cautiously. Indeed, more acutely, the question might be asked whether, if someone fell down under the power of the Spirit during a Toronto meeting, did that person get up again either healed or morally improved? If not, what was the point of the experience? Or, more generally, were reactions *to* the Holy Spirit being confused with manifestations *of* the Holy Spirit?

In any event little empirical research has been attempted by way of explanation of the phenomena. Dixon, while offering a positive theological account, attributed the underlying psychological basis for the occurrences to ASCs or 'altered states of consciousness' which, like dreaming or hypnosis, distort memory, perception, judgement, sense of space, time and emotion as a result of physical conditions like lack of food, hyperventilation or sensory deprivation.[44] A similar explanation is offered by Middlemiss who draws parallels between general charismatic experiences and hypnosis and treats the Toronto blessing as a special kind of charismatic experience.[45]

Academic psychologists are more tentative in offering similar conclusions while, at the same time, being careful not to devalue religious experience itself. They recognise a variety of triggers for such experiences, including music, meditation and even intense anxiety which, within a religious environment, result in an experience that is interpreted in a religious way. In other words, the experience itself, which they take to be related to the intuitive capacities of the brain's right hemisphere, is given meaning by the brain's left hemisphere. The remarkable sense of inner and outer harmony found in the experience is explicable by reference to the integrated functioning of the two parts of the brain.[46]

None of the four main Pentecostal denominations in Britain has made an official pronouncement on the Toronto blessing. There have been no 'position papers' or party lines issued by Executive Committees. Within Assemblies of God there have been manifestations of Toronto phenomena at Annual Conferences and these have been accepted without being propagated. The denominational magazine, *Joy*, has taken a more positive position, but this is as a

---

44 Dixon, 1994 242.
45 Middlemiss, 1996.
46 Beit-Hallahmi and Argyle, 1997.

result of the editor's own convictions. Within Elim, the largest single congregation, Kensington Temple in London, which is also the largest single congregation in the British Isles, took a very favourable position and this was echoed by other senior Elim ministers but, again, no official assessment was made. Schatzmann, quoted above, is an Elim minister, and the conference at which he presented his critical paper was designed as a joint Assemblies of God/Elim consultation on the entire matter. The impression given, though, is that Schatzmann is something of a lone voice. Within the Apostolic Church, while there has been discussion, no ruling has been made. The Church of God is similar. In terms of the denominational context, ministers have a free choice to accept or reject the blessing.

What do the data show?

Dealing first with healing, table 4.1 shows that most Pentecostal ministers (62 per cent) have been physically healed as a result of prayer, and a significant percentage (12 per cent) have been physically and mentally healed. Analysis of variance shows that there is no difference between Pentecostal denominations on this item. When Pentecostal preachers declare that God is able to heal, they do so with the conviction of people whose own experience has validated their doctrine.

Of those who had been healed in any way, 38 per cent said that this had taken place during a worship service, 15 per cent through a healing service, 27 per cent while praying with friends and 23 per cent while praying alone.[47] This shows that Pentecostal worship is seen to be an occasion for healing and any understanding of

Table 4.1 *Experience of healing*

Have you been healed as a result of prayer?	All ministers %
No	18
Physically	62
Mentally	1
Physically and mentally	12
Don't know	7

[47] These figures are not tabulated separately in the text.

Pentecostalism must take into account the close relationship between worship and any form of ministry, whether through the vocal gifts of the Spirit or healing. Worship, usually with music and often with singing in the Spirit, sets the scene for other engagements with the divine. Healing naturally takes place in this environment. Yet, having said this, healing may almost equally easily take place while praying with friends or alone. It is prayer that is the common factor here.

Theology and the practice of healing

Table 4.2 shows that Pentecostal ministers universally believe in an interventionist God who heals people today. Analysis of variance shows that there is no distinction between the denominations on these items. This is part of a shared Pentecostal heritage and an important element in the Pentecostal understanding and presentation of the gospel. Theologically, Pentecostals believe that it is perfectly acceptable to use modern medicine, indeed that it is a 'God-given blessing' that should be welcomed. There is no sectarian resistance to medicine in the minds of the vast majority of Pentecostals. All that they wish to proclaim is that God can and does heal the sick, but this proclamation carries an implicit recognition that God *may not* heal the sick and that, if this is the case, it is reasonable to resort to natural means or the means offered by medical science. It is true that a minority of Pentecostal ministers believe that it is actually sinful not to ask for divine healing, but this does not mean that these ministers condemn modern medicine: they simply assert that divine healing should be the first recourse of the Christian.

Table 4.2 *Theology and practice of healing (1)*

Item	Agree %	Not Certain %	Disagree %
I believe God heals the sick today	100		
It is a sin not to ask for divine healing if one is ill	14	17	69
I believe the Holy Spirit is active in healing the sick	99	1	
I believe modern medicine is a God-given blessing	94	5	1
I believe in the laying on of hands for healing	100		

Healing is imparted by the laying on of hands. This is also one of the few items that attracts 100 per cent agreement from Pentecostal ministers across the denominational spectrum. It is fundamental to their view of ministry. The Pentecostal preacher *expects* to be able to pray for sick people and *wants* to lay on hands. Ministry, in this respect, is quite literally a reaching out to those who are suffering. There is not intended to be a social or ecclesiastical gulf between minister and congregation.

The items in table 4.3.1 are those on which the Pentecostal denominations differ. More than half the ministers in the Apostolic Church and the Church of God believe that 'divine healing will always occur' so long as the sick person has sufficient faith. This is the unnuanced position held by early Pentecostals. Elim and Assemblies of God ministers are much more reluctant to put all the responsibility for healing on the faith of the sick person. The spread of opinion on this item shows that divine healing, though it is widely practised and though ministers frequently lay

Table 4.3.1 *Theology and practice of healing (2)*

Item	**Denom**	**Agree** %	**Not Certain** %	**Disagree** %
Divine healing will always occur if a person's faith is great enough	AC	55.1	21.4	23.5
	AG	19.7	21.5	58.8
	Elim	13.5	19.7	66.8
	CG	60.8	5.9	33.3
Physical healing is provided by Christ's atonement	AC	87.5	7.3	5.2
	AG	88.9	6.3	4.8
	Elim	80.9	10.5	8.6
	CG	98	2	
I believe in 'healing of the memories'	AC	68.8	22.6	8.6
	AG	47.4	29.2	23.3
	Elim	65.7	22.8	11.5
	CG	63	28.3	8.7
All Christians should be able to lay hands on the sick and pray for them	AC	86.7	4.1	9.2
	AG	93.4	2.8	3.8
	Elim	92.7	3.5	3.8
	CG	84.3	7.8	7.8

hands on people, is a matter of uncertain theology: about a fifth of ministers in three of the denominations are unsure whether faith *is* the key issue or not.

The ministry of all Christians in healing is accepted by nearly 85 per cent of ministers. Apostolic Church and Church of God ministers are the most reserved here and this probably indicates that these denominations have a greater tendency to take a traditional view of ministry, less one that flows from the body of a congregation and more one that comes down from the platform or pulpit.

The one theological foundation that over 80 per cent of Pentecostal ministers accept is that healing is provided by Christ's atonement (table 4.3.1). The wording here is deliberately general. Healing is not 'in' the atonement but is 'provided by' it. Nevertheless a sizeable proportion of ministers disagree with or are uncertain about this proposition (despite their fundamental truths or tenets). This implies that these ministers wish to offer another theology of healing, though what this is is unclear – after all they nearly without exception agree that the Holy Spirit is involved in some way (table 4.2).

There is more disagreement in their evaluation of the phenomenon of 'healing of the memories' which occurs when people suffering from persistent depression or guilt or another disorder are 'released' through prayer (table 4.3.1). The Assemblies of God ministers are more sceptical about the reality of this sort of healing than the others and less than half give it credence.

Faith teaching and healing

The Hagin/Copeland faith teaching is more likely to be held by older ministers and ministers who have not received full-time training.[48] Presumably training provides ministers with an opportunity to consider a diversity of views on the working of faith and to engage with the scriptural passages that are not preached by Faith teachers. These texts show faith is sometimes needed when coping with suffering (Heb. 11:36,37), for example, and is not simply a gateway to health and prosperity. There are, in other words, arguments for believing that healing cannot always be received simply

---

[48] Kay, 1999c.

because a certain critical mass of faith has been attained.[49] Moreover there is anecdotal evidence that the same results occur when a theology of suffering is preached in conjunction with a theology of healing as when healing is preached as being the will of God for everyone now.

Prevalence and correlates of the Toronto blessing

To gain an assessment of the prevalence of the Toronto blessing and of its acceptability to Pentecostal ministers a scale of four items was constructed. The items and psychometric properties of the scale are shown in table 4.4. High scoring on this scale shows approval of the Toronto blessing and its presence in the ministry of respondents. The scale has a minimum score of 4 and a maximum of 20.

Table 4.5 shows that there are sizeable differences in the acceptability of the Toronto blessing within the Pentecostal denominations. Elim and Assemblies of God are much more favourable than either the Apostolic church or the Church of God. The differences are large enough to register a highly significant chi-square.

Assessment of the support for the Toronto blessing within the various denominations was gauged by the ministers' responses to the single, specific item, 'I approve of the Toronto blessing (laughing in the Spirit)'. Altogether 46 per cent of the Apostolic, 59 per cent of the Assemblies of God, 76 per cent of the Elim and 27 per cent of the Church of God ministers agreed or agreed strongly with this statement. These figures give a clear indication of the general

Table 4.4 *Toronto blessing scale*

How often in the past three months have *you* . . .	**Item rest of test (r)**
Seen people 'slain in the Spirit' as a result of your ministry	.8009
Seen people 'laughing in the Spirit' as a result of your ministry	.8060
Seen manifestations of the Toronto blessing as a result of your ministry	.8937
Given a positive testimony about the Toronto blessing	.6690

Alpha .9091

[49] James 5:15,16 not only mentions forgiveness and confession of sin but also presumes that faith will be exercised by the minister (the elders) rather than the sick person.

Table 4.5 *Toronto blessing scale by denomination*

Denomination	**Mean**	**Std Dev**
Apostolic	6.37	3.34
Assemblies of God	8.12	4.56
Elim	9.84	4.75
Church of God	5.28	1.28

Chi square 22.446, $P < .000$

level of support for the Toronto blessing within the four Pentecostal denominations. In each instance more than 25 per cent of ministers support the blessing, and in the case of Elim more than three-quarters make this evaluation. As might be expected, level of approval of the Toronto blessing in each denomination exactly mirrors the ranking of Toronto blessing scale scores in the previous table.

To discover how the Toronto blessing functions in relation to other aspects of church life, correlations between items relating to healing and the Toronto scale were computed.[50] In the event the correlations that were found suggest that the Toronto blessing was associated with the *acceptance of prosperity teaching*. This is shown by correlation with the item 'all Christians should experience material prosperity' ($r = .1821$, $p < .000$). In respect of healing, items were also significantly related to the Toronto scale[51]. For instance, 'all Christians should be able to lay hands on the sick and pray for them' ($r = .1761$, $p < .000$) and 'I believe in healing of the memories' ($r = .1601$, $p < .000$) correlated positively and significantly with the Toronto scale.

This combination of correlations with experience of, and commendation of, the Toronto blessing suggests that there is a connection between the Faith prosperity teaching and the Toronto blessing. But more interesting is the linkage between the Toronto blessing and the belief that all Christians should be able to lay hands on the sick. The whole congregation, by holding out arms in a gesture of blessing towards those who need prayer, is involved in a

[50] Partial correlations were calculated, partialling out the effects of denomination, age and gender.

[51] Correlations between the Toronto blessing and healing were not calculated because of 100 per cent belief in healing shown in table 4.2.

single spiritual activity. The entire congregation can be experientially united.

Given this slant on the Toronto blessing it is no surprise to discover that the Toronto scale scores correlate positively with church growth ($r = .2644$, $p < .000$), the percentage of a congregation exercising spiritual gifts ($r = .1723$, $p < .000$) and with congregational size ($r = .3122$, $p < .000$). At its height, the Toronto blessing was particularly prevalent within large congregations where many people exercised spiritual gifts. Within a large congregation the Toronto blessing could be absorbed without overpowering members or frightening away more timid newcomers. Thus the Toronto blessing, despite the falling over and the laughing, functioned as a vehicle for empowering – all your problems can be drowned in 'heavenly' laughter – and mobilising churches. Christians could minister to each other, receiving a generalised sense of empowerment but, at the same time, the blessing was an image of revival because it was a group experience. It implied that if a whole congregation could be hit by the power of God simultaneously, then so could the street or the community. Stories were told of how when unbelievers came into church meetings they were bowled over by the presence of God. Conversion needed no preaching; God became tangible and real – heaven had come down to earth.

Conclusion

Healing has been part of the Pentecostal movement from the beginning of the twentieth century. Although the strong position on healing – that it is always available to those with enough faith and that medical provision is unnecessary – may be read off from the fundamental truths of Pentecostal denominations, there has always been, alongside this position, a more flexible, balanced and pragmatic line that has emphasised the initiative for healing as lying with God acting through the grace-gifts of the Holy Spirit. Although the strong position on healing has been asserted and reasserted by high-profile healing evangelists, more thoughtful commentators and, in recent years more academically competent commentators, have insisted on the validity of the alternative tradition.

The conception of the entire Pentecostal movement as being a revival, or the foretaste of revival, has been woven into the prayers and thoughts of Pentecostal ministers since its beginning. Revival is one of the recurrent themes of the Pentecostal movement and, though revival has often been confused with crusading, evangelism, church planting, prayer, restoration and renewal, the perennial attraction of revival stems ultimately from its place in eschatology. Revival is a way of bringing the kingdom of God into being through the impact of the power of God on whole communities, and even on whole nations, so that the church becomes visible and authoritative. Seen in this light the Toronto blessing can be understood as an analogue of revival, having an impact on both church and community at once. This said, its specific manifestations and effects are open to finer grade analysis that is important for a fuller understanding of the totality of its components. It certainly appears to be the case that its healing aspect leads to a greater likelihood that all Christians affected by it will be mobilised to pray for those who are ill.

Yet, just as there are alternative traditions concerning healing, one simple and direct and the other balanced and pastorally sensitive, so there are alternative traditions about the place of religious experience. One tradition emphasises experience, and almost any experience can be pressed into service so long as it has beneficial effects on the church and is not immoral, and the other tradition looks for a much more exact match between the paradigms and models of Scripture and contemporary events. This latter tradition is critical of the Toronto blessing, even if it acknowledges the church growth and 'loosening' effect that the blessing has brought. Since around 1998 the Toronto blessing has died down and been replaced by a much greater willingness to preach the gospel. Pensacola, the church that took over from the Toronto Airport Fellowship as showing what 'God is doing', has been described as 'Toronto plus preaching', experience coupled with strong, repentance-demanding proclamation of Christ in a mode that harks back to the early Billy Graham.[52]

[52] Poloma, 1998a.

5

Non-Charismatic Beliefs

Overview

This chapter examines beliefs about the Bible, creation, creationism, Jesus and the Trinity, eschatology, demons and finally women. It shows that within denominations there is both unity and diversity on these matters.

Beliefs about the Bible

The position taken by early Pentecostals with regard to the Bible was quite simple: they believed it from cover to cover and either ignored or dismissed critical literature. For instance, George Jeffreys distinguished between higher and lower critics of the Bible. The higher critic

> maintains the right to pick and choose the portions in the Bible which in his judgement are inspired. He does not allow his mind to accept anything that cannot be explained within the range of reason.[1]

The lower critic, on the other hand, is 'the one who unreservedly accepts the bible as the inspired Word of God, but who endeavours to show from its pages that we are not living in the days of miracles'.[2] This broad distinction between two kinds of critic would have been accepted by most Pentecostals during the 1920s and, since the early work of Pentecostal ministry did not capture academic attention, it

---

[1] Jeffreys, 1932.
[2] Jeffreys, 1932, 7, 8.

was the lower critics, the dispensationally-minded evangelicals and holiness advocates, who were most likely to pour scorn on Pentecostal claims for miracles and healing.[3] The lower critics, in other words, were distinct from Pentecostals in their interpretation of Scripture rather than in their evaluation of its authority or truthfulness.

The terminology used by Jeffreys had its roots in controversies of the previous century, particularly those within the Baptist community.[4] These controversies, as we shall see, were played out on a larger scale within the United States but many of the issues, including some of the finer points of detail, did have British protagonists. Both the Baptist F.B. Meyer (1847–1929) and the respected evangelical Bishop of Liverpool, J.C. Ryle (1816–1900), affirmed their belief in the verbal inspiration of Scripture and by this they meant that God revealed himself through the words of Scripture rather than in a general way through biblical revelation.[5] One of the best educated early Pentecostals, C.L. Parker, who became a member of faculty at the Hampstead Bible School but who also ran his own Bible Reading Institute in the early 1920s, outlined the doctrinal basis of his institute as standing for 'the verbal inspiration of the original Hebrew and Greek Scriptures', a form of words that recognised variation in English translations and, probably, the concept that the original autographs of Scripture, rather than any transmitted texts, were without error.[6] For the majority of Pentecostals such niceties were almost certainly not worth consideration.

Boddy received training for ordination from Bishop Lightfoot at Auckland Castle, though little information survives about the extent of the course the bishop offered.[7] It is possible that the

---

[3] Budgen, 1985 is a recent example. Harris (nd) is an earlier example.

[4] This seems to be the implication of Bebbington, 1989, and his reference to Spurgeon, 186.

[5] Bebbington, 1989, 189, 190.

[6] Parker, 1922. Percy Parker, who appears to have been no relation to C.L. Parker, considered the inspiration of the different translations and admitted copyist errors might have occurred. Parker, 1931, 57.

[7] Lightfoot, like C.J. Vaughan, offered training to men in his parish privately. They were known respectively as 'Lightfoot's lambs' and 'Vaughan's doves', see Moorman, 1980, 372. 'These men [Lightfoot, Westcott and Hort] brought the study of the Bible on to a new level – devout, reverent and fearless. Calmly accepting what was indisputable of the conclusions of the archaeologists and biblical critics, they guided scholarship into new channels

students considered matters of textual criticism but, if they did, then they would have concluded, as Lightfoot's massive scholarship concluded, that the Scripture was reliable and authoritative.[8] When Boddy edited *Confidence* he certainly made sure he included articles about the Bible in the early editions. A record of a sermon by Graham Scroggie that argues for verbal inerrancy appeared in 1909 and an article by Boddy himself was more practical and Pentecostal: it contended for the indispensability of Scripture in the Christian's life but suggested that the Bible was often not believed by contemporary sceptics because it was not confirmed by miraculous signs.[9] Within the ranks of evangelical Anglicans there were certainly disagreements about the nature and extent of the work of the Holy Spirit in relation to the text of Scripture. In a controversy dating back to 1912 the Bible Churchman's Missionary Society split from the Church Missionary Society in 1922 over the exact wording of a statement defining Christ's authority as a teacher. The CMS said 'we believe that His teaching, as recorded in the New Testament, is free from error, and that His authority is final' but the BCMS clergy wanted the words 'and utterances' to be inserted after 'His teaching' to convey the notion that the very words of Christ were in view.[10] To accommodate the liberal wing of the CMS, the insertion was not made and the split then took place.

Behind and beyond these verbal differences there were issues of substance about the kind of religion that Christianity was and its role within society. The Modern Church People's Union had been founded as a pressure group within the Anglican Church in 1898 with the intention of taking seriously the implications of 'modern thought'. The term 'modernist' was taken over from the Catholics after Pius X had condemned 'Catholic modernists' in an encyclical

---

[7] (*continued*) and did much towards bridging the gulf between science and religion, and between faith and scholarship'. Moorman, 1980, 377.

[8] Gilpin, 1976, 130, quotes but does not source, this interesting quotation from Lightfoot: 'verbal inspiration is involved in the conception of any inspiration at all, because words are at once the instrument of carrying on, and means of expressing, ideas'.

[9] See *Confidence*, April, 1909, 82–84 and *Confidence*, May 1909, 108–110.

[10] Manwaring, 1985, 25.

of 1907. Modernism restated the Christian faith and 'argued that belief in biblical inspiration must be wholly separated from belief in biblical infallibility' and recognised the validity of the conclusions of biblical scholarship to the extent that the virgin birth was treated as legendary, the resurrection of Christ was a non-literal event and the appearance of human beings and all life upon earth came about through the evolutionary process described by Darwin.[11]

Within the period from the emergence of Pentecostalism right through until the mid-1930s modernism became a cultural phenomenon that swept through novels, poetry, painting, sculpture and architecture. Religion, partly as a result of the traumatic events of the 1914–18 war, was thought to be out-moded and even 'shameful and distressing' to use the words of Virginia Woolf when she discovered that T.S. Eliot had become an Anglo-Catholic believer in God and immortality. The conventional wisdom placed religion, and particularly Anglicanism, within the sphere of decent or acceptable rituals – a kind of public respect for the discarded beliefs of Victorian grandparents – but which had no intellectual credibility or private value.[12]

Against all this Pentecostals stood firmly. Their interest in cultural trends was minimal and few of them belonged to the critical and artistic circles where modernism was eagerly embraced. Similarly, Pentecostal scholarship belonged to the type that depends upon self-taught men and women rather than university and college courses. When the Pentecostals drew up their fundamental statements of faith they were determined to affirm the reliability and authority of Scripture and the terminology they used was intended to make this unambiguous. The Apostolic Church, for example, spoke of 'the divine inspiration and authority of the Holy Scriptures', and Elim and Assemblies of God, and later the Church of God, were very similar. By asserting divine inspiration the writers intended to show that the text of Scripture was authoritative and trustworthy and, more than this, that it was the word of God. But they did not intend to take a position that related to divisions among Anglican evangelicals or Baptists, nor did they want to become

[11] Badham, 1998, 3, 4.

[12] Hastings, 1986, ch 12, where the above quotation from Virginia Woolf occurs.

involved in debating whether all the words in the Bible, even those spoken by the devil or by Job's unhelpful friends, should be classified in the same way. What mattered to Pentecostals was that God had caused the Bible to be written so that, through it, the gospel had been defined. This same God could still speak to today's generation as the text of Scripture was illuminated by the Holy Spirit or proclaimed by a Spirit-filled preacher.

For Pentecostals, as the argument over the validity of New Testament prophecy in Hutchinson's Apostolic Faith Church showed, the ability to speak in other tongues gave each Pentecostal believer an extraordinary sense of the closeness and reality of the Spirit. For the professional theologian the Holy Spirit might be an abstract concept or a useful solution to the interpersonal problems of the Trinity, but for Pentecostals the Holy Spirit was a genuine reality and, consequently, it was relatively easy to conceive of the means by which the Holy Spirit might inspire authoritative canonical utterance. Pentecostals were at home with the Holy Spirit as week by week prophecies were uttered, tongues were interpreted and believers came forward for healing prayer. The questions raised in the mind of a reflective believer about the gift of interpretation might also find an echo in his or her thinking about the Scripture. Interpretation was, as Pentecostals emphasised, just that: it was not the translation of an utterance in tongues but an approximation of what had been said.[13] When discrepancies, for example, were found between an Old Testament text and the citation of that text in the New Testament, it was relatively straightforward to invoke the notion of interpretation, though one carried out by divine sanction. Similarly, the fallible prophecies given in morning worship might be seen as simply a lower and lesser functioning of the work of the same Spirit who had inspired the Scriptures themselves. Qualitatively, however, they were the same.

---

[13] Parker, 1931, 31, 32, while making clear that he believed 'the inspiration of the original writings extended to the words and even letters of Scripture' was careful to explain that the style of writing reflected the character of the different writers but that this in no way prevented the inspiration of the Holy Spirit. Parker was Principal of the Christian Workers' Bible Correspondence School associated with Elim.

Wider arguments about the text of Scripture certainly took place in the United States and though these only slowly began to impinge on Pentecostals in Britain there is evidence that by the 1940s they had begun to register slightly. As we shall see, the science-religion debate, particularly over creationism, was aired in Pentecostal publications in the period after 1945 when religious education was statutorily required in British schools. In the United States the publication of *The Fundamentals* between 1910 and 1915 led to the self-conscious emergence of fundamentalism, a cross-denominational force which repeatedly attacked modernist theologians for distorting and betraying fundamental Christian beliefs so that, as a consequence, Christianity was being transformed into something quite different from what it had traditionally been. As fundamentalism became more sophisticated and rigorous, it defined its terms more sharply and this led to the fragmentation of fundamentalist ranks so that some fundamentalists insisted on inerrancy and others took a different approach. James Orr, the Scottish theologian, argued that:

> Though Christianity is neither a scientific system, nor a philosophy, it has yet a world-view of its own, to which it stands committed, alike by its fundamental postulate of a personal, holy, self-revealing God, and by its content as a religion of Redemption.

And this led him to see Christianity as a world-view centring on the incarnation of Christ rather than a scholastic mental framework.[14]

In the United States fundamentalist authors criticised Pentecostals for accepting spiritual gifts. Fundamentalists frequently accepted a dispensationalist position that denied the possibility of genuine miracles after the era of the first apostles. At the same time, fundamentalists pointed to the confusion and emotional extremism that often marked early Pentecostal meetings. Warfield, in his 1918 book *Counterfeit Miracles*, made the astonishing claim (for a Bible-believing Christian) that not a single miracle had taken place

[14] Dorrien, 1998, *passim*, gives an excellent account of this. Orr is quoted on page 43.

after the death of the last apostle.[15] There was real venom in the rejection of Pentecostals by the fundamentalist aristocracy.[16] So, whatever their debt to fundamentalism, Pentecostals found themselves forced into a different category and a different camp and, during the anti-modernist struggles of the 1920s, Assemblies of God in the United States was not formally welcomed by fundamentalists as an ally.[17]

This position continued for twenty years. Pentecostals in the United States claimed they were fundamentalist without being recognised as such by the fundamentalists themselves. There was rarely a temptation to embrace the sort of position that Orr advocated. Mainline fundamentalism insisted that it was the very words of Scripture which were free of error and this position was described as 'verbal inspiration' or 'plenary inspiration'. In 1942 the new National Association of Evangelicals (NAE) became the umbrella organisation for fundamentalist evangelicalism and in the mid-1940s sophisticated inerrancy claims were being made and defended by a new generation of scholars. The welcome invitation by evangelical leaders to Assemblies of God to the meeting that eventually led to the formation of the Association was an agreeable call in from the cold for Pentecostals who felt that they had been shunned by their evangelical brethren for too long. Once within the Association, Pentecostals found themselves seated alongside holiness and fundamentalist leaders who, in their attitude to the preaching of the Gospel, were their natural friends.[18]

In Britain the Inter-Varsity Fellowship broadened evangelical thinking and also discussed the meaning, mode and extent of

---

15 Synan, 1997, 209. It is difficult to account for any form of answered prayer using Warfield's logic. For a comprehensive rebuttal of Warfield, see Barnes, 1995.

16 Faupel (quoted by Hollenweger, 1997, 191) puts it this way, 'I believe Pentecostalism arose, in large part, as a critique directed at an emerging fundamentalism which was attaching itself to the Old Princeton Theology'; Faupel, 1993.

17 The story is told by Blumhofer, 1985, 102f.

18 The British scholar Jim Packer wrote *Fundamentalism and the Word of God* (IVP, 1958), to defend the term from its denigrators, and later *Keep in Step with the Spirit* (IVP, 1984) which gave the charismatic movement a cautious welcome.

inspiration. Hammond, whose *In Understanding Be Men* was reprinted sixteen times in five separate editions between 1936 and 1961, explained that 'plenary' inspiration was a term employed to avoid the criticism of those who saw 'verbal' inspiration as a purely mechanical transfer of information from God through human agents to the original scrolls upon which the text of Scripture was recorded. Sensibly, Hammond suggested that there was no important difference between the two terms and his conclusion was that Scripture is a divine-human product parallel in many respects to the divine-human Person of Christ himself. Such an incarnational model of Scripture in no way counted against the sufficiency of the biblical text for salvation and Christian living, and nor did it count against the perspicuity or transparent clarity of the text whose meaning becomes apparent to anyone willing to be taught by the Holy Spirit.

After the 1970s the charismatic movement became established in Britain and held a range of inter-denominational gatherings where Pentecostals participated.[19] It was rare for these gatherings to discuss the status of the biblical text but, obviously, there were Spirit-filled believers whose understanding of the Bible might be a little less than fundamentalist.[20] Would meetings between Pentecostals and charismatics lead to a modification of the predominant Pentecostal view on Scripture? The answer appears to be a clear, no. In 1993 the Elim Church revised its Statement of Fundamentals and the interim report of the Fundamentals Committee (1992) recommended the words:

> We believe the Bible, as originally given, to be the fully inspired and infallible Word of God and the supreme and final authority in all matters of faith and conduct.

But the 1993 Elim whole conference slightly *strengthened* this wording so that it read:

---

[19] Fountain Trust meetings or Spring Harvest meetings would be examples. Moreover, 'liberal evangelicalism' began to appear; a softer more accommodative offspring from evangelical stock, Cooling, 1984.

[20] Roman Catholic charismatics were a case in point.

> We believe the Bible, as originally given, to be without error, the fully inspired and infallible Word of God and the supreme and final authority in all matters of faith and conduct.

The words 'to be without error' were added and imply that an inerrantist position was acceptable. There is nothing strange about this apart from the fact that it coincided with the era of the admission of Pentecostal Bible colleges to university accreditation. And universities in Britain, without exception, had no time for inerrancy. It appears that while the move to accreditation was taking place, Pentecostals were becoming more educated and more sophisticated in their defence of biblical inerrancy, though whether such a claim could be made for the Assemblies of God is questionable. The British Assemblies of God statement of fundamental truths merely says, as it has always said, that the Bible is the 'inspired Word of God, the infallible and all-sufficient rule for faith and practice'. Certainly, Assemblies of God was moving on with its degree programmes, constructing both Bachelors and Masters courses and, after 1994, seeing its students graduate under the aegis of one of the foremost theology departments in Britain at Sheffield University.[21] But Assemblies of God in Britain simply continued with its high view of Scripture without either strengthening it in the direction of inerrancy or weakening it the direction of liberalism.[22] Though the Apostolic Church was slightly behind the other two denominations in the accreditation of its ministerial training courses, its *Manual of Belief, Practice and History* spelled out a clearly inerrant position.[23] Again, there seems to have been no detectable pressure from the theological or academic world to alter this position. The Church of God, having a more episcopal structure and links with the educational scene in the States, was less sensitive to changes within the theological scene in Britain.

---

[21] Sheffield's Department of Biblical Studies was a 5 rated department in the 1996 Research Assessment Exercise.

[22] Assemblies of God in Britain issued a discussion paper in the summer of 1999 with the intention of putting any changes that seemed necessary to its April 2000 conference. Some changes were made, but most of these were only to do with punctuation or the modernisation of expression.

[23] Published in 1988, see page 171.

Yet it, too, affirmed its belief in the 'verbal inspiration' of the Bible.

If Pentecostal beliefs about the nature of the biblical text were largely unchanged during the vicissitudes of the twentieth century, the area where change might most obviously be seen occurred in the realm of *hermeneutics*. Such is the nature of Pentecostalism, which for the most part is congregational-presbyterian in structure, that any changes within foundational documents are extremely difficult to secure, particularly as a movement grows larger and more and more people have to be persuaded as to the correctness of changes to statements which appear to have functioned satisfactorily for many years. Given this practical difficulty in making changes to doctrinal statements within Pentecostal denominations, it is not surprising that though the words of constitutions or fundamental statements may remain unchanged, their interpretation over a period of time can alter imperceptibly until many ministers believe something quite different from their predecessors.

In recent years hermeneutical issues have loomed large within the minds of Pentecostal scholars. Petts, for example, discusses how doctrine might be derived from the narrative portions of the New Testament, and he does so by dissenting from Fee who attempts to lay down rules about the transformation of historical precedents into experiential norms. Fee's rules, as Petts has little difficulty in showing, are only partially convincing.[24] A more prolonged and radical discussion by Smith argues that evangelicalism has become 'textualized': it has been turned into a religion where there is considerable danger of the believer loving the book more than the author of the book or, to put this another way, the believer loves reading the Bible and forgets that this is not the same thing as hearing God.[25] In Smith's view the history of Christianity over its first thousand years demonstrates a shift whereby texts received privileged status and the original hearing of the word of God through reading aloud or prophecy was gradually suppressed and forgotten. Consequently scribalism changed the character of Christianity. Prophetic communities died; the holy

---

[24] Petts, 1998.

[25] Smith, 1997.

text stopped being a letter from a living apostle and became a relic from another age; the importance of popular oral life was devalued by a literate and priestly elite.

Such changes had hermeneutical implications. 'It was not a matter of orality versus literacy, but rather the relationship between the two'.[26] Such tensions have momentous implications for a contemporary doctrine of Scripture. Contemporary Pentecostal communities emphasise the reality of the empowering presence of Christ but they do so largely within an evangelical theological framework. Smith and McGee,[27] who may be ahead of their denominations, argue for a re-working of the Pentecostal approach to Scripture. Whether this happens remains to be seen but, at the moment, and within the fundamental truths accepted by Pentecostal denominations, the standard formulae all come from a basis that fails properly to privilege Pentecostal experience. Conceptualised in this way there can be no Pentecostal doctrine of inerrancy: inerrancy demands textualisation, orality forbids it.

These issues raised hermeneutical questions about the role of Pentecostal experience.[28] Modern Pentecostal scholars argue that personal experience may be assigned a verification function at the end of the hermeneutical process. In other words religious experience confirms that a particular interpretation is true. A more complicated way of thinking about this is to argue for a kind of three-way conversation between Christian community, the activity of the Holy Spirit and Scripture itself. Thomas argues that the Council of Jerusalem in Acts 15 demonstrates this trialogue in action.[29] 'The community testifies to the experiences attributed to the Holy Spirit and then engages Scripture to validate or repudiate the experience.'[30] Coming at this issue from another direction, but pointing to a similar conclusion, Plüss argues that the testimonies (personal accounts of God's dealing with an individual) which are such a common part of all Pentecostal meetings necessitate a theology that takes human experiences seriously and accepts that shared

---

26 Smith, 1997, 55.

27 Quoted by Smith in his article.

28 An issue discussed by Stronstad as early as 1992.

29 Thomas, 1994.

30 Archer, 1996.

experiences have a place within the life of a community which has the right to interpret them.[31]

All these hermeneutical considerations raise a question about the future of Pentecostalism: is it to be fundamentalist or experientialist? A question posing such sharp choices may be over dramatic and arises from Harvey Cox's diagnosis of Pentecostalism as living in a post-modern world where rationality has broken down. Cox's analysis of the world context for Pentecostalism, fashionable though it is, may be prematurely confident because post-modernism is arguably a western academic presumption rather than a universal account of the status of knowledge. And, as the findings presented later in this chapter indicate, a form of fundamentalism, as evidenced by adherence to the verbal accuracy of Scripture and by creationism, co-exists within Pentecostalism quite happily with a belief in the self-authenticating reality of an experience of God mediated by the Holy Spirit.[32]

Creation

Like other beliefs which were not included within the fundamental truths of Pentecostal denominations, beliefs about the creation of the world are likely to be influenced by intellectual fashion. This is not to say that these beliefs chop and change frequently but they are open to challenge and variation as shifts take place within the wider alliances of church and society.

For some Pentecostals, what is striking about the opening chapters of Genesis is the order of events described. Life begins in the sea; it moves to the land; vegetation comes first; then animals; human beings come last. No other culture in the world at the time when Genesis was written preserved such a seemingly modern account. Certainly a comparison between the book of Genesis and Greek, Babylonian or Chinese myths shows that Genesis is infinitely superior. The order of events given in Genesis is precisely the order accepted by scientific explanation.

Yet historical analysis suggests that beliefs about the creation of the world, particularly in the USA, were strikingly influenced by

---

[31] Plüss, 1997.

[32] Cartledge, 1998; Cox, 1996.

the interaction between fundamentalism and Pentecostalism. In the 1920s, Pentecostalism had become institutionally established and accepted many of the tenets held by fundamentalists though differed, of course, on spiritual gifts and miracles. One interpretation of events might be that the expression of beliefs about creation which were integral to fundamentalism were simply appropriated by Pentecostal churches and accepted without criticism or examination. Fundamentalists offered a strong defence of their position and this was helpful to Pentecostals who were not forced then to produce their own arguments in favour of a six day creation.

This way of looking at things suggests that Pentecostals and fundamentalists were pushed together (though fundamentalists did not, as we have seen, join forces with Pentecostals until the 1940s) because of their common resistance to what they considered to be the sapping encroachment of modernism. However, there were also factors that kept Pentecostals and fundamentalists apart. In the United States it is generally agreed that the collapse of the 'monkey trial' of 1925 seriously weakened the fundamentalist position within the court of public opinion so that, whatever the merits of creationism, it was not one that attracted popular support. It was better for Pentecostals to emphasise their own distinctive beliefs rather than to become too closely identified in the popular mind with a movement that had attracted intellectual contempt.

In Britain fundamentalism was a more muted force and probably never built an institutional base. The natural allies of Pentecostals were denominational evangelicals whose position on the biblical account of creation could be subtle and flexible. What offended Pentecostals in Britain, and attracted comment from its leadership, was the BBC's 1949 broadcast of *How Things Began*, a series for schools, that tried to explain the theory of evolution.[33] From 1944 onwards, after the Education Act of that year, religious education

---

[33] Wolfe, 1984, 330. Carter, 1947, was already detecting the weakened state of Christianity in Britain and he picked up the acceptability of evolution to the BBC before the period of the schools programme mentioned above. Barrie, then editor of *Redemption Tidings*, wrote a forceful editorial (11 Nov. 1949), quoting from a letter written to the BBC by Drs Davies and Watson complaining that evolution was being propagated without any contrary argument having the chance to be heard.

became a statutory duty of all county and voluntary schools. The agreed syllabuses that regulated religious education were then drawn up by local consortia comprising representatives of the churches in local authority areas.[34] Pentecostals were rarely admitted onto these committees which did their work as well as they could by avoiding controversy and keeping the life of Christ and well-known Old Testament texts at the heart of their syllabuses. But anyone who taught the book of Genesis was bound to discuss universal and human origins in some way. So the issues tended to arise. And, if they did not arise in the primary school, they were likely to arise in the sixth form.

Sunday school influence within Britain was relatively high in the post-war era. One study carried out in the early 1970s showed that about 15 per cent of children under the age of six years attended Sunday School and that even for those aged 10 plus the figure was up to 4 per cent.[35] Another study carried out in the 1990s found that 40 per cent of children between the ages of four and nine years had had contact with Sunday Schools at some stage during their childhood.[36] Whether a study deals with contact or with attendance, it is clear that in the 1950s figures must have been higher than they became towards the end of the century, and a survey carried out for the BBC in 1954 showed strong support for Sunday School as being important for the young.[37] So there was always the possibility of a clash between what children learned in the church-related context and in the school. Moreover evolution, both in Britain and America, was, in the period between the accession of Stalin (1929) and the fall of the Berlin Wall (1989), seen as a natural bedfellow of communism and atheism. The Soviet Union had suppressed religion and crudely attempted to justify its deterministic view of history by recourse to a comprehensive evolutionary mechanism that purported to explain the emergence of human beings onto the face of the planet and the struggle between different kinds of societies.[38] So, as far as Pentecostals were concerned, to support evolution

[34] Kay and Francis, 1997, 189f.

[35] Reid, 1977.

[36] Francis, Gibson and Lankshear, 1991.

[37] Wolfe, 1984, 473.

[38] Kay, 1977.

was to take a step in the direction of supporting communism, and to support communism was to support atheism.

Creationism

The publication in 1859 of Darwin's *Origin of Species* gradually had an enormous effect on the way human life was understood. The study of the reception of Darwin's ideas within Victorian England and in the United States shows a complex pattern of acceptance and rejection. In the United States one of the most vigorous defenders of Darwin was Asa Gray, the distinguished naturalist and a pious and evangelical Congregationalist. He told Darwin in a letter, 'I am determined to baptise [*The Origin of Species*] . . . which will be its salvation.'[39] Gray was a moderate Calvinist and he saw in Darwin's argument the working out of divine purposes through the process of natural selection. 'God himself is the very last, irreducible causal factor and, hence, the source of all evolutionary change' he wrote.[40] For the Calvinist the beauty of the evolutionary theory was that it accounted for suffering within the world and enabled an explanation to be provided for pain in human and animal life: it was the cost of progress. To this extent, Darwin could be seen as offering an answer to the age-old question of why a benevolent and omniscient God would allow suffering to exist within the created order.

The objections to Darwin in Victorian England often came from non-religious sources that found the driving force of natural selection too prominent in the theory. The leading scientific opponent within America was the naturalist, Agassiz, whose religious views were mildly Unitarian and who believed that the categories by which we define animals are illusory. In his review of the *Origin of Species* he asked

> if species do not exist at all . . . how can they vary? And if individuals alone exist, how can differences which may be observed among them prove the variability of species?[41]

---

[39] Moore, 1981, 271

[40] Moore, 1981, 274.

[41] Moore, 1981, 209.

It is too simple, then, to portray Darwin's ideas as being an assault upon Christianity which the theologians of the nineteenth century were incapable of defeating.

One of the issues raised by Darwin's theory related to the age of the universe. Between 1862–68 Lord Kelvin had criticised the theory of evolution on the grounds that the universe was not old enough to allow the operation of natural selection to produce the current vast range of observable species. In this he drew on his calculations about the rate of planetary cooling and the frictional effects of tides in slowing the spin of the earth.[42] Earlier estimates of the age of the earth had been much more rough and ready and, before the science of geology was properly established, Archbishop Usher's calculations from the genealogical tables in the book of Genesis had dated the earth back only as far as 4004 BC. With the arrival of more sophisticated geology – and this was one of the features of Victorian science – estimates as to the age of the earth stretched further back in time and converged with Kelvin's date of about a hundred million years.

Before Darwin, what picture had been drawn of the creation of the world and the origins of human life? Certainly Augustine, in his *Confessions*, interpreted the opening chapters of the book of Genesis in a philosophical and poetic way, and he did so on the basis of his consideration of the nature of time and space rather than by reference to any biological or geological considerations. Forster and Marston in a perceptive survey showed that the standard and orthodox positions of Christians in patristic times allowed for figurative interpretations of the key words in the book of Genesis.[43] Both Origen and Augustine made the point that it was extremely difficult to imagine the first three days of creation described in Genesis as being 24-hour periods since the sun was not created until the fourth day. But these considerations and arguments were eclipsed in the debate that took place at the beginning of the twentieth century as evolutionism and Christianity collided.

Dorrien's study of the sources and factors making up modern evangelical theology shows how, in addition to the challenges posed by evolution, the coincidental arrival of re-evaluations of the

---

[42] Moore, 1981, 134.

[43] Forster and Martin, 1989, ch. 11.

texts of the Old and New Testaments laid the conditions for the emergence of fundamentalism.[44] In one sense the issues were very clear: either the Bible was true or it was not; either the text of Scripture was the word of God or it was a human product of no more value than any other ancient piece of writing; if the Bible could not be trusted historically, could it be trusted theologically? In another sense, the issues needed to be put into perspective. If the church had defended the view that the earth was the centre of the universe and remained stationary while the sun rotated round it, and if this view had been shown to be completely wrong, was it wise to wage war on the contemporary findings of science? Would it not be better to find a harmony between the biblical revelation and the best conclusions of the best scientists?

On the American continent fundamentalism emerged from the Calvinistic seminaries of Princeton and the Presbyterian and Baptist churches. Though the issues confronted certainly concerned science, they were also taken up with the reliability and accuracy of the text of Scripture. In this sense fundamentalism was a movement that fought on two fronts. The textual front was the one at which biblical scholars were much more adept. The scientific one demanded knowledge across a range of disciplines that few possessed and, anyway, science changed its conclusions and made a moving target. Consequently, the dispute between science and religion often became a matter of simplified entrenched positions. Forster and Marston trace the appearance of a branch of anti-evolutionary thinking that was wedded to a young earth position.[45] This position, picking up the weakness spotted by Kelvin, was committed to the notion that the chronology advanced by evolutionists was incorrect. But it also insisted that Genesis must be interpreted both to allow for the creation of the world within six 24 hour days and that Noah's flood was universal rather than local. No other interpretation was considered properly

---

[44] Dorrien, 1998.

[45] Forster and Martin, 1989, ch 11. Although their book ranges widely across biblical and philosophical issues, one of its consistent themes is that proponents of the young-earth are putting forward a theory that is unsupported by science and deviates from the traditional Christian understanding of Genesis.

biblical. For example the possibility that a gap of aeons existed between Genesis 1:1 and 1:2 was ruled to be inadequate even though the possibility of the gap offered a simple resolution of many differences between science and Scripture by allowing for an almost infinitely old universe and for the existence of pre-Adamic creatures. Instead, all the days within the Genesis account had to be a normal 24 hours long and the first three days, when there was no sun, had to be measured against the rotation of the earth in relation to a temporary supernatural light source which ceased to exist after the sun had been created.[46]

In a way the question of the origin of the universe and the creation of human beings became confused with issues of the accuracy of the text of Scripture. Even without the gap between Genesis 1:1 and 1:2 it was perfectly possible to accept the accuracy of Scripture and to interpret the meaning of Genesis so that there was an accommodation between it and science. For example Kidner's IVP commentary on Genesis allowed for the possibility that the divine command 'let the earth bring forth . . .' would permit some form of natural, possibly evolutionary, process.[47] Other writers also pursued the notion of theistic evolution: the belief that evolutionary processes had taken place under divine superintendence rather than, as atheists insisted, by chance.[48] Others took slightly different positions and mixed evolutionary accounts with the notion of the special creation of human beings.[49] Others insisted more generally upon 'the imperative necessity of a harmony' that paid due respect to both science and

---

[46] White, 1978, 40.

[47] 'If this language seems well suited to the hypothesis of creation by evolution (as the present writer thinks), this is not the only scheme it would allow . . .' Kidner, 1967, 48.

[48] Blocher, 1984, 24f. is concerned neither to venerate nor execrate science but to base faith on appropriate facts and only to read the text of Genesis literally where it demands this. In general Blocher is unconvinced by aspects of the creationist case (cf. 228f.) and sees its proponents as being anti-scientists in thrall to one interpretation of Genesis.

[49] Berry, 1999, 37, 'Thus there is no conflict in assuming that we have had a pre-Adamic history but that we are also special creations in God's image.'

Scripture.[50] More recent evangelical writing on Genesis has accepted the day-age theory of creation: seeing the days as a schematic device to describe particular stages of divine activity, and has made the powerful point that scientific activity presumes regularity and rationality within the universe and this is precisely what the opening chapters of Genesis, taken together, affirm.[51] Yet those who made the accuracy of the text of Scripture stand or fall with creation in six 24 hour days could appeal to the desire of Pentecostals not to compromise their faith. Rendle-Short, for example, makes precisely this appeal, and others could point out that to disbelieve in Genesis was to undermine the theology of the major Pauline epistles (Romans and 1 Corinthians) which both assign a key role to Adam.[52]

Forster and Marston admit that they would be proud to be called fundamentalists but would resist the young-earth theories put forward by 'creation science'.[53] Although there is no distinctively Pentecostal position on either the origin of the universe or the creation of human life, it is evident that a powerful belief in the Holy Spirit and in miracles, and therefore an interventionist God, predisposes Pentecostals to beliefs consonant with sovereign, divine originating actions, whether these take place over a period of time or through sudden demonstrations of creative power. Within the United States, Assemblies of God ministers from 1914 onwards have insisted that, although it was necessary to believe some things in order legitimately to call oneself a Christian, there was never any biblical statement defining exactly how Christians should hold the biblical doctrine of creation. What mattered was that God, and not chance, had created and that the whole universe was not 'an outcome of accidental collocations of atoms'.[54] Certainly there are American Assemblies of God ministers who believe in theistic evolution, and say so when they complete their

[50] Ramm, 1955, ch 1. According to Blocher, 1984, 223, Ramm prefers 'progressive creationism' to 'theistic evolution' because it allows for several divine interventions.

[51] Wenham, 1987, 40. Kidner, 1967, accepted the 'age-day' view.

[52] Rendle-Short, 1981.

[53] Forster and Martin, 1989, 330.

[54] Russell, 1953, 51.

annual forms.[55] The balance is conveyed by Zenas Bicket, who points out

> nothing is required of Assemblies of God ministers in this regard, meaning that a variety of creation scenarios would be accepted as long as they provide for fiat creation by God.[56]

Although there is a danger in trying to make terminology too precise, belief in the creation of the world in six 24 hour days is often called 'creationism' and the scientific arguments deployed to support this view are usually known as 'creation science'.[57] The point about creation science is that it is essentially science that is either carried out or presented with a theological conclusion in view and, in this respect, creation science differs from normal science since the latter is essentially open-ended and may come to any conclusions.[58] Creation science is supportive of the fixed theological interpretation of Genesis given above. And as the scientific arguments in favour of evolution or the origin of the universe develop using data that were not available at the beginning of the century (for instance, the construction of family trees derived from the analysis of DNA) so creation science engages in its critique, looking for weaknesses and assumptions that are not defensible.

One of these assumptions is that the universe behaves now in the way that it used to behave, the scientific doctrine of *uniformitarianism*, so that conclusions substantiated by sophisticated modern

---

55 Personal communication from Dr Calvin Holsinger. American Assemblies of God ministers must reaffirm their allegiance to fundamental truths annually.

56 Personal communication through Dr Calvin Holsinger. Dr Bicket goes on to point out 'Anything that smacks of evolution could be questioned, although I have heard some statements by A/G members that they believe in Theistic Evolution. That is a problem for many, because it doesn't actively proclaim a supernatural being active in creative acts', which shows where the balance lies.

57 Key texts here are found in the numerous publications of Henry Morris, e.g. 1974, 1976, 1977.

58 Kuhn, 1967.

tests are assumed to be relevant to conditions thousands of millions of years ago. But, of course, we cannot recreate conditions thousands of millions of years ago, or even conditions a century ago, and so the extrapolation of today's conclusions to the past must rest upon an untestable assumption. Nevertheless the belief that the past is like the present has, according to McGrath, assumed the status of a scientific dogma that simply must not be questioned, since to do so would bring the whole scientific enterprise to a grinding halt.[59]

Though creation science is not officially supported by British Pentecostal denominations there are indications that it receives a sympathetic hearing among some ministers. For instance a series of articles in the Assemblies of God magazine, *Redemption*, on the subject of the Bible and science argued for a well-defined creationist position.[60] The argument starts with the attitude of Jesus to Genesis and shows that he accepted the validity of its statements (often by reference to the passage dealing with marriage, Genesis 2:24). It then continues by arguing for a young earth and by suggesting difficulties within the evolutionary scheme, perhaps by showing that there is a scarcity of intermediate forms between different species or between scales and feathers, and finally by dealing with difficulties posed by the early chapters of the Bible, for instance by the long day in the book of Joshua (Joshua 10).

There is insufficient data to make a proper assessment of the attitude of Pentecostals to science but it would be reasonable to suggest that, as with British society as a whole, there is a general favourability to all the benefits that technology brings coupled with a lurking suspicion of its media-debated dangers, whether these be genetically modified crops, experiments on embryos or fossil fuel emissions. Translated into a Christian context, such an attitude produces both pleasure when science supports Christian belief and scepticism or irritation when it appears to do the opposite.

Beliefs about Jesus and the Trinity

The doctrine of the Trinity is unique to Christianity and defines its shape. The doctrine asserts that there is one God in three divine

---

[59] McGrath, 1992, 209–212.

[60] E.g. Cooke, 1994.

coequal and coeternal persons, Father, Son and Holy Spirit, and that the Son, Jesus, has two natures, one divine and one human, although he is one person. The doctrine of the Trinity, then, logically implies the divinity of Christ. If Christ were not divine there would be a binity rather than a Trinity. Moreover the orthodox formulation of the doctrine asserts that since the persons of the Trinity are coeternal, all coexist simultaneously and there is no sense in which the Father ever becomes the Son or the Son ever becomes the Spirit. The distinction between the persons remains, and will always remain and always has remained, at whatever point in historical time we reach.

When the Trinity is considered only as an intellectual truth, then the equation between the unity of God and the threeness of the persons appears puzzling but, as McGrath has recently argued, the doctrine grew out of the trinitarian experience of the early church.[61] It was their response to their rich and complex encounter with God as Father, Jesus as Saviour and the Spirit as a present reality. Perhaps not surprisingly, then, the arrival of the Holy Spirit in renewed power at the start of the present century led after a while to disputes about the nature of God. These disputes, it must be said, were largely played out within the Assemblies of God in America between 1914 and 1916 and, as a consequence, Britain was largely spared the trauma that the American Pentecostal churches suffered. Within the United States, Oneness Pentecostalism emphasised the name of Jesus not only as a baptismal formula but also as a way of indicating that Jesus, and especially the name of Jesus, unites all the designations of Father, Son and Holy Spirit.[62] Certainly British Assemblies of God, having been formed ten years after its American counterpart, was sufficiently far away in time and in space to learn

[61] McGrath, 1988.

[62] The issue is complex because there are at least two forms of Oneness Pentecostalism (see Reed, 1988, 650) and because the Oneness of God is reserved for his transcendence while the Threeness for his immanence. But Frank Ewart, an early Oneness preacher, used to say, 'There is only one person in the Godhead – Jesus Christ' (Blumhofer, 1985, 47). Suggestions for dialogue and united witness between Trinitarian and Oneness Pentecostals have been put forward by Del Colle (1997) and Reed (1997). These suggestions have not been acted upon. Brumback (1959) suggests why.

the lessons of the dispute. Trinitarian doctrinal statements were drawn up from the beginning. When, in the 1970s in Britain, independent Pentecostals tried to introduce 'Jesus only' water baptisms, they were given short shrift by the main Pentecostal denominations.[63]

In Britain, the declaration of belief in the Trinity within the Elim Church was made at the beginning and remained unaltered at the 1993 revision of fundamentals. Belief in the Trinity as existing coequally and coeternally in three Persons who are one God was reaffirmed; so was belief in the 'true and proper deity', virgin birth, real and complete humanity, sinless life and bodily resurrection of Jesus. The same may be said of the Assemblies of God Statement of Fundamental Truths, first set out in 1924, that continues to assert the 'unity of the one true and living God . . . who has revealed himself as one Being in three Persons'. Equally clear and forthright are the statements in tenets one and three of the Apostolic Church and in the second declaration in the Church of God Statements of Faith.

There is one other issue, however, that relates to the person of Jesus. It might be thought that the humanity of Christ scarcely needed attention being drawn to it. But where the miracles and the resurrection of Christ fill the believer's mind it is sometimes possible to forget his human nature. Indeed an important part of Pentecostal theology insists that the miracles of Christ came about as a consequence of the anointing of the Holy Spirit on his ministry and not simply or only by the hidden power of his deity. In this respect Jesus, as a man who was empowered by the Spirit, is a vital paradigm for the Pentecostal minister, and Allen is surely correct to draw attention to the neglected theology of Edward Irving for first broaching these issues.[64]

Eschatology

The original Pentecostals were certainly drawn from a variety of theological traditions that had in common the expectation that

---

63 Kay, 1989, 337.

64 Allen, 1994, 89 and *passim*, has seen Edward Irving's theology of the Person of Christ as appropriate for modern Pentecostals. See also Strachan, 1973, ch 9.

Christ would return to earth. The arrival of the Holy Spirit was understood as an indication that the return of Christ had drawn closer, that a milestone had been passed and that the church was now entering the final period prior to the glorious return of the crucified and ascended Jesus.[65] The biblical texts that speak of the return of Christ, like the texts which speak of his resurrection, run through the New Testament. They are to be found in the Gospels, in the book of Acts, in the Pauline and Johannine epistles and in the book of Revelation (e.g. Jn. 14:3; Acts 1:11; 1 Cor. 15:23; 1 Tim. 6:15; Jas. 5:8; 2 Pet. 3:4; 1 Jn. 2:28; Rev. 1:7). Alongside some of these texts are references to periods of intense suffering, pain, distress and panic (e.g. Mt. 24:21) and, to make interpretation more complicated, some texts refer to Israel and some to the followers of Jesus, to the church. In Revelation 20:4 there is reference to a millennium, a period of one thousand years in which Christ rules upon earth, and this too must be fitted into any satisfactory eschatological scheme.

Early church Fathers like Papias (c. 60–130), Justin Martyr (c. 100–165) in chapters 80 and 81 of the *Dialogue* and Iraneus (c. 130–200) in chapter 35 of *Against Heresies*, believed in a literal millennium after the return of Christ. Yet, it was the authority and argumentation of Augustine that transformed this expectation so that it became a glorious culmination to the *present* era as the church, having replaced Israel in the purposes of God, grew suddenly more powerful and extensive thereby bringing Christ's blessings to the whole human race. In Augustine's words, 'it follows that the Church even now is the kingdom of Christ and the kingdom of heaven'.[66] Thus, Augustine's position was amillennial since he did not believe there would be any dramatic new revelation of Christ before the whole church age was consummated. Gradual improvement could be confidently expected.

A different view was proposed in the nineteenth century by J.N. Darby (1800–92). Although the influence of Darby was undoubtedly important in the development of premillennial eschatology, Dayton, in a seminal study, has clearly shown that its origins can be put much further back, at least to the Puritans of the seventeenth

---

[65] Faupel, 1996.

[66] *City of God*, Bk. 20, ch. 9.

century.[67] This influence was then carried forward into the theology of Wesley and the thought of John Fletcher whose dispensational scheme was to have an impact on American revivalism and thus Pentecostalism. The points of divergence between Fletcher and Wesley were crucial for this development since Wesley was so focused on soteriology that his eschatology remained deliberately unelaborated. Fletcher, by contrast, devised a scheme in which the dispensation of the Spirit culminated in the return of Christ and, when this was combined with teaching on sudden sanctification, the framework was in place for the Pentecostal theology that came into being at the start of the twentieth century.

Darby divided human history into a series of dispensations during each of which God dealt with the human race on a different basis.[68] Each dispensation, though, was similar in that it posed a test for human beings which they inevitably failed so that each dispensation was concluded by a period of dreadful judgement. The dispensation of Noah ended with the flood, for example. The whole scheme had the advantage of allowing prophecies of judgement and blessing to be assigned to different dispensations and this made harmonisation easier. Darby taught that at the end of the church age there would be a period of judgement but that Christ would return to rescue his people from the earth and that judgement would then fall upon those who remained behind. Christ would return in the clouds of the air (1 Thes. 4:17) *for* his church and, after a period of seven years during which the anti-Christ would hold sway, Christ would return *with* his church to judge the wicked and set up his millennial kingdom (2 Thes. 1:7f.). These *two* returns of Christ, one before tribulation and one after it, were popularised by the *Scofield Reference Bible* (first published in 1909) and embraced by Pentecostals. The rescuing return was known as 'the rapture' after the Latin word meaning 'to seize' because it was then that Christ would seize his precious people from destruction. And the appearance of Christ at this moment was the 'parousia'. The Pentecostal Christian was able to face modern wars and disasters with a sense that the rapture was coming closer while being able to sing, 'This world is not my home, I'm just a-passing through'. Reference to the 1913 editions

67 Dayton, 1987.
68 Eaton, 1997.

of *Confidence*, where mention was made of the 'Soon-Coming of the Lord in the air' show that the hope of the rapture permeated British Pentecostalism from its earliest days.[69]

The psychological trouble with an expectation of a premillennial parousia was that it could lead to stoic defeatism when Christians felt that all they had to do was to hang on to their faith in trying and difficult circumstances and that, if they did this for long enough, Jesus would come to the rescue. This form of pre millennialism, in other words, could lead to a ghetto mentality where evangelism became unthinkable. As the years passed, and certainly in Britain during the 1950s, when Pentecostal churches remained small and struggled, there was a tendency to allow horizons to diminish and hopes to fade. When this kind of thinking was coupled with petty legalism that frightened away newcomers and resisted all forms of change, it was not surprising that the charismatic movement of the 1960s found another eschatological scheme altogether more attractive. These Christians, some of them coming from Reformed backgrounds, combined a vivid and exciting experience of the Holy Spirit with Augustinian amillennialism. They expected the church to grow stronger so that eventually it ruled the world and presented the nations to the triumphantly returning King Jesus. Such an expectation motivated evangelism and built faith and confidence within its ministers and congregations.[70] Where the older Pentecostal denominations came across this form of teaching – and it was usually younger Pentecostal ministers who had social contact with their restorationist colleagues – it became easy to throw aside premillennial doctrine and say, 'Jesus will rule no more in the future than he rules at present. Let me believe there will be steady improvement in the condition of the church and so bring Christ's kingdom into being.'

At the time when Pentecostal denominations were formed at the beginning of the twentieth century, amillennialism was not a live option and so in Britain premillennial belief is found in the Assemblies of God Statement of Fundamental Truths ('we believe

---

[69] Kay, 1989, 32. A study on the parousia by Pastor T.M. Jeffreys was published in the June, 1910, edition of *Confidence*, 149–151.

[70] Walker, 1985; Virgo, 1985.

in . . . the Lord Jesus Christ and his premillennial second advent'[71] and in Our Statements of Faith issued by the Church of God ('we believe . . . in the premillennial second coming of Jesus'). The third tenet of *The Tenets of The Apostolic Church* also records belief in 'his [Jesus'] second coming and millennial reign upon earth'. Only the Elim Pentecostal Church, which originally accepted premillennialism, now omits any mention of a millennium in its Fundamental Truths. This was a change made only in 1994 after heated conference debate. The change in no way denies the return of Christ. The new fundamentals state 'we believe in the personal, physical and visible return of the Lord Jesus Christ to reign in power and glory', but they allow a variety of evangelical views to be held about the circumstances leading up to this climactic event.[72]

Demons

When the first Pentecostals were filled with the Spirit, there was no doubt in their minds that they had received a gift directly from God. It came as an unpleasant shock to find themselves accused of being deceived and of having been taken over by evil spirits. There were modernist critics, of course, for whom such an accusation would have been beyond the pale since they denied the existence of any supernatural entities at all. By contrast, members of holiness churches who disliked the emotionalism of Pentecostals, but who could not deny the evangelical doctrines they preached, had to find some other explanation for what they took to be the spurious claim to spiritual gifts. The most obvious critic in Britain of this kind was Jessie Penn-Lewis (1861–1927) who appeared to specialise in seeing devils at work in Pentecostal phenomena. Her book, *War on the Saints*, is a classic of its kind in that it provides a series of subjective criteria for spotting demons at work in the lives

[71] Reasserted by David Allen in 'The Premillennial Return of Christ', a seminar given at the Assemblies of God General Conference at Minehead in 1987. In addition to patristic citations, Allen argued from the text of Acts 1, Daniel 7 and 1 Enoch.

[72] Wilson, 1961, 19. Lewis, 1976, 259–271, describes the original Elim position more graphically.

of other people, and particularly in the lives of people who think they are free from devilish influence.[73]

The International Advisory Pentecostal Council (which apparently met during the 1913 Sunderland convention) had to deal with Penn-Lewis's accusations and did so without becoming engaged in lengthy and bitter polemics. Yet more damaging to Pentecostalism within Europe was the influence of the Berlin Declaration that in 1909 condemned Pentecostalism as being 'from below'.[74] As a consequence German Pentecostal churches were ostracised by German evangelicals. As an example of the continuing attacks of this kind on Pentecostalism, the publications of Kurt Koch are a relatively modern instance.[75]

The issue of demons remained largely undiscussed in a period between the 1920s and 1960s. The emergence of the charismatic movement changed this and produced a climate where every kind of doctrine might be questioned. Gasson, a Christian Jew who had at one point been a spiritualist medium, wrote about the power of demons and about his subsequent deliverance from them and conversion to Christ.[76] Soon afterwards a series of high profile charismatic teachers argued for the possibility that Christians might be troubled by demons.[77] Until that time the classical Pentecostals had based their theology on the text of the Authorised Version

---

[73] Take this passage, for instance, 'when the believer is in any degree deceived by evil spirits he is liable to live in the body, give way to the sensuous, and to be dominated by the physical realm. This can become the case through "spiritual" experiences felt in the physical frame, but which are not really spiritual, because not from the spirit', 59. The criteria advanced here are unusable: everyone lives in the body, everyone is to some extent dominated by the physical realm. And what are we to do with the small 's' for 'spirit'? Is she talking about the Holy Spirit or some other spirit?

[74] See Hollenweger, 1972, 223f.

[75] Koch (nd).

[76] Gasson, 1966.

[77] Derek Prince issued tape recordings and Don Basham wrote *Deliver us from Evil*, first published in 1972, that is, relatively soon after the charismatic movement had begun. Lester Sumrall's *Demons: the answer book* (New York, Thomas Nelson Publishers, 1979), argued that a Christian could have a demon but would remain safe by being full of the Holy

which appeared to allow a distinction to be drawn between demon oppression and demon possession. It was argued, on this basis, that Christians might be oppressed even if they could not actually be possessed.[78] The difference between these two states was seen as a difference between being troubled by a demon from the outside in the case of oppression or, in the case of possession, being troubled by a demon from within. Oppression appeared to be an inevitable and occasional consequence of living a Christian life and the example of Jesus who was tempted in the wilderness appeared to provide a model of this kind of difficulty. But possession, when the human body was under the control of the demon, was altogether more sinister. Missionaries would return from abroad with stories of exorcisms but in the secular west such occurrences were rare and not spoken about.

Discussion of the role of demons was related to pastoral care. Where pastoral care appeared to fail, or where there were Christians who, despite ministry from their pastors appeared still to be addicted or tormented, the possibility of attack from demons seemed to be a biblical solution. Furthermore, although the Authorised Version made a distinction between demon possession and demon oppression, the New Testament Greek did not substantiate this distinction. The New Testament verb *daimonazomai* (literally, to be demoned) did not allow the reader to locate the demon precisely.

Classical Pentecostals agonised over the issue but eventually came to the conclusion that it would be incorrect to think that a born again Christian could be possessed by a demon. If this were the case then it would imply that the salvation offered by Christ was extremely fragile and that the triumph of Christ over evil was only temporary.[79] British Assemblies of God addressed the issue by

---

[77] (*continued*) Spirit, 103. A similar answer was given by Maxwell Whyte (1989), *Demons and Deliverance*, Springdale, Pa, Whitaker House, 109f.

[78] Compare Matthew 4:24 and Acts 10:38.

[79] Similarly, Assemblies of God in the States issued a 'position paper' stating, among other things, that 'the idea of a true believer being inhabited by a demon erodes the biblical concept of salvation and peace . . . it is certainly not in line with the freedom the Bible assures us we have'. Quoted by Duane Collins, 1994.

printing articles in its magazine *Redemption Tidings*, and this persuaded most ministers.[80] Elim issued a report to its 1976 conference concluding that Christians could not be possessed by the devil. The matter lay dormant for a while but was pressed by authors like Bill Subritzky who produced a handbook in 1986 on methods of deliverance, self-deliverance, the personality of demons, matriarchal spirits and other similar matters.[81] Oddly enough, his ministry appeared to receive the support of the official Assemblies of God magazine, then called *Redemption*.[82] It was perhaps not surprising that in 1988 the Yorkshire District Council of Assemblies of God felt it necessary to discuss the matter again. There it was argued that to be 'in Christ' precluded the possibility of being 'in' an evil spirit – the same Greek preposition being used to describe both states (compare the Greek of Ephesians 1:1 with Mark 5:2).[83] In a slightly different form the issue arose again in the 1990s in connection with spiritual warfare. Teaching about territorial spirits had asserted that the progress of the gospel could take place only after the spirits which controlled certain cities or geographical regions had been bound by appropriately aggressive prayer.[84] There was a link between the spiritual powers which were being bound and the demons that served them. In Wagner's demonology, the four levels of spiritual forces were 'principalities' (or individual demon spirits), 'powers' (captains of teams of spirits), 'rulers of darkness' (regional spirits) and 'strongmen' (dominating wickedness in high places).[85] In popular Christian

---

80 Richards argued against the possibility of the co-existence of the Holy Spirit and a demon within the same person (11 Oct. 1973). The veteran missionary Lawrence Livesey also wrote on the subject (24 Jan. 1980).

81 Subritzky, 1986.

82 Subritzky's visit to the UK was given space in *Redemption*, July 1988, 23.

83 One of the strongest repudiations of the possibility of Christians being demon possessed was given by C. Hurt (nd) in *Ministry*, 13, 1–2. Hurt argued that there is no biblical or patristic evidence to support the notion.

84 Wagner, 1991, *Territorial Spirits*, Chichester, Sovereign World. Continued interdenominational support for 'deliverance ministry' is also generated by the work of Peter Horrobin. See Horrobin, 1998.

85 Lawson, quoted in Wagner, 1991.

thinking the books of Frank Peretti[86] brought this entire conception to imaginative life, and it must be said that the *Screwtape Letters* of C.S. Lewis contributed to this genre and the world-view it projected.

Even within an academic milieu demonology has been given a respectful hearing. Ma describes how, as a doctoral student in 1995 at Fuller (in the USA), he participated in a course that included, as a practical demonstration, the exorcism of a thirty-nine year old man called Joe. The exorcist was Charles Kraft. The demons were interrogated during the session and their involvement with Joe's life unravelled. The session required Joe to travel imaginatively back in time to the crucial moments when the demons entered him and took control of aspects of his personality. Ma's reflection on what he saw from the perspective of a traditional Pentecostal leads him to point out that parts of Kraft's practice were directly contrary to Scripture while other parts may be relevant to the continuing development of Pentecostal doctrine.[87]

Within Britain a general consensus among Pentecostal denominations has been reached and maintained. What is interesting about the twists and turns in the argument, however, is that unlike the other topics mentioned in this chapter, demons are not mentioned in official statements of fundamental truth. To this extent belief about them is a matter of individual conviction and conscience. Theoretically, ministers could adopt any one of a number of positions on the subject but, in practice, as we have seen, there tended to be a large degree of unanimity. All this raises the question of the function of statements of fundamental truth within Pentecostal denominations.

In a recent study, using the database analysed in this book, ministers who believed that Christians are daily in conflict with demons were compared with those who do not believe this to see what sort of practical effects might be found.[88] It turned out that ministers who hold a demonised world-view are more likely also to emphasise healing, compassionate social action and prosperity. One way of understanding this is to argue that a demonised world-view

---

[86] E.g. Peretti, 1990.
[87] Ma, 1997.
[88] Kay, 1998.

produces a sense that life is a battle between good and evil and that this sense of conflict must be turned upon all that is negative in human life, whether it is illness or poverty. Thus, though a demonised world-view might be criticised from many angles, its positive outcome is a willingness to fight actively against evil. Or, to put this another way, compassion as a motivating force for Christian action may be less effective than the sense of struggle.

Women

Alexander Boddy recognised the ministry of his wife.[89] Mary Boddy had been affected by asthma during part of her adult life and during her husband's quest for spiritual renewal she had been healed in answer to prayer. As a result, when the Sunderland conventions (1908–1914) were organised, there was a role for Mary Boddy. She lectured at the seminars and also regularly contributed to *Confidence*. The impact of Mary Boddy's ministry, at the early formative stage of British Pentecostalism, would have been strong. Both the Carter brothers and George Jeffreys would have been aware of this and so would the powerful figure of Smith Wigglesworth, especially since she laid hands on him to receive the baptism in the Holy Spirit.

As elsewhere, Pentecostals in Britain took much of their understanding of the Holy Spirit from Acts 2 and from 1 Corinthians 12–14. The passage in Acts which describes the initial arrival of the Holy Spirit specifies the occurrence of glossolalia and also refers back to Joel's prophecy when it was said that the Spirit would be poured out on 'your sons *and daughters*' (verse 17). As a result of this, the giftings of the Holy Spirit were never seen as a matter of discrimination between the sexes. Both men and women might exercise any of the gifts the Holy Spirit bestowed. Discussion at the 1914 Sunderland convention agreed that women might manifest spiritual gifts, and many delegates considered that this possibility required the reinterpretation of those texts which either enjoined women to be silent in church (1 Cor. 14:34) or which forbade them

[89] It is probably relevant that Hannah Whitall Smith preached at the pre-Keswick Oxford conference of 1874. In other words, in holiness circles, the ministry of women was accepted. See Dayton's account of the ministry of Phoebe Palmer. Dayton, 1987, *passim*.

to teach (1 Tim. 2:12).[90] Moreover 1 Corinthians 12–14 included references to women praying and prophesying in a congregational setting. This also supported the gender inclusiveness of Acts 2.

Not only this, but the Pentecostal denominations, by their disapproval of clerical attire, took a strongly Protestant line with regard to the priesthood.[91] In general Pentecostal groups would have been glad to draw attention to the Lutheran emphasis on the 'priesthood of all believers' (1 Pet. 2:9).[92] The emphasis during the Reformation was a largely destructive one: it was intended to remove the privileges of the Roman Catholic hierarchy. But, when the same proposition was applied in a more peace-making sense, it implied that male and female ministry might be indistinguishable.

At the end of the nineteenth century the Salvation Army, following early Methodism, had made use of female evangelists and so the ground had already been broken with regard to the preaching of women.[93] Many of the new Pentecostals were influenced by the fervour of the Salvation Army and approved of much of its theology. Even in the 1950s at least 6 per cent of Assemblies of God ministers had a Salvation Army background.[94]

Equally relevant was the example of the Assemblies of God in North America. Its first constitutional statement in 1914 affirmed that women are called 'to prophesy and preach the Gospel' though not to act as elders.[95] However, in 1935 the prohibition on female elders was reversed.[96] Perhaps a more powerful endorsement of women's ministry was given by the extraordinary popularity of Aimee Semple McPherson (1890–1944) and, to a lesser extent, of Maria Woodworth-Etter (1844–1924). Despite McPherson's

---

90 *Confidence*, November, 1914.

91 Despite their disapproval of clerical attire, however, several distinguished Pentecostal ministers including Stephen Jeffreys, Fred Squire, Howell Harris and George Jeffreys Williamson would on occasion wear a clerical collar.

92 Hollenweger, 1972; Küng, 1994.

93 Lyon, 1985.

94 Kay, 1989, 270.

95 Gill, 1995a.

96 Hollenweger, 1997, 267 quotes commentators who think the diminution of women's ministry in American Assemblies of God may be due to the influence of evangelicalism.

divorces and gossip surrounding her disappearance in 1926, she retained a loyal following and a high public profile and the Pentecostal denomination she founded continues vigorously in existence. Her visit to England in 1926 identified her with Pentecostalism when she preached in the Royal Albert Hall during meetings arranged by Elim's George Jeffreys. Later she undertook successful campaigns in England and Scotland in 1928.[97]

In 1924, when the British Assemblies of God was formally founded, no objection was made to female ministers, and there were several women who, from the beginning, were accepted on to the ministerial list and functioned as pastors. They continued to do so and to participate in the annual conference on the same basis as men.

From its earliest years, British Assemblies of God gave prominence to ministerial and missionary training that supported the concept of female ministry. For example, Howard Carter's Hampstead Bible School (the forerunner of the main British Assemblies of God Bible College at Mattersey) had, in 1923, 15 men and 6 women students. In 1924 there were 13 men and 20 women, and in 1925, 33 men and 34 women. In 1926 there were 25 men and 24 women and a year later 51 men and 40 women.[98] Unfortunately, over the years the effects of this educational policy were diminished by the large numbers of ministers who entered full-time pastoral work without any training at all. In practice, though the Assemblies of God always had some women pastors and evangelists, the main preaching and teaching work of women was carried out on the mission field, a circumstance that led at least one woman to ask, 'If we are good enough to preach in Africa, why aren't we good enough to preach in England?'[99]

A survey carried out in 1990 on women's ministries in British Assemblies of God showed that of 232 women, 3 were pastors, 5 elders, 11 deaconesses, 50 counsellors, 16 musical directors, 15 were involved in youth leadership, 52 were involved in home or study groups, 39 in women's fellowships, 15 in administration and the others in evangelism, prayer groups, senior citizen groups and dance

---

97 Blumhofer, 1993.

98 Kay, 1989, 124.

99 Paraphrase of personal recollection.

and drama teams.[100] In open-ended comments provided on the survey form about 10 per cent said they had no objection to women holding aspects of governmental functions in the church provided these were supervised by constructive biblical leadership. Reservations about women's ministry were varied and among them were the dangers of isolationism (where women's groups become a church within the church), insecurity (making less gifted women feel inadequate), independence (overruling weak eldership) and imbalance (becoming trendy or willing to ignore the needs of home and family).

A survey carried out in 1995 of Assemblies of God ministers found that the majority of ministers thought the major spiritual contribution of women in their congregations was through prayer (60 per cent of ministers thinking this) and, after this, practical contributions (29 per cent thinking this) were most likely to be cited.[101]

Within the Elim Pentecostal Church women were admitted as ministers from the beginning, though very few became pastors and most worked in ancillary roles or on the mission field.[102] Wilson, writing in 1961, pointed out that all deacons and elders in Elim churches were always men.[103] The main distinction between male and female ministers was not in the functions they were allowed to perform – women could preside over communion, marriages, funerals, baptisms and also preach – but in the scope of their activity at the Elim conference. Women were not allowed to vote or to address the deliberations of ministers without special permission; in this they were treated like probationary and retired ministers. More hurtful was the failure to ordain women. Psychologically such a bar was daunting and sociologically it must have been disempowering. It was only in 1999 that women were granted ordination (by the laying on of hands at the annual conference) and so treated on an identical basis with men. The delay is largely attributable to a small faction of ministers who steadfastly resisted equalisation in the face

---

[100] Shelbourne, 1990.

[101] Kay and Robbins, 1999.

[102] Wilson, 1961, 102, pointed out that there were 34 women out of a total of 53 missionaries on the field.

[103] Wilson, 1961, 92.

of a series of reforming reports and committees that had pressed for change for many years.

In its earlier days the Apostolic Church accepted the ministry of women evangelists but has now settled to a position where women are given the opportunity to function as deaconesses and to preach and take part in evangelism and youth work without being able to function as elders, prophets, apostles or evangelists. Nevertheless the church has a recognised Women's Movement with an integrated system of national and local leaders.[104]

Unlike other Pentecostal groups, the Church of God places its ministers into ministerial ranks and women may function in the lowest of these ranks. They may look after local churches but not oversee groups of churches or hold authority at national level. At the present time there are about eight Church of God female ministers.

In all four of these Pentecostal groups there is an acceptance of the authority of the Bible and so, in theory, all organisation and activity is based on Scripture and subject to its critique. Since the role of women, both in the church and in the home, is addressed in the New Testament it would be reasonable to expect New Testament norms to prevail. Historically what appears to have happened is that Pentecostal churches and denominations were most aware of female ministry in those areas that touched on charismatic gifts and, in the early days, when there were few, if any, denominational or ecclesiological structures in existence, questions about authority were peripheral. Within American Assemblies of God a case has been made for the gradual slippage of female prominence once the early rapid phase of expansion was passed.[105] So Pentecostals accepted that spiritual gifts might be dispensed according to the will of God to males and females alike and to all human beings regardless of race or age but, when these gifts were formalised into ministries or embedded in administrative offices, then women were sidelined.

At the same time the teaching in the Pauline epistles about the role of women in relation to their husbands appears to have been accepted from the beginning and to have remained normative. The

104 *The Constitution of the Apostolic Church* (3rd edn.), 1987.
105 Benvenuti, 1995.

husband was the head of the wife and this, presumably, meant that the husband was the person with ultimate authority within the marriage relationship (Eph. 5:23). This said, there were nuances and qualifications to this position in the sense that the husband and wife were also understood to be 'one flesh' and therefore united in partnership. And most Pentecostal men who emphasised the headship of males also privately and sometimes publicly acknowledged that in practice many decisions within the marriage were shared. Conflicts occurred when women insisted that their ministerial callings superseded their family obligations. There are two ways to resolve this: first, in the sense that the call of God swept aside all other considerations; second, and more consistently, that a married woman's ministry took place under the authority and with the support of her husband.[106] In this respect Pentecostal women were not true sisters in the feminist cause. Rather, they saw the outpouring of the Spirit as empowering women only within a framework of biblically ordered relationships.[107] This is not as paradoxical as it seems, since Christ was understood as coming to set human beings free from sin and all its consequences. Gill could therefore write in an Assemblies of God publication about 'the biblically liberated woman'.[108]

Within the ordinary life of the church such issues often revolved around the teaching ministry of women. It is here that the most unambiguous statement appeared to apply. 'I suffer not a woman to teach' (appropriately quoted in the words of the Authorised Version, 1 Timothy 2:12) appears to rule out any kind of female Bible teaching ministry. Yet as more subtle exegetes noted, older women were certainly expected to teach younger women and, presumably, children (Tit. 2:4). The ban on the teaching ministry of women, therefore, could not be complete and must be conditional.[109] Moreover, if women were permitted to preach as evangelists – and how could a thoroughly evangelical movement deny this? – was it

---

106 Kwilecki, 1987.

107 A popular exposition of this basis for ministry is given by Virgo, 1985.

108 Gill, 1995b.

109 For an academic examination of the relevant biblical texts and conclusions that come closest to a feminist position established on evangelical premises, see Evans, 1983.

practical to try to draw a distinction between evangelistic preaching and expository teaching?

Again, these issues were not written into the fundamental statements of Pentecostal denominations and were a matter for a changing consensus that shifted over the course of time in response to wider social pressures. What appears to be the case, however, is that the ability of Pentecostal Christians to resist irreligious and atheistic cultural and social norms enabled them also to resist feminism and 'political correctness'. Feminism hardly featured in Pentecostal churches even through the 1980s and 1990s or, perhaps more accurately, it alerted Pentecostals to issues to which they responded in their own biblical way. Within the British Assemblies of God, for instance, during the first thirty years of the postwar period the Women's Missionary Auxiliary (WMA) raised money for the mission field through sewing clothes or by distributing collection boxes. Though this was a useful supportive function, it was clearly subservient to the more high-profile work done by pastors and evangelists. It was only in 1988 that a second phase began. The WMA was disbanded and relaunched as the Women's Ministry (WM) department to emphasise a less deaconal and more prayer-and-preaching set of activities. Instead of working in the background, women began to organise rallies and appear on conference platforms to speak and teach. Instead of being dressed unfashionably and working behind the scenes, women began to be smart and to preach, to wear make-up and to lead worship songs in a style and with a sophistication that matched the surrounding popular culture. They branched out into the taking of school assemblies and Jackie Bowler, the first WM National Director, become a leader of a newly planted church. Others gave themselves to social welfare schemes like church-based pregnancy centres for unmarried mothers. A few women found a role in both eras. In 1959 Muriel Shelbourne went with her husband as a missionary to the Congo but she later returned to Britain, helped establish a vibrant new congregation and then launched into an international preaching ministry.[110]

---

[110] Shelbourne, 1993.

What do the data show?

Table 5.1 shows how prevalent belief in the Bible as the infallible word of God is, but interpretation of this belief must be made in the light of the 33 per cent of ministers who accept that the Bible may contain verbal errors. In other words, about a third of Pentecostal ministers would not be classified as inerrant fundamentalists. This spectrum of opinion runs across Pentecostal denominations and perhaps reflects the meaning of the word 'infallible' in statements of fundamental truth. Infallibility speaks of authority rather than verbal precision.

Table 5.1.1 shows that Assemblies of God and Elim contrast with the other two denominations in their lower level of support for the Authorised Version of the Bible. Elim is even less likely than Assemblies of God to accept the Authorised Version as the best Bible for daily use. This finding fits with other figures elsewhere in this book showing that Elim is the best attuned of these denominations to the modern world.

Creationism is least strong among Elim ministers. Only just over half of them accept creation in six 24 hour days and they show the largest percentage of ministers who disagree with this theological position. Assemblies of God shows the strongest support for creationism, although even here 30 per cent of ministers either reject or are uncertain about its validity. What is perhaps most remarkable about responses to this item is the high degree of uncertainty found here. All told, the figures suggest Pentecostal ministers constitute a creationist majority and an uncertain or definitely anti-creationist minority.

Table 5.2 reveals unanimity about the person and work of Jesus and the Trinity. Pentecostal ministers almost without exception accept the deity, humanity, virgin birth, resurrection, miracles and sacrificial death of Jesus. The very small percentage of ministers who

Table 5.1 *Bible*

Item	Agree %	Not Certain %	Disagree %
I believe that the Bible is the infallible Word of God	99.5		.5
I believe the Bible contains no verbal errors	67	19	14

Table 5.1.1 *Bible*

Item	Denom	Agree %	Not Certain %	Disagree %
I believe the Authorised Version of the Bible is the best one for Christians to use	AC	46.0	7.0	47.0
	AG	19.5	10.3	70.2
	Elim	10.5	9.5	80.0
	CG	34.0	18.0	48.0
I believe God made the world in six 24 hour days	AC	67.4	23.2	9.4
	AG	70.3	23.0	6.7
	Elim	55.6	33.1	11.4
	CG	65.3	18.4	16.3

do not accept the full humanity of Jesus presumably do so because they wish to emphasise his deity even more strongly.

Table 5.3 shows almost perfect unanimity in a belief in the return of Jesus at some point in the future. Pentecostals almost without exception are adventists; they look forward to the return of Christ as their future hope.

Table 5.3.1 shows that the Apostolic Church and the Church of God are almost solidly believers in the millennium. Assemblies of God is not far behind and the Elim Church is furthest away from this belief. In both Assemblies of God and Elim there is a substantial minority uncertain of, or in disagreement with, the belief that there will be a millennium.

Belief in the rapture is held strongly within the Apostolic Church and Church of God and less strongly held in Assemblies of

Table 5.2 *Jesus and Trinity*

Item	Agree %	Not Certain %	Disagree %
I believe Jesus is fully God	100		
I believe Jesus is fully human	97		3
I believe that Jesus is the Son of God	100		
I believe that Jesus rose from the dead on Easter Day	100		
I believe that Jesus died for my sins	100		
I believe in the Holy Trinity	100		
I believe that Jesus really walked on water	100		
I believe that Jesus really turned water into wine	100		
I believe Jesus was born of a virgin	100		

Table 5.3 *Eschatology*

Item	Agree %	Not Certain %	Disagree %
Jesus will return to earth again in the future	99		1

God. The Elim Church, however, can only just muster half its ministers in favour of this proposition. Belief in the rapture is shown here to be a matter on which British Pentecostals are beginning to diverge. The two denominations which show most sympathy to a non-rapture position are also those which are less supportive of belief in a millennium. This implies that something like a fifth of Assemblies of God and Elim ministers are in a state of flux over eschatology.

There is a surprisingly high level of agreement about the lack of specificity in the Bible about end time events. In view of this acceptance of the Bible's lack of clarity here, the majority agreement about a millennium and a rapture must be attributed to the fundamental statements of belief to which Pentecostal ministers give assent. In other words, although the Bible may not be clear, fundamental statements provide a standard interpretation and ministers

Table 5.3.1 *Eschatology*

Item	Denom	Agree %	Not Certain %	Disagree %
I believe that there will be a millennium	AC	99.0		1.0
	AG	84.2	13.0	2.8
	Elim	77.2	18.4	4.3
	CG	94.9	2.0	3.1
The church will be taken from earth before the millennium	AC	91.8	5.1	3.1
	AG	71.6	21.0	7.3
	Elim	56.4	32.2	11.4
	CG	96.0	4.0	
The Bible does not make the order of end time events clear	AC	25.5	10.6	63.8
	AG	56.4	11.1	32.5
	Elim	64.4	8.7	26.9
	CG	32.7	12.2	55.1

Table 5.4 *Women*

Item	Agree %	Not Certain %	Disagree %
Women should obey their husbands	90	6	4

are generally willing to accept this. Over half of Assemblies of God ministers and nearly two-thirds of Elim ministers agree the Bible does not provide clarity, but even among the Apostolic Church ministers a quarter takes this position.

Table 5.4 reveals a high level of agreement about the headship of men within marriage relationships though, as can be seen, 10 per cent cannot accept this proposition, certainly in an unqualified form.

Table 5.4.1 reveals a range of opinions within the denominations about the role of women. In general Assemblies of God is the denomination most open to the ministry of women. Three-quarters of the Assemblies of God ministers think women should have exactly the same opportunities for ministry as men and over two-thirds are willing to accept that women may be in charge of congregations. In other respects, Assemblies of God and Elim are relatively similar. All denominations give strong support to women speaking in public meetings and to their preaching. The differences that occur tend to be over ministerial functions like presiding at communion (where 61 per cent of Apostolic ministers and 20 per cent of Church of God ministers agree that women should not preside) and over baptising people. The most critical differences, however, occur over holding authority. The Church of God is most willing to accept female governance of congregations (88 per cent), and this is followed by two-thirds of Assemblies of God ministers and smaller percentages of Elim (38.2 per cent) and Apostolic ministers. Yet, the Church of God position, given the percentages who do not accept women presiding at communion or baptising, appears to be one where women may be in charge but still not exercise the full range of ministerial functions. Such an interpretation would be in accord with the figures showing there is also a tendency among Church of God ministers to hold to the view that the wearing of headcoverings in public worship is right.

The Apostolic Church offers fewest opportunities for women. It has the highest percentage of ministers who believe that women

Table 5.4.1 *Women*

Item	Denom	Agree %	Not Certain %	Disagree %
Women should have exactly the same opportunities for ministry as men	AC	24.4	21.1	50.5
	AG	75.9	9.3	14.8
	Elim	54.1	14.1	31.9
	CG	68.6	11.8	19.6
Women should not preside at Holy Communion	AC	61.5	13.5	25.0
	AG	8.0	7.5	84.4
	Elim	13.5	6.5	80.0
	CG	20.0	12.0	68.0
Women should not speak in church meetings	AC	5.0	4.0	91.0
	AG	1.5	1.0	97.5
	Elim	2.4	1.1	96.5
	CG	2.0	4.0	94.0
Women should not baptise	AC	69.8	10.4	19.8
	AG	8.1	14.4	77.5
	Elim	12.5	14.5	73.0
	CG	29.2	8.3	62.5
Women should wear headcoverings in public worship	AC	41.8	14.3	43.9
	AG	15.7	11.9	72.5
	Elim	8.1	8.4	83.6
	CG	66.7	7.8	25.5
Women should not exercise a preaching ministry	AC	2.1	7.2	90.7
	AG	3.7	1.0	95.3
	Elim	5.7	5.4	88.9
	CG		4.0	96.0
Women should not be in charge of congregations	AC	59.6	17.0	23.4
	AG	21.3	11.0	67.7
	Elim	50.4	11.4	38.2
	CG	8.0	4.0	88.0

should not be in charge of congregations, should not preside at communion or baptise and should not speak in public meetings. It has the second highest number of ministers who think women should wear headcoverings in public worship.

Table 5.5.1 shows that there is disagreement over the issue of demons among Pentecostal denominations. None of the items relating to demons commanded a consensus across all denominations.

In some respects the Apostolic Church stands out from the other three denominations. The smallest number of ministers who believe that Christians are daily in conflict with demons is to be found within the Apostolic Church and the largest number of ministers who believe that Christians can be possessed by demons is also found among Apostolic Church ministers. This appears to suggest that while the Apostolic Church ministers do not consider demons to be a daily problem the majority do, nevertheless, believe that possession can and does occur with relative frequency.

In all the other three denominations more than half of the ministers believe that Christians are in conflict daily with demons. It is the word 'daily' which is startling to most people. This is not an issue

Table 5.5.1 *Demons*

Item	Denom	Agree %	Not Certain %	Disagree %
I believe Christians are daily in conflict with demons	AC	33.0	14.4	52.6
	AG	52.9	15.6	31.5
	Elim	55.9	15.8	28.3
	CG	68.6	5.9	25.5
I do not believe that Christians can be possessed by demons	AC	34.0	14.9	51.1
	AG	61.7	13.9	24.4
	Elim	59.3	12.0	28.7
	CG	68.0	6.0	26.0
I do not believe that Christians can be oppressed by demons	AC	9.3	9.3	81.4
	AG	11.5	3.8	84.7
	Elim	10.0	3.2	86.8
	CG	36.0	4.0	60.0

concerning occasional emergencies but one which is part and parcel of the everyday life of believers. Yet, again, the majority of these ministers – and it is a majority which goes over two-thirds in the case of the Church of God – does not believe that Christians can be possessed by demons. Such a finding suggests that these ministers have a strong doctrine of salvation.

On the other side of the equation, about a fifth of ministers in the Assemblies of God, Elim and the Church of God do believe that Christians can be possessed by demons. This is a significant minority of believers and points to an area of genuine dissent within Pentecostalism. The table presented here does not allow a clear analysis of the reasons why or how Christians might be possessed and all that can be said is that this is an area where future disagreements are likely to arise.

The Church of God is also strongest in its rejection of the notion that Christians can even be oppressed by demons. Thus the profile of the Church of God shows that, although over two-thirds of its ministers believe that Christians are daily in conflict with demons, high numbers believe that Christians cannot be possessed or even oppressed by demons. Again, the Church of God emerges with a strong doctrine of salvation. Once people become Christians there is protection from the power of evil supernatural entities. The other three Pentecostal denominations, Apostolic, Assemblies of God and Elim, all by a large majority of over 80 per cent believe that oppression can occur.

Conclusion

The non-charismatic beliefs of Pentecostals are certainly shaped by the Bible. Yet it would be a mistake to see these as being rigidly or woodenly transferred from the text of Scripture to the modern day. Pentecostals do not fall into the same category as the Amish people. Nor are they strictly speaking fundamentalist, as the sharp disagreements with fundamentalists early in the twentieth century demonstrate. Unquestionably, Pentecostals are conservative in their religious and social views, but this conservatism is played out within cultural contexts so that, in the United States, Pentecostals incline towards creationism whereas in Britain, where creationism is less prominent, approximately a third of ministers are not prepared to accept it.

In relation to the ministry of women, Pentecostals may be said to be progressive. Unlike the Church of England or the Roman Catholic Church, Pentecostals have always accepted the ministry of women as being biblically mandated. Yet this progressiveness coexists with conservatism because Pentecostals expect wives to function within the context of a husband's authority. In practice this authority may be non-existent and most Pentecostal ministers would not make a great fuss about this matter. What matters more to Pentecostal ministers is that their wives are genuinely supportive in church life.

Similarly, Pentecostal beliefs about eschatology are moderated by practical reality. Pentecostals by and large believe that there will be a millennium and that the church will be taken miraculously from the earth. Yet many agree that the exact order of end time events is unclear. In effect, Pentecostal ministers believe the fundamental truths of their denominations while simultaneously recognising that there are loose ends in Scripture that even the most comprehensive eschatological schemes have not managed to tie up convincingly.

Both in relation to the ministry of women and to eschatology there are variations between Pentecostal denominations. These variations are partly a consequence of historical factors but are also the result of the liberalising impact of modern culture. If this analysis is correct, it is reasonable to predict that the attitudes of the smaller Apostolic Church will move in the direction already taken by the Assemblies of God and Elim. It is more difficult to predict the future social attitudes of Church of God ministers since the Church of God began as a holiness movement set up in opposition to the trends and fashions of contemporary society. In addition, the Church of God is held together by a participatory and democratic structure that gives weight to factors outside the environment of each national church. This prevents national expressions of the Church of God being too easily adaptable to changes within their own cultures.

Belief in the reality of an experience of the Holy Spirit is accompanied by its logical opposite. Most Pentecostals believe in demons and many accept that they are in 'daily' conflict with them. The Pentecostal world-view is therefore dualistic: good, represented by the Holy Spirit, wages a constant battle against evil, represented by demons. Human beings are caught in the crossfire. But Pentecostal denominations, depending upon their understanding of the saving work of Christ, have dissimilar accounts of the security of Christians in the face of demonic attack. Some believe Christians are immune from possession by demons whereas others take the contrary view. Surprisingly though, despite this overall theological perspective, most Pentecostal Christians do not give a great deal of attention to the spiritual world in their ordinary lives. It is not a topic for casual conversation. Rather, it lies behind an analysis of human tragedies and extremities. It is a way of giving meaning to bereavements and accidents: it is the basis for theodicy.

6

Ethical Issues

Overview

This chapter deals with ethical issues, in particular divorce and remarriage, homosexuality and the holiness code governing leisure activities.

Divorce and remarriage

Pentecostal denominations, coming as they did from a Protestant, Methodist and holiness background, were always disposed to take a non-sacramental view of Christian marriage and to ignore or deny Roman Catholic teaching. Moreover, since their origins were strongly Protestant, Pentecostal denominations always accepted the right of ministers to be married even though they did not go as far as insisting that it was impossible to be a minister without being married.[1]

Against this generally biblical and Protestant background enormous social upheavals have occurred so that divorce, which was a rarity in the 1920s, has become much more common, particularly in Britain. A Legal Aid Act passed in 1945 opened the possibility of divorce to people who had previously been deterred by the expense. In 1947 divorces reached the peak of 60,000, ten times the pre-war figure. Even after the first rush of postwar divorces had taken place, the figures settled down to about 25,000 divorces a year in the mid-1950s.[2]

---

[1] On the basis of 1 Timothy 3:2.

[2] Marwick, 1982, 64. Another way of showing this is by seeing the percentage of people marrying in any year who divorced after ten years of

The moral and theological problems caused by a rising divorce rate, particularly a divorce rate that spilled over into the life of Pentecostal congregations, began to exercise minds in the Assemblies of God in the 1950s. When the matter was pointed out to them the Executive Council replied by drawing attention to the specifics of the Assemblies of God constitution and saying that they were unwilling to act unless a general feeling in the movement as a whole prompted it. When in 1954 one of the district councils asked for a ruling to be given on divorce and remarriage, the issue was discussed at the General Conference and a select committee was set up. The report was issued in 1955 but there was deliberately no debate on the document, presumably to prevent potentially divisive argument. In 1968 and 1969, as divorce within society as whole during the 'swinging sixties' began to gather momentum, the issue was raised again and a further committee reported but it could not reach a consensus and so, after outlining the various views that might be held, noted that 'there will always be especially involved cases which must be decided upon their own merits'.[3]

Family breakdowns in Britain continued through the 1970s and 1980s so that, with regard to divorce in Europe, Britain held the unenviable position of being one of the places where family life was least stable. Divorces in England and Wales had risen in 1971 to 74,000 a year and by 1993 they had reached 165,000 a year.[4] The graph of divorce within England and Wales in the postwar period appeared to climb inexorably upwards and only levelled off by the failure of people to marry in the first place. The number of marriages dropped from 404,700 in 1971 down to 283,000 in 1995.[5]

At the same time civil marriage solemnizations have grown in popularity. This is partly because many of those who have been through a divorce are denied a religious ceremony on the occasion

---

2 (*continued*) marriage. In 1951 in England and Wales this figure was 3 per cent, in 1961 7 per cent, in 1971 17 per cent and in 1981 23 per cent (Haskey, 1998, 26).

3 Kay, 1989, 253. The committee members were John Carter, Donald Gee, George Newsholme, T.S. Parfitt and Jimmy Salter.

4 Brierley, 1997, tables 4.8.1 and 4.8.2.

5 Brierley, 1997, table 4.8.1.

of the second marriage. In 1980 almost exactly half of all marriages (49.7 per cent) were solemnized by civil rather than religious means, and the religious means in this statistic include all kinds of religion within Britain, not only Christianity. In 1902, civil solemnizations as a percentage of all marriages only amounted to 16.3.[6] The rise from 16.3 to 49.7 per cent is in itself compelling evidence for the secularisation and fragmentation of British society in the twentieth century.

The application of biblical principles to the tangled and complicated lives of people living according to non-Christian standards is a matter of fine judgement. An individual minister may be faced with requests by congregational members that he or she can not, in conscience, accept. For example, ministers may feel they must refuse to offer a church wedding to someone marrying a divorcee. Moreover, for Pentecostal denominations, there are two further levels of complexity to consider. Pentecostal denominations have taken the position that it is vital that their ministers should set a moral and spiritual example so that what may be, in exceptional circumstances, permissible for members of congregations is impermissible for ministers. This results in a deliberate double standard but one designed to safeguard the purity of the ministerial list.

The second level of complexity occurs as a result of evangelical belief about the radical nature of conversion. As we shall see, the vast majority of Pentecostal ministers accept that what was done prior to conversion is forgiven when the sinner comes for the first time to the cross. All kinds of wicked acts are deemed to be completely washed away by the blood of Christ. This is the majority view. However, even on conversion, it has been pointed out that contractual obligations remain. Debts incurred before conversion must still be paid after conversion and, on this logic, marriages contracted before conversion are still in force after conversion. Consequently, it may be held that divorces and/or remarriages that occurred before conversion are still relevant to the consideration of ministerial status if the highest standards are to be maintained.

Two other factors further complicate issues of marriage and divorce in Britain. First, there is the question of the validity of

---

[6] Currie, Gilbert and Horsely, 1977, 224; 1980 figures taken from Social Trends 1995, table 11.11.

bigamous marriages contracted by converts to Christianity. A man who under Muslim law marries two wives and then converts to Christianity presents a problem to his minister. Is the second marriage invalid and, if it is, what should be done about the second wife, particularly if she has children, when through no fault of her own she finds herself a divorcee? Second, how are people who switch churches to be treated since they may have been advised one thing by a minister in one denomination and then find themselves being expected to live according to different standards after joining a Pentecostal congregation? This difficulty can also exist in a slightly different form when members of congregations are in receipt of tapes or books that press lines of teaching that are contrary to those held by their own minister. This issue arises in an acute form when one or both members of a married couple, one or both of whom has been married before, come to believe that the second marriage is invalid. Occasionally one member of such a partnership believes it is right to return to the first spouse.[7] If the first spouse of either party to the second marriage has also remarried such a course of action is completely out of the question. But, even if the spouse has not remarried, can any minister recommend divorce as a loving and biblical course of action? Such scenarios illustrate the pain and doubt that conflicting teaching can bring about.

Assemblies of God

Within British Assemblies of God the matter of divorce and remarriage was raised again in the early 1990s. Until then section 3.4 (b) of the Constitutional Minutes under the heading 'experience' and dealing with the subject of probationary ministers stated:

> No person after conversion having divorced and remarried or who is joined in matrimony to a person divorced after conversion during the lifetime of a former partner, shall hold status or be the leader of an assembly in our Fellowship.

Any person applying for ministerial status was first examined by the Regional Council who, after its representatives were satisfied that

[7] I know of two cases of this kind.

there was evidence of ministerial capacity, passed candidates forward to the Credentials Council, a national body that checked for consistency between the different regions and then brought the names forward to General Conference for ratification. Any breach by an applicant of the Constitutional Minutes on marriage and divorce would be picked up either at regional level or by the Credentials Council and would result in automatic rejection.

Nevertheless as a result of some uncertainty about the meaning of the Constitutional Minutes an appeal was made in the early 1990s to the Executive Council who ruled that the minute should be taken to mean that:

- someone who divorced before conversion but remarried after conversion would be ineligible for ministerial status;
- someone who divorced and remarried before conversion would be eligible for ministerial status;
- someone who divorces and remarries, for whatever reason, after conversion is not eligible for ministerial status;
- someone married to a divorcee where that divorcee went through divorce proceedings after conversion would not be eligible for ministerial status unless the former partner of the divorcee were dead.

Yet, in the light of the rapid social change within British society, and also in the light of the possibility that the biblical texts in Matthew 5 and 19 would permit divorce on the grounds of adultery and so, as a corollary, permit the innocent party to remarry without guilt, questions were raised about the justice and wisdom of the position that then pertained.

As a consequence, the 1993 Assemblies of God General conference decided to appoint a working group to report to the 1994 conference on the 'theological, pastoral and practical implications of the New Testament teaching on divorce and remarriage'.[8] The working group duly met and issued its report to all members of the Assemblies of God General conference, that is, all ministers

[8] Members of the committee (working group) were K. Munday, J. Bowler, J. Morgan, F.C. Weaver and W.K. Kay.

and missionaries eligible to attend the conference as voting members.

The report considered in detail the New Testament teaching on marriage, particularly focusing on the gospel texts and 1 Corinthians.[9] It rejected the view, advanced by some members of the earlier Assemblies of God committees dealing with the issue, that marriage automatically took place through sexual intercourse (1 Cor. 6:16) since this would produce anomalies in the case of incest. It took the view that marriage must take place when several conditions are satisfied and outlined four of these: exchanging of promises, public witnessing, legal requirements[10] and sexual intercourse and, on this account, it accepted that formal marriages made in non-British cultures or through non-Christian means were perfectly valid.

It examined four basic positions on divorce. The *indissolubilist* position holds that there are no grounds for a breach of the marital bond before or after conversion; the bond can only be broken by the death of one partner. The indissolubilist position argues on the basis of the absence of any mention in the Gospels of Mark and Luke of an exceptive clause and the general statement in Mark 10:9 that 'what God has joined together, let man not separate'. Those in favour of it argued that the indissolubilist position was the settled position of the patristic church – though it was agreed that the Reformers, seeing this stance as being contrary to Scripture, had rejected it.

A *modified indissolubilist* position is similar except that it argues that divorces and remarriages undertaken by anyone before conversion, though sinful, are forgiven with all the sins of the past life and

[9] It also considered previous documents issued by Assemblies of God committees in Britain (including a Select Committee set up by the Executive Council in 1981), notes prepared by Aaron Linford and John Carter (who took opposing views about the legitimacy of any form of divorce – Linford being against and Carter being in favour) and the Select Committee set up by the General Conference of 1954. In addition it considered the relevant statements of Australian Assemblies of God (1983) and American Assemblies of God (1987).

[10] A further complication impacting on this matter is that Scottish and English law differ. Any recommendation by a denomination working on both sides of the border has to take account of this.

so should not be grounds for refusing ministerial status to an applicant.

The *exceptive* position gives decisive weight to the exceptive clause given by Jesus and found in Matthew 5:32 and Matthew 19:9. This clause makes reference to *porneia*, a word connected with the English word 'pornography'. It means something that is sexually unclean and refers to adultery, and probably to other sexual sins. The exceptive clause is taken to mean that, whereas marriage is properly indissoluble, there is one important exception to this general rule. This exception is that if *porneia* has been committed, then the marriage may be terminated – indeed the 'one flesh union' has already been broken. Consequently the innocent party, that is the one who has not committed *porneia*, is free to divorce and remarry without sin or guilt. It is normal for those who adopt this view to point out that divorce always presumed the possibility of remarriage in the ancient world since it put the divorcee back in the legal position he or she had been in before the marriage had been contracted.

The *covenant* position emphasises the covenant nature of marriage (Mal. 2:14) and argues that, since marriage is a covenant freely made by both parties and made on the basis of promises exchanged, divorce is permissible if the promises are broken by one or other party. Normally this view is seen as giving permission for divorce on the basis of cruelty or desertion, which are viewed as serious breaches of the marriage covenant.

After reviewing the major commentaries on the relevant passages in the New Testament and showing that the majority of Protestant commentators accept the validity of the exceptive clause, the report recommended the setting up of a Marital Status Committee to consider applications where issues of divorce and remarriage arose. The Committee was to consider confidential information relating to the personal circumstances of applicants and, once having ruled, its decision would be final. The General Conference agreed to this proposal and the committee was set up and dealt with a few cases each year. It did not result in a flood of divorcees entering the ministry but, from time to time, one or two whose circumstances placed them as the innocent party in a marital breakdown were admitted to the ministerial list. In this way, the Assemblies of God in Britain was able to offer a less blunt solution than one that was completely rule-based but it did so without compromising its ministerial standards.

Elim

Elim considered divorce at its conferences in 1947, 1971, 1972, 1977, 1984, 1985 and 1988. The 1947 decision affirmed the sanctity of marriage as a lifelong union between husband and wife and recommended that, where problems arise, reconciliation and not divorce is the true remedy, even if there has been adultery. Nevertheless the conference recognised certain exceptions to the continuance of marriage both in Old and New Testament times, the possibility of divorce and remarriage and that, in any event, Christians should not initiate divorce proceedings.

The 1972 Elim conference agreed that 'no Elim Minister may officiate at the remarriage of a divorced person nor may any Elim Church property be used for such a ceremony'. But this decision was rescinded in 1977 and changed to the position held after the 1947 conference, which gave discretion to individual ministers. In 1985 the conference agreed again to place on record its commitment to the sanctity of marriage, but it also agreed that the remarriage of divorced persons in Elim churches and the admission of divorced and remarried persons to membership and leadership of a local church can be at the discretion of the Church Session and that the admission to the Elim ministry of a person who has been divorced and remarried, or whose spouse has been divorced and remarried, be at the discretion of the Executive Council.

A committee set up by the Elim Executive Council at the request of the 1983 Conference presented a report in 1988. The committee was asked:

> To make recommendations arising from the general views with particular reference to the admission and continuance in leadership and the ministry of those persons who had, or whose spouses had, been involved in divorce and/or remarriage. (Section 1.4.2.)

The committee considered its work in detail and began with a definition of marriage that agreed on its four elements. It is: covenantal, ratified by parents, a public witness and requires physical consummation. So far as marginal cases are concerned the committee agreed that a converted polygamist should not dispossess a wife of marital rights or legal status, but nor should he be admitted to church leadership.

The committee considered the consequences of 'no fault divorces' following the Divorce Acts of 1970 and accepted that if the law made no distinction between guilty and innocent parties in marriage breakdown, churches might also find it difficult to do so.[11] In dealing with the break-up of marriages within congregations, the committee offered pastoral advice based upon the aim of securing reconciliation but in the realistic knowledge that this might not always be achieved. In relation to ministers, the committee recognised the force of biblically-sanctioned grounds for divorce but took the trouble to point out the practical implications of divorce and remarriage and concluded that 'if Elim is willing to consider divorced men for the ministry, then they must enter with the understanding that divorce may still, for practical reasons, hinder their appointment to churches' (section 7.7.8).

Apostolic Church

The Apostolic Church, like the other Pentecostal denominations in Britain, has had to face the issue of divorce and remarriage. It has had to interpret the theological teaching of the New Testament and to find a way to apply this to particular situations. Its theological conclusions are similar to those of Elim and Assemblies of God in the sense that it does not support the indissolubilist position and its application of these conclusions is by means of a specialist committee. Its deliberations are set out in *When the Vow Breaks*, a booklet that arose out of four years of discussion by a team of Apostolic ministers actively involved in pastoral care. The publication of the booklet led to a reform of the Church's practice.[12]

---

[11] Members of the committee were J. Bristow, J. Burgan, T.G. Hills, B. Hunter, F. Lavender, I.W. Lewis, J.C. Smyth, G.L. Taylor, T.W. Walker, J.W. Ward.

[12] The ministers involved were D.R. Dicks, R.T. Brown, T.A. Dando, D.G. Daniel and G.G. Johnson. See Dicks (ed.), 1986, *When the Vow Breaks*, Penygroes, Apostolic Publications.

What now happens is that all problematic cases are referred to a Divorce Panel which considers the fine detail of reasons for marital breakdown and then, on the basis of either the exceptive clause or the desertion of a spouse for reasons of faith (1 Cor. 7), the committee will recommend that the innocent party in the marital breakdown be allowed to continue in, or be admitted to, ministry.[13] This recommendation is taken through to the Executive Council who, in disputed cases, may then go to the whole Council for a final decision. Normally, though, the recommendations of the Divorce Panel are acceptable to the Executive Committee. The same standards and values that apply to ministers apply to all members, so in this respect the Apostolic Church has a different policy from the Assemblies of God.

Church of God

In its Statements of Faith the Church of God affirms the sanctity of marriage, accepting 'the only clear biblical allowance for divorce being fornication (Mt. 5:32; 19:9)'.[14] In this the Church of God comes to a conclusion similar to the other Pentecostal denominations. It accepts that divorce may occur and stipulates that 'the remarriage of divorced persons should be undertaken only after a thorough understanding of and submission to the Scriptural instructions concerning this issue'.[15] Not that this decision was reached easily, as a record in its Book of Minutes for 1908 testifies, but it does have the distinction of having reached this position before any other Pentecostal group and of having maintained it without significant alteration for more than ninety years.[16]

Homosexuality

The issue of homosexuality has rarely, if ever, been discussed formally at Pentecostal ministerial conferences in Britain. There is

---

[13] Details are given in *The Constitution of the Apostolic Church.*

[14] *Our Statements of Faith* (nd), 12. 'Fornication' is the Authorised Version's translation of the Greek *porneia.*

[15] *Our Statements of Faith* (nd), 12.

[16] Conn, 1977, 83, quoting the Book of Minutes for 1908.

sufficient consensus among ministers for the issue not to need debating. The position taken by British Pentecostal ministers is that homosexuality is unbiblical and excluded by divine command from a Christian lifestyle. On the few occasions when homosexuality has been observed among church members or among ministers, it has been seen as a ground for church discipline. On those occasions when a married man has admitted to homosexual practice he has usually been advised to seek a reconciliation with his wife and counselling. This issue was, however, addressed in the Apostolic Church Constitution in May 1998 when it was decided that no practising homosexual could be a member of the Church or hold office.

Holiness Code

The biblical teaching on holiness is complicated. Holiness applies primarily to God and indicates a state of apartness, separation and difference. When applied to the human condition this translates into a sense of social distinction that is expressed by the avoidance of particular kinds of behaviour. In the Old Testament holiness was centred on the commands and prohibitions of the Mosaic Law, though the prophetic tradition distinguished between a kind of false holiness that was merely behavioural and a true holiness that included the inner thoughts and attitudes of the individual. 'These people come near to me with their mouth and honour me with their lips, but their hearts are far from me. Their worship of me is made up only of rules taught by men' (Is. 29:13) expresses this distinction pithily.

In the New Testament the dynamic for holiness sprang from the identification of the believer with the life and crucifixion of Christ. The most obvious text to support the New Testament conception is found in the epistle to the Romans where the believer, on baptism, is identified with Christ in his death in order to be raised (in baptism) to a new and holy life (Rom. 6). Again the distinction between behaviour and belief, between the outward and inward aspects of holiness, is present. The believer identifies with Christ by faith but acts out this identification by deeds, though these deeds are not based in religious law.

In theory the history of the church in all its forms and manifestations ought to include a doctrine of holiness but, in practice, the main thrust for holiness within Protestantism has come from Methodism. In the United States holiness teaching spread, as we have seen from Dayton's account, from Methodist beginnings.[17] It did this partly because Methodism contained a diversity of emphases. Along with the emphasis on spiritual experience, on the heart and on conversion, was an equally strong emphasis on life-style, disciplined living and upright behaviour. The correlation between the inner experience of God's love or God's cleansing power and particular forms of behaviour allowed the subsequent development of holiness teaching in the nineteenth century in the United States to stress one or other of these emphases without necessarily holding them in balance. Dayton's analysis of these emphases is borne out by Blumhofer who points out that teaching on holiness flourished after the Civil War through the creation of associations and new publications. 'Camp meetings became the settings in which thousands from all denominations professed the second religious crisis experience' and, despite an effort to shepherd these groups and associations back into the Methodist fold, several new denominations were formed.[18] These became the holiness denominations whose second blessing doctrine prepared the theological ground for Pentecostalism in the twentieth century.

These holiness denominations were capable of banning all kinds of innocent activities. 'At the general assembly of the Church of God it was decided that Coca Cola, chewing gum, rings, bracelets and earbobs were sinful and therefore prohibited to members of the church.'[19] Equally unholy according to the Pentecostal Holiness Church was the buying of life insurance, the joining of political parties or the support of labour unions. The point of this discussion is not to scorn the banning of such apparently harmless activities but to show how the concept of holiness could be interpreted positively and negatively as well as outwardly and inwardly.

Negatively and outwardly, holiness became the avoidance of social fripperies and fashions or, more seriously, the avoidance of

---

[17] Dayton, 1987.

[18] Blumhofer, 1985, 19.

[19] Synan, 1997, 81.

time-consuming organisations dedicated to social change. Positively and inwardly, holiness could be an attitude of love for God resulting in private devotion and praise. Sometimes one or other of these emphases predominated so that holiness was only seen in outward forms or, alternatively, so that it was only an inward, even introverted, tendency – a drawing away from 'the world' into quietism and pietism.

Early Pentecostalism encountered both negative and positive forms of holiness teaching. Early editions of *Confidence* had to warn against teaching denying the right of Christians to marry.[20] A more alarming case occurred at the Amsterdam conference of 1921 when the German Pentecostals introduced a teaching about the death of the self by incorporating it in prophetic utterance. As Gee points out, this use of spiritual gifts to underline the extreme form of a doctrine caused disagreement among the Pentecostals present and is used by him as an example of the need to avoid making modern prophecy the source of any Christian doctrine.[21]

Positive forms of holiness teaching occurred in the periodic calls to 'wait on God' or to engage in prayer and fasting and, in Pentecostal settings, such calls are often a preparation for manifestations of spiritual gifts. If believers meditate on passages of Scripture and are fervent and disciplined in their own prayers, then the fire of Pentecostal experience is stirred up and, within the worship and fellowship of congregations, prophecies, utterances in tongues and interpretations become more frequent.

The kaleidoscopic possibilities within the concept and application of holiness teaching are related to the state of the churches. Historically, teaching on holiness has tended to follow a cyclical pattern. When a denomination or a Pentecostal fellowship is in the first flower of its power and evangelism, believers are so taken up with exciting new accompaniments of church growth that no one notices what people wear or how exactly they live their lives. New and youthful Christians do not have established social norms. After a while, when the church begins to subside into routine and growth slows, someone begins to believe, and it is usually the older people who fall into this category, that the reason for decline is lack of

---

20 The so-called 'Bride teaching'.

21 Gee, 1967, 121.

holiness. Holiness is then preached as the path back to power. And since the holiness that can be seen is the holiness of behaviour, of abstention and regulation, it is this that is the preacher's most obvious target. Believers are told that true Christianity is evidenced by the many things they must avoid doing, and so congregations become cut off from society and isolated while believing themselves to be preparing for growth. Actually, however, in such a socially isolated state congregations are even less likely than ever to attract fresh converts, and so fall into further decline.

Assemblies of God and Elim

Assemblies of God and Elim are put together here because their histories run in parallel and the forces that moved the boundaries of holiness were in their case the same.

Assemblies of God has crossed the spectrum of holiness phases during its seventy-five years of existence. It certainly knew the early booming growth and the spiritual excitement that accompanied it in the period up to 1929. Equally, it knew retrenchment and retreat when some of its assemblies became small, isolated and routinised. At its best and most balanced it appreciated holiness as a central pre-condition for mission, evangelism, charismatic activity and church growth. When the charismatic movement began in the 1960s and it was clear that the Pentecostal churches were in need of a fresh infusion of life, attempts were made to remedy the problem by adjusting the constitutional mechanisms that governed the relationships between churches, between churches and councils and between churches and ministers. But the epoch-defining sermon preached by Donald Gee at the 1961 General Conference calling for 'another Springtime' was essentially a call for holiness because it urged believers to leave aside the attempts to tinker with the constitution and instead to repent and wait on God, replacing activity with spirituality.[22]

A decade later one aspect of thinking about holiness is found in the writing of David Powell, an influential though controversial Assemblies of God minister who for a while pastored a flourishing congregation in Yorkshire. Powell's teaching about holiness linked

---

[22] Kay, 1989, 262.

it with a doctrine of sanctification that related the believer's purity of life back to regeneration and, though he explained that holiness was developed by the activity of the Holy Spirit, he also thought

> Those people who say they are saved and belong to Christ and are dirty, dishevelled and undisciplined, are a disgrace to the name of Christ, because this is contrary to decency. God has a great deal to say about proper deportment and proper conduct in our dealings one with another.[23]

This suggests that, among other characteristics, he associated the doctrine of holiness with physical appearance, and in this he was probably representative of others of his era.

In its more negative and crusading forms, Pentecostalism also made holiness a matter of social ethics. From time to time there were attempts to influence the content of television programmes and to affect standards of public morality (for instance, pornography displayed on news stands), often by statements issued at the General Conference, as in 1975, and communicated through press releases to the media.[24] In this Pentecostals began to fasten onto the concerns of the National Viewers and Listeners Association which emerged from the 1964 Clean Up TV crusade and by 1975 had about 30,000 supporters.[25]

Holiness in its positive outward form can also include compassionate social action. And Assemblies of God, largely through the initiative of dedicated individuals, did take strides in this direction. Between 1960 and 1985 it set up five homes for elderly retired people, called Eventide homes,[26] and after 1977 began the Pentecostal Child Care Association because of concern for abused and neglected children.[27] Both these enterprises were largely funded by congregational giving, though as they became established, welcome support from local authority funds was also forthcoming.

---

23 Powell, 1976, 369.

24 See Cunningham's comments on these in *Redemption Tidings* after the 1975 General Conference.

25 Thompson, 1997, 164.

26 Kay, 1989, 301.

27 Kay, 1989, 333.

Elim churches were similar and the account given by Wilson of holiness precepts and practices in the 1960s has not been bettered.[28] What he said of the Elim churches almost certainly applies to the Assemblies of God. Using early copies of *Elim Evangel* and a series of interviews Wilson built up a picture of holiness thinking that, in his view, distantly reflects the Puritanism and Methodism of the nineteenth century. It sees anything that distracts the believer from God as fundamentally unholy, whether this distraction is personal or social. If it is personal, it may involve smoking and if it is social it may involve drinking alcohol. Wilson suggests that smoking is a far more likely lapse than drinking because drinking will normally involve special visits to licensed premises whereas smoking is a personal indulgence. If it is personal it may also involve gambling, but this is a behaviour rejected for reasons of stewardship. To gamble is to risk wasting money and, since all money is entrusted to the Christian by God, gambling is really the risking of God's precious resources.

Entertainment falls into a similar category. The cinema in the 1930s, 1940s and 1950s was a regular target for holiness advocates. To attend the cinema was to take the edge off one's spirituality and to allow oneself to be entertained by the glamorisation of crime, prostitution, violence, extramarital sex and godlessness. Even religious films were condemned as being a subtle Satanic deception: 'the devil is never more dangerous than when he professes to preach the gospel'.[29] Listening to the radio was also suspect but, according to Wilson, the possession of a radio usually depended upon the economic circumstances of the believer rather than on religious convictions. Sport was also a less than virtuous pastime, and examples were given of footballers who had lost their enthusiasm for the game once they had become converted.[30] Cycling and swimming were more acceptable because these were not undertaken with worldly people or in the spirit of competition.

---

[28] Wilson, 1961, 77–85.

[29] Wilson, 1961, 81 quoting *Elim Evangel*, 1927, 8, 229.

[30] Tom Woods had written to *Redemption Tidings* (March 1979) wondering more in sorrow than anger how a Christian could play cricket on Sundays.

The reading of novels could also be attacked as injuring Christian life, though this was seen as a less prevalent vice because Pentecostal Christians were not devoted to reading and so the temptation to relax with fiction was uncommon. Newspapers, however, could also arouse disapproval. 'By having Sunday newspapers you are spoiling your own sabbath by introducing into your own home papers that are full of beauty contests, football results and sensational stories.'[31] Children's reading was accepted and comics were allowed but, in an attempt to prevent children being led astray, children's stories were regularly printed in the *Evangel* and most of these had an underlying gospel message.

The arrival of mass television, particularly from the 1960s onwards, caused a shift in standards of outward holiness in the Pentecostal movement.

> We spend our time on Sunday afternoons watching the old black and white films on television that we were told we could not go to see when they were first shown at the cinema; someone has moved the goal posts.[32]

Television has homogenised the culture and brought the same sitcom and soap characters into millions of homes, spreading their attitudes and values and undoubtedly being used by the broadcasters, in some instances, to heighten public awareness of politically correct issues. The emotionally driven stories of the most popular soaps are non-judgemental and religion is rarely written into the script, implying that religious concerns are an irrelevance to ordinary people.[33] Soap characters are almost by definition irreligious. Occasionally stereotypical vicars appear, portrayed as effeminate and ineffectual human beings, and contrast with Irish-accented Catholic priests complete with cigarettes and a wry sense of humour. Where Pentecostals occasionally become visible in print or on screen, they are usually presented through hostile eyes and

---

31 Wilson, 1961, 84, quoting *Elim Evangel*, 1948, 29, 63.

32 Paraphrase of a comment made to me by Keith Munday in the 1990s.

33 The BBC website points out to potential script writers that soap scripts should be 'emotionally driven'.

shown to be brash, American, interested in money, insincere or strange.[34]

The spread of television within British culture can be demonstrated from the figures showing television ownership and audience ratings. Between 1951–64 ownership of television sets rose from 1 million to 13 million.[35] And this trend continued unabated: while 86 per cent of households had a television in 1970, by 1995 this figure had risen to 99 per cent.[36] By 1996 the ratings for favourite dramas consistently reached up to a third of the entire population of the United Kingdom. Casualty attracted 9.5 million viewers, while EastEnders could count on 16.9 million for each episode and Coronation Street 18.8 million.[37] As the old BBC/ITV monopoly begins to break up through satellite and cable television the situation is bound to change and viewing habits are likely to become more specialist and varied, but hardly to weaken.[38] Television itself is now seen as a necessary commodity to which everyone has a right, even the poorest within the community – as the ownership figures indicate.

Television affected all Pentecostal denominations but the unique factor that affected Assemblies of God and Elim were their General Conferences. Both Elim and Assemblies of God throughout their history, including the war years, had held (separate) conferences for their ministers but, as their fellowships grew, conferences that included business sessions for ministers and evening meetings for the general public – including day and weekly visitors drawn largely from the churches – were called. The response to these invitations, when up to about seven thousand people were in attendance, allowed the major British holiday

[34] Winterson's (1991) fictional account of a girl brought up in a religious sect was televised. Those who knew Wintersons's background saw the book as a veiled attack on Pentecostalism. Religious programmes about Morris Cerullo were in the main critical and questioned the reality of advertised healings.

[35] Hastings, 1986, 413.

[36] Brierley, 1997, table 5.14.4.

[37] *Radio Times*, April 10–16 1999, 126. This is roughly a third of the UK population.

[38] An insider's account of the emergence of satellite broadcasting is given by Neil, 1997, *passim*.

camp venues to be booked for a week in the off-season.[39] These great Pentecostal gatherings at Butlins or Pontins attracted young people and young families and, as the camp facilities were included within the cost of residence, it was natural for swimming and rides to be enjoyed by everyone who was not obliged to attend the ministerial business sessions. The camps were built for secular entertainment and Pentecostal preachers became accustomed to looking at the conference programme and discovering that they were meeting in a garishly decorated bar or ballroom. During these weeks alcohol was not served but it was certainly incongruous to insist on a world-denying form of holiness while occupying a world-enjoying venue. The very success of the conferences changed holiness norms. For example, when previously it had been expected that women would wear headcoverings for worship, it became difficult to police such a regime in a congregation of more than two thousand people. Moreover people wearing earrings and make-up could hardly be expelled from the site, particularly when young people who had not quite decided whether they were Pentecostal or not attended the camps to fulfil the evangelistic hopes of a particular pastor. For these reasons the holiness climate in Elim and Assemblies of God was changed in directions the conference organisers had not anticipated.

In addition to the changes brought about by television and through the enlarged attendance at the Assemblies of God and Elim general conferences, the impact of spiritual events outside Pentecostal boundaries was also felt.

In the 1960s the first signs of the burgeoning charismatic movement began to register on the horizon. From 1960 onwards reports were carried in *Redemption Tidings* of speaking with tongues in the older denominations. The editor, Aaron Linford, an experienced Pentecostal commentator noted:

> A strange phenomenon is taking place, both in this country and abroad. Christian ministers and members of churches outside

[39] In 1962 2,400 people attended the Assemblies of God Conference; in 1974 7,500 people attended; in 1982 the figure reached 7,916; in 1985 it again reached 7,500, but by 1997 less than 1000 came. I am indebted to Basil Varnam for these figures.

> Pentecostal circles are getting baptised in the Holy Ghost with the initial evidence of speaking with other tongues . . .
>
> The baptism of the Spirit is not the exclusive possession of the Pentecostal people; the Pentecostal movement is not the proprietor of the Holy Ghost. His baptism is the heritage of *all* God's people *everywhere.*[40]

Elim publications were quiet on the matter until 1963, but then the *Elim Evangel* drew attention to what was happening and, in a series of articles, presented it as a challenge to Pentecostals.[41]

One of the prime movers behind the spread of Pentecostalism across to the older denominations was David du Plessis whose roving ministry took him to the most unlikely destinations. He attended the 1954 World Council Assembly. He was received by three Roman Catholic pontiffs, John the XXIII, Paul VI and John Paul II and was invited to, and attended, the third session of Vatican II (1963–65). He attended all six assemblies of the World Council of Churches from Evanston 1954 to Vancouver 1983 that were convened during his lifetime.[42] Du Plessis spoke at the 1961 Assemblies of God General Conference and the matter of fact report of what he said gives the impression that the full import of his preaching was not grasped.[43] It was not until 1966 that the discussion at Assemblies of God formally discussed the 'problem' of 'fellowship with other Christian bodies'.

What Pentecostals in Britain first saw of the charismatic movement was its presence within the Roman Catholic Church. That was what astonished them. They appear to have failed to notice the effect of the charismatic movement within Free Church and Anglican settings and so were surprised at developments that followed.[44] The charismatic movement at its radical fringe resulted in the formation of new quasi-denominational groupings under

---

[40] Linford, 1960 (original italics).

[41] Hudson, 1998, 182, 183.

[42] Spittler, 1988, 250f.

[43] Kay, 1989, 267.

[44] The best account of the unfolding charismatic movement in Britain is to be found in Hocken, 1984.

apostolic figures.[45] These new groupings were Pentecostal in their appreciation of the Holy Spirit but their ecclesiology was fresh. They did not support the apparatus of voting, committees, councils, constitutions and agendas but simplified everything by a stress on relationships. 'Relationship' became a buzz word and men (it was almost always men) began to relate together in Apostolic teams or to relate as local church ministers to a particular apostle who acted as their 'cover' (a term that implied both authority over and care for). Sociologically, the advantage of this new structure was that it avoided tiresome argument over procedures and the best way to make decisions and put everything into the hands of the apostle. New structures were simpler, more streamlined in decision making and more flexible since they combined decisiveness with pastoral care.

Their history can be dated back at least as far as 1953 when Arthur Wallis and David Lillie arranged a small conference on the Holy Spirit where 'Arthur took a non-Pentecostal stance, emphasising the baptism in the Spirit as an anointing of power for service'.[46] In 1958 Arthur Wallis convened a conference at Exmouth on the subject of 'the Church of Jesus Christ: its purity, power, pattern and programme in the context of to-day'. At this invited gathering papers were read by Arthur Wallis, Cecil Cousen, David Lillie, Metcalfe Collier and Roger Forster and an attempt was made to sketch out the kind of church that would come into existence if the traditions which conditioned the thinking of most Christians were subjected to a testing by Scripture. Two further conferences followed, one in 1961 and another in 1962, and at these further doctrinal foundations were put in place. The church was to follow the pattern of the New Testament and each local church was to be an expression of the body of Christ: powerful, enjoying complementary charismatic gifts and ministries, united and controlled by an oligarchy of men who met the qualifications outlined in the pastoral epistles.[47] Emphasis upon 'the kingdom message' – making known the authority of Christ through the authority of the church – appeared in 1961[48] and teaching about the

---

45 Walker, 1985.

46 Wallis, 1991, 106.

47 Wallis, 1961, 27.

48 Lillie, 1961.

Holy Spirit was amplified in 1962. The view taken accepted the importance of the Holy Spirit for ministry and rejected the cessationist position that confines tongues to the era of the New Testament. In the years that followed, Wallis went on to become a father figure to many of the new church apostles whose ministries began to make an impact in the 1970s and 1980s.

In relation to holiness the new house church or restoration groupings were much freer than the Pentecostals. This was partly a matter of theology. At least one of the new groupings (led by Terry Virgo) espoused a more Calvinistic doctrine than was common among Pentecostals who, because of their evangelistic and Wesleyan heritage, tended to be Arminian in theology. Arminianism underlines the necessity for human decision and, in holiness terms, human effort. Unlike Calvinism, there is a danger that the Arminian might not feel that his or her salvation is secure. So the Arminian might be less willing to break holiness taboos than the Calvinist. Certainly the Calvinistically inclined group led by Terry Virgo emphasised the grace of God in a way that cut against legalism or Sabbatarianism. Similar unwillingness to allow and accept legalism in other branches of the restoration movement were also observable, particularly as some of its leaders had broken free of restrictive forms of Christianity and were only too glad to move out into fresh pastures untrammelled by the old holiness codes.

The impact of the Restoration movement upon Pentecostals was considerable. Some of the best Pentecostal ministers were strongly attracted to the new associations and at least two influential congregations left Assemblies of God to join them.[49] Other ministers were equally attracted and, even where they did not formally identify with the new movement, they imbibed its teachings and its attitudes and became impatient with the cautious rule-bound approach that seemed to have invaded the souls of their own Pentecostal denominations. By the mid-1970s the situation was becoming clearer. The restorationist groups were, in some instances, veering towards 'heavy shepherding', a tag that described a form of pastoral authority over church members that left little room for personal decision making.[50] Ministerial authoritarianism

[49] Kay, 1989, 340.

[50] Hunter, 1988.

led to abuses and considerable psychological damage was done. Several individual congregations were broken up; an unknown number of families were made to move house or in other ways disrupted.[51] Attempts were made to rectify the situation and these largely succeeded.[52] But what had begun as a radical charismatic fringe was briefly perceived by the traditional Pentecostals as an organised and aggressive threat. By the mid-1980s an equilibrium was established. The new churches were less authoritarian and the Pentecostals were more flexible and open; in this atmosphere mutual respect could be reached.

By the 1990s the new churches developed an identifiable family resemblance that had become a familiar influence on the Christian landscape in Britain. With an approximate numerical strength of 150–200,000 adult members they were larger than the long-established Baptist Union and probably similar in size to the classical Pentecostals. According to Bonnington, worship as 'the moment of Spirit-inspired awe that is the locus of God-encountering, energising, life-transforming grace' is completely central to their vision of church life, more central than preaching or celebration of the Lord's Supper.[53] And, when theology is engaged, though it follows from a conservative evangelical position, its form is usually 'narrative' in the sense that the story of the Bible is believed to continue in the life stories of today's believers.

From a different angle the effects of the charismatic movement within the established denominations led to a similar result. As Anglicans, Methodists, Baptists and others began to experience the flow of the Holy Spirit, and speak with other tongues, so their exploration of the gifts of the Spirit, of prophecy and healing, began to lead to new growth and sometimes to new forms of worship. But these experiences did not necessarily change the lifestyle to which they had been accustomed. An Anglican charismatic might still drink a glass of sherry before his Sunday lunch and saw no reason to stop occasionally going to the cinema. Pentecostals could not but help observe that 'the Lord seems to be blessing the older denominations' even though their lifestyle, in Pentecostal terms, lacked the

---

51 Chambers, 1997.

52 Prince, 1976.

53 Bonnington, 1997; 1999.

marks of holiness. Perhaps holiness conceived as a set of rules and taboos was not the way forward after all.

Ironically, once the effects of the large general conferences had been felt, conference attendance dropped rapidly when the holiday camp venues became unavailable, or unavailable on the preferred dates, as the charismatic groups banded together under the Spring Harvest banner and booked the sites ahead of Assemblies of God and Elim. At its peak in 1982, Assemblies of God had mustered just under 10,000 people, but this dropped rapidly in the years that followed reaching a low of just over 1000 in 1997.[54] Spring Harvest could muster far larger numbers of people and could take several venues over a longer period of time – perhaps altogether accommodating around a hundred thousand visitors, a turnout that the Pentecostal denominations simply could not begin to compete with. Consequently, the Pentecostal General Conference shrank down to a largely ministerial gathering and the excitement and crowds that had attended in the 1980s melted away. But the impression made on holiness teaching across the churches could not be undone.

Apostolic Church

The Apostolic Church was, like Elim and Assemblies of God, touched by the increasingly secular culture that permeated the British Isles in the twentieth century. It was, however, different in three respects. First, the Apostolic Church was based and centred in Wales rather than in England and this meant that it was, to an extent, insulated from the main cultural currents that flowed through the United Kingdom. Particularly in the period up to the 1970s, there were parts of Wales that were rural and more family-based than was the case in the great urban sprawls of central England and, especially after the 1988 Education Reform Act when Welsh became part of the National Curriculum in Wales, and when Welsh culture was emphasised and supported by government spending, more culturally conservative than the rootless English cities.[55] In such an environment Pentecostal churches could almost escape time and fashion and remain as they had been many years before.

---

[54] Private communication from Basil Varnam.

[55] Jones, 1997.

Second, the annual conference held by the Apostolic Church was always in the same place on a site owned by the denomination and this meant that there were no extraneous influences, no funfairs and ballrooms, as there were at British holiday camps. The Penygroes conference took place at roughly the same time each year and, situated as it was in rural west Wales, the effects of secular culture were minimised. Holiness norms of dress and behaviour could be maintained and inculcated without compromise or variation. This said, the conference is an international one and delegates attend from all over the British Isles as well as other continents and countries (especially Nigeria) where the Apostolic Church flourishes.

Third, the Apostolic church in the United Kingdom remained much smaller than Assemblies of God or Elim. The 1995 *Apostolic Church Directory* mentions only 76 'pastors and workers' as servicing the 116 churches. The Assemblies of God would claim about 950 ministers in Britain, and Elim a slightly lower number, but certainly a figure well in excess of the Apostolic figure. The smaller Apostolic ministry list is less likely to contain a spread of opinions on holiness simply by virtue of its restricted length. In this respect the Apostolic Church has not, in the UK, had to face the problems caused by numerical growth that the two larger Pentecostal denominations have had to address.

Church of God

The Church of God is different from the other denominations considered here because it comes from a recognised holiness tradition. It is also much more likely to cater for black congregations than the others are. These two considerations give its holiness doctrines a distinctive character. In its Statements of Faith, for example, there is a printed resolution, passed in 1960, which reaffirms its commitments to the principle of biblical holiness. Among other things this statement says

> The subtle encroachment of worldliness is a very real and unrelenting threat to the Church . . . we hereby remind ourselves the Scriptures enjoin us at all times to examine our own hearts . . . be it resolved that we, as ministers, maintain this standard in our own lives, in our homes,

> and in our pulpits . . . as ministers and members, rededicate ourselves to this purpose and guard our lives against conformity to the world in appearance, in selfish ambition, in carnal attitudes and in evil associations . . . as ministers and members, seek to conform to the positive virtues of love, mercy, and forgiveness as taught by Jesus Christ.[56]

This comprehensive statement and the commitment it enshrines contains positive and negative elements and also, within it, an affirmation that it is necessary for holiness to be brought about by self-examination rather than by a condemnatory preaching or legislation. During its history the Church of God has clearly appreciated the dangers of legalism and attempted to get round them in a biblical way. Certainly temperance is endorsed though it is temperance of the general kind set in the context of abstention from 'activities and attitudes which are offensive to our fellowman or which lead to addiction or enslavement',[57] and so excludes alcohol and tobacco without specifically listing them. In the same context the Church of God affirms the need for correcting social injustices to 'improve the situation of those who are underprivileged, neglected, hungry, homeless and victimised by prejudice, persecution and oppression'.[58]

The predominantly black membership of this church has, in Britain, been seen in the Caribbean origin of many of its people. And, since these members came to Britain as immigrants, often in the 1950s, they traditionally took low-paid jobs and found themselves socially disadvantaged. By the 1980s improvements were observable, but Church of God members often found themselves struggling against social deprivation and prejudice that degenerated into racism. Efforts were made to address unemployment, family breakdown and the alienation of black youth. The Church of God set up a Department of Social Responsibility in 1986 to help develop cooperation among Afro-Caribbean churches. Some of this was funded by government money and much of it depended upon local ministerial initiatives in a series of separate projects within Britain's inner cities: in Leicester, in the

---

56 *Our Statements of Faith*, 17, 18.

57 *Our Statements of Faith*, 13.

58 *Our Statements of Faith*, 16.

Handsworth area of Birmingham, or in Brixton. This work was recognised nationally and Bishop S.E. Arnold's book *From Scepticism to Hope* which tells the story of these events is prefaced by the Archbishop of Canterbury.[59]

What do the data show?

Table 6.1 shows that there is general agreement that the minister who is an innocent party to divorce should be allowed to continue to serve as a minister. Despite this general agreement, approximately one Pentecostal minister in eight takes the opposite point of view and, presumably, considers that any divorced minister, whatever the grounds of the divorce, should cease to function in a ministerial capacity.

Table 6.1.1 shows that about a fifth of all Pentecostal ministers are clear about their rejection of the ban on divorce and remarriage for ministers. This item, the first in the table, does not specify the grounds for a divorce but only allows us to see that a general veto on ministerial divorce and remarriage does not command their support. On the other hand, the majority of ministers in three of the denominations do take the view that divorce and remarriage disqualifies a person from acting as a minister. The Elim Church is more open to the possibility of ministerial divorce and remarriage than the other three denominations, as can be seen by the high percentage of its ministers (nearly a third) in the 'not certain' category.

A minister who commits adultery loses support consistently within all four Pentecostal denominations. The pattern of figures is very similar, though there is slightly more likelihood of acceptance within the Apostolic Church and the Church of God. While only

Table 6.1 *Divorce and ministry*

Item	**Agree** %	**Not Certain** %	**Disagree** %
A minister who is the 'innocent' party in a divorce should not continue to serve as a minister	13.1	16.7	70.1

[59] Arnold, 1992.

4.8 per cent of Assemblies of God ministers think that a minister who commits adultery should continue to serve, the corresponding figure is twice as high in the two latter denominations.

Divorce prior to conversion is largely seen as irrelevant to ministerial office or ordination but the Apostolic Church is significantly different from Elim, the Church of God and Assemblies of God in this respect.[60] More than twice as many of its ministers consider that divorce prior to conversion is sufficient to bar a candidate from ordination. But the great majority of ministers, in all four denominations, do give primacy of place to conversion, which is seen as obliterating past sin of any kind, even marital sin.

Table 6.1.1 *Divorce, remarriage and ministry*

Item	Denom	Agree %	Not Certain %	Disagree %
A minister who, after ordination, divorces and remarries should not continue to serve as a minister	AC	60.0	18.9	21.1
	AG	56.7	23.0	20.3
	Elim	38.4	32.3	29.3
	CG	53.1	24.5	22.4
A minister who commits adultery should not continue to serve as a minister	AC	82.5	5.	12.4
	AG	88.2	7.0	4.8
	Elim	83.0	8.9	8.1
	CG	80.4	7.8	11.8
Divorce prior to conversion should prevent ordination	AC	11.2	14.3	74.5
	AG	4.7	10.7	84.6
	Elim	4.9	8.6	86.5
	CG	4.0	22.0	74.0
Divorce prior to conversion and remarriage after conversion should prevent ordination	AC	10.3	22.7	67.0
	AG	11.0	15.5	73.5
	Elim	5.7	12.4	81.9
	CG	18.0	24.0	58.0

60 $F = 5.8$, $p < .001$; confirmed using the Bonferroni post hoc tests.

Table 6.2.1 *Homosexuality*

Item	Denom	Agree %	Not Certain %	Disagree %
A minister who practises homosexuality should not continue to serve as a minister	AC	95.9		4.1
	AG	99.2	0.3	0.5
	Elim	97.8	0.8	1.3
	CG	100		

Divorce prior to conversion and remarriage after conversion attracts a slightly unexpected pattern of responses. While the majority of ministers in all four denominations consider that this is not a bar to ministerial office, rather more Church of God ministers than in the case of the other denominations see remarriage after conversion as particularly culpable. Whereas only 4 per cent of Church of God ministers thought divorce prior to conversion should prevent ordination, the figure in this denomination jumps to 18 per cent when remarriage after conversion is included. For two of the other denominations, Assemblies of God and Elim, remarriage after conversion is also seen to be an obstacle to ordination more than divorce before conversion. The unexpected pattern is found in the Apostolic Church which, on this particular issue, yields a lower percentage of ministers than related to the previous item and a rather higher percentage in the 'not certain' category.

Taken together, the items in tables 6.1 and 6.1.1 show that there is widespread agreement that ministers who commit adultery are not fit for office and that there is general sympathy with ministers who are innocent parties to divorce proceedings. Conversion is seen as a spiritual watershed but otherwise there is sufficient variability of opinion to suggest that individual personal circumstances must play a part in any proper judgement of a particular case.

Table 6.2.1 shows practising homosexuality is seen as disqualification for Pentecostal ministry.

Table 6.3 demonstrates a consistent and heavy majority of ministers who believe that Christians should not smoke or gamble. Although these items refer not to the behaviour of ministers specifically but to all Christians there is little or no legislation in

Table 6.3 *Holiness code (lifestyle)*

Item	Agree %	Not Certain %	Disagree %
Christians should not smoke	91.4	3.3	5.3
Christians should not gamble	94.0	3.4	2.6

Pentecostal churches about these two signs of personal holiness since there is long-standing support for both of them.[61]

Table 6.3.1 reveals a consistent pattern across three lifestyle items. In each instance the Church of God shows the largest percentage of ministers who agree with the prohibition, the Apostolic Church the second largest percentage, the Assemblies of God come third and the Elim ministers show the lowest percentage. The right-hand column of the table displays an identical implication. Taken together these items show that the holiness code of the Church of God is much more restrictive and rigorous than that of the Apostolic Church and that this in turn is more rigorous than the code governing Assemblies of God and Elim. The figures, in other words, support the holiness origins and commitments of the Church of God.

When the figures are looked at in more detail it becomes clear that cinema-going is more acceptable than social dancing or drinking alcoholic beverages.

One way to interpret these findings is to suggest that the two larger denominations in Britain have relaxed the older holiness code and moved closer to the social norms observed by the rest of society. In this respect Assemblies of God and Elim are easier to join and to become part of for new members since there is less of a contrast between believers and unbelievers. Assemblies of God and Elim members will find it more straightforward to socialise with non-Christian friends than will the Apostolic and Church of God members. Nevertheless, this pattern of figures should not disguise the general spread of opinion that exists within Pentecostal denominations. When, for example, almost equal numbers of Apostolic ministers can take opposite views about cinema attendance and when almost equal numbers of Assemblies of God ministers can

61 See Poloma, 1989, 177, for a similar comment about Assemblies of God in the USA.

Table 6.3.1 *Holiness code (lifestyle)*

Item	Denom	Agree %	Not Certain %	Disagree %
Christians should not attend the cinema	AC	43.9	9.2	46.9
	AG	18.0	12.9	69.1
	Elim	10.8	5.7	83.5
	CG	58.0	12.0	30.0
Christians should not take part in social dancing	AC	59.8	13.4	26.8
	AG	35.8	19.3	44.9
	Elim	22.8	11.4	65.9
	CG	84.0	4.0	12.0
Christians should not drink alcoholic beverages	AC	56.8	11.6	31.6
	AG	43.0	10.9	46.1
	Elim	35.3	12.0	52.7
	CG	66.7	8.3	25.0

take opposite views about drinking alcoholic beverages, it is clear that there is the possibility of conflict between ministers of the same denomination. But it is also true that where figures are fairly equally balanced, and therefore a majority is difficult to find, denominations will avoid attempting to legislate for their ministers or members in the interest of maintaining unity.

Table 6.3.2 shows that the Apostolic Church is the most likely to consider Sunday to be a special day akin to the Jewish Sabbath. The Apostolic Church ministers are most likely to be against buying or selling on Sundays, to be against sporting activities on Sundays and to be against the watching of television on Sundays. Behind them come the ministers of the Church of God and then, more lax than the other two denominations, are ministers of Elim and Assemblies of God. The Elim ministers are the least likely to support a sabbatarian approach to Sunday though, as the 'agree' column on watching television shows, there is a small core of ministers even within the Elim and Assemblies of God who take a fairly strict line on Sunday activities.

Altogether these tables support the general finding that there is a shift within the holiness tradition in Pentecostal churches and that

Table 6.3.2 *Holiness code (Sundays)*

Item	Denom	Agree %	Not Certain %	Disagree %
Christians should not buy or sell on Sundays unless absolutely necessary	AC	80.6	6.1	13.3
	AG	56.4	10.5	33.1
	Elim	46.5	10.5	43.0
	CG	80.4	3.9	15.7
Christians should not engage in sporting activities on Sundays	AC	74.0	11.5	14.6
	AG	40.9	17.5	41.6
	Elim	27.3	19.5	53.2
	CG	60.8	17.6	21.6
Christians should not watch TV on Sundays	AC	13.5	19.8	66.7
	AG	7.5	13.3	79.1
	Elim	6.5	10.2	83.3
	CG	3.9	17.6	78.4

the two faster growing denominations are those leaving the holiness tradition behind most rapidly.

Such a shift may be interpreted as a departure from the old standards held by Pentecostal denominations though many ministers would interpret it as a proper realisation of the teaching about grace within the New Testament. They would not see themselves as forsaking the older standards of social behaviour but rather as understanding that Christianity is a religion of grace and not of law and that prohibition is no substitute for the inner sanctity of heart and mind. They would support the restorationist or charismatic emphasis prevalent since the 1970s.

Conclusion

In his highly publicised Reith Lectures broadcast on the BBC in 1999, Anthony Giddens discussed globalisation and summarised his assessment of changes brought about by this phenomenon:

> Two basic changes are happening today under the impact of globalisation. In the western countries, not just public institutions but

> everyday life is becoming opened up from the hold of tradition. And other societies across the world that remained more traditional are becoming de-traditionalised. I take it this is at the core of the emerging global cosmopolitan society. (Lecture 3: Tradition.)

This weakening of tradition is connected with the family since it is the family which is the protector and transmitter of tradition. He puts it like this:

> I would turn the argument of the political and fundamentalist right on its head. The persistence of the traditional family – or aspects of it – in many parts of the world is more worrisome than its decline. For what are the most important forces promoting democracy and economic development in poorer countries? Well, they are the equality and education of women. And what must be changed to make these possible? Most importantly, what must be changed is the traditional family. (Lecture 2: Family.)

Pentecostal Christians would agree with Giddens but they would interpret the social changes he describes in the opposite way to him. What he sees as good, they see as bad. While he sees the persistence of the traditional family as 'worrisome', they would see it as a reason for celebration. While he sees equality and the education of women as being hindered by the traditional family, most Pentecostals would argue that it is the traditional family, particularly among poorer people, which provides the financial security to allow education to take place.[62] Moreover, where he sees religious tradition as resistant to democracy, many Pentecostal Christians would see the church as an ideal preparation for participation within democratic organisations. Unfortunately, there are Pentecostal congregations that are authoritarian and closed, but within existing democratic societies, these churches invariably decline. This is not a particularly religious phenomenon since the same sort of tension might exist within a trade union: some are run democratically and others by an authoritarian caucus. But, within the Pentecostal denominations described here, it is the annual conference structure that all four of them have

---

[62] A point supported by Hollenweger (1998) reviewing Harvey Cox's *Fire from Heaven* (1996).

adopted which is essentially democratic in its effect. Where each participating member carries only one vote in the forum where all important decisions are made through ballots, democracy reigns.

In respect of divorce and remarriage the four Pentecostal denominations described here have all, by different routes, reached similar procedural conclusions. They unconditionally accept the sanctity of marriage and the importance of the family while at the same time recognising the complexity of modern life to the extent of allowing cases of marital breakdown to be dealt with individually. Their particular concern is to maintain the moral integrity of their ministerial lists. The implicit assumption here is that if the ministerial list is degraded, then it is impossible to continue defending the biblical institution of marriage and the vitality of the traditional Christian home.

In respect of holiness within the four Pentecostal denominations, there are distinctions to be drawn between the three groups indigenous to Britain (Elim, Assemblies of God and the Apostolic Church) and the Church of God which originated outside Britain and from a pre-Pentecostal holiness tradition. The data show there is a gradual accommodation to leisure activities that previous generations of Pentecostals would have shunned. The barrier between Pentecostal congregations and an ungodly world has been lowered. Pentecostalism has re-thought its approach to worldly life and entertainment. Condemnatory preaching is rarely heard, though, because of the busy round of weekly meetings expected of the average Pentecostal Christian, there may be little time left for anything beyond the watching of television at home in the evening. Gambling and smoking are still almost universally rejected but cinema attendance and drinking alcohol are less forthrightly forbidden. Sunday observance only retains residual support. Nevertheless, where there is support for the traditional holiness code, this tends to be found within the Church of God and, to a lesser extent, the Apostolic Church.

This trend naturally raises a question about its possible limit. Will the accommodation between the Pentecostal congregations and the multimedia, entertainment-crazy western world continue until there really is no difference between what goes on inside and what goes on outside church? The likely answer to this question must be 'no' because the churches have been able to resist pressure for cultural accommodation by offering Christian versions of secular culture. Christian rock concerts are not uncommon and, where fairground-type facilities are required, denominations have been known to hire part or all of these facilities for their young people. In a sense the process began at the Assemblies of God and Elim conferences in the 1970s. The older, more legalistic forms of Christianity find scant biblical support and have difficulty in coexisting with the charismatic freedom in worship that Pentecostalism at its vibrant best encourages. If Pentecostalism continues to attract new converts and to grow, it is hard to see how its old holiness code can survive except as an historical relic. But if Pentecostalism falters, then legalistic holiness is always offered as a remedy and circumstances can be conceived where this might occur.

7

Ministers: Background, Material Conditions and Spirituality

Overview

This chapter begins by considering the place of religion in British society and explores the material conditions of Pentecostal ministers. It presents information on the marital status of ministers, their pay, their age, the organisation of congregational life, the size of congregations and other data of this kind and then considers the personal and devotional life of ministers including their childhood and their theological education.

Churches in Britain

Despite argument between social commentators, there is general agreement that the position of religion has declined within British society over the past 100 years.[1] It is difficult to measure this decline exactly because some of it is dependent upon an assumption about attitudes and values in the past that are no longer accessible. Yet what can be measured speaks consistently about a shift in the importance of religion and the way it functions in the lives of most people.

In measuring these changes, the most usual figures referring to religion are those of church membership and attendance, religious solemnisation of marriage, infant baptism, or the number of ordained ministers in relation to the general population. Most of

[1] Martin, 1976; Wallis and Bruce, 1992; Hamilton, 1995.

these figures are relevant to Anglican or Roman Catholic clergy but are less easy to apply to Pentecostals, partly because Pentecostal churches have not been in operation in Britain for a sufficient length of time and partly because their record keeping is less efficient than that of the older churches. In addition, church membership means different things in different denominations and this makes comparisons problematic. The most trustworthy figure is one that records church attendance but, even here, complications arise since, in most churches, some Sundays in the year are better attended than others and, unfortunately, there is no agreement about how adults should be distinguished from children. Should we count everyone below the age of fifteen as a child or everyone from secondary school age upwards as an adult? Or should we leave it to the person who counts to decide whether someone is an adult or a child since it is hardly practicable to go round the congregation asking everyone what their age is? In the figures given later in this chapter it is this strategy that has been adopted – pastors were asked how many adults attended their average Sunday morning congregations (see table 7.11.1).

Within the sociological literature on religion, debates about secularisation have assumed three basic positions. One group of sociologists argues that all the figures about religion tell a consistent story.[2] It has declined in importance as a personal practice (fewer people read the Bible, pray, say grace at meals, attend church), as an institutional force (fewer people get married in church, are buried by the church, value the pronouncements of senior clergy) and, more subtly, as a world-view or philosophy of life. The Christian account of the creation of the world, the sinfulness of human beings, the judgement of God and the reality of heaven and hell has been modified and pushed aside in favour of alternative evolutionary or pan-religious accounts of the place of human beings within the cosmos.

Another group of sociologists disputes these conclusions and argues that religion has remained as an important feature of British life but that it has been displaced into novel activities and expressions.[3] Religion has an enduring reality because it expresses a

---

[2] Bruce, 1995, for instance, has consistently and vehemently argued this.

[3] Greeley, 1973. Or from another point of view, Gill, 1993 and Berger, 1970.

fundamental feature of the human psyche. Consequently we should look for religion in the new rituals by which people give meaning to life, whether these rituals are overtly religious or not, and we should treat secular or humanistic stances as being disguised but genuine outcomes of the religious impulse. According to this account, religion has been transformed rather than eradicated. It still exists and it is now poured into the cultural structures and forms created for it by contemporary social relations.

A halfway position between these two extremes suggests that religion is an altogether more complicated, multidimensional entity than it seems.[4] This means that some aspects of religion may be declining and vanishing under the pressure of secularisation but other aspects of religion may be growing and flourishing. At the same time, two contradictory things are happening: religion is disappearing and growing.

Whatever the niceties of the sociological debate about the place of religion within Britain, Pentecostals almost instinctively would have accepted the secularisation thesis. The original Pentecostals felt themselves to be working 'against the grain' and many of the early calls to holiness and separation drew strength from the apocalyptic sense that the world, equated with the kingdom of darkness,[5] was heading for the judgement of God. Pentecostals did not distinguish between a process of secularisation and a process of paganisation. As far as they were concerned the church in its institutional forms was in trouble: it was lukewarm, weakened by modernist theology and resistant to the gracious movings of the Holy Spirit. And the world, as far as they were concerned, was rushing after the false and ultimately pagan gods of materialism and hedonism.

The original Pentecostals, and even subsequent post-Second World War Pentecostals, did not make a connection between the religious ambience of society and the ease with which people might become Christians. They did not assume that, if religion was thriving across the board, Pentecostalism would share in this spiritual prosperity. On the contrary, many assumed that the growth of Pentecostal churches was most likely to be due to a sovereign, all

---

[4] Gilbert, 1994.

[5] Cf. Colossians 1:13.

powerful, sweeping move of the Holy Spirit that would make cultural conditions irrelevant.[6] Prayer for revival was based upon the premise that it was God, and God alone, who caused the church to grow and human effort was either a small or non-existent part of the process. In short, there was a danger that belief in an interventionist God would result in the corollary of the church being largely reduced to a spectator role.

Yet, though only a minority of Pentecostals perceived it, the Pentecostal movement was not an isolated phenomenon.[7] Donald Gee particularly understood the place of Pentecostals within the larger body of the church and he lived long enough to see the beginnings of the charismatic movement and to welcome these new tongues-speaking Christians. On the other side of the theological spectrum, his invitation to the World Council of Churches assembly in Delhi in 1961 testified to the recognition by the great non-Pentecostal bodies that Pentecostalism belonged within Christianity as a whole.[8]

For these reasons it makes sense to look at the position of Pentecostal ministers in Britain within the social and cultural matrix of which they were an inevitable part. In the period from 1900 to 1990 the total Protestant community in Britain dropped from 5.4 million to 3.4 million, although the population as a whole rose. The Roman Catholic community in the same period of time remained roughly static, moving from 2.0 million in 1900 to 2.2 million in 1990. When Protestant and Roman Catholic communities are added together and presented as a percentage of the adult population of Britain, the decline of Christianity is easy to see. In 1900 30 per cent of the adult population were accounted Christians; in 1990 this figure had shrunk to 12 per cent. When these figures are related

---

[6] Despite a predominantly Arminian theology, a more Calvinistic belief in the sovereignty of God in relation to revival could be detected. See also the discussion in Kay, 1990, 245–258.

[7] David du Plessis was the most prominent communicator of the Pentecostal message as it began to be welcomed by non-Pentecostal churches in the period from 1952 onwards, the year that du Plessis addressed the International Missionary Council.

[8] Gee declined the invitation under pressure from Assemblies of God in Britain and the States, Kay, 1990, 292.

to the Protestant population alone the drop is even more dramatic. In 1900 21.9 per cent of the adult population were Protestant but by 1990 this had dropped to a mere 7.3 per cent.[9]

These figures can be illustrated by reference to Anglican and Methodist church membership. In 1900 Church of England membership ran at about 2.8 million and Methodist membership 727,000. The former fell to 1.5 million by 1990 and the latter to 416,000. As church membership in Britain has declined during the course of the twentieth century, so the number of ministers has also declined.[10] One set of figures suggest that the Anglican ministry declined by 20 per cent between 1900 and 1968; another set shows that this decline proceeded rapidly in the years that followed: by 1984 the number of Church of England clergy was only just over half that recorded in 1900, and this swift decline has to be seen against the approximate doubling of the population during the century.[11] Even when a shorter span of time is investigated the same kind of results are apparent. Membership of the Anglican Church declined in the years 1975 to 1995 by 25 per cent, the Baptist Church by 14 per cent, the Roman Catholic Church by 23 per cent, the Methodist Church by 27 per cent and the Presbyterian Church by 27 per cent.[12] And, when these figures are related to the age profile of the population, it is apparent that the largest number of church attenders is to be found in the under 15 or over 65 age groups. In each age category women significantly outnumber men. The lowest church attendance is found in those aged 22 to 29 years. Not surprisingly the number of ministers also declined between 1975 and 1995. Anglicans lost 2700 clergy, Roman Catholics 1200 and Methodist 100. Of the old churches, only the Baptists in this period saw an increase in the number of their clergy by some 500. Moreover, because new clergy were not recruited, the average age of clergy who remained in post increased. Church of England clergy in 1994 averaged 52 years of age while the modal age of Roman Catholic parochial clergy in England and Wales lay in the decade 55 to 64 years of age

---

[9] Bruce, 1995, 37.

[10] Bruce, 1995, 36.

[11] Towler, 1968; Bruce, 1995, 32.

[12] Francis and Brierley, 1997.

– indeed over a quarter of Roman Catholic priests were aged over 65 years.[13]

When the figures for social class are examined in relation to church attendance across Great Britain it is clear that non-manual workers are more likely to attend than manual workers, another indication that the church as a whole (including all Protestant and Roman Catholic congregations) is more likely to attract a middle-class clientele.[14]

While the numerical strength and significance of religion has been declining, there has also been a measurable decline in the status of clergy. In the United States a piece of research asked a sample of the population to place 90 occupations in order of rank and clergyman came twelfth. A comparable British study placed clergy fourth among 30 occupations, only coming behind surgeons, medical doctors and solicitors. Evidence that suggests (or suggested in 1962 when the research was done) that clergy were still held in relatively high esteem.[15] A more recent study (1992) asked people to rate the degree of confidence they placed in different institutions and non-churchgoers ranked the church as tenth, above the social security system, the trade unions and the press but below the civil service, the education system, the legal system, the police and the armed forces. And, when a Euro-wide perspective is taken, a similar ranking of institutions showed that the church had lost several percentage points of confidence in the period between 1981 and 1990.[16]

According to one line of sociological analysis it is best to think of status as being either ascribed or achieved.[17] If it is ascribed then it is given to people on the basis of some form of honours system and there is little relationship between the status they receive and their actual performance at work or in the community. An achieved status, by contrast, is based upon some clear achievement, whether sporting, academic or commercial. According to the general

---

[13] For Anglican ages see Francis and Lankshear, 1994 and for Roman Catholic ages see Louden, 1998.

[14] Kay, 2000c.

[15] Wilson, 1966, 82, 83.

[16] Barker, Halman and Vloet, 1992, 11.

[17] Towler, 1968.

population clergy are recipients of ascribed status. Any status they have is not a result of what they have accomplished but of who they are. This distinction between two kinds of status tends to break down in the Pentecostal community. Status in this setting is more likely to be achieved. The minister who has taken a small and dying congregation and managed to encourage it into new life or the evangelist who held successful crusades is acclaimed by his or her peer group. This is partly a consequence of the congregational nature of much Pentecostalism. Among Elim and Assemblies of God there is no ecclesiastical rank. Everyone is notionally at the same level – simply a minister of the gospel. Successful ministers, having achieved status, are recognised at conferences and in ministerial gatherings, often by being asked to speak.

Sociologically, status is linked with the notion of religious authority. Authority is usually thought of as being either legal-rational or charismatic.[18] If it is legal-rational then it depends upon the deployment of power within a system, whether bureaucratic or legal. The judge has this kind of authority since, on the basis of law, he or she may pass binding judgement on a plaintiff. Similarly, within a religious context, it is possible to exercise this type of authority on the basis of religious law or precedent. Sometimes this sort of authority derives from the power of a religious bureaucracy attaching itself to the church or a religious movement. But there is another kind of religious authority, much more dynamic and creative, that is characteristically to be found in the early stages of religious movements. This is the authority of a charismatic individual where the word 'charismatic' does not need to have a technical theological meaning but simply refers to an individual who by virtue of his or her gifts is recognised as important. Religious founders are considered to have this sort of authority since they innovate and do not depend upon any established legal or bureaucratic framework. Within Pentecostalism, George Jeffreys is usually seen as an example of a charismatic leader who, through his extraordinary ministry, brought a whole set of churches into existence and established his authority over them. Yet, at local congregational level, most Pentecostal pastors would also expect to exercise charis-

---

[18] A major theme in the work of Weber. See MacRae, 1974; Berger, 1963.

matic authority, again where the word 'charismatic' need not be taken in its full New Testament sense. The pastor is someone who preaches and knows what do in perplexing situations and, because of this, is invested by congregational members with high status.

Material circumstances

Status and pay tend to belong together. Within Pentecostal denominations the payment of ministers is almost invariably made from the pockets of their congregations. Within Assemblies of God there is little or no central provision for the payment of ministers. If the congregation is small, the minister is likely to be poor. If the congregation is large, the minister may be better off. Levels of payment are usually entirely within the hands of a local church council or a board of deacons and, though the denomination may issue pay guidelines to churches, there is usually no necessity for the churches to observe them.[19] In this respect the relationship between the Pentecostal minister and his or her congregation is quite unlike that found within the Anglican or Roman Catholic traditions where substantial funds are generated by investments and there is little or no need for the minister to raise money through an offering. Moreover, within the Anglican and Roman Catholic traditions there are extensive property holdings to ensure that ministers are housed to the end of their lives.

The Apostolic Church is more centralised than other Pentecostal groups in its approach to finance. All salaries are paid by the central office from funds that are sent in by the individual congregations. In each assembly the running expenses (heating, lighting, and so on) are deducted from the tithes each Sunday and then 10 per cent of the balance is deducted for local funds and the surplus sent to headquarters. The church also contributes to a pension scheme for its ministers, allowing them to retire with a supplement to the state

[19] Where individual congregations are classified as charities (as is the case in British Assemblies of God), the church council has legal obligations to the minister and to the running of the charity. Normally members of the church council cannot be paid by the charity, but in the case of ministers this is allowed as long as they are in a minority on the council.

pension. Ministers who complete twenty years full-time service can take a sabbatical year from the age of sixty-four. Ministers are given the opportunity to purchase their own manse during their full-time service. Moreover, local councils are obliged to accommodate anyone who, on retirement, loses 'tied accommodation', that is accommodation that is tied to a particular job. This means that an Apostolic minister can retire from a manse in one part of the country to council property in another part of the country and the only restriction on the minister's free choice of a place to live derives from the level of rent in an area. It may be too high and he may prefer to go elsewhere where rent is cheaper.[20]

Such long-term financial security is less common within other Pentecostal denominations and, although Elim has a pension fund and makes provision for ministers in their old age, Assemblies of God advises all its ministers to make their own arrangements. Earlier attempts at an Assemblies of God denominational pension scheme came to nothing because ministers could not afford the premiums. There is a small amount of Assemblies of God housing available at eventide homes, but no guarantee that all ministers will be catered for in this way. The figures provided later in this chapter show the current position and also suggest that, along with the rest of society, Pentecostal ministers are seeking to become home owners. Only 50 per cent of houses in the UK in 1970 were owner-occupied but this percentage rose steadily until in 1996 it had reached 68 per cent. Correspondingly, accommodation rented from local authorities accounted for 30 per cent of the market in 1970 and only 19 per cent of the market in 1996.[21]

During the same period of time considerable government attention has been given to occupational pensions since projected population figures show that, as the proportion of retired people rises in relation to the working population, there will be insufficient tax money available to fund future pensioners. The government answer to this demographic problem is to encourage individuals to invest in personal pension schemes and not to rely upon the state scheme which, in relation to future wages and prices, is bound to become less valuable. Most pension schemes are invested with large

---

[20] I am grateful to Revd Gordon Weeks for this information.

[21] See Brierley, 1997, table 5.14.3.

pension companies that took advantage of the steady growth of the stockmarket during the 1960s and 1970s. However, where a denomination wishes to start up an occupational scheme for its ministers, that period of postwar growth is disadvantageous because the current rate of economic performance is much less impressive.

By the mid-1990s, of the 35 million people in Britain of working age, approximately 10.5 million were members of occupational pension schemes and about 10 million personal pension plans were held (it is not clear how many people have more than one pension plan).[22] Even if we could assume that there is no overlap between people with a personal pension plan and people with an occupational pension, then we could only say that at the most about two-thirds of people of working age in Britain are entitled to a pension in addition to the state's pension scheme.[23]

In Pentecostal thinking the linkage between status and pay is not straightforward because it is refracted through a theological lens. From the very beginning of the Christian tradition there has always been an emphasis on the value of poverty. Poverty and spirituality belong together. It is the poor to whom the kingdom of God belongs and wealth may be a positive disadvantage.[24] This theological imperative frequently works out in two equal and opposite directions. Either the underpayment of ministers is made a virtue by congregations and denominations that wish to spend money on buildings or evangelism or, when ministers feel the system is treating them unfairly, they may be attracted to the theology of prosperity and seek to improve their material circumstances, often by trying to increase congregational giving.[25]

It is always difficult to assess the exact earnings of ministers since the payment of phone bills, rent, petrol or other allowances of this

---

[22] Information given by Frank Field MP (letter dated 19 May 1999) in reply to my enquiry.

[23] It is not legitimate to assume that all occupational pension scheme holders do not have personal pensions even though it is not legal to be in an occupational pension scheme and to have a personal pension at the same time. People may have started a personal pension scheme, held it in abeyance while in an occupational pension scheme, and then changed jobs and restarted their personal pension scheme.

[24] Matthew 19:24; 1 Timothy 6:10; Matthew 5:3.

[25] See, Kay, 1999b, for a brief discussion.

kind boost the minister's effective salary while making the take-home pay seem low. During the period from 1970 to 1996 salaries increased sharply. The average weekly earning for a man in full-time manual employment in 1970 was £27 and this rose in 1985 to £164 and in 1996 to £301. Non-manual males also enjoyed a similar lift. In 1970 non-manual males were earning £36 a week, in 1985 this had risen to £225 and by 1996 this became £465. In these 26 years average earnings rose by a factor of 11 or 12. In a sense, however, average salaries are not a good guide to the salaries of Pentecostal ministers since these averages contain a small number of very high salaries generated in the City of London that tend to pull the figures up unrealistically. In addition, differential tax rates make it difficult to calculate take-home pay. Yet, as a reasonable estimate one can deduct approximately a third of the salary for tax and superannuation payments to arrive at a takehome figure.[26] In 1996, on this basis, an average male in non-manual employment would be taking home £325 and a male in manual employment would be receiving £210 per week.[27] Pastoral salaries almost certainly did not keep pace with these rises although no detailed figures are available to verify this impression.

A further piece of evidence relevant to the payment of ministers occurs in relation to the social class of typical congregations. A survey of Assemblies of God ministers showed that 41.5 per cent of ministers assessed their congregations to be 'mainly working-class', 6.6 per cent assessed their congregations to be 'managerial/professional' and 43.7 per cent of ministers assessed their congregations to be equally mixed between 'working-class and non-working class-people'. A further 1.6 per cent estimated their congregations to be made up mainly of unemployed people.[28] Data are not available on the social class composition of the other Pentecostal denominations but the impression is that the Apostolic and the Church of God congregations would draw from similar social strata. Only Elim might be slightly more middle class in its orientation.

Whatever the connection between the status and pay of the Pentecostal ministers and the status and pay of other clergy within

26 In the lower tax bands.

27 Brierley, 1998, table 5.14.2.

28 Weaver, 1999.

western society, Pentecostal denominations would draw a deliberate and sharp line between these issues and those of sexual morality. Undoubtedly the traditional marriage and the nuclear family are losing their normative force in Britain and across the world. It is now extremely common for couples to live in a stable relationship for many years and to bring up children without ever having undertaken formal marriage vows. The question now is not 'Is this your husband or wife?' but 'Is this your partner?' Pentecostal ministers, however, would not accept this as a legitimate basis for personal relationships among church leaders or, almost certainly, among congregational members. In this respect, Pentecostalism stands against prevailing norms and is to be seen as a conservative social influence, defending the value of marriage and upholding the virtue of the nuclear family.

Pentecostal ministers would accept the biblical teaching on marriage and family relationships and see it as part of their mandate to teach and exemplify this lifestyle, however old-fashioned or criticised it might become. And the strength of Pentecostal convictions in this direction are not only based upon the text of Scripture but also upon their own experience of helping people who have suffered emotional pain as a consequence of family breakdown. Whatever goods the sociological pundits might find in the advancement of liberalism within global society through the breakdown of religion,[29] Pentecostal ministers would be inclined to rebut by drawing on a range of pastoral experiences that are not easily incorporated within sociological theory.

Congregational organisation

The traditional method by which ministers are supported in Pentecostal churches is from the tithe. This is a concept drawn from the Old Testament when priests were supported by a 10 per cent offering taken from harvest and other produce. There were 12 tribes of Israel, and only one of these was priestly, so by ensuring that a 10 per cent offering was given, these priests lived at approximately the same material level as the rest of the nation. This system

[29] Giddens, 1999. See also the conclusion to the previous chapter.

of supporting a minister suggests that one minister can be fully funded by ten wage-earners but, in practice because of the costs of running the building and other incidental expenses, ministers normally require a rather larger base of support. Pentecostal congregations of about 50 adults would probably contain sufficient wage-earners to support a minister. Since Pentecostal congregations tend to be fewer than a hundred people, and certainly historically were often considerably smaller than this, the traditional pattern was for one minister to be in charge of each congregation.

The support of a minister within a denomination also depends upon the generosity and adventurousness of previous generations. Pentecostal churches in Britain are about three generations old (allowing 25 years for generation). The first generation, born in the heat of the Pentecostal revival, perhaps bought a small piece of land or a building; the second generation perhaps bought a house for a minister so that, by the time the third generation arrives, the cost of the building and house may well have been cleared and such income as comes in from the congregation is theoretically available to support the minister comfortably. But at this point the church building may have become too small and the house may be in need of repair so that the material purchases of the previous generations are in need of upgrade. In many cases, too, the original church building will have been in a poorer part of town and so may be unsuitable for the aspirations of what is now an established denomination.

Moreover, as congregations grow and as Britain becomes less of an industrial and more of a service culture, there is a recognition that congregations need a quality of pastoral care beyond the capability of one over-busy individual. Pentecostal theology, with its emphasis upon the work of the Holy Spirit within the whole congregation, naturally leads to a recognition that lay ministries will emerge. New positions within churches begin to appear. Music leaders, youth leaders and housegroup leaders come to the fore and the solo Pentecostal pastor is transformed into the manager or leader of a team of people with diverse functions and strengths. In a sense the switch into housegroups is an indication of the modernity of a congregation. It shows that the pastor has relinquished some of his (or her) authority to others, a development that only works smoothly if the pastor can cultivate and maintain good, loving relationships with these new leaders. If the pastor finds this sort of delegation problematic, then the congregation is unlikely to grow beyond a certain size and the church may be pastorally impoverished. Whatever the size of a Pentecostal congregation its members will expect their minister to preach or teach several times a week. Ministers need to remain fresh to sustain this ministry. Using the text 'For anyone who speaks in a tongue does not speak to men but to God' (1 Cor. 14:2), most Pentecostal ministers would take the view that speaking in tongues is a form of prayer that has the effect of edifying, building up or strengthening the person who prays. For this reason the Pentecostal pastor would expect to speak in tongues as a means of preparing him or herself for ministry to others. Since Pentecostal pastors preach a great deal they would also expect to speak in tongues a great deal and many find this an indispensable aid to ministry, as we shall see.

Education

The place of formal education within the Pentecostal churches is ambiguous. On one hand Pentecostal churches and Pentecostal denominations have from their very beginnings provided ministerial training and invested large sums of money in this project. At the beginning, this was to ensure that the doctrinal position of Pentecostal ministers was in accord with the fundamental truths espoused by their denominations. But it was also felt that Pentecostalism, though born out of intense reliance upon the Holy Spirit, was also a movement founded on the Bible and so a knowledge of the Bible was imperative.

The Hampstead Bible School set up in about 1921, the Bible College founded by George Jeffreys in Clapham in 1925[30] and the training College at Penygroes are all examples of Pentecostal educational institutions. For the first 60 or so years of their lives these institutions largely offered short courses based almost entirely upon the study of the text of Scripture, though occasionally subjects such as Christian journalism or public speaking were also taught. In more recent years Pentecostal colleges have swum with the current of

[30] Moving to Capel in 1965 and to Nantwich in 1987. I am grateful to Neil Hudson for this information.

higher education in Britain so that they now all offer degrees validated by secular institutions. Undoubtedly part of the impetus for this change came from the realisation that public funding was available to support students enrolled for examinations accredited in this way. Having begun the process of educational development, Pentecostal Bible Colleges are embarked upon a journey with an uncertain destination. Certainly their staff have been required to obtain recognised qualifications and most of them now have masters degrees or doctorates. Courses themselves, accredited as they are by secular institutions, have to conform in a measure to the requirements of the secular institutions raising inevitable tensions between vocational training for ministry and the purely academic criteria related to free inquiry and secular scholarship. It is possible to predict that Pentecostal Bible Colleges will continue to develop their vocational courses and retain their distinct Pentecostal heritage. This appears to be the most likely scenario. Another projection suggests that the Pentecostal colleges might be unable to maintain their student numbers and so will allow themselves to be integrated within secular structures as has now happened to several Anglican institutions of higher education whose campuses, libraries and facilities are controlled by the governing agencies of institutions to which they are affiliated.

What do the data show?

Material circumstances

Table 7.1.1 indicates that the vast majority of Pentecostal ministers are married, showing that their own lifestyles suit them for the defence of traditional family values. The slightly larger number of single ministers in Elim is almost certainly due to the younger average age of Elim ministers while the larger number of widowed ministers in the Apostolic Church is almost certainly due to their higher average age (see table 7.6.1). Differences of denominational policy on divorce and remarriage are indicated by the presence of a small minority of divorced and remarried Elim ministers and the complete absence of any such ministers in the other three denominations.

Table 7.1.1 *Marital status*

Denom	Single %	Married %	Widowed %	Divorced %	Divorced and remarried %
AC		94.0	6.0		
AG	3.0	96.3	0.7		
Elim	4.6	93.2	0.5		1.6
CG	2.1	95.8		2.1	

Table 7.2.1 shows that the great majority of ministers live within a couple of miles of their churches. In each denomination apart from the Church of God more than 50 per cent of ministers live up to two miles from their church. The Church of God presents a slightly different picture presumably because, as table 7.3.1 shows, it has a larger proportion than the other three denominations of ministers who are in full-time secular employment. The location of the minister's home is likely to be determined by his or her main place of work.

Table 7.3.1 also shows that Assemblies of God and Elim are the denominations most able to support their ministers on a full-time basis since only 13 per cent of their ministers find it necessary to take full-time secular employment.[31] The Apostolic ministers are slightly less well provided for in this respect by their churches though, as can be seen by the right-hand column in the table, about three-quarters of Apostolic, Assemblies and Elim ministers are supported full-time by their congregations.[32]

The level of finance provided for ministers presents a compatible picture (table 7.4.1). The Apostolic Church has the largest percentage of ministers earning under £125 per week and the Elim church the least. At pay levels up to £200 per week the Apostolic Church again shows the largest proportion of ministers (76 per cent) and the

Table 7.2.1 *Living distance from church*

Denom	< 1 mile %	1–2 miles %	3–5 miles %	6–10 miles %	10+ miles %
AC	18.3	40.8	25.4	11.3	4.2
AG	27.4	31.5	21.0	14.3	5.7
Elim	28.7	33.8	21.2	8.5	7.8
CG	21.9	12.5	31.3	12.5	21.9

31 Weaver, 1999.

32 Weaver, 1999.

Table 7.3.1 *Secular employment*

Denom	Yes, full-time %	Yes, part-time %	No %
AC	24.5	4.3	71.3
AG	13.0	12.0	75.1
Elim	13.2	10.0	76.8
CG	37.5	8.3	54.2

Elim Church the smallest (38 per cent). This suggests that the Apostolic Church contains the largest proportion of financially struggling ministers. At the top end of salary levels there is a slight alteration to the balance. There are more Elim ministers (12.7 per cent) earning more than £325 per week than in any other denomination, but there are also a fair number of Apostolic ministers (9.5 per cent) at this level. This suggests that the most senior ministers of the Apostolic Church are relatively well paid considering the pay given to the rest of their denomination.

When these data were collected, average male workers in Britain were receiving approximately £325 (non-manual) and £210 (manual) in wages per week. As these figure show, the majority of Pentecostal ministers were earning at the level of average non-manual males or below. As pointed out earlier, take-home pay would normally be supplemented by allowances but, given the generally higher than average age of Pentecostal ministers, this compensation is partly cancelled out and certainly does not make the job attractive

Table 7.4.1 *Weekly take-home pay*

	Apostolic %	Assemblies of God %	Elim %	Church of God %	All %
less than £100	18.2	16.3	10.1	20.0	14.1
£100 to £124	13.6	6.6	6.9	6.7	7.4
£125 to £149	16.7	6.0	4.3	6.7	6.4
£150 to £174	21.2	11.3	6.9	13.3	10.5
£175 to £199	6.1	8.6	7.6	3.3	7.7
£200 to £224	6.1	13.0	13.0	16.7	12.5
£225 to £249	4.5	8.6	9.4	10.0	8.6
£250 to £274	3.0	8.6	12.7	3.3	9.5
£275 to £299	1.5	5.3	9.1	3.3	6.4
£300 to £324	1.5	6.0	8.3	10.0	6.7
more than £325	7.6	9.6	11.6	6.7	10.1

on salary grounds alone and, indeed, disguises the real hardship of young ministers at the bottom of the pay ladder.

Table 7.5.1 produces, in the left-hand column, slightly different figures from table 7.3.1 because it shows responses to a question asking whether the minister's ministry was 'primarily' paid or unpaid. There will be a number of ministers working on pensions or perhaps disability allowances so, for example, while 71.3 per cent of Apostolic ministers are not in secular employment only 46.2 per cent of them report their ministry as being primarily paid. In each denomination there is a mismatch between the number of ministers being financed by their congregations and the number not in secular employment, but in the case of the Assemblies of God and Elim this shortfall is only a few per cent.

In relation to the ownership of property, Pentecostal ministers are generally ahead of their contemporaries and those at similar levels of pay to themselves. While 68 per cent of homes in England and Wales are owner occupied, a larger percentage of Pentecostal ministers in three of the denominations has bought property. Such a finding suggests, probably correctly, that Pentecostal ministers are normally disciplined in their handling of personal finance and it may also be connected with the generally stable marriages Pentecostal ministers enjoy, marriages in which it is common for wives to take on some form of paid secular employment. According to Weaver's figures, 16.4 per cent of Assemblies of God minister's wives are in full-time secular employment and 30.8 per cent are in part-time secular employment.[33]

Table 7.5.1 *Current financial position*

Denom	Ministry Paid %	Accommodation provided by church %	Own property %	Pension %
AC	46.2	42.1	56.9	92.8
AG	67.9	10.0	77.6	62.4
Elim	74.7	18.9	74.9	83.3
CG	40.0	14.9	93.9	74.2

[33] Paul Weaver, Assemblies of God General Superintendent, carried out a survey in 1999 using a database of 318 Assemblies of God ministers.

Nevertheless, although many wives of Pentecostal ministers are employed in secular work, nearly half (47.8 per cent) have a major role within the church that is recognised by their congregations. In this respect Pentecostal ministry is frequently a husband and wife partnership and it is not uncommon for congregations looking for a new minister to take into account the potential contribution of the wife when making a choice.

Pentecostal ministers in Britain are predominantly male. Of the Apostolic ministers 100 per cent are male, of Assemblies of God 97.5 per cent, of Elim 97.9 per cent and of the Church of God 90.2 per cent. Putting this another way, just 2.5 per cent of Pentecostal ministers are female.

Table 7.6.1 shows the age distribution of ministers in the different denominations. The Apostolic Church clearly has the largest number of older ministers – nearly a fifth of its ministers are more than seventy years old. At the other end of the scale the Elim ministry is the youngest. It has the highest percentage of ministers under twenty-nine years old, the highest percentage between thirty and thirty-nine and the highest percentage between forty and forty-nine. The Assemblies of God profile shows the second highest number of ministers under twenty-nine and then the second highest number between forty and forty-nine. Like Elim, about a third of its ministers are in this age bracket.[34] By contrast, a third of Church of God ministers are a decade older in the 50 to 59 band. This table helps to explain some of the social attitudes and theological beliefs of the four denominations. Elim is most go-ahead while the Apostolic Church appears more cautious and traditional.

Table 7.6.1 *Age of ministers in years*

Denom	**Under 29** %	**30–39** %	**40–49** %	**50–59** %	**60–69** %	**Over 70** %
AC	2.0	12.1	15.2	29.3	24.2	17.2
AG	4.8	18.5	30.8	25.8	15.3	5.0
Elim	6.8	27.0	35.1	20.7	7.9	2.5
CG	2.1	20.8	16.7	35.4	20.8	4.2

[34] Paul Weaver found their average age was 49.36 years, their median age was forty-nine years and their modal age forty-seven years. This set of figures fits satisfactorily with the age profile of Assemblies of God ministers found here.

Table 7.7.1 *Length of ordained ministry in years*

Denom	Under 9 %	10–19 %	20–29 %	30–39 %	Over 40 %
AC	38.4	21.2	18.2	9.1	13.1
AG	44.0	26.4	13.7	9.7	6.2
Elim	47.2	30.7	13.5	6.4	2.2
CG	48.9	27.7	12.8	10.6	

Assemblies of God comes somewhere in between. When these figures are compared with those of Anglican and Roman Catholic clergy cited earlier, it is evident that, certainly in Assemblies of God and Elim, Pentecostal clergy tend to be somewhat younger.

Table 7.7.1 matches the age profile of the four denominations except that it indicates the Church of God tends to recruit its ministers rather later than the other Pentecostal churches. This explains why, although about a third of Church of God ministers are aged between fifty and fifty-nine years, nearly half have only been ordained for less than nine years. On the other hand, the Apostolic Church has a long tail of elderly, experienced ministers and shows more than twice as many (13.1 per cent) men to have been ordained for more than 40 years. Again, the younger profile of Elim is confirmed in that it has the largest percentage of ministers ordained for between 10 and 19 years.

Table 7.8.1 gives an indication of the pressure felt by ministers as a consequence of their work, though these figures probably need to be read in conjunction with the age profile already discussed. This would explain why the Church of God ministers are the most unlikely to have considered leaving the ministry (many of them are older and have only come to ministry relatively late in life). A similar explanation would cover the Apostolic ministers. Younger ministers presumably feel that there are other employment

Table 7.8.1 *Have you considered leaving the ministry?*

Denom	No %	Less than twice %	Several times %	Frequently
AC	63.9	26.8	8.2	1.0
AG	51.9	32.6	12.2	3.3
Elim	47.1	34.0	15.1	3.8
CG	79.1	14.6	6.3	

Table 7.9.1 *Leadership position*

Denom	**Not in charge of congregation %**	**Yes, in sole charge %**	**Assistant to senior minister %**	**Part of team %**
AC	26.0	47.9	2.1	24.0
AG	19.9	47.5	5.1	27.5
Elim	19.9	54.0	8.7	17.7
CG	36.0	48.0	4.0	12.0

opportunities for them which they are not too old to decline. Nearly a fifth of Elim ministers and 15 per cent of Assemblies of God ministers have 'several times' or 'frequently' considered leaving the ministry. Nevertheless, among Apostolic, Assemblies of God and Elim ministers together this is clearly an important issue.[35] A small but significant number of younger ministers has considered going back on their vocation and ordination. They are likely to be in need of pastoral help.

Table 7.9.1 shows that roughly 50 per cent of ministers are in sole charge of congregations in all four denominations. Elim and Assemblies of God contain the largest percentage of ministers who function as assistants though the differences between denominations are not great. The position of assistant minister is one that presumes both a training regime and sufficient funds within the congregation to support a second person. Team ministry is most popular in the Assemblies of God though not uncommon in the other denominations. Ministers who are not in charge of congregations may be operating as supplementary preachers or teachers, but earning a living through secular employment and, when these figures are compared with those in table 7.3.1, this seems a reasonable explanation. Roughly the same number of Apostolic and Church of God ministers are not in charge of congregations and are in full-time secular employment.

Congregational organisation

Table 7.10.1 shows that housegroups are popular across the Pentecostal spectrum. They are most popular in Elim churches but about

[35] Weaver, 1999, found that the average age at ordination ('receiving ministerial status') for Assemblies of God ministers in Britain is thirty-six years, the median age thirty-four years and the modal age thirty years.

Table 7.10.1 *Housegroups*

Denom	Use housegroups %	Median number of housegroups
AC	51.4	2
AG	65.6	4
Elim	73.5	4
CG	51.6	2

two-thirds of Assemblies of God churches also make use of them. Housegroups are partly a function of the size of congregation but also important in that they allow a fine-grain form of pastoral care by promoting lay members of the congregation to a position of pastoral responsibility. In the 1960s and early 1970s Pentecostal pastors often resisted housegroups since housegroup leaders were seen as potential challengers to the authority of the minister. Such worries have now largely dissipated and it is reasonable to see housegroups as normal within all but the smallest Pentecostal congregations. When table 7.10.1 is compared with table 7.11.1 there is a reasonable match between average congregational size and the presence of housegroups.

Table 7.11.1 indicates the average adult attendance for Sunday morning congregations. The table shows that 68 per cent of Apostolic congregations attract fewer than 50 people and that the same is true of 59 per cent of Church of God congregations. About 44 per cent of Assemblies of God congregations and 40 per cent of Elim congregations fall into this size category. These figures alone indicate that the Apostolic congregations are generally smaller than Assemblies of God and Elim and a little smaller than the Church of God. No

Table 7.11.1 *Adults attending average Sunday morning congregation*

	Apostolic %	Assemblies of God %	Elim %	Church of God %
less than 25	24.3	19.8	13.6	28.1
25 to 49	44.3	23.3	26.2	31.3
50 to 74	18.6	16.9	18.4	15.6
75 to 99	5.7	11.2	10.5	9.4
100 to 149	2.9	9.9	10.2	
150 to 199	1.4	8.9	8.2	6.3
200 to 249		2.9	4.4	9.4
250 to 299	1.4	3.8	2.0	
300 to 349		1.3	1.7	
350 +	1.4	1.9	4.8	

data are available on the location of Apostolic congregations but, given their concentration in Wales, a rural environment, this pattern is not surprising. The figures given here apply to adult attendance so that the visitor arriving at a Pentecostal Church on a Sunday morning would expect to find children and young people who might make up a quarter of the total congregation, ensuring that even a congregation of, say, 40 would actually have 50 people present.

The figures can be looked at from another perspective to see what percentage of congregations are above 100 adults. Here we find that the Apostolic Church has only 7.1 per cent of its congregations of this size and the Church of God twice as many (15.7 per cent) of its congregations at this level. For Assemblies of God (28.7 per cent) and Elim (31.3 per cent) nearly a third of its congregations reach this numerical strength.

Spiritual Life

There is almost universal agreement among Pentecostal ministers that they have been baptised in the Spirit. All the ministers in this sample except two said that they had been baptised in the Holy Spirit; one said he did not know whether he had been baptised or not and the other said 'no'.

When asked whether they prayed by themselves, 94.4 per cent said that they did so 'nearly every day', 4.1 per cent said that they did so 'twice a week', 0.9 per cent said that they did so 'at least once a week' and the remaining less than 1 per cent prayed at least 'occasionally'. None never prayed on their own.

Table 7.12.1 relates to the frequency of a minister's speaking in tongues. It shows that the Apostolic Church, Assemblies of God and Elim are similar in that 80 per cent or more of their ministers

Table 7.12.1 *Do you speak in tongues?*

Denom	Never %	Used to %	Occasionally %	At least once a month %	At least once a week %	Every day %
AC			5.1		13.1	81.8
AG			2.0	0.5	6.7	90.8
Elim	0.5	0.5	3.5	1.1	14.2	80.2
CG			37.5	12.5	29.2	20.8

Table 7.13.1 *Do you read your Bible by yourself?*

Denom	Never %	Occasionally %	At least once a month %	At least once a week %	At least twice a week %	Every day %
AC					6.1	93.9
AG				1.0	5.0	94.0
Elim		0.8		1.3	9.7	88.2
CG				4.0	8.0	88.0

would expect to speak in tongues every day. Church of God ministers show a different pattern in that only 20 per cent of their ministers would expect to speak with tongues daily. The most frequent response by Church of God ministers is 'occasionally', which implies these ministers do not see speaking in tongues as a vital part of their spiritual preparation or life of prayer. By contrast, Assemblies of God ministers place great emphasis on speaking with tongues – a finding that is in line with the Assemblies of God emphasis on tongues as being the initial evidence of baptism in the Spirit – and only 2 per cent report themselves as speaking 'occasionally'. There are a few Elim ministers (about 5 per cent) for whom tongues appear to be relatively unimportant but the majority value the gift.

Table 7.13.1 deals with personal Bible reading and the figures show that well over 80 per cent of all Pentecostal ministers would expect to read the Bible every day. This stress on Bible reading is almost universal, though there is a maverick Elim percentage (0.8 per cent) that disregards evangelical norms. Taking the two tables 7.12.1 and 7.13.1 together it is evident that around nine Pentecostal ministers out of ten will pray in tongues and read their Bibles each

Table 7.14.1 *Do you prophesy in church? (where prophecy is not understood as preaching)*

Denom	Never %	Used to %	Occasionally %	At least once a month %	At least once a week %
AC	24.5	9.2	44.9	17.3	4.1
AG	5.0	1.3	39.6	36.1	18.0
Elim	5.4	2.2	51.8	25.6	15.1
CG	18.8	4.2	66.7	4.2	6.3

Table 7.15.1 *Sudden acceptance of Christianity*

Denom	Sudden acceptance %
AC	37.7
AG	48.6
Elim	42.2
CG	29.0

day, suggesting that they see their ministries as being disempowered without these spiritual disciplines.

Table 7.14.1 concerns the frequency of ministerial prophecy. Assemblies of God ministers show themselves most likely to prophesy: over half (54 per cent) will prophesy once a month or more. Elim ministers are similar and about 40 per cent of them will prophesy with the same frequency. Apostolic Church ministers prophesy at about half this level (21 per cent) while Church of God ministers are the least likely to bring this sort of utterance to their congregations (10.5 per cent only). The particular status of prophecy within the historical development of the Apostolic Church is perhaps reflected in the quarter of its ministers (24.5 per cent) who never prophesy.

Personal spiritual background

When asked whether their Christian commitment had begun in childhood, 51.5 per cent said 'yes'. And when asked whether their acceptance of Christianity was sudden the figures distinguished between denominations as table 7.15.1 shows.

Table 7.16.1 reveals an interesting and unexpected finding. Apostolic ministers report a church-attending father far more frequently than any of the other denominations. Nearly three-quarters of Apostolic ministers report that their father attended

Table 7.16.1 *During childhood father attended church*

Denom	Never %	Once or twice a year %	Sometimes %	At least once a month %	Nearly every week %
AC	16.7	1.5	9.1	1.5	71.2
AG	34.7	10.3	7.4	3.9	43.7
Elim	35.1	10.7	11.0	2.7	40.5
CG	19.4	16.1	25.8	3.2	35.5

church during their own childhood, a statistic that, while it may reflect generally high church attendance in rural communities, also points to the influence of a male Christian role model as being important for these ministers. The other three denominations all show much lower paternal church attendance during childhood and approximately one-third of both Elim and Assemblies of God ministers report that their fathers never attended church. When we take this finding in conjunction with table 7.17.1 it is again evident that Assemblies of God and Elim ministers tend to come from much less strongly Christian homes than the other two groups of ministers. It is reasonable to assume that between a quarter and a third of Assemblies of God and Elim ministers (that is taking the maternal and paternal childhood church attendance figures as markers) came from non-Christian homes. Or, to look at this in another way, these Assemblies of God and Elim ministers were converted from secular or pagan or non-Christian religious environments to become fully committed to the Christian faith. Such a transformation is one that encourages evangelistic preaching: 'If God could change me, he can change you.' Church of God ministers are much more likely to come from homes where the mother attended church in childhood. Only 3.9 per cent of Church of God mothers *never* attended church, a lower figure even than that found among Apostolic ministers.

The other way of interpreting these figures is to see that in all four denominations half of the Pentecostal ministers had a mother who attended church weekly. It is evident that church-attending mothers tend to produce sons who feel a call to full-time ministry.

There is one further finding these two tables suggest. The gap between maternal and paternal church attendance in childhood is between 8.2 per cent and 11.9 per cent in the Assemblies of God, Apostolic and Elim experience. But it runs at twice this (21.4 per cent) in the Church of God experience, a discrepancy that suggests

Table 7.17.1 *During childhood mother attended church*

Denom	Never %	Once or twice a year %	Sometimes %	At least once a month %	Nearly every week %
AC	6.2	6.2	6.2	2.0	79.4
AG	25.6	9.3	9.3	4.0	51.8
Elim	23.0	8.1	12.7	3.8	52.4
CG	3.9	9.8	25.5	3.9	56.9

lower male attendance at Church of God congregations than is the case with the other three denominations.

A further exploration was carried out to discover whether there was a connection between paternal and maternal church attendance during childhood and the date at which Christian commitment began and the nature of the onset of this commitment. Was it sudden or gradual? The statistics showed that there was, indeed, a significant statistical connection between maternal and paternal church attendance and the date when Christian commitment began.[36] For those whose mothers attended church during the years of primary education Christian commitment was much more likely to have begun in childhood, and the same finding applied with respect to fathers. When the nature of the onset of this commitment was inspected, it became clear that ministers who in childhood had church-attending mothers or fathers were much more likely to make a gradual Christian commitment. Sudden conversions were more likely to be recorded by ministers from non-church-attending homes.

When asked whether they had been healed *as a result of prayer* (original italics in questionnaire) 17.9 per cent of Pentecostal ministers said 'no', 62.2 per cent said 'physically', 1.2 per cent said 'mentally', 12.3 per cent said 'physically and mentally' and 6.4 per cent did not know.

The healing of Pentecostal ministers is all part of the experiential nature of Pentecostalism. The great majority of Pentecostal ministers have experienced some form of healing, whether mental or physical, and this must give them confidence as they pray for others who are ill. The correlation between doctrine and experience strengthens convictions about the reality of healing, as it does about the reality of conversion. Table 7.18.1 shows that in most instances healing followed worship rather than special healing services and this highlights the centrality of worship and the understanding of worship in Pentecostal churches. Worship is 'meeting with God' and, if meeting with God is accompanied by charismatic vocal gifts of tongues, interpretation or prophecy, then it becomes harmonious to anticipate the manifestation of similar charismatic gifts of power – including gifts of healing.

---

[36] In all four comparisons oneway analysis of variance was significant at the .001 level.

Table 7.18.1 *Circumstances of healing*[37]

Healing followed	**Yes** %
prayer during a worship service	37.8
prayer during a special healing service	15.1
prayer with a few friends	26.6
prayer by oneself	23.4

Education

The education of Pentecostal ministers is denominationally varied (table 7.19.1). Elim and the Church of God make formal training for ministry a much more rigorous requirement than do the Apostolic Church and the Assemblies of God. Only 13.7 per cent of Elim ministers and 14.3 per cent of Church of God ministers have *not* received formal training for ministry. The comparable figure relating to Apostolic ministers is over two-thirds (69.1 per cent) and a surprisingly high 44.7 per cent for Assemblies of God. Over two-thirds of Elim ministers have received full-time training for ministry, but the other Pentecostal denominations give much less priority to this kind of education. Less than half of the ministers of each of the other denominations have received full-time training, a finding that may be related to a theology of the Holy Spirit that sees his 'anointing' or 'empowering' qualities as sufficient to transform the uneducated into vibrant servants of Christ. Not surprisingly theology degrees and higher degrees are relatively rare among Pentecostal ministers (table 17.20.1).

Table 7.19.1 *Formal training for ministry*

Denom	**Yes, full-time** %	**Yes, part-time** %	**No** %
AC	17.5	13.4	69.1
AG	41.1	14.2	44.7
Elim	69.4	16.9	13.7
CG	30.6	55.1	14.3

[37] Figures do not add up to 100 per cent because some ministers will have been healed more than once and in more than one way.

Table 7.20.1 *Academic qualifications*

Qualification	%
Theology degree	9.9
BTh	1.5
BA	2.9
BD	2.4
MA	0.8
MTh	1.1
MPhil	0.3
PhD	0.8

Conclusion

The three indigenous British Pentecostal denominations are all approximately seventy-five years old. During the course of three generations each of these denominations has acquired traditions, history, property and recognition from the wider evangelical community. The acquisition of property has made an impact upon all these denominations. Indeed, in the case of the Elim Pentecostal Church it was the acquisition of property which contributed to the pressure for the formation of a legal identity.[38] Without such an identity it would have been impossible for property to have been willed to it.[39] Yet, though property provides stability and essential solidity to any Christian group, it also drains resources from evangelism and the payment of ministers. To continue expansion, Christian groups are often forced to minimise the payment of ministers so as to pour resources into buildings and other aspects of the material infrastructure. The argument is very frequently one to do with economics and theology: from an economic point of view renting property is wasting money; from a theological point it is sometimes meanly assumed that ministers should have sufficient faith to disregard the benefits of a regular salary.[40]

---

[38] Cf. Wilson, 1961, 36.

[39] Boulton (see Cartwright, 1999) points out that an attempt to leave money to the growing Elim work before 1915 was legally disputed (31). The formation of the Elim Pentecostal Alliance was so that the 'property should be safeguarded for the Lord's work' (38).

[40] Donald Gee was Principal of the Assemblies of God Bible College (1951–64) at Kenley and took no salary. He supported himself by Sunday

Thus, if they survive, and over the course of several generations, Christian denominations gradually accumulate resources. For instance, the Elim Pentecostal Church has set up a pension fund for its ministers while the Assemblies of God has connections with a large but independent financial agency, the 'Property Trust'.[41] What begins in a small way as the initiative of one or more ministers becomes over several years a substantial pool of money worth many million pounds. The challenge facing a denomination in its third generation is to maintain the zealous and pure commitment with which its founders were endowed while, at the same time, husbanding the resources they so carefully acquired *and* treating contemporary ministers justly and generously. Such a balancing act is easier within some denominational structures than others. Assemblies of God, with its emphasis upon local congregational autonomy, is the most difficult to bring into line but each denomination has had to solve problems peculiar to itself.

Although most Pentecostal denominations would be reluctant to face this possibility, it is reasonable to suppose that recruitment to full-time Pentecostal ministry is partly dependent upon the likely financial position of its ministers. And, again, there is a difficult balancing act to achieve. If complete financial security is guaranteed, ministers may be tempted into a kind of empty professionalism that turns them into the purveyors of civil religion or, at best, a type of specially dedicated social work.[42] If no financial security is offered, only the most hardy ministers will survive and many of these will be so individualistic that they will not naturally show the team-building qualities necessary to make a denomination function smoothly.

The issue of financial security is linked with the issue of full-time ministerial training. Where training is a requirement of the denomination, someone must pay for it. If this someone is the minister him

[40] (*continued*) preaching. Similar arrangements had been followed by Howard Carter in the 1920s.

[41] The Trust is recognised by the Charity Commission and has assets of at least £10 million. Most of this is used to provide mortgages at favourable rates to congregations wanting to buy, build or extend premises.

[42] This is the sort of accusation levelled against ministers supported by automatic tax deductions in Switzerland.

or herself then there must be a way by which the cost of education can be recouped. The minister who attends a two or three year full-time course and leaves with a debt of £10,000 will have difficulty in accepting a position in a small and struggling congregation unable to pay a good salary. Consequently, two basic conditions favour full-time training. First, a system that moves trainee ministers from their full-time courses into guaranteed employment. Where this kind of 'moving staircase' is in place, dedicated Christians are willing to offer themselves for full-time training. Second, where this guarantee can be put in place, it is possible for a denomination to insist on the training provided by its designated college that teaches according to its established fundamental statements of faith. In the absence of these conditions the most likely people to 'risk' full-time training are single men or women without family responsibilities or, alternatively, those who have acquired sufficient financial assets, often in the form of a house they are willing to sell or an early retirement package they have received from secular employment, to allow them to pay for their education without incurring a debt.

Where full-time residential education is impossible, trainee ministers can make use of church-related options. Larger churches occasionally offer informal 'on the job' training from the senior pastor. More ambitiously, ministers of the most prosperous or visionary congregations have set up Bible schools that use their church premises during the day, sometimes functioning alongside a Christian school for children of primary age in the same building. Alternatively, denominational initiatives using regional networks have offered training on Saturday mornings by drawing on the teaching expertise of local ministers. And, because of the existence of housegroups within most large congregations, opportunities for lay ministry are extensive. Men and women can retain full-time secular jobs while still making valuable contributions to the life of their local churches and exercise pastoral responsibilities of a limited but satisfying kind in the process.

By virtue of these background considerations, Pentecostal ministers must minister well to survive and prosper. The spiritual resources to which their convictions direct them are prayer and Bible reading. Pentecostal ministers need to preach well to move their congregations forward, and to preach well they feel they must spend time in prayer of all kinds. It is no surprise, therefore, that the figures show that most Pentecostal ministers read their Bibles and speak in tongues each day. These are the means by which their faith is kept fresh and their preaching is empowered.

The socio-cultural situation against which the Pentecostal churches described here have made progress is one where most other religious groups within British society have suffered decline. During this period, when British society has become more secularised, Pentecostal churches, preaching 'an old-fashioned gospel', have grown. This growth may not have been as spectacular as it has been in other parts of the world where Pentecostalism has taken root, but it has been consistent. Moreover, Pentecostalism has been able to cope with the transition from early leaders born in the Victorian era to a more modern generation of leaders born during the radical 1960s. These denominations, whatever may be the criticisms of the constitutional structures, have at least solved the problem of selecting leadership by methods with which everyone can broadly agree. Further, they have adapted themselves to new fashions in music, worship and church life. They have introduced housegroups and so made use of the intimacy of the Christian home while also accommodating themselves to the working patterns stamped on secular life by the migration from factory to office. In addition, they have adjusted to the world that offers high employment prospects for women outside the home. Some of this adaptability has been generated by the ability the Pentecostal churches have acquired in retaining the children of previous generations. It is these children, now grown up and assuming leadership, who very often have the confidence to make changes to structures and attitudes at which they balked when they were younger.

8

Ministerial Experiences, Roles and Satisfaction

Overview

This chapter deals with the experiences ministers find most helpful to their faith, the way they prioritise the roles they carry out, the conflicts that can exist between expectations laid on the minister and the minister's own wishes and the levels of satisfaction the minister gains from his or her work.

Ministry gifts

When the Pentecostal movement began at the start of the twentieth century it quickly formulated a theology of restoration.[1] The Holy Spirit had been poured out afresh upon the church. The gifts of the Spirit, for so long invisible and apparently unattainable, had once more graced the waiting people of God. The miracles recorded in the pages of the New Testament might be repeated in the modern era and, with them, we might expect to see the kinds of ministries the New Testament had recorded. True, while the gifts of the Spirit in 1 Corinthians were *charismata*, manifestations of the Spirit for particular occasions and purposes, the gifts spoken of in Ephesians 4 were *people* given by Christ to the church, and therefore enduring and permanent. Consequently, Gee argued that 'holding steadily before us the vision of the supernatural gifts

---

[1] Land, 1993, 65f.

of the Spirit, and their resultant ministry-gifts, is of vital importance'.[2]

For instance, there was a gift of prophecy mentioned in 1 Corinthians 12 and 14 but also the fully-fledged ministry of prophet.[3] Ssimilarly, the gifts of the Spirit included 'the word of wisdom'[4] and this looked as though it might belong with the ministry of the teacher.[5] Likewise, 1 Corinthians spoke about 'gifts of healings'[6] and elsewhere the New Testament spoke of the ministry of the evangelist.[7] In 1 Corinthians miracles[8] were an important part of the repertoire of the Holy Spirit and these might justly be expected to accompany the ministry of the apostle.[9] In other words, there was a correlation between the charismatic chapters of 1 Corinthians (12 through 14) and Ephesians 4, and all this was illustrated in the book of Acts.

The five ministries listed in Ephesians 4 are those of the apostle, prophet, evangelist, pastor and teacher. Most Pentecostals believe these five ministries are essential to the perpetual expansion and renewal of the church. The apostle plants congregations; the prophet communicates revelation on the basis of which other leaders can act; evangelists preach the gospel without flagging and are able to change their message to suit all kinds of audiences; the pastor gathers and looks after a congregation; and the teacher systematically explains and applies the doctrines of Scripture. Of these ministries the apostle and evangelist are most likely to be itinerant and the pastor most likely to be static. The prophet may travel (as was the case with Agabus in Acts 11) and so may the teacher (as was the case with Apollos in Acts 18) but, equally, these ministries may function within a local church and there is a view that the pastor and teacher may be different aspects of the same ministry since the pastor is expected to be able to teach (1 Timothy 3:2).

---

2 Gee, 1930, 14.
3 Ephesians 4:11.
4 1 Corinthians 12:8.
5 Ephesians 4:11.
6 1 Corinthians 12:28.
7 Acts 21:8.
8 1 Corinthians 12:10.
9 2 Corinthians 12:12.

Assemblies of God and Elim

Gee, as the most articulate and perceptive spokesman within British Assemblies of God, argued for the persistence of all the Ephesians 4 ministry gifts and their continuation to the twentieth century. He was careful to stress, however, that these gifts are appointed by Christ himself and not badges, labels or ranks that depend on purely human disposition. Moreover, the apostle is demonstrated to be so by certain signs, the first of which is 'outstanding fruit of the Spirit' and only after this 'outstanding gifts of the Spirit' and that 'the sufferings of an apostle are such as demand the fullest possible exhibition of all the fruit of the spirit'.[10] With regard to the work of apostles, Gee drew the usual distinction between the twelve apostles of the Lamb (Rev. 21:14), the later apostles within the canon of the New Testament and then subsequent apostles working today. In each case he saw the apostle as being sent by Christ to 'establish churches' and, for this reason, possessing a variety of ministerial abilities – pastoral, evangelistic, teaching – necessary for beginning and nurturing a new or young congregation. But with regard to the authority of the apostle, Gee only saw it as existing in the relationship between the apostle and the church he had founded. In this sense the authority of the apostle is logical and natural and does not need to be insisted upon or enshrined within a constitution.

In speaking of these ministries Gee was also insistent upon their mutual interdependence. It was quite wrong for the teacher to criticise the evangelist for being shallow or for the evangelist to criticise the teacher for being dry and stodgy since both needed the contribution of the other to maintain the health and vitality of the church. Each ministry has its own strengths and limitations and each is equally a gift from Christ to the church. The point of this discussion was to show that all the ministry gifts are important, not just the ones that appear to carry authority, and that each is supernaturally endowed.

The line taken by Gee in the 1930s was usually maintained by Assemblies of God and Elim in the years that followed. Admittedly, the constitutions of both denominations were more inclined to speak

---

[10] Gee, 1930, 30.

of pastors than of any other gift, but in conference or private discussion it was usual to admit that modern apostles existed, and the case of W.F.P. Burton whose exceptional ministry in the Belgian Congo produced more than a thousand churches was usually cited.[11] More pertinently and publicly, an illuminated address given to George Jeffreys on behalf of the Elim church in gratitude for his ministry over the previous 25 years, carried the inscription:

> As an Apostle, you have pioneered the Full Gospel message and established churches in the largest cities and towns of the British Isles. As an Evangelist, your ministry has been signally owned and blessed of God.[12]

But the rarity of the designation 'apostle' provides evidence of the reverence in which Jeffreys was held in this period and does not detract from the general case that Elim and Assemblies of God contented themselves by speaking mainly of pastors.

In the 1970s Eldin Corsie, writing from an Elim perspective, accepted the existence of contemporary apostles but he was keen to underline the notion that they 'did not rule the church' and pointed to the choice of deacons in Acts 6 by the body of the congregation rather than by the diktat of the apostles. Similarly the Council, of Jerusalem in Acts 15 was an egalitarian discussion of policy rather than an audience to receive a decision handed down by a ruling group of apostles.[13]

Taking a broader view, again from within the Elim Church, John Lancaster asserted the importance of the New Testament concept of the 'body of Christ' where every member contributes to the total ministry to avoid the 'minister-centredness' that robs congregations of the variety intended for them. He also discussed the work of elders alongside the pastor and their collective functioning in a church council that should be preoccupied with

---

11 Whittaker, 1983.

12 Hudson, 1999. According to Cartwright the word 'apostle' was spelled with a small 'a' and, when a question was asked about its use at the 1936 conference, the answer was given 'the term "apostle" was used only in its etymological sense and not in its official meaning'.

13 Corsie, 1976.

'the total condition of the assembly' and not simply with practical matters like a new gutter or heating system.[14]

The Apostolic Church

The Apostolic Church historically took a different view of the ministry gifts from that of the rest of the Pentecostal movement. The Apostolic Church, as the name suggests, vested authority within apostles who were considered to be given specific duties that elevated them above their peers and contemporaries. This prominent position was regularised by giving them the *constitutional* right to attend any service or meeting of the church and to take a leading role, including the chair of a meeting if they felt it appropriate to do so. In relation to each other, apostles were thought to be equal. Only in the case of specific business meetings, for instance executive meetings of the Apostolic Church (which might include some apostles and not others), would all apostles not be allowed to intrude.

In the view of the Apostolic Church the distinctive work of the apostle is the ordination of other ministries. Only apostles may ordain prophets, evangelists, pastors and teachers. By this means the apostle's governmental function is obvious to the rest of the church, and apostles are able to offer 'leadership, revelation and government of a super-local character'.[15] This emphasis on the governmental role of the apostle ensures that the Apostolic Church is not democratically run, and deliberately so, because it aims for theocracy, the government of God mediated through divinely chosen men.

The Apostolic Church has a high estimation of New Testament prophecy and prophets. Rowe speaks of the majestic and powerful nature of these gifts which find their source in God alone.

> Standing on the prophetic craft in mid-ocean, our eyes sweep the azure vault of the heavens, the far and rimless horizon and the deep, mystic waters beneath: feeling the imprint of infinity upon our souls we cry – God! The prophet . . . is one who is enveloped by the Holy Spirit and in ecstasy spiritually appropriates the revelation of God . . .

---

[14] Lancaster, 1973, 53.

[15] Rowe, 1988, 243.

> Prophecy comes from the depths of the inner-being of the channel, deeper than mind and consciousness.[16]

Following 1 Corinthians 14:3 the Apostolic Church fully expects prophecy to help build up the church by exhortation and consolation, but it does not downplay the predictive possibilities of prophecy or the exposition of prophetic utterances by apostles (taking 1 Tim. 4:1 as its legitimation). This said, a prophet is understood to be subservient to apostolic ministry and answerable to the judgement of other prophets. 'Apostles play a vital part in the government of prophecy'[17] and they apply or interpret prophetic utterances to church issues. In this respect prophets are seen as functioning alongside apostles but without the authority of an apostle to make judgements or decisions.

The authority given to apostles and the revelatory gifts attributed to prophets within the Apostolic Church might be thought to be a sufficient means of governing and guiding the church. Oddly enough, this is not so. The Apostolic Church has an important and strong constitutional base that defines the scope of each ministry and the links between each section and level of the church. This contrast, on the one hand, between charismatic ministry and authority and, on the other, between constitutional and quasi-legal authority looks contradictory. Why should apostles need to be bound by a constitution since they may act according to the wisdom God gives them and the immediate revelation of the prophets who stand by them? The answer to this question is not to be found in the pages of the New Testament but must come from common sense and sociological analysis. Rowe's biblical exposition, recommended by the presidents of the General Councils of the Apostolic Church in Australia and in Great Britain, has only a brief reference to its Rules of Conduct and Belief and its constitution. Common sense suggests that the constitution provides a quick and easy way of resolving disputes and regularising perennial issues: it is not necessary to return on every occasion to first principles, to reinvent the wheel. Sociological analysis suggests that the constitution provides a means to

---

[16] Rowe, 1988, 256, 266, 267.

[17] Rowe, 1988, 273.

control the prophets and apostles themselves by laying down a strict framework derived from the practice of the first generation of the church. In this sense, the early apostles wanted to control the later ones and, certainly, there was in the first generation a recognition that churches decline, modernising their original evangelical doctrines and diluting their strong standards of holiness with fads and fashions. So, to try to combat this tendency, fundamental beliefs were sharply formulated and solemnly laid down, and once this had been done it was a relatively short step to write down procedural rules and codify them as a constitutional document.[18]

A further but unexpected and unintended consequence of these constitutional definitions of apostolic and prophetic ministries was that all other ministers – pastors, evangelists and teachers – knew exactly what the 'senior' ministries entailed. Open-ended aspirations to the glories of apostolic ministry on the scale of St Paul's were unlikely to arise. On the contrary apostolic ministry was visible to the ordinary pastor and did not seem especially miraculous and glorious.

The Church of God

The position of the Church of God on the structure and type of ministries it recognises stems from a decision taken at its second General Assembly in 1907. After some delegates favoured 'the congregational system for selection of pastors; others called for appointment by higher church authority, as in the episcopal system' and the eventual compromise 'paved the way for a strong episcopal government' that allowed the Church of God to develop the 'most centralised government of all the holiness or Pentecostal denominations in America'.[19] Its episcopal figures are called Overseers and the most senior of these is the General Overseer. At local church level Licensed Ministers operate as pastors and there is little or no tradition of itinerant apostolic or prophetic ministries.

[18] Worsfold, 1991, 215.
[19] Synan, 1997, 79.

Obligations

All four of these denominations have faced the conflict between charismatic authority and constitutional formality and each has attempted to grant freedom and encouragement to its Spirit-filled ministers while at the same time creating stable administrative structures to facilitate consistent policy for purposes of education, credentials, missionary work, publications and property holding. At the local church level these issues barely impinge upon the life and work of the ordinary minister except insofar as they may define his or her aspirations.

But being the minister of a local church creates the outlines of the job. Ministers are inducted into pastoral positions by leading figures within their denomination: the Scriptures are read; prayers are prayed; hands are laid upon the new incumbent; a sermon is preached; welcomes are said and the minister takes up the appointment. The job of the minister is usually only defined by the pattern of meetings within the church and, in Pentecostal churches, there are only likely to be three or four such meetings in a week, and no liturgy or prayer book to follow. The minister is free to use his or her time most profitably and no one checks at 8.30 on Monday morning to see whether he or she is doing something useful. There can hardly be any other job where the holder has so much freedom to shape the pattern of the week. Yet, in contrast to this freedom are the inner obligations: from the minister's conscience; from the sense that he or she is serving God and ultimately is responsible to Christ to carry out the duties of the pastorate conscientiously; from the expectations of the congregation. Can you visit my mother in hospital? Is my son old enough to attend the youth meeting? Who is going to speak at the women's meeting? Perhaps not surprisingly, then, a survey of Anglican clergy found that 42 per cent were stressed by 'always having to please others'.[20]

Pentecostal ministers are, in some respects, like self-employed craftsman or businessmen. They are free to run their lives how they will but, if they wish to prosper financially and, more importantly to see their congregations come to spiritual life and flourish, then they must use all their gifts and skills to make the church succeed. In

---

[20] Beit-Hallahmi and Argyle, 1997, 68.

other respects Pentecostal ministers feel themselves to be responding to the narrative of Scripture, to be sensitive to the Holy Spirit and to be 'walking with the Lord'. Scripture contains a huge number of instances of people whose relationships with God, covering every conceivable circumstance, provide insights and examples about how the Christian life should be lived and how the minister should proceed. Anyone, like these Pentecostal ministers who reads the Bible practically every day, is bound to become saturated by the scriptural roles. There is a natural tendency and desire to shape one's life according to what are seen as divine principles. Abraham trusted God; Philip preached the gospel; Paul founded new churches; one was an evangelist and the other an apostle and, pre-eminently, Christ gave his life for sinners as the ultimate pastor – these are the models by which to live.[21] This is the language Pentecostal ministers talk.

Satisfaction

Pentecostal ministers are familiar with the biblical texts which speak of giving thanks in all circumstances, with being content in all situations and with learning to offer a sacrifice of praise to God.[22] These texts, along with others which instruct Christians to 'rejoice ever more' or to be glad if they are persecuted or to be unworried about a lack of material possessions, should allow ministers to cope effectively with the ups and downs of life.[23] At the same time there are biblical texts and examples that suggest the possibility of pain and unhappiness within the Christian life – Paul speaks of having 'great sorrow and unceasing anguish' in his heart over the condition of the Jewish people.[24] Psychological studies suggest that there is a 'religious buffering of uncontrollable negative events' meaning that religious people are able to cope with traumatic events better than

[21] This theory is developed by Sunden and discussed by Hood, Spilka, Hunsberger and Gorsuch, 1996, 190, 197. See also Beit-Hallahmi and Argyle, 1997, 63.

[22] 1 Thes. 5:18; Phil. 4:11; Heb. 13:15.

[23] 1 Thes. 5:16; Mt. 6:25; Mt. 5:11.

[24] Rom. 9:2.

irreligious people and, though religious people can become saddened and depressed, the depths of despair are reduced allowing religious people to regain an even keel more rapidly than others.[25]

What is unclear, though data presented later in this chapter helps to throw new light on the situation, is what gives clergy, and in this case Pentecostal ministers, the greatest amount of satisfaction in connection with their work. Clearly, if material factors were the most decisive, we might expect the most satisfied ministers to be the best paid, or those with the largest congregations but, as we shall see, this is not the case.

What do the data show?

Table 8.1 shows in ranked order elements that Pentecostal ministers believe are important to their faith. Altogether 54 items were listed. Ministers were asked the question 'How important are the following experiences to your faith?' and given a rating scale between 1 'means nothing at all' and 5 'means a great deal'. The scores on these items were compared to discover whether there were denominational differences between them.[26] The items reported in table 8.1 are only those on which no denominational differences were discovered. In other words, all Pentecostal ministers rate these items in very much the same way.

The table shows that the three top items are all strongly evangelical. Ministers rate most highly being born again, accepting Jesus as Saviour and Lord and having a conversion experience. This shows that Pentecostalism is committed to the evangelical experience of conversion. The next two items, not far behind, are those relating to the work of the Holy Spirit: being baptised in the Holy Spirit and being renewed by the Holy Spirit – items that are almost synonymous – and these show the commitment of Pentecostal ministers to the distinctive doctrines of Pentecostalism. Below these, also at a very high level, are a series of items related to sharing the Christian faith with other people, whether by word of mouth or by baptism (which in the Pentecostal churches is carried out by the total

---

25 Beit-Hallahmi and Argyle, 1997, 190.

26 By analysis of variance.

Table 8.1 *Experience and faith*

How important are the following experiences to your faith?	Mean (1–5)	Sd
Being born again	4.96	.35
Accepting Jesus as Saviour and Lord	4.96	.35
Having a conversion experience	4.90	.49
Receiving the baptism of the Holy Spirit	4.80	.54
Experiencing the renewing work of the Holy Spirit	4.77	.56
Witnessing to others about salvation	4.76	.58
Being baptised	4.75	.65
Giving personal testimony to faith	4.74	.60
Attending Sunday worship at church	4.73	.62
Finding God's word for me in the Bible	4.69	.74
Praying for others to be saved	4.68	.69
Hearing God speak to me	4.66	.73
Feeling God's Spirit within me	4.56	.82
Meeting with other Christians for open prayer	4.49	.77
Listening to an inspiring sermon	4.47	.75
Singing spiritual songs	4.30	.89
Hearing the Bible read in church	4.21	.97
Attending praise and sharing meetings	3.95	.95
Seeing healings happen	3.84	1.06
Laying hands on someone for insight or healing	3.80	1.10
Receiving a word of knowledge	3.71	1.05
Being prayed over	3.61	1.09
Being in a state of mystery outside my body	1.14	.55
Making the sign of the cross	1.06	.37
Using incense in worship	1.03	.32

immersion of adults – an act of witness). Below these are items relating to prayer, worship and sensing the presence of the Holy Spirit.

Other items relate to healing and the laying on of hands as well as at least one of the gifts of the Holy Spirit (receiving a word of knowledge).[27] And then right at the bottom of the list are two items that belong to a completely different Christian tradition; one both sacramental and symbolic. One other item relates to a mystical state of being 'outside my body' which, for Pentecostal ministers, is suspiciously occult and so rejected.

[27] 1 Cor. 12:8.

These items provide a useful way of mapping Pentecostal priorities; of showing what Pentecostal ministers value. It is clear that, whatever might be the perception of Pentecostals from outside, Pentecostals themselves rate evangelical distinctives above Pentecostal distinctives.

Once the items on which there was no difference between denominations had been tabulated and inspected, there was a further large group of items on which the denominations clearly could be separated. But it would have been tedious and fragmentary to comment on each item in turn and so the remaining items were grouped together by statistical means (factor analysis), some of them were dropped and the remainder were collected together to form a scale that turned out to cohere nicely (alpha .7717) and to relate to an underlying sense of unity with the created universe and the church (table 8.2). The items in the scale refer to an experience of beauty, ineffable unity and to spiritual experiences like being forgiven for sin, singing gospel hymns and receiving communion.

The scale was an unexpected discovery and does indicate that Pentecostal ministers, though they clearly reject many aspects of a 'high church' worship, do nevertheless draw sustenance from a complex appreciation of divine-human harmony. This harmony is

Table 8.2 *Mysticism scale*[28]

How important are the following experiences to your faith?	**Item rest of test (r)**
Experiencing something I could not put into words	.49
Feeling forgiven for sin	.37
Receiving Holy Communion/Eucharist	.27
Seeing the beauty of the church	.30
Sensing God in the beauty of nature	.52
Singing gospel hymns	.48
Feeling at one with the universe	.39
Feeling moved by a power beyond description	.56
Being overwhelmed with a sense of wonder	.56
Seeing healings happen	.41

Alpha .7717

[28] The mean score of the sample on this scale was 33.37, the median 34 and the standard deviation 6.41. The maximum possible score was 50 and the minimum 10.

Table 8.3 *Mysticism scale scores*

Denomination	Mean	Sd
Apostolic	34.13	6.46
Assemblies of God	33.02	6.45
Elim	33.04	6.27
Church of God	38.00	5.14

'beyond description' (this item has the highest item-rest of test correlation indicating that it is at the heart of the scale in table 8.2), a finding that may throw new light on the practice of speaking with tongues: what is beyond description must be responded to through a linguistic instrumentality beyond human language.

When the scale scores for the four different denominations were inspected and analysed it was immediately clear that the Church of God ministers were significantly more likely than the other three groups to value this sense of mystical harmony (table 8.3).[29] Similarly, older ministers were significantly more likely than younger ones to appreciate and value this mystical sense of unity[30] though there were no significant differences between male and female ministers.[31]

Roles

Table 8.4 is designed to show what sort of ministerial roles Pentecostal ministers want to fulfil. Ministers were asked how much priority 'do you *want* to give to the following aspects of ministry?' (original italics) and given a seven point scale ranging from 1 (very little) to 7 (very much) on which to rate twwenty different roles. The items in this table are ones on which no differences between the four denominations were found. These six roles give an insight into the spiritual desires of Pentecostal ministers. These are the six things they want to do. Preaching comes top of the list. Fundamentally and primarily Pentecostal ministers view themselves

---

[29] Using analysis of variance with denomination as the main effect and scale scores as the dependent variable, $F = 6.279$, $p < .000$.

[30] $T = 5.35$, $p < .000$. Blockwise multiple regression analysis, entering age before denomination, showed denomination still to be a significant predictor ($p < .007$) of mysticism scores.

[31] $T = .29$, non significant (NS).

Table 8.4 *Priority given to ministry gifts/aspects of ministry*

How much priority do you *want* to give to the following aspects of ministry?	**Mean (1–7)**	**Sd**
Preacher	6.33	.98
Man or woman of prayer	5.99	1.29
Pastor	5.80	1.57
Fellowship builder	5.62	1.34
Pioneer	4.61	1.99
Apostle	4.19	2.09

as preachers and many of them will travel long distances to fulfil invitations to speak. Not far behind this is the hidden and quieter role of prayer. The balance Pentecostal ministers reveal by these two items shows there is an outward face of the ministry (in preaching) and an inward face (in prayer) and it would be a mistake to see either without the other.

Below these items come two others showing the pastoral concern of Pentecostal ministers. They want to be pastors and understand this as being fellowship builders, people who tend to the needs of their congregations and so build up the worshipping community. Below these two items come the roles of pioneer and apostle, both of which are seen as being important but more ground-breaking than the pastoral ministry. The apostle ventures into difficult situations, hence the connection with pioneering, while the pastor cares for a known congregation.

The items in table 8.4 have also been presented to full-time stipendiary parochial clergy within a rural Anglican diocese and their ratings show a slightly different pattern. Anglican clergy rated being a pastor and counsellor highest, followed by leading public worship, being a preacher and then being a teacher. Pentecostal ministers, by contrast, rate preaching and prayer above pastoring though, interestingly, both groups of ministers give pastoring a rating of 5.80. This comparison simply points to the prominence of preaching within Pentecostal churches.[32]

Attitudes towards the remaining three ministry gifts mentioned in Ephesians 4 are itemised in table 8.5.1 and show differences between the denominations. In general it is clear that the teaching gift is valued above the other two gifts, as can be seen by the mean scores, and the

[32] Francis and Rodger, 1996, 70.

Table 8.5.1 *Priority given to ministry gifts*

How much priority do you *want* to give to the following aspects of ministry	**Denom**	**Mean (1–7)**
Prophet	AC	3.98
	AG	4.72
	Elim	4.98
	CG	4.42
Evangelist	AC	5.62
	AG	5.03
	Elim	5.06
	CG	5.74
Teacher	AC	5.26
	AG	5.61
	Elim	5.75
	CG	6.22

prophetic gift is valued least highly. This measure of ministerial aspirations can be expressed in a slightly different way: about 61 per cent of these ministers rate being a teacher in the top two categories; about 68 per cent rate being a pastor; about 48 per cent rate being an evangelist; 40 per cent being a prophet and only 33 per cent being an apostle.

Table 5.6.1 shows how the different ministries overlap with other roles. Making use of a correlation matrix the five ministry gifts (apostle, prophet, evangelist, pastor and teacher) were grouped with the items most closely correlated with them and formed into a cluster of roles.[33] The role of apostle correlated with evangelist, pioneer and prophet. The role of pastor correlated most closely with minister of sacraments, fellowship builder, visitor and counsellor. The role of teacher correlated most closely with theologian, preacher and spiritual director. Since the evangelistic and prophetic roles had already been found to correlate with the apostolic role, a further cluster was created making use of the role of administrator which was found to correlate with the roles of fund-raiser and manager.

---

[33] The administrative cluster was put together of items with a higher correlation (r) than .222, the apostle cluster higher than .312, the pastoral cluster higher than .288 and the teaching cluster higher than .370. In each case the level was chosen by looking for a natural break in the sequence of cohering items.

Table 8.6.1 *Ministerial clusters: mean scores*

Denomination	Pastor	Admin	Apostle	Teacher
Apostolic	24.75	8.72	18.74	19.56
Assemblies of God	22.03	9.41	18.16	20.70
Elim	22.50	9.37	19.00	21.42
Church of God	26.33	12.70	18.92	22.84

By looking at the clusters it is possible to see how ministers broadly conceive of different kinds of ministry. The person who feels called to be an apostle is also attracted to evangelistic and prophetic ministry as well as to pioneering, that is, starting a church where none exists at the moment. Because these roles cluster together we can validly make the assumption that the evangelist may also feel called to apostolic ministry or that the prophet may find an affinity with evangelistic ministry. What is common to these ministries is their preaching impact and their visibility. The role of the pastor, by contrast, is much less proclamatory and confrontational and more suited to one-to-one encounters by visiting and counselling. The teacher sees him or herself as a preacher with theological expertise: this ministry is less attracted to personal contact, more study orientated.

Each cluster (apostle, pastor, teacher and administrator) was arranged into a scale and then denominational comparisons were made.[34] Of the four, there was no significant difference between denominations in relation to the apostolic scale. In other words being an apostle was equally attractive, or unattractive, to all the ministers surveyed here. There were significant differences in the administrative, pastoral and teaching roles where Church of God ministers scored more highly than the others.[35] The Church of God ministers valued these roles more highly than ministers in other denominations. Note that because the clusters were composed of unequal numbers of

---

[34] The 3 item administrative cluster recorded an alpha coefficient of .6503; the 5 item pastoral cluster an alpha of .7057, the 3 item teaching cluster an alpha of .6402 and the 4 item apostolic cluster an alpha of .6762.

[35] In each case analysis of variance was carried out. The scales were dependent variables and the denomination was the main effect: admin $F = 12.101$, $p < .000$; pastoral cluster $F = 11.850$, $p < .000$; teaching cluster $F = 7.659$, $p < .000$; apostolic cluster $F = 1.542$, NS.

items, direct comparisons between the columns cannot be made; comparisons can only be made within columns.

Desires and ministerial expectations

In addition to being asked the question 'How much priority do you *want* to give to the following aspects of ministry?', ministers were also asked 'How much priority do you feel you are *expected* to give the following aspects of ministry?' (original italics). Exactly the same ministerial roles were presented in exactly the same order to ministers on both occasions and the same seven point rating scale was available. This allows a clear comparison to be made between ministerial desires and the expectations placed on them.[36]

Clearly, if ministers *want* to give priority to role X and are *expected* to give priority to role Y, there is every likelihood of frustration, particularly if the expectations are created by congregations and these force the minister to carry out his or her ministry in a way that goes against inner convictions or natural or charismatic giftings. Since the denominations are different from each other, it makes sense to present the configuration of role desires and expectations separately.

In the case of the Apostolic ministers the great majority of roles were matched between the ministerial desires and the expectations placed on them. In only five roles was there a mismatch, and these were administrator, fund-raiser, manager, social worker and spiritual director. In each case the Apostolic minister felt expected to give more priority to these roles than he wanted to give. In this denomination the picture is of a good and comfortable psychological space where ministers work. For three-quarters of their roles they want to do what they are expected to do. Only in the less distinctly ministerial tasks do they feel they must carry out roles that are unattractive to them.

The picture of Assemblies of God ministers is more complicated. Desire and expectation are matched in a mere three roles. These are the roles of leader in the community, pioneer and preacher. In

---

36 The comparisons were carried out by paired t-tests for each role, treating the denominations separately. Significance tests and t values were inspected and it is on these that the next few paragraphs are based.

fifteen roles the Assemblies of God minister feels expected to do more than he or she wants to do. In two roles, those of apostle and prophet, the ministers want to do more than they are expected to do. The positive side of these findings is that Assemblies of God ministers have aspirations to apostolic and prophetic ministry, they are reaching out for greater effectiveness in two of the key areas specified in Ephesians 4. The negative side of this finding is that the Assemblies of God ministers feel expected to do far more in the way of everything from administration, to prayer, to managing, to pastoring, to visiting, to being theologians than they want. The typical Assemblies of God minister feels caught in a network of expectations. The saving feature of this configuration, though, is that the role of the preacher, one of the most central to the Pentecostal minister's perceived task, is one where there is no discrepancy between desire and expectation. These are preachers who want to preach and their congregations want them to preach.

The picture of Elim ministers is similar to that of Assemblies of God ministers except that there is a slightly longer list of roles in which there is no mismatch between desires and expectations. These roles are evangelist, fellowship builder, leader in community and preacher. On the other side of the coin it is the roles of apostle, pioneer and prophet that Elim ministers aspire to. And, again, all the other roles are those in which they feel expectations are higher than desires. So, there is roughly the same tension within the hearts and minds of Elim ministers as there is within Assemblies of God ministers. For about three-quarters of the roles presented here Elim ministers feel obligated to do what they do not really want to do. But at least preaching is not in this list.

The Church of God ministers are identical to the Apostolic ministers. Again there is a common pool of roles where desire and expectation are matched and the same small set of mainly administrative roles where expectations, presumably congregational expectations, are higher than ministerial desires.

Obligations

A slightly different way of exploring the obligations felt by Pentecostal ministers is shown by the items in table 8.7. All ministers during the course of the questionnaire were presented

Table 8.7 *Ethical expectations*

My church ought to be fully involved in giving practical help to . . .	**Agree %**	**Not Certain %**	**Disagree %**
the poor	92.3	5.7	2.1
the elderly	93.1	4.7	2.2
unmarried mothers	86.2	10.4	3.4
drug addicts	85.0	11.0	4.0
AIDS sufferers	73.8	20.7	5.5
the unemployed	80.8	14.3	4.8
ethnic minorities	78.1	16.3	5.6

with a set of items to which they could respond with strong agreement, agreement, uncertainty, disagreement or strong disagreement. These items all had the same stem: 'My church ought to be fully involved in giving practical help to . . .'. After testing to see whether there were any significant denominational differences in responses to this item (which there were not[37]), what is astonishing about the figures given in the table is the overwhelming concern that all ministers have for different groups of these disadvantaged or needy people within society. The highest levels of concern are for the elderly and for the poor; the lowest levels are for AIDS sufferers and ethnic minorities, but even the lowest level of agreement still draws the support of around three-quarters of Pentecostal ministers. These Pentecostal ministers, then, feel that they ought to ensure that their churches are involved in compassionate social action. What they are responding to is human need.

When we attempt to disentangle the obligations placed upon Pentecostal ministers, it becomes clear that they stem from congregational wishes and expectations *and* from wider social needs. They feel that they must listen to the concerns of their congregations, even if this involves them in administration or social work, and that they should not close their eyes to human suffering outside the door of the church.

Satisfaction

Table 8.8 lists twenty separate roles carried out by ministers assessed on a seven point scale. A score approaching 7 indicates great

[37] Using analysis of variance.

Table 8.8 *Satisfaction from roles*

Satisfaction derived from being a . . .	All	AC	AG	Elim	CG
preacher	6.39	6.12	6.40	6.45	6.28
man or woman of prayer	5.80	5.91	5.77	5.74	6.39
pastor	5.78	6.03	5.76	5.74	5.76
teacher	5.75	5.42	5.77	5.79	6.02
fellowship builder	5.64	5.60	5.56	5.73	5.70
evangelist	5.23	5.45	5.14	5.22	5.64
leader of public worship	4.92	5.11	4.79	4.94	5.57
spiritual director	4.82	4.44	4.63	5.07	5.22
prophet	4.68	4.12	4.67	4.84	4.40
counsellor	4.67	4.83	4.48	4.74	5.33
pioneer	4.64	4.98	4.51	4.72	4.42
visitor	4.30	5.24	4.11	4.10	5.60
theologian	4.18	4.29	4.02	4.27	4.72
apostle	3.92	4.07	3.73	4.04	4.37
manager	3.73	3.21	3.72	3.78	4.30
administrator	3.49	3.68	3.52	3.30	4.43
leader in local community	3.10	2.76	3.00	3.18	4.07
minister of sacraments	2.91	3.82	2.80	2.71	3.84
social worker	2.72	2.75	2.47	2.81	4.02
fund-raiser	2.49	2.40	2.38	2.47	3.81

satisfaction with that particular role and score approaching 1 indicates very little satisfaction. The different roles have been arranged in order of satisfaction using the whole sample. So, when all 930 ministers are treated together, the average satisfaction obtained from preaching is 6.39. This average is biased towards the two biggest groups, Elim and Assemblies of God, and so the ratings for each denomination are also given separately. Before the table was constructed tests were run to discover whether there were differences in ratings between denominations and the seven items italicised – pastor, teacher, fellowship builder, evangelist, pioneer, theologian, apostle – are those on which there are no significant denominational differences in rating. These commonly rated items tell a story about the similarities between Pentecostal ministers. For example, they all find pastoring and teaching to be very satisfying activities, a finding that is not surprising considering most of them chose to go into Pentecostal ministry expecting to be caring for congregations. They also find the role of the evangelist satisfying and this combination between pastoral and evangelistic ministry gives an insight into many Pentecostal congregations. They are both inward and outward looking; striving to maintain a balance between caring for existing members and attracting new ones.

The roles of pioneer, theologian and apostle are less satisfying to most of these ministers, perhaps understandably because of the difficulties attached to them. The apostle and pioneer must usually start a new congregation from scratch and this is a lonely and demanding assignment. Being a theologian seems detached from the everyday problems of congregational members.

When the ratings are looked at generally, it is evident that satisfaction is gained from the core ministerial tasks involving Scripture and people and that the unpopular tasks like being a fund-raiser or social worker are those that force the minister into a different mode. The fund-raiser must preach on giving, often making himself or his congregation feel uncomfortable, or write letters to beg for money. It is an arduous, often thankless, undertaking and goes against the grain for most ministers since it appears to be an admission of a lack of faith.

The differences between the four denominations in their rating of these roles is relatively small. For instance, Church of God ministers rate being a man or woman of prayer above being a preacher while all the other denominations rate being a preacher first of all. Similarly, Church of God ministers rate being a social worker slightly more favourably than the other denominations, but these differences are minor. The slight difference in the rating of being a leader of public worship within Elim and Assemblies of God as against the Apostolic Church and Church of God is probably due to the frequent delegation, in Elim and Assemblies of God, of the role of leading worship to groups of musicians. Again, the Church of God and the Apostolic Church give a higher rating to being a visitor than do the larger denominations, but this also is probably due to the internal structure of congregations in the larger denominations which tend to give responsibility for visiting to housegroup leaders.

Table 8.9.1 treats these items by looking at average satisfaction ratings for each denomination. It is immediately obvious that Church of God ministers rate their overall satisfaction with their work much more highly than the other three denominations and that the Assemblies of God ministers are least satisfied with their

Table 8.9.1 *Satisfaction by denomination*

Denom	**Mean**	**Sd**
AC	89.53	20.54
AG	86.58	16.57
Elim	89.89	16.41
CG	98.50	18.81

ministries.[38] When tests were run to discover what factors were associated with satisfaction they showed that neither age, weekly take-home pay, size of congregation, gender or the percentage of the congregation exercising spiritual gifts were relevant.[39] One of the two factors that was significantly associated with satisfaction is shown in table 8.10. Church growth of zero is associated with the lowest level of satisfaction and there is a steady progression in satisfaction levels in the next two steps of growth, from 1–5 per cent and from 6–10 per cent, which is where the majority of congregations are placed.[40]

A previous study had suggested that there is a connection between ministerial satisfaction and charismatic activity.[41] A scale of charismatic activity was constructed from six items. Ministers were asked 'How often in the past three months *you* have . . .' (original italics) and given a set of charismatic items that included giving public utterances in tongues, interpreting tongues, singing in tongues, prophesying and dancing in the Spirit. These items were

Table 8.10 *Satisfaction by church growth*

Growth %	**N**	**Mean**	**Sd**
None that I know of	129	84.12	17.19
1 to 5	265	88.30	17.51
6 to 10	167	92.62	15.79
11 to 20	82	91.87	16.13
21 to 30	40	91.27	14.01
More than 30	59	92.96	15.82

[38] $F = 6.878$, $p < .000$.

[39] Again using analysis of variance. In each case the F values were not significant. An attempt was made to connect size of congregation with satisfaction by using a restricted congregational size, but even this failed.

[40] $F = 5.086$, $p < .000$.

[41] Kay, 2000b.

Table 8.11 *Ministerial charismatic activity scale*

How often in the past three months *you have* . . .	**Item rest of test (r)**
Given a public utterance in tongues (glossolalia)	.31
Interpreted tongues (glossolalia)	.43
Sung in tongues (glossolalia)	.44
Prophesied	.60
Danced in the Spirit	.48
Given a 'word of wisdom/knowledge'	.52

Alpha .7194

arranged into a scale by adding responses to them together. The psychometric properties of the scale are shown in table 8.11. The items provide a sample of spoken and non-spoken charismatic activity with a scale mean of 12.77 (Sd 4.29). Since a charismatic activity between one and six times in three months was scored as a two, it is reasonable to suppose that the average minister carried out most of these activities at least once in three months (6 × 2 = 12).

Once the charismatic activity scale had been constructed it was divided into four separate bands. In the first and lowest were ministers with a score of nine or less, in the next band were ministers scoring between 10 and 12, in the next band were ministers scoring between 13 and 15, and the top band contained ministers with scores of 16 or more. By making the divisions at these points in the scale the sample of ministers were divided into four roughly equal groups. An analysis of variance was then computed where charismatic activity divided into these four bands was the main effect and the results are shown in table 8.12.[42] The table indicates that where frequency of charismatic activity is low, satisfaction is also low but, as frequency of charismatic activity increases, so satisfaction increases significantly until the most charismatic group of ministers register the highest mean score in the satisfaction scale (93.02).

Charismatic activity is associated with ministerial satisfaction and two reasons can be advanced for this. First, charismatic activity allows the Pentecostal minister a form of self-expression. Second, charismatic activity represents a direct and close contact with God. To prophesy, as Pentecostal ministers understand it, is to speak in an unpremeditated way into the life of the congregation.[43] It is a

---

[42] $F = 4.996$, $p < .002$.

[43] Kay, 1991.

Table 8.12 *Satisfaction by level of charismatic activity*

Frequency of charismatic activity	**N**	**Mean**	**Sd**
Less than 9	160	86.65	19.10
10 to 12	197	86.94	17.22
13 to 15	185	88.54	16.02
more than 16	163	93.02	15.46

creative spiritual utterance that can lift the congregation to a new burst of worship or speak to the unseen concerns of an individual. As such it is an expression of divine power and ministerial sufficiency.

Conclusion

Pentecostal ministers shape their lives by reference to biblical patterns of ministry and in response to congregational demands and, beyond these, to the needs of disadvantaged or deprived groups outside the church. Apostolic and Church of God ministers appear to be least troubled by a conflict between what they want to do and what they feel obliged to do, Assemblies of God and Elim ministers are most troubled. Perhaps, though, the tension between obligation and aspiration is ultimately beneficial to the progress of the church in that it ensures ministers strive for personal growth.

Levels of satisfaction with the ministerial life are difficult to compare with those of other occupational groups. Ministers' material conditions that might be thought to be influential such as take-home pay, age or size of congregation turn out to be not relevant to ministerial satisfaction. Though there are some denominational differences and the figures shown here indicate that Church of God ministers are most satisfied with their work, when the whole sample is taken together, ministers can be seen to find satisfaction through church growth and the exercise of charismatic ministry. Ministers whose churches grow most and who exercise charismatic ministry most frequently are those most likely to be satisfied with their work.

9

Charismata and Church Growth

Overview

This chapter looks at a model of church growth developed by Margaret Poloma in relation to Assemblies of God in the United States. It explores the factors associated with church growth in Britain to see whether they are similar to those applicable to American Pentecostal churches.

Pentecostal growth

The astonishing growth of the Pentecostal movement is a matter of statistical record. In 1900 Pentecostals and charismatics amounted to 0 per cent of the world's population. In 1970 they amounted to 2 per cent of the world's population, a figure that rose in 1998 to 8 per cent and which is predicted to rise by 2025 to 9 per cent. In terms of numbers, there were 74 million Pentecostals or charismatics in 1970, 471 million in 1978, 502 million in 2000 and there are predicted to be 740 million in 2025.[1] The figures, though they include a variety of religious groups, are all legitimately included within the general Pentecostal/charismatic fold and they raise questions about how this phenomenon has occurred. After all, whereas the world-view of communism has spread rapidly and widely within the twentieth century, it has been supported by the apparatus of the state, particularly in China and Cuba, and formerly in the USSR, but Pentecostalism has not had this advantage. It has not been taught in schools or supported by flag-waving parades or

[1] Barrett and Johnson, 1998.

tax revenues.[2] The advances of Pentecostalism have been, like the advances of early Christianity, largely unseen and unnoticed by academic, political and cultural commentators.

It is usual to distinguish between separate waves of the Holy Spirit.[3] The first of these resulted in the Pentecostals, or 'classical Pentecostals' as they are sometimes called, who formed denominations in the period after the Azusa Street revival of 1907. Each of these denominations has built into its foundation documents an emphasis on the experience of the Holy Spirit and, though there may be differences concerning crisis experiences of holiness and church polity, they belong together as a single identifiable group. Following them in the second wave are those within the charismatic movement from approximately 1965 onwards.[4] These are Christians who have been renewed within the older denominations and who have, in most cases, shared the same experience of the Holy Spirit that Pentecostals claim. The charismatic movement has changed the style of worship within the old denominations and, in Britain, is usually advanced by separate agencies within each denomination: for example, Anglican Renewal Ministries (from 1980), the National Service Committee of the Roman Catholics (1973), Mainstream among Baptists and the magazine *Dunamis* distributed among Methodists. Estimates as to the charismatic movement's size in Britain vary but up to 20 per cent of Anglican and Baptist churches have been positively affected by it and about 10 per cent of Methodist ministers would take a strongly Pentecostal line.[5] Catholic charismatics continue to be active though they are harder to quantify.

The third wave, especially in Britain, is usually dated from the Third Wave Conference held by John Wimber in October 1984 at the Methodist Central Hall, London, though there is evidence that the third wave was already rolling before then.[6] The third wave is usually thought to comprise those who are neither classical

---

[2] The entire curriculum of Soviet schools was shaped by Marxist-Leninism in the period up to glasnost; Kay, 1977.

[3] Barrett, 1988.

[4] Hocken, 1984.

[5] Kay, 2000a; Haley, 1999.

[6] Walker, 1985.

Pentecostals nor charismatics within the older denominations; a new set of people within a new set of churches: the house or new churches. Nevertheless, the third wave has had a strong impact on the charismatic movement and also made an impression on the Pentecostals. A report on the London conference of 1984 revealed the denominational representation of its participants. Over 40 per cent of them were Anglican. The next largest groups were Baptist with 25 per cent and house churches with 16 per cent; Pentecostals amounted to only 4 per cent.[7] By 1988, although these waves were identifiably intact, their global proportions were understood by the most knowledgeable analyst as being made up of thity-eight separate categories.[8]

Alongside these megatrends within the religious domain were underlying socio-economic changes that included the crumbling of the Soviet empire, the continued growth of the world's population and its accompanying migration to expanding cities. In 1900 only 14 per cent of the population were urban dwellers but by 1970 this had risen to 36 per cent and by 1998 to 45 per cent. The predicted figure for the year 2025 is 61 per cent. Indeed early in the current millennium the proportion of the world's population within cities will, for the first time, overtake the proportion living in rural areas.[9] Pentecostalism within the Third World has been welcomed by the urban poor and, in many densely populated areas, cell churches have been knitted together to allow many thousands of people to belong to congregations under a single leader or leadership team. But these adaptations and growth patterns hardly apply to Britain or to the USA where more conventional church structures are in place.

A great deal has been written on church growth. Gibbs and McGavran have argued for a necessary compatibility between congregation and the surrounding community and for the authoritative and participatory leadership of the minister.[10] Wagner particularly stresses the need for full-time ministers to be leaders and equippers and for the congregation to be followers and lay

---

[7] Hunt, 1997, 94.

[8] Barrett, 1988, 119.

[9] Barrett and Johnson, 1998.

[10] Gibbs, 1981; McGavran, 1955, 1959, 1970, 1983; Wagner, 1976, 1984, 1987.

ministers.[11] The minister teaches and empowers the congregation so that it becomes a ministering entity.[12] This is the dynamic of church growth that seems most appropriate to Pentecostalism in Britain where it has been effective to an extent, but not to the spectacular extent that has been witnessed in Asia or Latin America. This is partly because the first wave crashed against the rocks of existing denominationalism without much impact. And this was also true in the rest of Europe. By contrast, the numerically powerful second wave has been welcomed as a refreshing new force, able to sweep away dust and deadness.[13] Yet, whichever wave has been successful, the remarkable diffusion of the Pentecostal/charismatic movement needs to be examined and understood. It cannot be simply explained as a matter of evangelical doctrine since, as Johnstone is able to show, the growth of Pentecostalism has easily outstripped that of non-Pentecostal evangelicals.[14] Indeed, non-Pentecostal evangelicals have been in decline according to his figures since about 1980. Other explanations for Pentecostal growth must be invoked.

Weber and Poloma

The sociologist Max Weber (1864–1920) in his voluminous writings distinguished between traditional, legal and charismatic authority.[15] In his view charismatic authority stems from the extraordinary religious powers of special individuals and, though he broadened his theory to apply to all religions, it may, without prejudice, be applied to Pentecostalism. To his mind religion may operate in a legal mode and attempt to bring order to our experience of the unpredictable and tragic world by laws and rituals. Alternatively, it may enable us to survive by fixing our eyes on a transcendent heavenly realm. The prophetic charisma, associated with this mode, enables a message of new transcendent meaning and salvation to be proclaimed.

---

[11] Wagner, 1984, 169.
[12] See also Kay, 1999a.
[13] Barrett, 1988, 122.
[14] Johnstone, 1998, 113.
[15] See Poloma, 1989, 88.

Pentecostalism can obviously be understood in this way. The very word charisma, which Weber took from the New Testament – his Calvinistic family acquainted him with the religion of the Reformation and he was a member of the Evangelical Social Union from 1890 onwards[16] – describes the kind of authority which a preacher like Seymour or Jeffreys possessed. Moreover with its ability to make a plausible connection between modern historical events and the biblical sweep of world history, Pentecostalism is able to provide a message of salvation that not only centres on Christ but also gives the current generation an experientially-validated motive for preaching the gospel: the Spirit has been poured out so that the church can once more bear witness to the ends of the earth.

Yet Weber pointed out that charisma can be routinised and transformed into the other forms of authority, whether legal or traditional. The process is familiar to church historians. The first blaze of revival burns away dull routines and unexamined attitudes. Old practices are discarded; formality and unemotional habits are replaced by excited zeal and joyful renewal; and then, quite suddenly, normality returns and all that remains of the revival is a new set of habits and procedures that fail to engage either the intellect or the emotions. The habits become traditions and the procedures become rules, and charismatic authority has become traditional or legal authority. Moreover this transition is often accompanied by the process of creeping bureaucracy. The charismatic figure at first needs no office staff or secretary, but gradually they are put in place and eventually the authority of the charismatic figure is transferred to them. When he or she dies, the bureaucracy holds sway and dedicates itself to visionless self-perpetuation.

This process can be observed over more than one generation on a national scale. Margaret Poloma, writing about Assemblies of God in the USA, entitled her book *The Assemblies of God at the Crossroads* because she saw the third generation of Pentecostals in the 1980s as having to tussle with the pull of bureaucracy on the one hand and charismatic life and power on the other. The dilemma for Assemblies of God, as she saw it, was that bureaucracy had provided stability and denominational efficiency that allowed its churches to

16 MacRae, 1974, 25.

be co-ordinated and accepted within the wider evangelical constituency. In these circumstances to get rid of bureaucracy would have been dangerous. But not to get rid of bureaucracy would also be dangerous. It would be to risk following the road leading to decline and eventual decay. Somehow, in her view, Assemblies of God in the United States had to find again the charismatic thrill of the founding years while retaining a slimmed down version of denominational bureaucratic structures.

> Paradoxically, although charisma has long been recognised as a factor in the revitalisation of religious movements, it seems to depart quickly once it has completed the task of institution-building. Now it is more fragile than ever, for modern institutions are prone to favour efficiency and pragmatism rather than charisma's illusive spirit. Charisma and institutionalisation thus appear to be at odds, with charisma quick to take on the routine forms that stem its free flow.[17]

Poloma Tests her analysis on US data

Poloma made use of ministerial and congregational questionnaires covering a wide range of topics. Some of the items in her questionnaires have been repeated within the questionnaire distributed to Pentecostal ministers in Britain. Her findings show that there is a linkage between charismatic experience and evangelism and she argues, on this basis, that charismatic experience is vital to the continued growth of Pentecostal churches. She writes:

> What I have attempted [in this chapter] was, first, to build a theoretical case for the importance of including religious experience in any study of institutional religion. I then went on to describe the alleged importance of religious experience in launching the early Pentecostal movement. Finally, I used survey data collected from Assemblies of God congregations to test a model relating such experiences to behaviour that would facilitate church growth.[18]

---

17 Poloma, 1989, 232.
18 Poloma, 1989, 33.

Her scale of congregational charismatic experiences included seven items: frequency of praying in tongues, frequency of receiving definite answers to prayer requests, being divinely inspired to perform some specific action, giving a prophecy in a church service, giving a prophecy privately to another, frequency of being slain in the Spirit, personal confirmation of scriptural truths (alpha .74).[19] Her scale of congregational evangelism included eight items: inviting a non-member to church, inviting an inactive member to church, offering transport to church services, inviting children of non-members to church, involvement in witnessing, talking about church to others, offering pastor's services to someone in need, visiting inactive members (alpha .82).

Once these scales were constructed Poloma was able to correlate them and she found a significant positive relationship between congregational charismatic experience and congregational evangelism ($r = .45$).[20] This indicates that the two things, charismatic experience and congregational evangelism, occur together. It does not indicate whether one causes the other but the likelihood is, considering that congregational evangelism can occur in non-Pentecostal contexts also, that it is charismatic experience that strengthens evangelism and not vice versa. This is the model of church growth that Poloma has advanced.

She also included other items in her congregational questionnaires relating to the age, gender, education, income, holiness outlook, orthodoxy, religious devotion and church attendance record of the respondents. Having established the general positive correlation between charismatic experience and congregational evangelism she also reported on the items that correlated with charismatic experience and found, using multiple regression which allows a series of correlations to be carried out simultaneously, that education, orthodoxy and religious devotion correlated significantly and positively with charismatic experience. In a second, more complex analysis, she attempted to discover whether it is charismatic experience rather than the background variables like religious devotion, age and education that influence evangelism. Again, using multiple regression she was able to demonstrate that

---

19 An explanation of alpha is given in the introduction to this book.

20 For an explanation of correlation look in the introduction.

the strongest relationship with evangelism was with charismatic experience rather than with the background variables, even when they were present in the same equation. She concluded that charismatic experience is what leads to evangelistic activity, and she presumed that evangelistic activity leads to church growth.

The analysis reported in this chapter substantially repeats Poloma's investigation, though modifications have been made both to the scales she used and to the model she constructed. As we shall see her findings *are* applicable to a British context: charismatic activity is associated, in the main, with evangelism and church growth.

The first main difference between this study and Poloma's is that she made use of data collected from ministers and from congregations. This study makes use only of data collected from ministers but within this collection is information given by the ministers about the congregations. Secondly, this study puts forward the eminently Pentecostal thesis that Pentecostal ministers produce Pentecostal congregations. In other words, that there is an empowering of the congregation by the Pentecostal minister and this is part of the work, the deliberate work, of the minister. By prophesying for instance, the minister encourages members of the congregation to do likewise. This notion that the minister within Pentecostal settings has the privilege and task of empowering the congregation is taken from biblical data. Christ gave authority to the apostles to heal the sick (Mk. 6:7); Peter and John went to Samaria so that the disciples there could receive the Holy Spirit (Acts 8); Paul prayed for the first Ephesian Christians so that they could speak in tongues and prophesy (Acts 19). Thirdly, this study contains variables relating to evangelism and to church growth so that it is possible to see not only whether charismatic activity is connected with evangelism but whether evangelism is connected with church growth. Fourthly, Poloma made use of measures of the educational achievement of congregational members to discover whether educational sophistication, or the lack of it, was associated with charismatic gifts. The current survey did contain questions on the academic qualifications of ministers but discovered that these measures were not sufficiently nuanced to be informative about the present sample. Moreover, there is considerable difficulty in equating the different qualifications, some technical and some academic, some at an uncertain diploma level and others of an honorary nature. Finally, this study refers to four separate denominations and not just to Assemblies of God, the one studied by Poloma.

What do the data show?

A scale of ministerial charismatic activity was constructed using items very similar to those employed by Poloma. The six items in the scale were based upon answers to the questions 'How often in the past three months *you* have . . .' (original italics) given a public utterance in tongues, interpreted tongues, sung in tongues, prophesied, danced in the Spirit, given a word of wisdom/knowledge? To each of these items ministers could reply: none, 1 to 6, 7 to 12, 13 to 18 or 19+. The items were tested for scale properties by computing the alpha coefficient (.7131), a satisfactory indication of the scale's reliability and slightly higher than that recorded by Poloma in her equivalent measure of charismatic experience. The mean scores for each denomination are shown in table 9.1.1. The scores vary with the Church of God ministers being lowest and the Assemblies of God ministers highest. The analysis of variance statistics data at the foot of the table indicates that the differences between denominational means are significant. High scores indicate that ministers record themselves as being frequent in their manifestation of charismata.

A similar procedure was adopted for the ministerial evangelism scale. The items were again based upon responses to the question 'How often in the past three months *you* have . . .' (original italics). And the items were: talked with friends or neighbours about Christ, talked with friends or neighbours about church, invited a new person to an activity at your church, invited a backslider to return to church, offered to drive a new person to church, invited children of new

Table 9.1.1 *Ministerial charismatic activity by denomination*

Denomination	**Mean**	**Sd**
AC	10.30	3.37
AG	13.35	4.40
Elim	12.98	4.21
CG	10.16	2.99

$F = 15.122$, $p < .000$

Table 9.2.1. *Ministerial evangelism by denomination*

Denomination	Mean	Sd
AC	13.94	4.22
AG	14.70	4.57
Elim	14.28	4.52
CG	16.43	16.21

$F = 3.203$, $p < .023$

people to children's meetings, prayed for the salvation of specific people. The properties of the scale were assessed using the alpha coefficient and this was computed at .8337, again a slightly higher figure than achieved by Poloma's equivalent scale although a lower number of items were used. Table 9.2.1 shows the mean scores for each denomination and the analysis of variance statistics indicate that these mean scores are significantly different from each other. The Church of God ministers record themselves as being more evangelistically active than the others and the Apostolic ministers record themselves as being least active in this respect.

Poloma used three items in her devotional scale, one about frequency of prayer, another about frequency of Bible reading and another about the frequency of reading religious literature. The devotional scale used here only included two items: frequency of prayer and frequency of Bible reading. These items correlated significantly ($F = .237$; $p < .000$) and function as a mini-scale. The three items assessing religious mores used by Poloma, relating to attendance at the cinema, approval of alcohol and social dancing, were all included within the current study and combined as a scale with an alpha coefficient of .8370, again a slightly higher value than the original study achieved.

Table 9.3.1 *Ministerial evangelism by ministerial charismatic activity*

Ministerial Charismatic activity	AC	AG	Elim	CG
Low	12.12	13.15	12.12	13.35
Low medium	13.65	13.53	13.11	17.57
High medium	14.85	14.29	14.85	17.00
High	19.25	17.48	16.81	22.00
F	7.684	16.918	16.384	4.164
P	.000	.000	.000	.016

Table 9.3.1 shows the relationship between ministerial charismatic activity and ministerial evangelism. The charismatic activity scale was broken down into four levels so as to divide the sample into four roughly equal groups. The table shows how evangelistic activity increases in step with charismatic activity and it does this significantly within each denomination. This table gives powerful support to the notion that it is ministers who are most involved in charismatic activity who are also most involved in evangelism. Of course this does not show, by itself, that the most charismatic ministers produce the most charismatic congregations or that the most charismatic congregations are also the most evangelistic congregations. Nor does it show that the most evangelistic congregations are the congregations that grow fastest. All these connections are steps in a chain of argument. But it is important to establish the connection between charismatic activity and evangelistic activity in the life of the minister. Once this can be established, the other steps can be taken with greater confidence.

Ministers were asked to assess the percentage of their congregation publicly exercising spiritual gifts in large meetings or prayer groups. The range of six possible percentages were offered from none, through 1 to 5 per cent, 6 to 10 per cent, 11 to 20 per cent, 21 to 30 per cent, and more than 30 per cent. The assessments were rated between one and six, with six being the highest. The results of this analysis are given in table 9.4.1 where the impression that the differences between the denominations is small is confirmed by the non significant F ratio.

Table 9.5.1 shows the relationship between ministerial charismatic activity and congregational charismatic activity. In three of the denominations, the Apostolic Church, Assemblies of God and

Table 9.4.1 *Per cent of congregation exercising spiritual gifts by denomination*

Per cent of congregation	**AC**	**AG**	**Elim**	**CG**
None that I know	2.2	1.7	1.2	6.8
1 to 5	36.7	31.7	30.9	38.6
6 to 10	33.3	26.7	27.7	13.6
11 to 20	11.1	19.6	15.3	22.7
21 to 30	8.9	7.4	8.7	6.8
More than 30	7.8	12.9	16.2	11.4

F = 1.982, NS

Table 9.5.1 *Congregational charismatic activity by ministerial charismatic activity*

Ministerial charismatic activity	AC	AG	Elim	CG
Low	2.75	2.74	2.80	2.79
Low medium	3.35	3.21	3.38	2.88
High medium	3.00	3.49	3.46	6.00
High	4.50	4.01	4.28	3.75
F	3.031	12.34	14.410	2.168
P	.036	.000	.000	NS

Elim, there is a clear and significant connection between the level of charismatic activity of the minister and the percentage of his or her congregation exercising spiritual gifts. For example, within the Apostolic Church a score of 3.0 indicates that for the high medium group of Apostolic ministers 6 to 10 per cent of the congregation exercise spiritual gifts and this number rises to between 11 and 30 per cent in the most charismatically active group of Apostolic ministers. This table establishes the connection between the charismatic activity of a minister and the charismatic activity of the congregation. The more the minister is active, the more the congregation is active. The only exception to this finding appears, at first sight, to be within the Church of God, but the last column in table 9.5.1 shows there is a positive association between the minister's charismatic activity and that of the congregation. However, this relationship is not as smooth as occurs within the other denominations and so fails to reach statistical significance.

As part of the questionnaire ministers were asked to assess the extent to which their congregations had grown during the previous twelve months. They were given a set of six percentage ranges, 0, 1 to 5 per cent, 6 to 10 per cent, 11 to 20 per cent, 21 to 30 per cent, and

Table 9.6.1 *Per cent by which congregation has grown within the last year by denomination*

Per cent of congregation	AC	AG	Elim	CG
None that I know	25.8	16.2	18.4	18.6
1 to 5	40.4	38.7	30.5	48.8
6 to 10	19.1	20.1	25.4	16.3
11 to 20	5.6	10.9	11.8	11.6
21 to 30	4.5	5.0	6.3	2.3
More than 30	4.5	9.2	7.5	2.3

$F = 3.289$, $p < .020$

Table 9.7.1 *Church growth by per cent of congregation exercising spiritual gifts*

Per cent of congregation exercising spiritual gifts	**AC**	**AG**	**Elim**	**CG**
None that I know	3.00	2.33	3.25	2.33
1 to 5	1.76	2.45	2.40	1.82
6 to 10	2.60	2.70	2.76	2.17
11 to 20	1.80	3.12	2.74	2.78
21 to 30	3.38	3.50	2.83	2.67
More than 30	3.83	2.91	3.64	3.60
F	5.897	3.548	5.922	2.753
P	.000	.004	.000	.033

more than 30 per cent. The assessments were rated between one and six, with six being the highest. Table 9.6.1 shows the percentages by which congregations in the different denominations have grown over the past twelve months. The figures suggest that growth is largest within Elim and then Assemblies of God. For example, 25 per cent of Elim ministers consider that their congregations have grown by between 6 and 10 per cent whereas only a fifth of Assemblies of God ministers makes the same judgement, and the other two denominations have lower proportions than this. The differential growth rates between the denominations confirmed by the significant F ratio beneath the table.

Table 9.7.1 establishes the linkage between the percentage of a congregation that exercises spiritual gifts and church growth. The table shows that in the case of each denomination, there is a linkage between the two factors. As the percentage of the congregation exercising spiritual gifts increases, so there is a tendency for church growth also to increase.[21]

This table completes the link between ministerial charismatic activity and church growth. It helps establish the cross-cultural similarities (at least between the USA and Britain) between Pentecostal churches that are growing and to suggest the dynamics of this growth. It is not simply engendered by the Pentecostal experience in and of itself nor does it arise solely by the evangelistic

[21] This finding can also be expressed using correlation. For the Apostolic Church, Spearman's rho was .342, $p < .001$; for Assemblies of God it was .226, $p < .000$, for Elim .241, $p < .000$ and for the Church of God, .460, $p < .002$.

exertions of the minister. It arises through a combination of charismatic activities within the life of the minister, evangelistic example within the life of the minister and these two factors at work within the congregation.

Extended testing of the analysis on British data

Table 9.8.1 presents the means and standard deviations of the ministerial devotion scale. There are sufficient differences in the frequency of Bible reading and prayer between ministers for these figures to just attain statistical significance.

Table 9.9.1 presents the responses of ministers to the holiness code and here the figures show how different the four denominations are. The most lax is the Elim group of ministers, followed closely by Assemblies of God. The other two denominations show a much tighter and tougher view about traditional worldly pursuits. Differences between the denominations are highly significant statistically and one would expect that visitors to churches would become aware of these differences quite quickly.

Table 9.10 provides a correlation matrix showing the relationship between the minister's charismatic activity and the other variables so far considered. The first thing to notice is that all the variables are significantly related but that adherence to the holiness code and age are negatively related to charismatic activity, implying that older ministers and ministers who more strictly adhere to the holiness code are less likely to be highly charismatically active. Of the positive correlations, the highest is with evangelistic activity, suggesting that these two factors are most closely related, but the percentage of the congregation exercising spiritual gifts is also highly correlated with the minister's charismatic activity. The minister's devotion is also a significant correlate of charismatic

Table 9.8.1 *Ministerial devotion by denomination*

Denomination	**Mean**	**Sd**
AC	11.90	.42
AG	11.85	.55
Elim	11.75	.73
CG	11.76	.66

$F = 2.710$, $p < .044$

Table 9.9.1 *Mores (holiness code) by denomination*

Denomination	**Mean**	**Sd**
AC	10.19	3.41
AG	8.43	3.07
Elim	7.26	2.88
CG	11.45	2.91

$F = 43.858$, $p < .000$

activity but not nearly as powerful as the other positive factors. This table takes the analysis a little further than the previous section. It shows that age and holiness are negatively linked to ministerial charismatic activity and reveals the strengths of correlation between ministerial charismatic activity and the various factors.

Table 9.11 takes the analysis to another level. Following Poloma's more complex testing of relationship between charismatic activity and evangelism, a multiple regression equation was computed.[22] This allows lots of variables to be related to each other simultaneously rather than in pairs. The three variables relating to devotion, the holiness code (mores) and age were entered into the equation in a block and together significantly predicted evangelistic activity. But when the level of charismatic activity was added into the equation there was a sharp increase in the significance of the multiple correlation and the beta values for each variable show that, as with the American data, charismatic activity is the most powerful predictor of evangelistic activity even when other variables are simultaneously at work contributing to the variability of evangelism. The pattern discovered by Poloma and relevant to American Assemblies of God is found to be similar to that existing within British Pentecostalism. This confirms the notion that charismatic activity is the most important stimulant to evangelism.

Table 9.10 *Correlations with ministerial charismatic activity*

	Devotion	**Holiness (Mores)**	**% Congreg Spiritual gifts**	**% Congreg growth**	**Evangelistic activity**	**Age**
Charismatic activity	.141	-.163	.346	.229	.371	-.122
P <	.000	.000	.000	.000	.000	.001

[22] Multiple regression is discussed in the introduction.

Table 9.11 *Multiple regression significance tests exploring influence of four variables on minister's evangelistic activity*

Independent variables Minister's . . .	**R^2**	**Increase in R^2**	**F**[23]	**P <**	***Beta***	***T***	**P <**
Devotion					.046	1.34	NS
Mores					.196	4.91	.000
Age	.030	.030	7.229	.000	-.102	-2.62	.009
Charismatic activity	.202	.172	151.345	.000	.427	12.30	.000

Two other questions need to be addressed before completing this analysis. The first is whether there might be examples of churches within Pentecostal denominations that appear to be growing as a result of the minister's charismatic activity alone but without any great evangelistic example from the minister. We could imagine a situation where charismatic activity becomes almost an end in itself, and even a frightening or strange barrier to newcomers, which puts them off joining the church. But equally, we could imagine a church fully involved in charismatic activity that was warm-hearted and welcoming, but not evangelistic in any traditional sense, which still managed to grow by virtue of the community created by the charismata. So the question is, can a Pentecostal church grow through ministerial charismatic activity alone?

The second question relates to the possibility that congregational charismatic activity (with ministerial evangelism) and church growth might not be related to each other in any simple way, but that within particular bands of congregational size charismatic activity (with evangelism) might be more or less effective. The very small congregation, for example, that was highly active charismatically might be one that did not grow because people within it were seen by potential converts as extreme or weird while, within a much larger congregation, charismatic activity might be more diffuse and acceptable to visitors. So the question is, are charismatic activity and evangelism related to church growth differently depending on the size of the congregation?

---

[23] The F ratio in this table shows the significance of the increase in R, the beta values refer only to the final equation that includes all the variables simultaneously.

Probably the simplest way to discover the answer to the first question is by calculating a partial correlation. By this procedure one can remove the effects of one variable from the relationship between two others. If the relationship between the minister's charismatic activity and church growth is recalculated removing the effects of the minister's evangelistic activity, then an indication is given of the pure relationship between ministerial charismatic activity and church growth. The coefficient (.1554, $p < .000$) is highly significant. The evidence is that ministerial charismatic activity on its own *does* appear to have a church growth effect even when a ministerial example in evangelism is not given to congregational members.

When ministerial example in the spheres of charismatic activity and evangelistic activity are taken together but divided up for the purposes of analysis into four separate congregational sizes, then an interesting and different pattern of results emerges. Again, however, this analysis was carried out using multiple regression and, to equalise possible differences between different denominations, the variance attributable to denomination was entered as the first block into the equation. Following this the ministerial charismatic activity and evangelistic activity variables were entered. The results are shown in table 9.12.

For the smaller churches with fewer than 49 adults in attendance, both the minister's charismatic activity and his or her evangelistic example are significant contributors to church growth. For congregations between 50 and 99 people and for congregations of between 100 and 199 people only the minister's evangelistic example is significant. But above the size of 200 neither the evangelistic nor the charismatic example of the minister are related to the congregation's growth. This, on reflection, is not an unexpected set of findings. In small congregations the minister's example, whether charismatic or evangelistic, is important. As the church grows larger the evangelistic example of the minister is most important for church growth. And by the time the congregation reaches more than 200 the minister has become a rather more distant person for most members of the congregation; and his or her example is less apparent.

At first sight it might seem odd that the charismatic example of the minister is related to church growth in the sample of ministers as

Table 9.12 *Multiple regression significance tests exploring influence of minister's charismatic and evangelistic activity on church growth*

Independent variables	R^2	F	P<	Beta	T	P<
Less than 49						
Denomination				-.024	-.443	NS
Minister's charismatic activity				.163	2.633	.008
Minister's evangelistic activity	.078	8.661	.000	.164	2.666	.009
50 to 99						
Denomination				.086	1.162	NS
Minister's charismatic activity				.108	1.325	NS
Minister's evangelistic activity	.062	3.745	.012	.170	2.088	.038
100 to 199						
Denomination				.074	.863	NS
Minister's charismatic activity				.127	1.361	NS
Minister's evangelistic activity	.177	8.235	.000	.345	3.712	.000
200+						
Denomination				-.054	-.463	NS
Minister's charismatic activity				.078	.622	NS
Minister's evangelistic activity	.024	.613	NS	.081	.645	NS

a whole but that, when the figures are broken down into four sizes of congregations, it is only the smallest in which this result can be observed. But the reason for this is that 45.5 per cent of the ministers' congregations have under 49 adults. Consequently the effects found in the small congregations are transferred to the whole sample by sheer weight of numbers.

These findings suggest that the church is likely to grow, certainly for congregations below 200, where the minister sets a good evangelistic example. Above this ceiling, other factors – presumably those to do with the structure of the congregation for instance – are going to be decisive.

One other way of investigating the relationship between church growth and the factors that contribute to it in the four different bands of congregational size is by making use of the variable referring to the percentage of the congregation exercising spiritual gifts and putting this in a multiple regression equation with the minister's evangelistic example (table 9.13). Among the smaller churches of below 49 people we find that both the percentage of the congregation exercising spiritual gifts and the evangelistic example of the

Table 9.13 *Multiple regression significance tests exploring influence of per cent of congregation exercising spiritual gifts and ministerial evangelistic activity on church growth*

Independent variables	R^2	F	P<	Beta	T	P<
Less than 49						
Denomination				-.051	-.996	NS
% congregation exercising spiritual gifts				.201	3.884	.000
Minister's evangelistic activity	.095	12.052	.000	.209	4.049	.000
50 to 99						
Denomination				.030	.434	NS
% congregation exercising spiritual gifts				.193	2.675	.008
Minister's evangelistic activity	.064	4.326	.006	.119	1.650	NS
100 to 199						
Denomination				.071	.844	NS
% congregation exercising spiritual gifts				.107	1.267	NS
Minister's evangelistic activity	.172	8.215	.000	.373	4.430	.000
200+						
Denomination				-.019	-.189	NS
% congregation exercising spiritual gifts				.369	3.541	.001
Minister's evangelistic activity	.142	4.728	.004	.021	.203	NS

minister are important to church growth. Among churches in the next band, up to 99 people, we find that the percentage of the congregation exercising spiritual gifts is important but that the evangelistic example of the minister does not register as being significant. In the next band, between 100 and 199, we find that the significant variable is the evangelistic example of the minister. Finally, in the largest churches it is the percentage of the congregation exercising spiritual gifts that is the only significant variable and the evangelistic example of the minister has no bearing on church growth.

The figures are a little perplexing at first sight but the general interpretation is that in the smallest churches, growth is associated with the evangelistic example of the minister and the spiritual life of the congregation, whereas in the largest churches, it is the spiritual life of the congregation which is the crucial factor. In the two intermediate bands there is no clarity, although it would be possible to suggest that for churches of between 100 and 199 the evangelistic example of the minister still counts for a great deal. Indeed, the notion of a ceiling of 200 adults for Sunday morning congregations is not unheard of and it may be that, to break through this ceiling, the minister needs to press forward with evangelistic zeal rather than becoming weighed down by administrative and other burdens. Once this ceiling has been broken, however, the congregation's life takes over as the main factor in causing growth.

Conclusion

This chapter has used the detailed studies of Poloma as a starting point for an exploration of the factors leading to church growth. The thesis that church growth and charismatic activity are related has been borne out by the data. If Pentecostal churches wish to continue growing, they should continue to be charismatic. This general finding can be unpacked. A causal sequence can be found. The charismatic activity of the minister is linked with the evangelistic activity of the minister. Both these activities are reflected in the behaviour of the congregation. Charismatic and evangelistic congregations are likely to grow. Once the congregation has reached approximately two hundred people, the charismatic life within it appears to be attractive to newcomers and to lead to church growth even if the minister is not obviously evangelistic in his or her own lifestyle. A model of church growth developed in relation to Assemblies of God in the United States appears to be transferable to the main Pentecostal denominations in Britain, a finding that provides evidence about the similarity of the dynamics of church growth, and about Pentecostalism, in both cultures.

10

Personality

Overview

This chapter describes psychological understanding and measurement of personality and then applies Eysenck's dimensional model of personality to Pentecostal ministry, first in the field of church growth and then picking up the themes that have been explored in earlier chapters.

Personality

A girl asked what she was looking for in her ideal boy might reply: 'He's got to like music, animals and have a great personality.' What does she mean by 'a great personality'? In everyday use the term probably refers to the ability to mix with other people, tell jokes, stand out from the crowd and be a 'well-marked character'.[1] But in psychological terms personality is something that everyone possesses. Personality refers to combinations of habits and traits that, in every individual, are formed into a unique configuration. In the psychological sense personality refers broadly to the inner, dynamic workings of the mind and emotions and to their outer expression in the social world.

One of the problems with the measurement and discussion of personality, however, is that its expression is dependent, to some extent, on situations. For example, in a library everyone behaves in more or less the same way. They sit quietly and read. No difference in behaviour can be observed. At the football match, on the other

---

[1] See *Chambers English Dictionary*, Cambridge, Chambers, 1989.

hand, everybody is shouting, singing or cheering and, again, everybody behaves in more or less the same way. So, while there is no argument over the impact of situations on our behaviour, there are also many situations when people behave quite differently and these differences are easy to detect. Moreover these differences are persistent. In ordinary language we often refer to these persistent or consistent differences as traits. A man may be persistently late for meetings. A woman may consistently worry about her children's health. These traits occur in a variety of situations and one way of describing the character of people is by enumerating the traits they show. John is honest, punctual, generous and thoughtful. Elisabeth is shy, artistic, musical and careful. These traits are partly a matter of character but they may also refer to certain abilities – as in the case of Elisabeth who is artistic and musical.[2]

The psychological study of personality is extremely diverse. There are all kinds of approaches to it including those that attempt to describe the workings of personality as a system of integrated parts developing from the experiences of childhood. In the Freudian approach it is the ego, the I, the rational self, that is in contact with reality and responds both to the restraint of the conscience, or superego, and to the promptings of the id, or unconscious. This Freudian system, developed as it was by a man utterly opposed to religion, is of limited help to anybody interested in the personality of religious people. This is partly because Freud considered religion to be a form of illness, or at least closely related to it, operating to prevent people facing the grim reality of the human condition.[3]

A more friendly approach to religion was developed by the Swiss psychologist C.G. Jung who, though his own religious opinions were complicated and unorthodox, accepted the importance of religion within the human psyche.[4] Writing in 1921, Jung proposed the existence of psychological types and developed the idea of

---

[2] In Eysenck's scheme intellectual abilities are not included among personality traits, but other conceptualisations of personality do take note of abilities; see McCrae and Costa, 1997, 828.

[3] Freud wrote *The Future of an Illusion* in 1927 about religion. Even the title tells the reader about Freud's attitude to religion.

[4] McLynn, 1996; Storr, 1973. Jung's father was a pastor in the Swiss Reformed Church.

extraversion (where the extravert relates primarily to the outer world of society and events) and introversion (where the introvert relates primarily to the inner world of thoughts and feelings). In Jung's theory introversion and extraversion are rather like right and left-handedness. The right-handed person can, with difficulty, write with the left hand and vice versa, but the right-handed person prefers to use the right hand. It is the hand of greatest skill, the natural hand. Similarly the extravert prefers the outer world but, with practice and opportunity, can develop an ability to explore the inner world. It is a mistake to think that extraverts are incapable of quiet thought just as it is a mistake to think that introverts are incapable of joining in laughing and joking with groups of people. The point is that the extravert finds it easier to relate outwardly – it is less tiring and less stressful – and the introvert finds it easier to relate inwardly. In addition to his perceptive description of psychological types Jung also described a form of religious development that most traditional Christians would find unacceptable.

A religiously neutral and therefore more promising approach to personality, and the one adopted in this book, stems from a biological understanding of human beings. The research of the British psychologist Hans Eysenck has been widely used internationally and has the advantage of making use of certain aspects of the psychodynamic approach to personality, particularly the use of the ideas of extraversion and introversion.[5] Whereas Jung saw extraversion and introversion as types – you were either an extravert or an introvert – Eysenck understood extraversion and introversion as belonging to the same continuum or scale so that it was possible to be more extravert and less introvert without having to be placed in one box or the other. And he did this by grouping together sets of traits so that they could be seen as belonging to these broad dimensions. This had the advantage of allowing him to make use of the insights of Jung's type theory while at the same time incorporating the traits we use in popular descriptions of people. Moreover, and importantly, Eysenck developed his description of personality by reference to the nervous systems all human beings possess.

---

[5] Many aspects of Eysenck's work are conveniently summarised in his autobiography; Eysenck, 1990.

The main control of muscles in all human beings is carried out by the sending of messages from the brain through the spinal cord to the nerves in every part of the body; and, similarly, messages are carried back from every part of the body through the sensation of touch and feeling to be interpreted by the brain. This communication network from the brain to the rest of the body and from the rest of the body back to the brain is called the central nervous system. Without it we could not function as free agents. But Eysenck noticed that the input of information to the brain is itself controlled through a structure in the brain stem and that some people's brains tend to function at a higher level of arousal than others. The level of arousal of the brain has, he suggested, an impact on whether someone operates as an extravert or an introvert. For the extravert, whose natural level of arousal tends to be lower, there is a desire to seek stimulation in the events of the outer world. For the introvert, whose natural level of arousal tends to be higher, the stimulation of the outer world may be altogether too much, and it is for this reason that the introvert turns inwards to his or her thoughts and feelings.

When the typical state of arousal of the brain is considered over the course of an individual's development from childhood, it is not surprising that the low-aroused extravert develops social skills, hobbies and interests that depend upon noise, colour, excitement and risk and that the high-aroused introvert develops intellectual skills and interests and is wary of risky, complicated social situations; is, in other words, shy.

Human beings also possess a second nervous system that deals with automatic bodily functions like breathing, heart rate and digestion. This nervous system is responsive to hormones and is associated with emotional stability. Wherever a situation arousing anxiety occurs this nervous system is activated. Individuals vary in the extent that they perceive situations to be worrying and also in the extent to which, after worrying, their bodily functions return once again to normal levels. Consequently some individuals are much more prone to emotional instability than others. Once having become worried and responded with an increased heart rate and more rapid breathing, they remain worried and only gradually lose their anxieties. Others, by contrast, are rarely worried and, even when they are, quickly return to an even keel. This second nervous system, the autonomic nervous system, is associated with neuroticism or emotional stability.

There is a third personality dimension that Eysenck proposed and this is less well understood but may be associated with male hormones or with a particular part of the brain.[6] Eysenck described this dimension of personality as being expressed by the extent to which someone is uncaring, asocial, quirky, cold and impulsive. He called this dimension psychoticism or tough-mindedness.

These three dimensions, extraversion-introversion, neuroticism-stability and tough-tender mindedness, were isolated through the use of questionnaires and were shown by Eysenck to be independent of each other. In other words, someone's position on one dimension did not help to predict their position on either of the others. A person could be a neurotic introvert or a stable extravert or any combination of these dimensions with any scores on the psychoticism dimension. Moreover, these dimensions changed slightly and at different rates over time so that during the ageing process most people became less extraverted and less tough-minded. In addition, the mean scores of men and women, when studied in large populations, differed. Men tended to be more extravert, more stable and more tough-minded.

In a long series of studies over more than forty years Eysenck was able to devise items that related to these three underlying personality dimensions and to show how they helped to predict and understand human behaviour. For example, smokers tend to be extraverts looking for stimulation or neurotics looking for something to calm them, or to combine these needs as neurotic extraverts.[7] Extraverts tend to answer 'yes' to the question 'Can you get a party going?' while neurotics tend to answer 'yes' to the question 'Does your mood often go up and down?' Or, to take another example, drug users tend to be high on the psychoticism scale, as do pupils who play truant from school. Psychotics tend to answer 'no' to the question 'Would you feel very sorry for an animal caught in a trap?'

In this theory it is important to be aware that the three personality dimensions identified by Eysenck are not to be thought of as a

---

[6] Funder, 1997, 162.

[7] Eysenck, 1990, 168.

prison into which individuals are placed at birth. Rather, they are predispositions that tend, like abilities, to shape our lives. But also like abilities, we can capitalise on them or develop them in various directions. Someone with an artistic flair might become a painter, a graphic designer, a fashion expert or a landscape gardener. An extravert might become a disc jockey, a worker in public relations or a salesman – or any of a number of other jobs that require risk and interaction with people. In other words, the personality of an individual is able to carry forward many gifts and talents and, in this respect, is easily compatible with a Christian theology of personhood.

In addition to the three main dimensions, Eysenck's personality questionnaire also carries a lie scale. The lie scale was, as the name suggests, originally included as a method of checking that items were being honestly answered. The theory was that if you asked someone whether he or she had ever stolen anything (even a pin or a button), then the person who categorically denied this must be a liar. The assumption is that everyone has at some time or other taken something that does not belong to them. But the scale proved to function in interesting ways that were not anticipated by its constructors. When this was discovered a question arose about the interpretation of like scale scores. What did the lie scale really measure? Eysenck suggested that correlations between the lie scores and other personality dimensions gave a useful clue to choosing between different interpretations of the scale. A negative correlation between neuroticism and lie score would suggest a *tendency to deceive* since, when instructions to people filling in the questionnaire were given to 'fake good' or when groups were told their lie scores would be relevant to job applications, neuroticism scores declined and lie scores increased, so creating the necessary correlation. On the other hand, a negative correlation between extraversion and lie score would indicate a tendency to *social conformity* because introverts tend to be more socially conformist than extraverts.

These two main interpretations do not seem to function well with highly religious populations who often appear to score high on lie scales, that is, they denied wrongdoing. This denial, in the case of religious groups, particularly when there were no correlations between lie scale and neuroticism or extraversion, had to be explained in other ways. In the case of highly religious and morally honest subjects, it may be that the lie scale indicates that they are telling the truth: in this instance high lie scores would indicate *moral probity* because religious subjects really have not, for example, ever stolen anything. Alternatively, it may be that low lie scale scores indicate a lack of self-insight, a disposition to *immaturity*. The reason for this final interpretation is found in the tendency for lie scores to increase with age among most populations.[8]

Previous findings

A long series of studies has been carried out by Francis to discover the relationship between the different personality dimensions and attitude toward Christianity.[9] The main findings of the studies can be expressed quite simply: in the general population there is no significant relationship between extraversion and attitude toward Christianity or between neuroticism and attitude toward Christianity. There is, however, a consistent negative relationship between psychoticism and attitude toward Christianity. In other words people scoring high on the psychoticism scale (being quirky, uncaring, impulsive, insensitive, aggressive and lacking in empathy) are likely to have a negative attitude toward Christianity.

There is a question mark above the direction of causation here. Does a low score on the psychoticism dimension predispose people to accept Christianity, or is it that when people become Christians they lose some of their tough-minded traits under the impact of the gospel? If we accept Eysenck's view of personality that it is rooted in the physical constitution then the suggestion must be that the personality dimension is a 'given', something that is hard to change, and so this would favour the first explanation. Less tough-minded people are more likely to become Christians. This may well be so but the other explanation is also valid and it is reasonable to propose that, though less tough-minded people are predisposed to become Christians, when they do actually take this step then the work of the Holy Spirit within their lives begins to erase the callous and

---

[8] Francis, Pearson and Kay, 1983; Francis, Pearson and Kay, 1988.

[9] A summary is given in Kay and Francis, 1996. But see also Francis and Pearson, 1991, and Francis and Thomas, 1992.

aggressive corners of their personalities and so to make them even more tender-minded.

The lie scale also tends to show a consistent pattern of relationship with attitude toward Christianity. Previous findings usually indicate that people with a positive attitude toward Christianity also score high on the lie scale. At first sight this seems to suggest that Christians are bigger liars than other people! But, because of the different ways of interpreting the lie scale, a series of studies have been carried out with different versions of the scale and by inspecting the correlations between lie scale scores and those of the other personality dimensions. Two general conclusions have been drawn from this set of findings. The first is that highly religious people are, paradoxically, more likely to be truthful than others and that when they report their behaviour, they do so accurately. They really have not stolen anything from others, for instance and, though psychologists assume that people who deny stealing are in fact lying, in the case of highly religious people this is not so. The second conclusion, based on the fact that lie scores tend to go up as people grow older, is that the lie scale is a measure of maturity or self-insight.

This discussion about highly religious groups provides a transition into a consideration of personality findings about religious professionals – the clergy. While the findings reported above have generally been drawn from studies of young people of school age, investigations into Anglican clergy show them to be distinct from religious people generally. Studies have shown that male Anglican clergy are more likely to be introverted than is the case with the population as a whole or with religious people as a whole. Similar studies have shown that female Anglican clergy tend to be more extraverted than the general population and more tough-minded than is usual among women.[10] An interpretation of these findings with regard to Anglican female clergy is that, since they have had to fight for the right to ordination, it is the tougher minded women who have persisted in this struggle and that, as a consequence, the more tender-minded candidates have been weeded out in the selection process, or have simply declined to put themselves forward as ministry candidates. Male introverts, perhaps attracted by

---

[10] Francis, 1992.

the predictable liturgical structure of services, have been drawn to Anglican ministry.

There are also findings about neuroticism levels among religious professionals and highly committed religious groups and these tend to show that such groups are less neurotic than the population as a whole. The reason for this, it has been suggested, is that surety of religious faith produces stability in the personality.

What predictions might be made about Pentecostal ministers? A series of early studies on Pentecostals, dating back to the 1920s, was almost uniformly hostile to speaking with tongues.[11] They assumed that tongues-speakers were neurotic, mentally unstable or deranged in some other way. Even as late as the 1960s researchers could suggest that glossolalia is 'a dissociative expression of truncated personality development'.[12] Others, while they did not question the general normality of people who spoke tongues, argued that the whole experience was one arising from the suggestibility of tongues-speakers whose behaviour was learned rather than spontaneous or supernaturally inspired.[13]

More recent studies investigating these assertions found no difference on measures of suggestibility between those who spoke in tongues and those who did not and later, largely following the emergence of the charismatic movement, still other researchers considered speaking with tongues as positively healthy and a means by which anxiety might be reduced. None of the studies, however, focused specifically on Pentecostal ministers.

For this reason in the early 1990s a study of 364 Bible college students drawn from the Assemblies of God and Elim colleges was carried out.[14] The study compared the students both with the general population and with Anglican clergy. The study found that the students were different from the general population in several respects. With regard to the men, the finding was that Bible college students scored significantly lower on the neuroticism and psychoticism scales but significantly higher on the lie scale than the general population. With regard to the women they only differed

---

11 Mackie, 1921; Cutten, 1927; Vivier, 1960.

12 See Lapsley and Simpson, 1964.

13 Kildahl, 1972, 1975; Samarin, 1959, 1973.

14 Francis and Kay, 1995; Kay and Francis, 1995.

from the general population in scoring significantly lower on the neuroticism scale.

Both Pentecostal men and women training for ministry, then, recorded greater emotional stability than is found in the population generally. Such a finding supports the argument that speaking with tongues is associated with mental health rather than the contrary. It would be a mistake to characterise Pentecostals as being especially erratic or peculiar. In comparison with the general population Pentecostals are actually more stable, more reliable and less emotional than their counterparts outside the churches.

The male Pentecostal students scored lower on the psychoticism scale than the general population and this indicates that they are more tender-minded than their contemporaries and less antisocial. In this respect the Pentecostal students are similar to all those who are positive in their attitude toward Christianity and they support the finding that of the personality dimensions it is psychoticism which is fundamental to attitude toward Christianity. The female Pentecostal students were no different from the general population in their scores on the psychoticism dimension. They were neither higher nor lower. This suggests that female Pentecostal ministers may be, comparatively speaking, slightly tougher-minded than their male colleagues – a finding that would fit with the generally greater determination women need to show in order to secure a place within the ministry. But this difference between males and females on the psychoticism dimension has another implication.

The argument that glossolalia is a learned experience depends upon the notion of conditioning. Conditioning is a form of unconscious learning that may depend upon low psychoticism scores. In other words, the tender-minded person is more likely to be shaped by social conventions or church-related pressures. However, the difference between the male and female Pentecostal students suggests that speaking with tongues is not a learned behaviour – if it were, then we might expect both males and females to score lower on the psychoticism dimension, an indication of their openness to conditioning. After all, no one suggests that males and females come to speak with tongues in different ways. Thus the different levels of psychoticism among male and female Pentecostal students in relation to their respective population norms is an argument *against* a learning theory explanation of speaking with tongues.

The other difference between the male and female Bible college students is in relation to the lie scale scores. The men score higher than the general population norms on the lie scale but the women are no different. To find a suitable interpretation of the lie scale in respect of Pentecostal ministers a series of correlations was computed between the lie scale and the three other personality dimensions, gender and age.[15] The lie scale correlated negatively with extraversion, neuroticism and psychoticism and positively with gender and age. In other words, as age increased lie scale scores also increased, females tended to score higher on the lie scale than males, introverts than extraverts and tender-minded than tough-minded. The most satisfactory explanation for this set of correlations is that the lie scale indicates the tendency to social conformity. Extraverts are known to be less socially conforming than introverts and tough-minded people are also generally less socially conforming than those who are tender-minded. Females also are usually more inclined to conform to social norms than males while, in the case of these Pentecostal ministers, the older among them are more conformist than the younger.

No research has been carried out on Pentecostal ministers using the personality scales developed by Eysenck. For this reason the first set of figures presented below are given to allow Pentecostal ministers to be placed against the general population norms.

The means for the different age groups provided by the Eysenck manual for each of the four personality dimensions were compared with the means within this sample of Pentecostal ministers. Means were only calculated on males since there were insufficient females in the sample for a proper comparison. The Pentecostal ministers are, at every age level, less neurotic than the general population. This set of figures confirms the findings based upon Pentecostal Bible college students. Pentecostal ministers are generally very stable people. On the other hand, there are few differences between Pentecostal ministers and the general population on the psychoticism means and the lie scale means. Pentecostal ministers score slightly lower than the general population on the lie scale means in the oldest age cohort

---

15 With extraversion ($r = -.185$, $p < .000$), with neuroticism ($r = -.183$, $p < .000$), with psychoticism ($r = -.242$, $p < .000$), with gender (female scored high) ($r = .079$, $p < .018$) and with age ($r = .304$, $p < .000$).

Table 10.1 *T-tests comparing neuroticism and psychoticism scores between Pentecostals and the general population*

Age	EPQN mean	Pent mean	Pent Sd	t	Sig	EPQP mean	Pent mean	Pent Sd	t	Sig
20–29	9.81	7.74	4.31	3.14	.001	4.19	3.91	2.71	0.66	NS
30–39	9.33	7.65	4.86	3.22	.001	3.27	3.24	2.25	0.10	NS
40–49	9.17	6.80	4.77	4.42	.001	3.09	2.85	1.82	0.94	NS
50–59	10.12	6.61	4.69	4.96	.001	2.57	2.82	2.77	-0.70	NS
60–69	8.51	6.35	4.28	2.84	.001	2.56	2.60	3.06	-0.10	NS

but otherwise these groups are indistinguishable from each other, a finding that suggests Pentecostal ministers are generally similar to the general population on these two dimensions. On the extraversion dimension, Pentecostal ministers are, at three age levels, different from the general population: they are more extraverted. On the basis of these figures it is reasonable to say that Pentecostal ministers are usually stable extraverts who are neither more nor less tough-minded than the general male population. In this respect male Pentecostal ministers are distinct from Anglican ministers whose personality norms are distinguishable from the general population, being more introverted and more tender-minded.

So far as a comparison between the Bible college students and the ministers is concerned, the one finding that remains the same is to do with neuroticism. Explanations for the differences between the students and ministers are not difficult to find. The Bible college sample was no different from the general population in its extraversion scores but the young Pentecostal ministers sampled here are more extraverted than the general population, a finding suggesting that Pentecostals who go to study full-time at Bible colleges are slightly less extraverted than their contemporaries in full-time ministry. So far as the psychoticism levels are concerned the

Table 10.2 *T-tests comparing lie scale and extraversion scores between Pentecostals and the general population*

Age	EPQL mean	Pent mean	Pent Sd	t	Sig	EPQE mean	Pent mean	Pent Sd	t	Sig
20–29	6.50	6.09	2.59	1.02	NS	13.72	16.51	3.75	-4.82	.001
30–39	7.53	8.28	3.80	-1.61	NS	12.85	14.38	4.49	-3.20	.001
40–49	8.07	8.68	3.84	-1.41	NS	12.38	13.18	4.65	-1.49	NS
50–59	9.10	9.68	3.78	-1.08	NS	10.76	13.30	4.60	-3.66	.001
60–69	11.58	9.69	4.20	2.65	.001	10.44	11.60	4.99	-1.57	NS

Pentecostal ministers do in fact score lower than the general population; it is just that these differences are not statistically significant.

Having established where Pentecostal ministers stand in relation to the general population, it is reasonable to turn to specifically church-related issues. For instance, what expectations would this theory suggest about personality and church growth? Given that there is a connection between the charismatic activity of the minister and the minister's evangelistic activity and church growth (chapter nine), there ought to be a connection between extraverts and church growth. Extraverts will find it easier to engage in evangelistic activity involving speaking to new people about the church and about Christ and, presumably, extraverts will find it easier than introverts to express themselves through charismatic gifts like prophecy or prayer for healing. This prediction is simply based on the preference introverts have for a lower social profile.

What do the data show?

Before carrying out a series of crosstabulations the four personality dimensions were reduced to four separate categories. The frequency distribution for each personality dimensions was displayed and then approximately 25 per cent of ministers were selected to belong to each of the four levels chosen. Thus ministers scoring more than 18 on the extraversion scale are in the top category but ministers scoring more than 10 on the neuroticism scale are in the top category, even though both scales have the same range. This procedure simply breaks the sample up into roughly equal groups for each dimension but it says nothing about the relationship between this sample of Pentecostal ministers and the wider population as a whole.

Church growth and size by personality

Table 10.3 presents a crosstabulation of church growth by the extraversion of ministers. The most striking figures occur among the ministers who score low and high in extraversion. Approximately a third of ministers whose churches have grown by more than 11 per cent come in the top quarter of the extraversion

Table 10.3 *Church growth by extraversion*

Church Growth (%)	**Low %**	**2 %**	**3 %**	**High %**
none	34.5	28.4	21.6	15.5
1 to 5	25.4	34.2	24.4	15.9
6 to 10	14.2	33.3	25.7	26.8
11 to 20	12.8	29.1	23.3	34.9
21 to 30	25.6	11.6	27.9	34.9
more than 30	17.5	30.2	22.2	30.2

Chi-square 49.429, $p < .000$

distribution. Conversely, among the ministers whose churches have not grown at all about a third are in the low extraversion, or introvert, section of the scale. The distribution shows that there is a tendency for more extraverted ministers to be associated with churches which are growing most. It also shows that some introverted ministers are associated with church growth. There is no iron law connecting extraversion to church growth but simply a tendency for more extraverted ministers to see more church growth and less extraverted ministers to see less church growth. The chi-square statistic indicates the strength of the relationship.

The relationships between church growth and the dimensions of neuroticism and psychoticism were investigated but, in both cases, were found not to be significant.

Table 10.4 presents a crosstabulation of congregational size and extraversion. Again there is a clear association between size of church and extraversion. Over a third of ministers whose congregations

Table 10.4 *Sunday morning adult attendance by extraversion*

Sunday morning (adults)	**Low %**	**2 %**	**3 %**	**High %**
less than 25	35.1	33.1	17.5	14.3
25 to 49	22.1	32.4	22.5	23.0
50 to 74	21.8	36.6	22.5	19.0
75 to 99	20.3	26.6	26.6	26.6
100 to 149	14.5	26.3	34.2	25.0
150 to 199	17.2	27.6	32.8	22.4
200 to 249	9.7	19.4	45.2	25.8
250 to 299	8.3	33.3	12.5	45.8
300 to 349	16.7	25.0	33.3	25.0
350 and over	17.2	34.5	13.8	34.5

Chi-square 54.941, $p < .000$

amount to more than 350 members on Sunday morning are in the high extraversion category while the opposite is true of churches with less than 25 members. Again the figures demonstrate tendencies of association rather than unbreakable rules. There are introverted ministers in charge of large congregations but the big congregations are predominantly the province of more extraverted ministers. Again the chi-square value shows that the tendency is statistically significant.

Table 10.5 shows the connection between the lie scale and Sunday morning attendance. It is clear that ministers scoring high on the lie scale tend to be those with the smallest churches while ministers low on the lie scale tend to be those with the larger churches.

What do the lie scale figures indicate about personality and congregational size? Given that the lie scale within this population is indicative of social conformity, the best interpretation of this table is that ministers with large congregations are less socially conforming than ministers with smaller congregations. More than half of the ministers with congregations of 100 or more are in the lower categories of lie scale scores while the opposite is true for the smallest congregational band. Such a finding makes sense. Ministers of larger churches are likely to have to be decisive and authoritative characters who set trends rather than bowing to them and who, if anything, make other people conform to their wishes rather than the other way round.

Table 10.5 *Sunday morning adult attendance by lie scale*

Sunday morning (adults)	**Low** %	**2** %	**3** %	**High** %
less than 25	17.3	25.6	21.8	35.3
25 to 49	18.9	35.6	23.9	21.6
50 to 74	29.8	36.9	14.9	18.4
75 to 99	16.7	38.5	26.9	17.9
100 to 149	32.9	35.5	17.1	14.5
150 to 199	17.2	46.6	24.1	12.1
200 to 249	19.4	45.2	25.8	9.7
250 to 299	16.7	54.2	20.8	8.3
300 to 349	8.3	50.0	25.0	16.7
350 and over	10.3	51.7	24.1	13.8

Chi-square 57.759, $p < .000$

Charismatic activity and personality

Following the investigation into the association between church growth, church size and personality, statistics were computed to discover what relationships, if any, existed between the personality dimensions and the scale of charismatic activity. Table 10.6 shows that the relationship between ministerial charismatic activity and extraversion is significant and strong. Ministers scoring low on the extraversion scale tended to be less charismatically active than ministers scoring high. So, for instance, nearly 42 per cent of ministers in the lowest quarter of charismatic activity were also more introverted, while over 35 per cent of those in the high activity row are in the highest quarter of the extraversion scale. Again, there is no complete rigidity here since some introverted ministers are charismatically active and some extraverted ministers are charismatically inactive but the trend is clear and shown to be significant by the chi-square statistic.

No significant relationship was found between neuroticism and ministerial charismatic activity or between psychoticism and ministerial charismatic activity though, if the tests were made less rigorous, it was possible to see a trend coupling lower neuroticism and higher psychoticism with higher charismatic activity. What these findings suggest is simply that the more stable and slightly more tough-minded ministers are more willing to risk becoming involved with charismatic activity than those who are more tender-minded and more unstable.[16] A similar set of figures using

Table 10.6 *Minister's level of charismatic activity by extraversion*

Minister's charismatic activity	**Low** %	**2** %	**3** %	**High** %
Low activity	41.8	31.3	17.6	9.3
Low medium activity	23.0	31.1	22.0	23.9
High medium activity	18.9	31.1	28.1	21.9
High activity	9.5	29.0	26.0	35.5

Chi-square 74.207, $p < .000$

[16] If a one tail rather than a two tail significance is chosen, that is, if the direction of the relationship is predicted rather than being left open, it is legitimate to read the chi square of 16.542 (for neuroticism and charismatic activity) as being significant (p becomes $< .025$) and the chi square

the lie scale suggests that it is the less conformist ministers who are likely to become charismatically active.[17]

It is possible to see the Toronto blessing as a special case of charismatic activity, similar in its emphasis on the Holy Spirit but dissimilar in that its support in the biblical text is questionable and its position within Pentecostal tradition fluid. A series of items relating to the Toronto blessing were formed into a scale and these were crosstabulated with the personality dimensions.[18] The results are striking. There is a marked relationship between support for the Toronto blessing and the extraversion scale and a significant relationship between support for the Toronto blessing and the lie scale. Table 10.7 shows how this support works out. About a third (34 per cent) of ministers who are highly supportive of the Toronto experience are highly extraverted ministers while more than a third (38.9 per cent) of ministers more reserved about the Toronto experience are more introverted. A slightly less significant association was found between support for the Toronto experience and the lie scale, suggesting that it is the less socially conformist ministers who are supportive of the experience.[19]

On the basis of these figures it is possible to form an explanation for the Toronto blessing which, while it does not address the

Table 10.7 *Support for Toronto blessing by extraversion*

Support for Toronto blessing	**Low** %	**2** %	**3** %	**High** %
Low support	38.9	32.7	17.9	10.5
Low medium support	22.2	34.6	25.3	17.9
High medium support	17.2	28.3	24.7	29.8
High support	15.8	25.5	23.9	34.8

Chi-squared 60.003, $p < .000$

---

[16] (*continued*) of 16.047 (for psychoticism and charismatic activity) as being significant (p becomes $< .033$).

[17] Chi-square 15.774 and p becomes $< .035$.

[18] The four items were based on responses by the minister to a question asking how often in the past three months he or she has: 'seen people slain in the Spirit as a result of your ministry'; 'seen people laughing in the Spirit as a result of your ministry'; 'seen manifestations of the Toronto blessing as a result of your ministry' and 'given a positive testimony about the Toronto blessing'.

[19] Chi-square 23.395, $p < .005$

theological content of experience, does provide a way of understanding what was happening when the Toronto phenomena was at its height. More extraverted ministers were looking for spiritual experiences and, when they found these in the form of being 'slain in the Spirit' and/or being overcome with 'divine laughter' that were characteristic of the Toronto experience, they were happy to commend the experience to others. In this way the experience was received and transmitted through churches with extraverted ministers and only the more introverted church members were likely to stand aside from what was happening.

Healing and personality

Table 10.8 provides figures showing the relationship between personality and an answer to the question 'Have you been healed . . .?' Not unexpectedly there is a reasonable relationship between neuroticism and either mental healing or physical and mental healing together.[20] Physical healing on its own, however, is not related strongly to neuroticism and the largest group of ministers who have been healed physically are in the low neuroticism category. A similar picture emerges with ministers' scores on the psychoticism scale. It is the high scorers who are most likely to have been healed mentally and physically together.

Table 10.9 shows the relationship between views of divine healing and the lie scale. Here ministers scoring high on the lie scale are more likely to agree that divine healing will occur if the person's faith is great enough; and conversely ministers low on the lie scale are more likely either to disagree with this proposition or be

Table 10.8 *Type of healing by neuroticism*

Have you been healed?	**Low** %	**2** %	**3** %	**High** %
No	14.5	21.8	19.4	18.9
Physically	79.1	68.6	61.7	58.5
Mentally		.4	2.9	1.8
Physically and mentally	6.4	9.2	16.0	20.7

Chi-square 38.090, $p < .000$

[20] Type of healing and psychoticism were related by a chi-square of 18.730, $p < .028$.

Table 10.9 *View on divine healing by lie scale*

Divine healing occurs if a person's faith is great enough	**Low** %	**2** %	**3** %	**High** %
Disagree	24.9	38.2	18.2	18.7
Not Certain	18.6	36.7	26.0	18.6
Agree	9.1	29.7	26.3	34.9

Chi-square 41.992, $p < .000$

uncertain about it. Since we interpret a high score on the lie scale as an indication of social conformity, the table indicates that there is a sense in which ministers who take this position are those who have conformed to Pentecostal norms, whereas those who resist these norms are more inclined to take a position that does not hinge on the ill person's level of faith. It might be thought, since the older ministers are known to score high on the lie scale, that what table 10.9 really shows is the difference between older and younger ministers. Older ministers might be thought simply to have a more 'old-fashioned' Pentecostal view of divine healing. But this is not the whole story since, when a partial correlation controlling for age is computed between the lie scale and this view of divine healing, the resultant coefficient is still statistically significant ($r = .1577$, $p < .000$). Consequently, an element of social conformity appears to be one of the underlying reasons for holding a 'strong' view of divine healing. And this is confirmed by another partial correlation, this time between tough-mindedness and the item 'I believe modern medicine is a God-given blessing' ($r = -.0752$, $p < .029$); it is the tough-minded, those not inclined to be socially conformist, who reject modern medicine.

A series of computations were carried out to discover whether any significant relationship could be found between a belief in healing of the memories and personality dimensions but all the measures of association proved to be non-significant. In this area, at least, there is no effect of personality dimensions on beliefs about divine healing.

Non-charismatic beliefs and personality

In presenting the relationship between beliefs and personality it would be extremely time-consuming to provide a series of tables showing how the personality dimensions related to each of the items specifying particular clusters of belief. For example, three items were used to detect creationism and since there are four personality dimensions (including the lie scale) this would generate twelve different tables. Consequently, it makes more sense to present relationships between personality dimensions and different groups of beliefs through partial correlation coefficients which can be included within a passage of text much more easily. The partial correlation coefficients in all the cases quoted in this section have 'partialled out', or removed, the effects of denomination, age and gender. Consequently, the reported relationships between variables are not influenced by imbalances within the sample between the variant sizes of denominational contingents or by similar differential effects of gender and age.

The item 'I believe the Bible contains no verbal errors' correlated negatively with neuroticism ($r = -.1186$, $p < .001$), and positively with the lie scale ($r = .0686$, $p < .049$). The item 'I believe the Authorised Version of the Bible is the best one for Christians to use' correlated positively with neuroticism ($r = .0915$, $p < .009$) and with the lie scale ($r = .1437$, $p < .000$). The item 'I believe that God made the world in six 24-hour days' is not significantly associated with any of the personality variables. One way of interpreting these findings is to suggest that belief in verbal inerrancy is held by very stable individuals who are not socially conformist, while ministers who prefer the Authorised Version of the Bible are socially conformist and more inclined to worry than the rest of this ministerial population.

Beliefs about demons were only correlated with the psychoticism dimensions of the personality scale. All the other dimensions recorded non-significant correlations with the items in question. But a positive and significant correlation was found between 'I believe Christians are daily in conflict with demons' and psychoticism ($r = .0894$, $p < .009$), indicating that it is the tough-minded ministers who perceive their Christian lives as being ones of 'daily' conflict. This gives an insight into the world of the tough-minded individual. He or she perceives the world as a place of battle, of struggle, of victory and defeat. It is this perception of winners and losers that produces toughness in dealings with other people.

Beliefs about the ministry of women are only significant in relation to extraversion and the lie scale. In general, the introverted ministers were opposed to the ministry of women as were the high scorers on the lie scale, the more socially conforming ministers. In relation to the items 'Women should not baptise' ($r = -.0725$, $p < .037$), 'Women should wear headcoverings in public worship' ($r = -.1308$, $p < .000$) and 'Women should not be in charge of congregations' ($r = -.0786$, $p < .024$) the correlations with extraversion were all significant and negative, indicating that it is the introverted ministers who agree with these restrictions or conditions for women. The item on headcoverings was also positively correlated with the lie scale ($r = .1262$, $p < .000$) and in addition the lie scale correlated with the item 'Women should not preside at Holy Communion' ($r = .0800$, $p < .021$). This pattern of correlations suggest that it is the more socially conformist ministers – perhaps conforming to traditional Pentecostal beliefs or to the pressure of congregational hard-liners – who are inclined to place restrictions on women and that it is introverted ministers who may feel most threatened by female authority. Again, it is important to note that these correlations indicate trends only and cannot confidently be applied to every single individual. There will be introverted ministers who are extremely favourable towards the ministerial authority of women and there will be socially conforming ministers who are also supportive of the ministry of women. These correlations simply indicate tendencies within British Pentecostalism in the 1990s, but they also show that there *is* a detectable linkage between personality and certain doctrinal or social beliefs.

There are also correlations between personality dimensions and eschatological, or end time, doctrines. There are positive correlations between the item 'I do not believe the Bible makes the exact order of end time events clear', neuroticism ($r = .0715$, $p < .038$) and psychoticism ($r = .0740$, $p < .032$), and negative correlations with the lie scale ($r = -.1630$, $p < .000$). The lie scale, however, correlates positively with a belief in the rapture, 'I believe that the Church will be taken from the earth before the millennium (1000 year reign of Christ on earth)' ($r = .1102$, $p < .001$) and with 'I believe that there will be a millennium (a 1000 year reign of Christ on earth)' ($r = .0738$, $p < .03$). The psychoticism score is negative in relation to this last item ($r = -.0980$, $p < .004$). Tough-minded believers accept a lack of clarity within the Bible and also are disinclined to accept a belief in the millennium while the more conformist ministers dislike the notion of a lack of clarity within the Scripture and accept both the millennium and the traditional Pentecostal doctrine of a rapture. The more neurotic ministers are also more inclined to think that there is a lack of clarity within Scripture.

Holiness code and personality

An investigation of the holiness code and personality factors showed that the ministers most likely to support the code were introverted and socially conformist. A series of negative correlations with extraversion and of positive correlations with the lie scale point firmly in this direction. For example, the item 'Christians should not engage in sporting activities on Sundays' showed a negative correlation with extraversion ($r = -.0912$, $p < .008$) and a positive correlation with the lie scale ($r = .1401$, $p < .000$). This pattern was repeated for the item 'Christians should not watch television on Sundays', for 'Christians should not attend the cinema' and 'Christians should not take part in social dancing'. The item, 'Christians should not drink alcoholic beverages' only correlated with the lie scale ($r = .1872$, $p < .000$) as did 'Christians should not smoke' ($r = .0800$, $p < .020$). These correlations are self-explanatory. Ministers most likely to find social and sporting activities unpleasant or boring are also most likely to accept the ban on them. The linkage here with social conformity suggests that the holiness code was prevalent within Pentecostal churches during the period when the social attitudes of these ministers were formed. Of course, it is important to state that introverted ministers are not hypocritical in their support for a holiness code but, clearly, such ministers will find this aspect of the code easier to observe than extraverted ministers who are much more attracted to all kinds of social activity.

Views on divorce and remarriage also appeared to be slightly influenced by personality factors. It is the more introverted ministers who agree with the item 'Divorce prior to conversion should prevent ordination' ($r = -.0811$, $p < .017$) and the more socially conformist ministers who agree that 'A minister who divorces before ordination and remarries after ordination should not continue to serve as a minister' ($r = .0768$, $p < .026$). Certainly agreement with the first of these items is difficult to explain theologically and is not supported by the official position of the Pentecostal denominations to which these ministers belong. Yet the most introverted ministers, whatever their official denominational position, are inclined to support this rigorous ban.

Leaving ministry and personality

Partial correlations were calculated for the four different personality dimensions and answers to the question, 'Have you, since ordination, ever considered leaving the ministry?'. Ministers could answer 'no', 'once or twice', 'several times' or 'frequently'. Each of these answers was coded on a range where 'no' was scored 1 and 'frequently' was scored 4. There was no significant correlation between extraversion and thoughts about leaving the ministry. There was, however, a positive and significant correlation between neuroticism and thoughts about leaving the ministry ($r = .2294$, $p < .000$). The positive correlation indicates that as neuroticism increases so thoughts of leaving the ministry increase significantly. This is intuitively likely: unstable ministers are prone to intense inner emotional battles about their professional lives. The relationship between the lie scale and thoughts of leaving the ministry is negative, suggesting that less socially conforming ministers have more frequent thoughts about leaving the ministry – again an apt scenario ($r = -.1310$, $p < .000$). Two main conclusions may be drawn from this set of figures. The first is that extraversion is the one personality dimension that is unrelated to leaving the ministry. Extraverts and introverts are equally likely either to think about leaving the ministry or not to think about leaving the ministry. The second is that personality *is* an important factor in predisposing Pentecostal ministers to think about leaving the ministry.

Table 10.10 provides an example of the relationship between thoughts of leaving the ministry and personality dimensions. The crosstabulation indicates that of the ministers who have frequently thought of leaving the ministry nearly two-thirds (59.3 per cent) are in the top quarter of scorers on the neuroticism scale. Conversely, it indicates that only 3.7 per cent of ministers in the bottom quarter of

Table 10.10 *Have you ever considered leaving the ministry by neuroticism*

Have you ever considered leaving the ministry?	**Low** %	**2** %	**3** %	**High** %
No	23.6	36.0	20.2	20.2
Once or twice	19.4	31.4	19.8	29.3
Several times	14.3	22.3	18.8	44.6
Frequently	3.7	14.8	22.2	59.3

Chi-square 47.754, $p < .000$

scorers on the neuroticism scale have frequently thought of leaving the ministry.

Satisfaction and personality

When personality variables were correlated with the satisfaction scale (chapter eight), extraverted ministers were easily the most likely to find satisfaction within Pentecostal ministry.[21] The correlation itself was high ($r = .1559$, $p < .000$) and when analysis of variance was computed, the contrast between the satisfaction levels of extraverted ministers compared with introverted ministers were easy to see, as table 10.11 shows. Not only are Pentecostal ministers generally more extraverted than the population as a whole but also the more extraverted among these ministers are more satisfied with their work. In many ways this is not at all surprising. Pentecostal pastors are constantly involved in the lives of other people, whether visiting, organising meetings, attending committees, preaching, praying for those who are ill, taking Sunday School classes and so on. In other words, Pentecostal ministers are usually not attracted to the quiet world of books or administration and a visit to the annual conferences of most Pentecostal denominations would offer noisy occasions for worship, lengthy and often loud sermons and a dawn-to-dusk round of committees or seminars. Extraversion is essential for survival!

Satisfaction for tough-minded ministers is more difficult to obtain ($r = -.0707$, $p < .049$). The tough-minded minister as defined by the Eysenck personality scale is one whose enjoyment of intimate personal relations is limited. He or she is usually

[21] Again a partial correlation was used, removing the effects of age, gender and denomination.

Table 10.11 *Satisfaction by extraversion levels*

Extraversion	Satisfaction mean	Satisfaction sd
Low	84.59	16.99
Low medium	88.62	17.70
High medium	91.47	16.29
High	90.91	17.15

Chi-squared 6.088, $p < .000$

anti-social and quirky, qualities which tend to put other people off. The correlation here shows that the more tough-minded ministers are, the less satisfied they are with their overall ministerial role.

More conformist ministers, by contrast, are likely to report satisfaction ($r = .0861$, $p < .017$). These ministers are willing to accept the obligations placed upon them by their congregations or by others and, learning to do this, find satisfaction in the life of service to which they are drawn. The minister who conforms is likely to avoid conflict and criticism but, drawing upon the resources of the New Testament, to feel that his or her duty is to walk a path that avoids personal gain or glory. The Christian doctrine of discipleship is one that emphasises the need to follow Christ by denying oneself.

The satisfaction scale is made up of assessment of satisfaction on twenty different ministerial roles but its items can be taken individually to see the relationship between personality and satisfaction in respect of the five ministry gifts of apostle, prophet, evangelist, pastor and teacher. Partial correlations between satisfaction in these roles and the four personality dimensions show extraverts are most satisfied with the roles of apostle ($r = .1572$, $p < .000$), evangelist ($r = .1785$, $p < .000$) and prophet ($r = .1444$, $p < .000$) and that introverts are most satisfied with the role of teacher ($r = -.1121$, $p < .002$). More neurotic or unstable ministers report no significant levels of satisfaction with any of the five ministry gifts. Perhaps it is no wonder that, in general, Pentecostal ministers are extremely stable! Tender-minded, or low scorers on the psychoticism scale, find satisfaction in pastoring ($r = -.1472$, $p < .000$) and teaching ($r = -.0773$, $p < .030$). More socially conformist ministers find satisfaction in pastoring ($r = .0903$, $p < .011$).

Ministry gifts and personality

When desires and obligations concerning the five ministry gifts are inspected by partial correlation coefficients in relation to the four personality dimensions, the results show that extraverts *want* to exercise the ministries of apostle ($r = .1153$, $p < .001$), evangelist ($r = .1924$, $p < .000$) and prophet ($r = .0930$, $p < .008$) and that introverts are attracted to the ministry of a teacher ($r = -.1210$, $p < .001$). The most striking correlation is between extraversion and desire to be an evangelist, which immediately suggests that it is those ministers who are most inclined to seek stimulus and change who find that evangelism is naturally appealing to them. Conversely, extraverts are not attracted to the ministry of the teacher, presumably because they see it as being too book-bound.

The more neurotic ministers have no particular leaning one way or another in relation to these five ministry gifts. But the high psychoticism scoring, or tough-minded, ministers are not attracted to the ministry of pastor ($r = -.1321$, $p < .000$) or teacher ($r = -.0782$, $p < .027$). The negative correlations shown here indicate that pastoring is attractive to tender-minded ministers. This corresponds with findings reported earlier where pastoring is a ministry that especially appeals to ministers who want to be involved in the lives of other people and in caring for them. Similarly, it is the tender-minded who are more attracted to teaching than the tough-minded. In respect of social conformity (or the lie scale), the correlations show that those who are most conformist are also most attracted to the work of a pastor ($r = .0988$, $p < .005$). And, surprisingly, the social conformist also indicates that he or she wants to work as an apostle ($r = .0760$, $p < .031$).

There is an interesting pattern between the personality dimensions and the sense of *obligation* ministers have about fulfilling the five ministerial roles. It is reasonable to deduce that the happiest ministers are going to be those whose desire for particular ministerial roles corresponds exactly with the obligations they feel towards the fulfilling of those roles. Among the extraverts this match occurs in the sense of obligation felt towards the roles of apostle, evangelist and prophet, suggesting that extraverts are not unduly pressured to perform roles they do not want. By contrast, the higher neuroticism scorers feel an obligation to perform two of the roles they do not wish to perform. High neuroticism scorers feel expected to be both evangelists ($r = .0712, p < .043$) and teachers ($r = .0809, p < .022$). This finding points to the kind of anxieties to which high neuroticism scorers are prone: they are sensitive to obligations, real or imagined, and then fret about whether or not they should fulfil them. The tender-minded ministers react to social obligations differently and there is no role they feel obliged to fulfil that they do not want to fulfil. Finally, the social conformists, like the more neurotic ministers, feel expected to fulfil more roles than they want and, in this instance, it is the role of the evangelist that burdens them most ($r = .0750, p < .033$).

In summary, there is a very good match between desire and expectation among extraverted ministers, but the more neurotic ministers and the more socially conformist ministers feel expected to perform more roles than they want to perform. By contrast the tender-minded ministers want to perform more roles than they feel expected to perform. These findings are explicable in the light of personality theory: extraverts want to be involved with people; introverts want to be involved with study and scholarship; the tender-minded want to be responsive to people's needs and social conformists shape their lives to meet the expectations of others. This suggests that there is a linkage, independent of vocation, between personality and ministerial role.

Mysticism and personality

Mysticism has been a subject of research ever since William James' classic book, first published in 1902, *The Varieties of Religious Experience*. Subsequent scholars have modified and developed James' work by clarifying the concept of mysticism and by developing scales by which its various types can be measured. In essence, though, mysticism is seen as a sense of unity where the objects of consciousness are brought together into a striking harmony and, in this, mysticism is the opposite of analysis which breaks everything down into simple, constituent parts and tries to discover their intricate inter-relations.[22]

---

[22] Russell, 1918.

Two kinds of mysticism have been identified.[23] The first is that of an overwhelming experience of unity within the world such that the person involved feels absorbed, or at one with all things, sometimes feeling as if everything is conscious, or united in a single whole, and sometimes feeling during this experience that time and space are meaningless. This kind of experience is classified as 'extravertive mysticism' because it is orientated to the outer world, often a world of nature where all living things plus the landscape, and sometimes the sky and stars, are brought into the consciousness of the mystic.

The second kind of mysticism is an experience of unity devoid of perception. It is unity without image, almost a unity of thought itself, sometimes described as a 'pure conscious experience' and because it does not relate to the external world is called 'introvertive mysticism'.

Many scholars have contrasted mystical experience with numinous experience. A numinous experience is an awareness of someone or something holy, other and beyond nature. The experience of Moses at the burning bush illustrates the point exactly. After seeing and coming close to the bush, Moses experienced the power and presence of the God of Israel but this experience was not one that could be called mystical. He did not feel united with the bush or the landscape or even with God. On the contrary, God was beyond him and the bush and the landscape; able to speak to him quite apart from any of these things, persuading him to do what he had no desire to do by commanding him to return to Egypt.

Mystical and numinous experience are sometimes placed at two ends of a spectrum. Mystical experience is a sense of awesome unity while numinous experience is a sense of awesome presence. Mystical experience may be fundamentally impersonal while numinous experience may result in an apprehension of the personal nature of God.[24] However, although the two kinds of experience can be separated, and although mystical experience can itself be divided into two categories, there is an underlying similarity between all three of these conceptually diverse entanglements with reality; they belong on the same spectrum.

---

23 Hood, Spilka, Hunsberger and Gorsuch, 1996, 225.
24 Hood, Spilka, Hunsberger and Gorsuch, 1996, 226.

Research carried out by survey in 1978 in England and Wales has shown how widespread these types of experience are. Hay and Morisy found that 36.4 per cent of a national sample in Britain could answer 'yes' to a question about remembering being 'aware of or influenced by a presence or power, whether you called it God or not, which is different from your everyday self?' – the question being asked in this way so as to include both mystical and numinous experiences.[25] An advertisement placed in the national press by the Alister Hardy Centre elicited over 3000 reports of religious experience of one kind or another within the British population and of these reports 5.6 per cent were mystical and 12.3 per cent numinous. In a sample of pupils from selected schools and universities, considerably more than half reported feelings of being at one with nature and the universe.[26]

Attempts to relate disposition towards mystical or numinous experiences and personality have been limited and some of the best conducted tests have simply been designed to show that a propensity for unusual experiences need not be related to mental instability or pathology.[27] Indeed, it has been argued that religious experiences are important because they are actually signs of mental health or an aid to mental health.[28] One of the most persuasive findings of this kind concerns the association between mystical experience and well-being or, in Maslow's terminology, self-actualisation. In Maslow's work human needs are arranged into a hierarchy, at the top of which is self-actualisation. It is characteristic of healthy and creative individuals who have an accurate perception and acceptance of reality, spontaneity, freshness of appreciation, creativity in everyday activities, relative detachment from immediate physical social conditions, satisfying interpersonal relations, sympathy for other human beings, a democratic way of working, an ability to concentrate on problems lying outside themselves and clear ethical standards.[29] It refers to the ability to express the personality effectively but without self-consciousness or selfishness.

---

25 Wulff, 1991, 505.

26 Quoted in Hood, Spilka, Hunsberger and Gorsuch, 1996, 234.

27 Hood, Spilka, Hunsberger and Gorsuch, 1996, 261.

28 Hood, Spilka, Hunsberger and Gorsuch, 1996, 241; Wulff, 1991, 505; Beit-Hallahmi and Argyle,1997, 86.

29 Wulff, 1991, 603.

The data derived from the Pentecostal ministers in the sample enabled a relationship between mystical experience and personality to be investigated. Again, partial correlation coefficients (partialling out age, denomination and gender) were calculated between the four personality dimensions and scores on the mysticism scale detailed in chapter eight. Only extraversion proved to be significantly related to mysticism ($r = .1651$, $p < .000$), suggesting that the kind of mystical experience enjoyed by these ministers was one of unity with the church, nature and ultimately God. In other words, extraverts experience an extravertive mysticism that is not directly numinous though through holy communion and gospel hymns – items on the scale – they feel themselves drawing closer to God.

The absence of any correlation between neuroticism, psychoticism, the lie scale and mystical experience is itself informative. Neither stability nor instability, neither tough-mindedness nor tender-mindedness, neither social conformity nor social non-conformity is associated in these Pentecostal ministers with mystical experience. The one relevant dimension is extraversion and it is arguable that mystical experience, this apprehension of wholeness or harmony, is the basis for creative self-expression that may lead to charismatic gifts or engagement with the needs of others (see the next section). Moreover this expression of extraversion can be interpreted as a type of self-actualisation.[30]

The high mean score on the mysticism scale (33.34) and the relatively low dispersion of scores (sd 6.4) testifies to the general openness to such experience among Pentecostal ministers, a finding compatible with surprisingly widespread reports of religious or mystical experience in the population as a whole mentioned earlier.

Compassionate social action and personality

The items relating to compassionate social action reported on individually in chapter eight were combined to form a very satisfactory scale (table 10.12). This scale was then correlated with the four personality dimensions, partialling out, as before, age, gender and denomination. Compassionate social action correlated strongly and significantly with extraversion ($r = .1058$, $p < .002$), slightly less

---

[30] Kay, 2000b.

Table 10.12 *Compassionate social action scale*

My church ought to be fully involved in giving practical help to . . .	**Item rest of test (r)**
the poor	.77
the elderly	.80
unmarried mothers	.85
drug addicts	.85
AIDS sufferers	.79
the unemployed	.84
ethnic minorities	.78

Alpha .9421

strongly with neuroticism ($r = .0768$, $p < .025$), negatively with the lie scale ($r = -.0792$, $p < .021$) and not at all with psychoticism. This pattern of figures indicates that the extraverted ministers are those most likely to lead their churches in a direction of compassionate social action and that more neurotic ministers are also responsive to human need outside the church and feel that they should ensure that their congregations are committed to alleviating suffering. The lie score suggests that it is the less conformist ministers who are most inclined to see compassionate social action as a priority. Presumably socially conformist ministers are disposed to hear the voices of congregational members rather than deprived or marginalised members of the secular community. We can put this another way by saying that introverted and socially conformist ministers are unlikely to call their congregations to ease general human suffering.

Conclusion

Extraverts prosper within the Pentecostal environment. They tend to be more satisfied and more successful in terms of church growth, more likely to exercise spiritual gifts, less wedded to the old holiness code, more attracted to the five main ministry gifts mentioned in Ephesians 4 and more likely to be open to mystical experience. They are less likely than neurotics to think about leaving ministry and they are more inclined to lead their churches to compassionate social action.

What is surprising about the correlations and associations discussed in this chapter is how widely personality theory can be applied to ministerial life. Nearly every aspect can be covered in a way that suggests, as personality theorists have often argued, that personality may be more important than ability. In Pentecostal preaching the characteristic emphasis has been on the gifts of the Spirit but the more thoughtful expositors (like Donald Gee) also give attention to the fruit of the Spirit (Galatians 5.22) – the love, joy, peace, patience and forbearance of the mature Christian, and all these qualities are obviously related to personality. Or, to put this another way, the New Testament itself is concerned with the personality of Christians as much as it is concerned with their gifting and empowerment. Modern personality theory expands this concern since the qualities of love and joy, for instance, may simply be differently expressed by extraverts. The extravert and introvert both feel joy but, whereas the extravert will communicate this boisterously to others, the introvert will be quietly happy.

These findings also provide evidence on which a form of careers guidance for Pentecostal ministers might be offered. Again, to prevent misunderstanding it is important to stress that such guidance ought not to be seen as obstructive or rigid, and there will be some Pentecostal ministers who will hate the idea of an apparently natural method by which spiritual guidance may be offered. But consider the parallel with musical ministry: it would be foolish to advise a person who was tone deaf to become a worship leader in a church. Similarly, the suggestion these data support is that ministers who are unhappy in various aspects of their work may find help through a discovery of their own personality profiles. More introverted ministers may well be more successful in administrative tasks where they have failed in evangelism. The problem, however, with this kind of approach is that ministers who feel an aversion to one kind of work may never make themselves face challenges that could cause them to grow in the extent of their capability. The introvert who finds some Sunday School work difficult ought not to be encouraged simply to give this up straight away; similarly the extravert who dislikes sitting quietly to read ought not to be discouraged from wrestling with intellectual difficulties. The knowledge of personality theory provides insight; it is one further factor to consider in the placement of round pegs in round holes and square pegs in square holes.

Perhaps more strikingly these data also provide a way of explaining why it is that there may be disagreement between ministers over moral guidelines. Introverted ministers appear to be those most willing to embrace restrictive holiness practices. Such practices, while in some cases they may find support from the New Testament, are not always defensible in this way. Introverted ministers therefore need to ask themselves whether the banning of a particular practice is being carried out because this is in line with New Testament teaching or because it is in line with their own preferences. Equally, extraverts need to ask themselves whether their desire for social activity may cause them to overlook New Testament precepts. The knowledge of personality theory thus helps to bring more clearly into focus the teaching of the New Testament itself.

11

Burnout

Overview

Approximately 10 per cent of Pentecostal ministers may be in danger of burnout. This chapter explores the factors associated with it and the strategies Pentecostal ministers can adopt to avoid or reduce it.

Burnout

The concept of burnout goes back probably to the 1961 novel by Graham Greene, *A Burnt-out Case*, though it may well have its origins even earlier in the notion of 'cracking up' exemplified by the novelist Scott Fitzgerald.[1] The general idea is simple enough. Men or women are burnt out when they become prematurely old, unable to work and incapable of proper personal relationships. The victim of burnout is a little different from the victim of a nervous breakdown since in burnout there is often no obvious moment of crisis and, indeed, whereas the victim of a nervous breakdown is unable to work at all this is not necessarily the case where burnout is concerned. The burnt out person simply goes through the motions of work.

The other distinguishing mark of burnout is that its victims often begin as highly talented and promising people. They enthusiastically give more to their job than they strictly need to and are creative in the way they tackle problems. When burnout is reached, and it may be a condition carried by a slow-burning fuse,

---

[1] Fichter, 1996.

enthusiasm, energy and creativity disappear. One of the most systematic and extensive writers on the subject is Christina Maslach who has analysed the experience of burnout in relation to work as being characterised by three themes: an erosion of engagement with the job; an erosion of emotions; a problem of fit between the person and the job.[2]

Erosion of the emotions is one of the hallmarks of burnout. There is a sense of frustration, even anger and this fuels negative reactions that may lead to aggression and meanness. These negative emotions can also lead to lack of self-esteem and anxiety about working conditions and the future. The presence of negative emotions about work are unhelpful but the absence of positive emotions prevents creativity or the generation of enthusiasm. Negative emotions also damage relationships by producing rudeness, sarcasm, criticism and irritation and, worse still, they can affect the burnt out person's sense of judgement of people and events.

These negative emotions then result in a failure to fit into the world of work. The burnt out person refuses to adapt, to change his or her ways, to respond to new challenges and fails to take advantage of any opportunities that may arise. This failure to adapt leads in a vicious circle to further negative emotions.

Burnout can then be described as having three separate components each of which can be measured on a scale. First, there is *emotional exhaustion* that robs the burnt out person of satisfaction with work and an ability to feel relaxed and confident. Second, there is a *depersonalisation* that makes the victim of burnout lacking in concern for the predicaments and needs of those for whom they have a professional care. For example, burnt out people might agree that their ministry is hardening them emotionally or that they can not really be bothered with the problems of other people or that they are becoming impatient with those who confront them day by day. Thirdly, there is a *lack of personal accomplishment*. The burnt out minister feels that nothing is being achieved, that his or her ministry is not making any positive impact upon the church or the community. The first two scales have been tested against alternative measures of burnout and found to be in agreement with them.[3]

---

[2] Maslach and Leiter, 1997, 23.

[3] Corcoran, 1995, found convergent validity.

Causes of burnout

Burnout can affect young school teachers, for example, who at the start of their careers bring with them dedication to pupils and interest in the curriculum but who, after a while, having put in long hours and agreed to do all kinds of extras over and above the strict requirements of the job, feel undervalued, exhausted, cynical and determined to do no more than is strictly necessary to keep getting paid. According to Maslach's analysis burnout in the case of a young school teacher begins with work overload but this is made worse by lack of control over the policies and practices of teaching that prevent the teacher taking any kind of evasive action to improve her situation. Following this there is a feeling of insufficient reward for all the work that has been done and this lack of recognition leads to the belief that there is an inherent unfairness in the system ('Why am I working so hard, doing so much, and yet getting so little in return?'). This, in turn, leads to a sense of a breakdown of community as the teacher becomes alienated from other members of staff or from parents. Lastly, there is a growing value conflict between what the teacher is trying to achieve in the classroom and the wearisome extra duties being imposed by the school.

Taking these factors one at a time, it is evident that workload in the caring professions (such as teaching, nursing, social services) can increase in several ways. For instance, it can become more intense as more people have to be dealt with in a shorter space of time, because rest gaps are reduced or simply as more complex roles – being simultaneously a counsellor, preacher and fund-raiser, perhaps – have to be undertaken. If any or all of these changes to the nature of the job occur then workload will become heavier.

Lack of control is relative. No one has complete control over a working environment but as demands are made upon the minister in the workplace, either from the denomination or from the congregation, the minister may feel unable to 'get a grip' on the schedule of the week. His or her diary is filled without apparently offering an opportunity to control the flow of events, the endless meetings with people or the pressures of administration.

Insufficient reward is usually translated into economic terms. Salaries for most Pentecostal ministers remain below what they might hope to earn in secular employment (chapter seven). However, it is unnecessary to think of rewards entirely in cash terms and the most dangerous failure of reward occurs when ministers feel that pastoral work itself is without value. Once intrinsic satisfaction disappears ministers do not easily feel compensated by slight increases in pay.

The breakdown of community, for the Pentecostal minister, is one of the final steps in a process of disintegration. Once personal relationships and teamwork disappear and ministers find themselves involved in factions and feuds, then burnout is desperately close.

The impression that the world of work is unfair can nag the minister. 'Why should Pastor X enjoy all the advantages of a successful church when I struggle here unrecognised and unrewarded? Why should I work so hard and receive so little when others work less hard and receive more?' These searching questions can undermine the faith of the minister who begins his or her vocation with bright hopes and an idealistic willingness to make financial sacrifices.

Finally, conflicting values occur when the minister wishes to take the church in one direction, perhaps towards greater openness or to missions or to a new building, and the congregation is unwilling to move. But other examples can occur where the minister finds one style of leadership or worship preferable but powerful members of the congregation prefer something contrary. These conflicts of values can lead to the breakdown of community and so compound the problem. However, on another level, changes in the demands at work may also lead to 'role ambiguity', another form of value conflict, where the minister is unable to decide which value to prioritise and therefore which role to emphasise. In other words, the minister becomes unsure how to do his or her job.

What do the data show?

Candidates for burnout are aware that their working lives are going wrong and can adopt two basic strategies to put matters right. They may try palliative measures and look for emotional, social or intellectual support. In the research literature some attention has been given to warding off or preventing burnout through the social support of colleagues or family.[4] Alternatively, changes to the working environment can be made to remove the organisational causes of burnout but, of course, this may be impossible because one of the causes of burnout stems precisely from lack of control over the situation at work.

These two responses sidestep the issue of whether burnout is somehow the responsibility of the person who becomes burnt out.[5] Maslach and Leiter take the view that the fault lies squarely with the managers of working environments[6] but studies linking burnout with personality point the other way.[7] Citing a range of longitudinal studies, Maslach and Schaufeli noted that the chronic nature of burnout supports the idea that personality is implicated. Whereas job conditions change, personality remains relatively stable.

The three Maslach scales help formulate an explanation of the burnout process. Burnout may be seen as 'progressing from emotional exhaustion to depersonalisation to lack of personal accomplishment'.[8] In other words, emotional exhaustion occurs first and leads to depersonalisation which, in turn, prevents or diminishes personal accomplishment. On the other hand, the inner dynamics may function differently. Depersonalisation may be either a symptom of burnout or a coping mechanism to prevent burnout. Thinking about the problem in this way, depersonalisation can be seen as an adopted defence mechanism to prevent further emotional exhaustion.[9] Whether or not this is the case, Maslach and Schaufeli point out that emotional exhaustion is related to depression but distinct from it, and is also related to depersonalisation and lack of personal accomplishment but in a different way from depression.[10] Nevertheless, there is general agreement that emotional exhaustion

---

[4] E.g. Greenglass, Fiksenbaum and Burke, 1995.

[5] Dewe, 1996.

[6] This is the main theme of Maslach and Leiter, 1997.

[7] Though both Maslach and Schaufeli, 1993, and Dolan, 1993, agree that job and organisation are more strongly related to burnout than personality.

[8] Corcoran, 1995.

[9] Wallace and Brinkerhoff, 1991.

[10] Maslach and Schaufeli, 1993.

is at the heart of the burnout concept, and this explains its direct relevance to the caring professions.[11]

The ostensible conditions of Pentecostal ministers vary enormously. Some look after large congregations, others have very few in their churches; some work alone, others as part of a team. Where they are similar, however, is in their dependence on their congregations for financial support. There is little centralised funding for ministerial stipends (apart from within the Apostolic Church and in special circumstances in the others) with the result that ministers whose congregations are small tend to be poorly paid and to suffer the lack of self-esteem and worry that such conditions bring. There is a constant incentive to increase congregational size. Ministers in larger congregations may have no concerns about their own living standards but may instead be in such great pastoral demand that they risk overwork. Thus the possibility of burnout exists whatever the size of a congregation. In addition, ministers who began their lives with small congregations and who eventually manage to build their congregations to a financially viable size may continue the work routines they established in youth; they may work harder than they need to by force of habit.

Taken together these considerations suggest burnout would be most prevalent among more introverted and more neurotic ministers and that the effects of burnout would be seen in emotional exhaustion and in a consequent lack of personal accomplishment. Lack of personal accomplishment in Pentecostal ministers would readily translate into church growth. Ministers whose churches failed to grow would feel they had accomplished less than those whose churches flourished numerically. Because of similar work patterns it is difficult to predict the effects of the minister's age on his or her burnout. Support from a ministry team might be expected to reduce burnout levels.

Table 11.1 shows the intercorrelations between the three burnout scales. Although they belong together because of the strong intercorrelations, they are also meaningfully distinct. Emotional exhaustion correlates most highly with depersonalisation, suggesting that if there is a causal linkage between the operation of different facets of burnout, emotional exhaustion leads most strongly to

[11] Crandall and Perrewé, 1995.

Table 11.1 *Pearson correlations between burnout scales*

	Emotional exhaustion	Lack of personal accomplishment
Depersonalisation	.613	.440
P<	.000	.000
Emotional exhaustion		.438
P<		.000

depersonalisation. Depersonalisation then leads to lack of personal accomplishment, a path proposed above.

Table 11.2 shows the psychometric properties of the three different scales. The means are similar to each other and the alpha coefficients are high in each case, showing the scales perform satisfactorily.

Table 11.3 provides comparisons between males and females on the scales and shows that, while the sexes are similar in their recording of depersonalisation and emotional exhaustion, the females demonstrate a significantly higher feeling of personal accomplishment than the males.

Table 11.4 provides comparisons between four age groups within the sample (as in previous tables of this kind the four age categories have been selected so as to divide the sample into four groups of roughly equal size). The table shows that depersonalisation is significantly higher among the younger ministers and that there is a gradual decline in depersonalisation as ministers grow older. This is one of the advantages of ageing! Conversely, however, it indicates the pressures under which young ministers operate. A similarly dangerously significant pattern is observed with regard to emotional exhaustion. Again the most emotionally exhausted are the younger ministers and the least emotionally exhausted are the older ministers. Some of the younger ministers, many of them with young families and some of them poorly paid, feel themselves to be emotionally spent. These men and women are most at risk from burnout. Finally, lack of personal accomplishment is unrelated to age. The young ministers, despite their levels of

Table 11.2 *Means, standard deviations and reliability coefficients of burnout scales*

Maslach Scales	Mean	Sd	Alpha
Emotional exhaustion	20.03	5.59	.8387
Depersonalisation	20.77	4.64	.7885
Lack of personal accomplishment	21.24	3.78	.7446

Table 11.3 *Gender differences on burnout scales*

Maslach Scales	Gender	Mean	Sd	F	P
Depersonalisation	Male	20.82	4.82		
	Female	18.86	4.15	3.426	NS
Emotional exhaustion	Male	21.99	5.64		
	Female	22.26	4.63	.045	NS
Lack of personal accomplishment	Male	21.22	3.73		
	Female	18.60	4.10	9.600	.002

exhaustion and depersonalisation, are similar to the older ministers in their evaluation of their personal accomplishments.

In addition to the exploration of gender and age differences in respect of the burnout scales, computations were also carried out to look for differences between the four Pentecostal denominations. Church of God ministers demonstrated a slightly but significantly greater sense of personal accomplishment than the other three denominations.[12]

Table 11.4 *Age differences on burnout scales*

Maslach Scales	Age	Mean	Sd	F	P
Depersonalisation	Under 39	21.77	5.00		
	40–49	21.01	4.62		
	50–54	20.93	4.69		
	55+	19.60	4.63	8.74	.000
Emotional exhaustion	Under 39	23.01	5.83		
	40–49	22.64	5.52		
	50–54	21.79	5.86		
	55+	20.45	5.01	10.30	.000
Lack of personal accomplishment	Under 39	21.20	3.57		
	40–49	21.47	3.60		
	50–54	21.04	3.75		
	55+	20.98	4.10	.782	NS

[12] Multiple regression on all three of the burnout scales, entering age and gender in the first block, showed denominational differences in personal accomplishment (t= −2.343, p <.019). When means were inspected Church of God ministers were approximately two points lower on the lack of personal accomplishment than the others.

More arresting were calculations showing what percentage agreed with a statement about feeling 'burnt out' (9.4 per cent).[13] This indicates that a little under 10 per cent of Pentecostal ministers are either feeling burnt out or are in danger of doing so. Although this is not a large figure, it is an alarming one.

When the factors that might be related to burnout were inspected partial correlation coefficients were calculated. Table 11.5 shows that there is a significant correlation between all three of the burnout scales and answers to the question 'Have you, since ordination, ever considered leaving the ministry?' This triple correlation is a good indication of the validity of the burnout scales: one would expect burnt out ministers to consider leaving the ministry. The next column of figures displays what appears to be, at first sight, a paradoxical piece of information As depersonalisation increases the Sunday morning congregation decreases but, equally, as the Sunday morning congregation decreases emotional exhaustion increases. To put this the other way round, as the Sunday morning congregation increases emotional exhaustion decreases. In other words, there is no connection here between emotional exhaustion and the size of the Sunday morning congregation. It is not the case that the ministers with the largest congregations are also the most emotionally exhausted, quite the opposite. This suggests that the size of the Sunday morning congregation is a source of emotional stimulus and pleasure to the Pentecostal minister. He or she is encouraged by looking out over a large sea of faces. Consequently,

Table 11.5 *Partial correlation of burnout scales with four variables*

Maslach Scales	**Considered leaving ministry**	**Size of Sunday a.m. congregation**	**% Congregation charismata**	**% Congregation growth**
Depersonalisation	.2378	–.0187	–.0798	–.1183
P<	.000	NS	.03	.001
Emotional exhaustion	.3617	–.0839	–.0879	–.1176
P<	.000	.023	.017	.001
Lack of personal accomplishment	.2149	–.1877	–.1208	–.1599
P<	.000	.000	.001	.000

[13] For copyright reasons Maslach items may not be reproduced. Several other items were inspected individually and gave similar percentages.

it is not a surprise to discover that the size of the Sunday morning congregation is also linked with personal accomplishment. The larger the congregation the greater the minister's sense of personal accomplishment.

Similarly, the annual growth of the congregation is negatively correlated with the burnout scales. The more the congregation grows, the less the minister is likely to succumb to burnout. Indeed the relatively large size of the correlation coefficient at the bottom of the last three columns of the table indicates how important congregational growth and charismatic activity is to the Pentecostal minister. Personal accomplishment is quite directly measured by these indices.

As a further confirmation of the importance of charismata, the scale measuring ministerial charismatic activity was correlated with the three burnout scales and in each instance significant and negative relations were found.[14] Burnout, or the slide towards burnout, reduces the charismatic effectiveness of the minister.

These findings demonstrate that the size, growth and charismatic activity of the congregation are factors relevant to the potential burnout of the minister. But what of the material rewards of ministry? Are these related to burnout? Correlations were computed between the average weekly take-home pay of ministers and the three burnout scales. In each case the results were shown to be non-significant. The material rewards of being a Pentecostal minister are thus not related to burnout at all.

If material conditions are not related to burnout, then might there be a linkage between these scales and role conflict? Role conflict indicates the presence of cross currents within the life of the church and, perhaps, within the heart of the minister. The twenty different ministerial functions (administrator, apostle, counsellor, evangelist, fellowship builder, fund-raiser, leader in local community, leader of public worship, man or woman of prayer, manager, minister of sacraments, pastor, pioneer, preacher, prophet, social worker, spiritual director, teacher, theologian and visitor) were presented twice to ministers. On the first occasion ministers were

---

[14] With ministerial charismatic activity partial correlations are: depersonalisation ($r = -.0816$, $p < .03$), emotional exhaustion ($r = -.1669$, $p < .000$) and lack of personal accomplishment ($r = -.2558$, $p < .000$).

asked 'How much priority do you *want* to give to the following aspects of ministry?' On the second occasion they were asked 'How much priority do you feel you are *expected* to give the following aspects of ministry?' (original italics). On each occasion ministers could respond on a seven point scale from 'very little' to 'very much'. Role conflict was assessed by subtracting scores on each of the twenty different roles from each other. So the score on the role of administrator relating to what the minister was expected to give was subtracted from the score on the role of administrator relating to what the minister wanted to give. Since these differences might in some cases be positive and in other cases be negative, all results were squared to make them positive and then added up to make a single scale. However, the squaring of the results produced some high scores and so the scale was divided into four parts corresponding with four roughly equally sized groups of ministers. The four parts were then correlated with the three burnout scales. The results are displayed in table 11.6.

The table shows very clearly how, in the case of each scale, there is an increase as role conflict increases. For example where role conflict is low the mean of lack of personal accomplishment is 20.38 but, where role conflict is high lack of personal accomplishment rises to 22.02. The same sort of gradation is found with the other two burnout scales. This finding illustrates as clearly as anything

Table 11.6 *Burnout and role conflict*

Role Conflict		**Mean**	**Std Dev**	**F**	**P**
Depersonalisation	Low	20.31	4.43		
	Low medium	20.42	4.52		
	High medium	21.27	4.55		
	High	21.94	5.52	4.920	.002
Emotional exhaustion	Low	20.72	5.44		
	Low medium	21.69	4.94		
	High medium	22.55	5.52		
	High	23.97	6.51	11.195	.000
Lack of personal accomplishment	Low	20.38	3.52		
	Low medium	21.39	3.42		
	High medium	21.19	3.63		
	High	22.02	3.89	6.423	.000

could how it is role conflict that really induces the conditions which precipitate burnout. This finding is all the more stark considering that the expected pressures of work derived from a large and growing congregation or from low pay are unrelated to burnout. If there is a message here for the superintendents who care for young ministers – given that young ministers are most at risk – it must be that role conflict within the church should be reduced as much as possible.

A further set of correlations were computed to discover whether the burnout scales corresponded with the minister's assessment of his or her denomination. Table 11.7 shows that depersonalisation and emotional exhaustion both correlated with the items, 'I think my denomination is too centralised' and 'I am worried about the future of my denomination'. It seems unlikely that worry about the future of the denomination could lead to burnout and much more probable that a burnt out minister would feel jaundiced about the denomination. This interpretation is borne out by the lack of correlation between the two statements about denomination and lack of personal accomplishment. A minister *can* enjoy a sense of personal accomplishment even though he or she is unhappy about the progress of the denomination. What this suggests is that the minister on the brink of burnout becomes disillusioned with the denomination.

In order to investigate for other possible causes of burnout table 11.8 was computed. It shows that the personality dimensions are all significantly implicated in burnout. As might be expected from the findings in the previous chapter, the extraverted minister is the least at risk. He or she is least likely to be afflicted by depersonalisation, by emotional exhaustion and by a lack of personal accomplishment. The more neurotic minister, on the other hand, is extremely likely to be affected by burnout, as the level of correla-

Table 11.7 *Partial correlation of denominational items and burnout*

Denomination items	**Depersonalisation**	**Emotional exhaustion**	**Lack of personal accomplishment**
I think my denomination is too centralised	.0912	.1145	.0429
P<	.009	.001	NS
I am worried about the future of my denomination	.1407	.1301	-.0105
P<	.000	.000	NS

Table 11.8 *Partial correlation of burnout scales with personality dimensions variables*

Maslach Scales	Extraversion	Neuroticism	Psychoticism	Lie Scale
Depersonalisation	-.0735	.3095	.2415	-.2341
P<	.037	.000	.000	.001
Emotional exhaustion	-.1519	.4607	.0811	-.1123
P<	.000	.000	.021	.001
Lack of personal accomplishment	-.3155	.2461	.0250	-.1727
P<	.000	.000	NS	.000

tions indicates. The unstable minister is likely to be affected by depersonalisation, emotional exhaustion and lack of personal accomplishment. The tough-minded minister is also, logically enough, affected by depersonalisation: indeed this is almost a definition of tough-mindedness, decisions being made without regard to the feelings of other people. Unexpectedly, though, the tough-minded minister is also prone to emotional exhaustion. The socially nonconforming minister, scoring low on the lie scale, is like the extraverts also likely to resist burnout. This is not in the least bit surprising since the socially nonconforming minister is the type who will not put up with social and emotional pressures either from the congregation or from the denomination but will be determined to do what he or she thinks is right. The ability to resist pressure enables this kind of minister to carve out a space for ministry free from the dangers of burnout.

Coping with burnout

One way that Pentecostal ministers might expect to cope with incipient burnout is through personal prayer. It is reasonable to anticipate that ministers who spend more time in personal prayer, drawing upon the spiritual resources of the Christian faith, might be less likely to come close to burnout. Table 11.9 shows that this proved to be the case; those who pray more frequently are less likely to become burnt out. A similar test was run making use of the record of the frequency of the minister's reading of the Bible and, as might be predicted, those who frequently read their Bibles were also less likely to be burnt out. And a similar pattern of findings was

Table 11.9 *Partial correlation of burnout scales with devotional activities*

Maslach Scales	Frequency of prayer by yourself	Frequency of speaking in tongues	Frequency of Bible reading by yourself
Depersonalisation	-.1123	-.0990	-.0815
P<	.001	.005	.019
Emotional exhaustion	-.0620	-.0881	-.0815
P<	NS	.012	.019
Lack of personal accomplishment	-.1084	-.1524	-.0886
P<	.002	.000	.011

also associated with speaking with other tongues: frequent speaking in tongues was associated with lower burnout scores.

Interpretation of these findings might, of course, be made the other way round by arguing that those ministers who are not burnt out are also those who engage in the spiritual disciplines of prayer and Bible reading. There is no conclusive way to decide in which direction the causation flows: it may be that burnout leads to neglect of spiritual resources or, alternatively, it may be that the use of spiritual resources prevents burnout. The reason for leaning in favour of the presumption that burnout is prevented by drawing upon the spiritual resources of prayer and Bible reading is that there seems to be no logical connection between personal accomplishment, or lack of personal accomplishment, and these disciplines. It is possible to see a connection between emotional exhaustion and even depersonalisation and lack of prayer and Bible reading but how can a lack of personal accomplishment either interfere with or promote personal Bible reading? Thus it seems reasonable to take the spiritual resources mentioned here, and emphasised within the training of Pentecostal ministers, as antidotes to the spectre of burnout.

Conclusion

Although the problem of burnout is far from endemic among Pentecostal ministers, figures cited earlier suggest that approximately 10 per cent of ministers are in the danger zone. Explorations of patterns within the data show that it is younger ministers who are most at risk from the effects of burnout and, on reflection, this is not surprising since young ministers lack the perspectives that may come from experience and, at the same time, may be coping with low wages, young children, the adjustments of a recent marriage, a new job and a new home. Thus despite the resilience of youth, young ministers are in need of the care and support both of their congregations and of their denominational supervisors.

But what these figures also suggest is that the most stress-inducing set of experiences faced by ministers arise from role conflict. Ministers who wish to exercise their ministry in particular ways but who feel pulled in competing directions experience many of the classic causes of burnout. They sense conflicts of values and a lack of control over their situations. They may even attempt to do too much work in order to try to fulfil the contradictory roles being asked of them or which they ask of themselves.

On the positive side, it appears that the size and growth of churches is not a potential cause of burnout. Ministers are not in a position where, the larger the church, the more burnt out they become; quite the opposite. Ministers enjoy working with big congregations. They thrive on the life and excitement generated by all the potential of well resourced congregations and, where the congregation is charismatically active, this is a further stimulus towards creative engagement with work – the opposite of burnout.

For ministers who are struggling, the support of a team or a spouse does not show up as being a statistically significant palliative. Rather, it is the traditional spiritual resources of the minister, prayer and Bible reading, that provide the inner renewal that fend off the outer dysfunctions of burnout. Even on a non-spiritual interpretation of prayer and Bible reading this is an explicable conclusion since these disciplines reading offer solitude and quietness, two of the very things which can help prevent emotional exhaustion.

12

Conclusion

Preamble

I completed *Inside Story* in 1990. The book gives an account of the growth and development of British Assemblies of God from its formation in 1924 until the Annual General Conference of 1989. In the final chapter I took note of the extensive changes that had occurred since the mid-1970s. A larger Executive Council had been voted into existence with a more active role. The internal administration of the denomination had been altered so that instead of having a large number of small District Councils with twenty or so churches in each, the basic unit became the Regional Council, a larger unit of about sixty churches. This alteration from districts to regions was intended to generate enough money locally to fund twelve new full-time Regional Superintendents. Essentially, the administrative changes were intended to lead to better pastoral care for ministers and, through this, to stimulate effective church planting in each new region.

Along with these changes, important adjustments were made to the Annual General Conference itself. For many years it had been a mixture between a ministerial business conference and a conference where visitors might enjoy preaching and teaching in the evenings. The new format was intended to reduce the lengthy business sessions, to release ministers from arduous hours of debate and voting and to enable them to receive inspiration in a range of seminars. However, as a consequence of reducing the business at the Annual General Conference, it was necessary to convene a separate additional Business Conference to be held at a different time of year and to last for a mere two days instead of the traditional week.[1]

Alongside these changes was a willingness to examine the theological basics of Assemblies of God. Was there a millennium predicted in the Bible or not? Should speaking with other tongues be seen as the 'initial evidence' of the baptism in the Holy Spirit? To what extent might one minister have authority over another? Should interpretations of tongues be directed from God to the congregation like prophecies or should they be directed from the congregation to God like praise? These theological issues might be discussed within the denominational magazine. The title, *Redemption Tidings*, was thought to be too old-fashioned and its weekly nature to result in flimsy and preachy content. Many Assemblies of God members only subscribed out of loyalty. So *Redemption Tidings*, renamed *Redemption*, turned itself into a glossy monthly magazine and one that was intended to appeal more widely across the Christian denominations than had been the case in the past. As a result local Assemblies of God news about Sunday schools and conventions was dropped and more column inches were given to interviews with preachers from 'rival' denominations, particularly those from a restorationist background. Naturally these preachers did not always see eye-to-eye with Assemblies of God on matters of doctrine and so the newly launched magazine became a force for change rather than merely a method of reinforcing existing convictions.

Administrative changes could only be made on the basis of constitutional changes and constitutional changes were always difficult to secure because they required a two-thirds majority at the Annual Conference. All the changes that took place in the Assemblies of God in the 1970s and 1980s – the simplification of the constitution, the new style Executive Council, the new role for the Executive, the creation of regions and regional superintendents – not only needed big conference majorities but also took place against a background in which other newer and palpably successful

[1] The adjusted format did not last. Eventually a kind of compromise was reached. Ministerial business sessions would take place at the Annual General Conference, but they would be restricted as far as possible and a new National Business Committee would be the forum for detailed debate and meet at other times of the year than the Annual Conference.

Christian groupings, usually of a restorationist stance, were teaching strongly that the day of denominations had passed and that God was calling all Christians out into a fresh form of kingdom unity.[2]

Having enumerated and described the changes that had taken place within Assemblies of God, and having noticed how the changes of the 1970s and 1980s were far greater than those in any previous decades since 1924, I ended the book with a relatively upbeat assessment of future prospects. I saw that the necessary constitutional changes had eventually been agreed. I presumed that the denomination was in good shape for the 'decade of evangelism', the 1990s, and sat back with cautious optimism waiting for growth and blessing. Now, ten years on, the condition of Assemblies of God remains slightly ambiguous.

I had not foreseen, nor could have foreseen, a problem that arose as result of a commitment made by an Assemblies of God missionary to purchase a building in Germany. This building proved to be far more expensive than originally anticipated and its eventual cost ran to more than £600,000. Assemblies of God honourably agreed to fulfil the financial commitment made 'in faith' by its missionary, but the drain on its resources in Britain was great. The general offices had to be sold to cover part of the debt and money that might have been be spent on evangelism or church planting or missionary work was diverted to fill an apparently bottomless financial pit. Similarly, I had not foreseen, though with hindsight might have foreseen, the criticism that was levelled at the new *Redemption* magazine and its editor. Quite suddenly he was voted out of office and the previous editor was recalled to repair damage to the circulation. The content of the magazine became much more neutral and uncontroversial and it ceased to be a voice for radical change. But the incident showed how matters could go awry.

Similarly, it might have been possible to predict that the transition to Regional Superintendency would not go completely smoothly. The problems were often financial. As money was diverted into the regions, the administrative centre was starved – particularly in light of the overseas debt. And even then the money available in the regions was too little. Regional Superintendents either had to be largely funded by their own congregations and then released to work round

---

[2] *Forgive Us Our Denominations* by John Noble exemplifies this theme.

and about or else regions had to be made much larger than originally envisaged. In either case the system did not work as well as had been hoped. One region, for example, ended up with about 130 churches, far more than had been expected and far too many for a single superintendent to sustain. Consequently some regional superintendents came in for criticism and, furthermore, churches could see no reason to pay for a pastoral service they did not receive. This only made the problem worse.

These difficulties, discouraging as they were, were less damaging than the diminution of attendance at the Annual General Conference. Despite attempts to make the conference more attractive (more ministry, less business) and to raise the standard of accommodation and reduce its cost, conference attendance plummeted in the 1990s. This was probably a consequence of the loss of the prime week in the Easter holidays and of the Butlin's site at Minehead but was also brought about by an alternative conference offered by a number of old Assemblies of God ministers who rejected many of the changes that the previous decades had brought into being. Once the Annual Conference lost its pulling power, it became a financial liability. Even ministers began to relegate it in their priorities and, when this happened, the possibility of retaining denominational unity was seriously threatened.

Approximately two hundred new congregations were started in the early 1990s. Though the target of a thousand churches by the year 2000 was always going to be difficult to achieve, considerable progress was made and Regional Councils, in the main, accepted their responsibilities in this direction. It may seem odd to see this as an unplanned outcome of regionalisation but the point to note is that the creation of regions was really proposed to the Annual General Conferences of the late 1980s on the basis of the benefits that would accrue to ministers who needed pastoral care themselves. Gains in the area of church planting were secondary and resources and plans to ensure that this happened were not detailed or substantial. That church planting was successful and regionally supported this was due to the outstanding individuals at national level who gave themselves to the work.[3]

---

[3] Warwick Shenton, Assemblies of God General Superintendent, was passionately concerned for church planting at the start of the decade. Later, George Ridley, as church planting director, was highly effective.

In education, after 1994, academic courses at the Assemblies of God Bible College at Mattersey were validated by the University of Sheffield with the result that, in the mid-1990s, students received mandatory grants from local education authorities. Quite suddenly students who came to study at Mattersey were funded by public money because the courses they could undertake were publicly recognised. Large numbers of students took advantage of this and the college quickly became financially buoyant and had sufficient funding to erect a new teaching block and make other modernisations. Yet towards the end of the decade, this source of income dried up as the government phased out educational grants and insisted on student loans. New non-residential arrangements for ministerial training became more urgent.

More intangible problems inherent in Assemblies of God in the 1980s continued into the 1990s. By the mid-1990s over twenty-five of the most go-ahead and radical ministers considered leaving. Warwick Shenton the General Superintendent who helped to pilot constitutional changes through Assemblies of God in the late 1980s and early 1990s stood down in 1994. He was a man of wide sympathy and a passionate preacher and was able to hold together all the elements within Assemblies of God. With his departure, and unexpected and sad death the following year, the future again became uncertain. The new General Superintendent, Paul Weaver, found himself having to continue the pace of reform while, at the same time, generating a new unity. He did this by obtaining an agreement the General Conference in 1997 that Assemblies of God should have a corporate vision, a strategy that linked all different parts together coherently. In 1998 this vision was presented to acclaim at the General Conference and for the first time in many years it became apparent that the separate departments and strands within the movement might be knitted together in a mutually supportive way. *Joy* magazine was given the role of helping to disseminate a sense of purpose, and a fresh emphasis upon ministry gifts – apostles, prophets, evangelists, pastors and teachers – helped to downplay the role of committees and constitutional procedures. The more radical and go-ahead ministers were supportive of these emphases which were presented in the context of the importance of the denomination in its entirety. In effect, the purpose of denominational cooperation was woven into the corporate vision so that ministers could see what they gained from belonging and what they might lose if they left, and they could see that they stood to achieve more together than apart.

Following this breakthrough, in 1998 a UK-wide Pentecostal alliance (PCUK) was launched with the mission 'to promote the Kingdom of God through our Pentecostal distinctives and contribute to the Church in the United Kingdom'. PCUK included all four main Pentecostal denominations and its formation indicated the willingness of Pentecostals to see themselves as being able to make an impact on national consciousness, whether by addressing social needs and evangelistic projects or by speaking prophetically to the wider church.[4] Its first project was a detoxification unit for Teen Challenge.

The point of this reflection is to show that prediction about the future of denominations, Pentecostal or otherwise, can never take account of completely unexpected events. Yet, outstanding individuals in one realm sometimes compensate for desperate setbacks in another. Sometimes trends that appear to be substantial, like the growth in attendance at the Assemblies of God annual General Conference, turn out to be fragile and reversible. Sometimes the dire predictions of apparently spiritual individuals ('God has finished with denominations') fall flat and turn out to be the product of their own anxieties or imaginations. The best that can be said is that denominations that have survived for the best part of a hundred years are likely to continue.

With these reservations in mind it is apparent that of the four denominations considered here, the healthiest appears to be the Elim Pentecostal Church. It has the youngest group of ministers, the best and the most consistently applied form of training, apparently secure financial arrangements and a promising mixture between old and new styles of Pentecostalism. Assemblies of God, though similar to the Elim Pentecostal Church in many respects, looks slightly less healthy. Its ministers are older, some of them are poorly paid, its training schemes are not yet balanced between its

[4] Its members were Assemblies of God, Church of God of Prophecy, Connections, Elim, New Testament Assembly, New Testament Church of God, New Wine Church, The Apostolic Church and The Redeemed Christian Church of God.

Bible college and what can be offered part-time in the regions and there is a slightly greater diversity of views on moral, social and doctrinal issues than is found within Elim. The Apostolic Church, though it has become more open than used to be the case, and though its training schemes have been upgraded, still lags behind Elim and the Assemblies of God. Nevertheless, the care taken of its ministers is sufficient to secure their devotion, though the fact that 50 per cent of them think their denomination is too centralised and nearly two-thirds are worried about their denomination's future shows that further reform is crucial. The Church of God, originating as it did within the United States, is always going to march to a slightly different drumbeat from that of the indigenous Pentecostal denominations within Britain. Yet, as with the other denominations, the progress it makes in Britain is likely to depend upon the quality of a few outstanding individuals rather than the administrative structure that it has evolved.

Disappointments

Taking the period from the beginning of the century until the present, it is clear that some of the expectations of the very earliest Pentecostals for an immediate end to human history with the return of Christ have been disappointed. The eschaton, the second coming, has not occurred and the outpouring of the Holy Spirit at the beginning of the century signalled more a phase in the life of the church than a climactic moment.[5] Some, but not all, of the earliest Pentecostals expected to be part of the last generation, an expectation that certainly surfaced among the Millerites of the nineteenth century and, from time to time, appear within restorationist circles.[6] Such disappointments, in the nature of things, lead to rationalisation. Perhaps the end will come tomorrow, perhaps next year, but it is not cancelled – rather it is just beyond our experience.

So, although the failure of history to end within the first Pentecostal generation was felt deeply by some believers, others took a

5 Land, 1993.

6 Personal conversation with Pentecostals in the 1970s about Pentecostals in the 1930s shows this to have been the case.

more robust view and planned for a long-term future. Barratt argued for the founding of Pentecostal denominations precisely because he felt that they would be necessary in the years that lay ahead. Others, like the missionary W.F.P. Burton, set out to evangelise what was then the Belgian Congo and were aware that the gospel could hardly be said to have been preached all over the world, a requirement before the end could come (Mt. 24:14). Burton's urgency was certainly tempered by practical common-sense and at some point in the middle of his life he changed his eschatological views and the timescale associated with them.[7]

However, within Britain it would have been possible for disappointments to arise out of the failure of an immediate Pentecostal revival. Although the Welsh revival had shown how a whole nation might be rapidly and powerfully shaken by the proclamation of the gospel and spiritual phenomena, there was little evidence that the great bulk of the English or Scottish populations were ready for such religious fervour. Instead what happened was that hopes for a revival became transformed into enjoyment of crusades. Particularly in the 1920s and 1930s when George and Stephen Jeffreys were at the height of their powers, there were local mini-revivals in many British cities that resulted in numerous conversions and the relatively speedy planting of new congregations. When this phase of Pentecostal existence ceased, as it did after about 1935, the most far-sighted and perceptive Pentecostal preachers, especially Howard Carter and Donald Gee, expanded their own acquaintance with Pentecostalism by travelling round the world and seeing the extent of Pentecostal life in different countries. Therefore, although there might have been disappointments about the scale of Pentecostal success within the United Kingdom, Pentecostals were assured by leaders they trusted that on other continents and in other circumstances more wonderful and irresistible outpourings of the Spirit were being enjoyed.

Successes overseas could have a less than comforting effect, however. If Pentecostalism could sweep everything before it, why was this not taking place in Britain? With hindsight it is possible to see how the first wave of Pentecostal revival succeeded or failed in different parts of the world depending upon the reaction to it by

---

[7] Kay, 1989.

the existing churches and by the disruption to growth caused by the onset of war.[8] In most of Europe Pentecostal churches were rejected by existing Protestant denominations. The exception here was in Scandinavia where nominal Lutheranism was not strong enough to resist, and in some cases embraced, Pentecostal preaching. In the rest of Europe, especially in Germany, Pentecostalism fared far less well because of its frosty reception by respected theological denominational authorities.[9] In Holland, traditionally a religiously open country, Pentecostalism found early success but was hampered by two world wars, as was the case in the rest of Europe. Later the communist block hindered Pentecostalism and prevented evangelism in parts of Europe. In Britain during the First World War conscription and disagreement over the merits of pacifism divided Pentecostals.[10] In Holland, Belgium and France the German occupation made normal church life almost impossible and Pentecostal congregations struggled there both organisationally and evangelistically. In Britain, the Second World War restricted church attendance and made church planting practically impossible.

These things were not clear at the time. All that British Pentecostals knew was that they were not sharing in the spiritual prosperity of their American cousins or Swedish counterparts and, when from the vantage point of the 1950s they looked back on their own history, they rued the loss of commanding evangelists (again the Jeffreys brothers in particular) and there was always a tendency to try to find a new key figure who would draw the crowds, heal the sick and make the hard work of denominational expansion easier. Certainly the Executive Council of British Assemblies of God spent time in the 1950s, especially after the success of Billy Graham, looking for a Pentecostal evangelist of equal stature whom they could let loose on the British people.[11]

When Pentecostal churches failed to grow as rapidly as their ministers had hoped and when disputes and defections troubled Pentecostal denominations it was easy to become discouraged. In

---

8 Barrett, 1988.

9 Hollenweger, 1972.

10 Boddy accepted the necessity of British military engagement in the 1914–18 war but Donald Gee and Howard Carter were pacifists.

11 Kay, 1989.

such circumstances heartsearching questions were asked. Was the old-time Pentecostal power really present in the modern church? If it was, why was it not being seen? Was lack of holiness the root of the problem? These questions, and the tensions they induced, led some ministers to stop praying for those who were ill or to devalue charismatic gifts and others to attribute real Pentecostal power to particularly anointed individuals among whom they could not count themselves. In other words, there was a tendency to look round the horizon for the powerful (and presumably exceptionally holy) minister who would do what the struggling pastor found impossible. Even in the 1970s many Pentecostal ministers considered that healing was more likely to be achieved by visiting preachers and evangelists than by ministry within their own congregations or at their own hands.

Hypotheticals

One way of trying to assess the course of any form of history is to ask the question 'What would have happened if. . ..?' The question sharpens perception of events and allows one to probe for real turning points.

What would have happened if Elim and Assemblies of God had merged in 1924 and become a single denomination as was suggested at the time? The original suggestion was that Elim should become the evangelistic arm of Assemblies of God. The combined denomination, if it had been brought into existence, would have had an evangelistic arm directed, presumably, by George Jeffreys aided by his brother Stephen who would not have been able to leave Elim to join Assemblies of God, and a missionary work derived from the Pentecostal Missionary Union (PMU) that would have been supported from a larger base of churches. It would have developed links with the Assemblies of God in the United States and this, according to one reading of events, would have produced a similar form of government to that which Assemblies of God in Britain uses today. In other words, it would have continued to safeguard the autonomy of local Assemblies and to have de-emphasised the power of central administration.

Such a configuration would have presumably satisfied George Jeffreys whose departure from Elim revolved in large measure around this issue. So we could reasonably suppose that the combined British Pentecostal denomination would have retained the important services of George Jeffreys who would have crusaded for the British Pentecostal churches after 1945 as well as in the 1930s. In addition, it is reasonable to suppose that it would not have been necessary to run two Bible colleges, with the expense that this produced, as well as two sets of magazines and two general conferences. Some money would therefore have been saved and, if the benefits of the Elim system had been transplanted into Assemblies of God, then we might have anticipated a pension scheme to support the older ministers and some of the administrative capability that E.J. Phillips brought to Elim would have been applied to the whole larger group.

On this analysis the combination of Assemblies of God and Elim would have been to the benefit of both and would have prevented the damaging loss of George Jeffreys. Yet, at the time, the reason given for failure to amalgamate was that if one Pentecostal group failed then at least the other might succeed; putting all the Pentecostal eggs into one basket was a dangerous strategy. Whether this reason was a true reason cannot at this distance in time be verified, but it might well be misleading to presume that the combination of the two groups would have resulted in harmonious development. There were strong personalities both in Elim and in the Assemblies of God and it is difficult to believe that Howard Carter, who clashed with Nelson Parr and to some extent with Donald Gee, would have been able to keep free of a dispute with George Jeffreys. Consequently, the dangers of fragmentation after an initial amalgamation would have been greater and, had fragmentation taken place, the psychological outcome might have been devastating for the sundered denomination.

Unquestionably the decision to join together or to remain separate was a vital one for Pentecostalism within Britain. Had the amalgamation taken place and had it been entirely successful, then it is reasonable to envisage a larger and more successful Pentecostal presence within Britain than is the case today. Had the denomination failed, then it is possible that the fragments would have formed themselves into two or more relatively small groups, each of which would have been headed by a leading figure and we would be in a position similar to that reached by the restoration groups in the

1980s, but simply with more groups on the scene. Both these outcomes, depending on one's viewpoint, might be thought preferable to the present position.

What would have happened if the original teachings of the Apostolic Church had been accepted more widely within Elim and Assemblies of God? If this had happened there would have been a far greater recognition of the role of ministry gifts within Pentecostal churches. Not only would there have been an emphasis on pastors, and to a lesser extent upon evangelists, but the ministries of prophets, apostles and teachers would have been given a higher profile. Had this happened, then the government of Pentecostal denominations would undoubtedly have been opened to a greater range of ministerial impetus. It is difficult to believe that the current more constitutional form of government would have survived intact. Decision-making processes, instead of being driven by debates followed by votes, would have been more likely to have occurred through more intuitive and, in theory, more spiritual means.

Certainly the Apostolic Church, because of its original teachings about ministerial giftings, accepted the authority of ministry much more readily than did Elim and Assemblies of God, all of whose ministers had one vote at the General Conference. At its best the acceptance of ministry gifts within British Pentecostalism would have produced enormous vibrancy and almost certainly a greater emphasis on charismatic gifts and on church planting. This was the experience of similar groups that functioned in parts of Africa, especially those associated with Nicholas Bhengu.[12]

In fact, as it turned out, within the Apostolic Church the emphasis on the ministry gifts began to be counterbalanced by an emphasis on constitutional regulations and rules and, as a consequence, the main result of giving a free rein to ministry gifts is seen in the enormous success of the Apostolic Church overseas. An apostle or prophet could simply send a lesser-rated minister to another country. Within Britain, the Apostolic Church has moved closer to the other two indigenous Pentecostal denominations so that there is very little difference between them. All the denominations attempt to place ministry gifts within a constitutional framework, balancing ministerial freedom against an agreed structure.

---

[12] McGee, 1988, 57.

We can put this hypothetical issue another way by asking whether it is more important to recognise ministry gifts, even though sometimes these gifts are misdirected and abused, or more important to conduct business matters and decision making using the integrity and reasoning abilities of ministers. Of course this is a false dilemma. Pentecostal denominations need integrity and rationality as well as ministerial giftings but if one has to choose between the two it is clear that it is possible for a denomination to function, albeit in a very dreary way, using constitutional machinery alone. Ministerial gifts tend to produce networks of churches rather than denominations.

What would have happened if the Pentecostal denominations had foreseen and welcomed the charismatic movement? To answer this question is to presume a different state of affairs than that which existed in the early 1960s. We must presume that the Pentecostal churches were alert to life outside their own confines. We must assume that Pentecostal churches had concerns for the Baptist, Methodist, Congregational and Anglican churches down the road. In other words, we must assume that there was greater ministerial interchange than existed then when Pentecostals were, by and large, isolated from the main flow of life in the older denominations. We must also assume that Pentecostal churches, as a consequence of their relationships with other Christian groups, adopted lifestyles that were much closer to those of the other churches.

If we make these two assumptions then it becomes reasonable to envisage a scenario in which the Pentecostal churches, seeing the outpouring of the Spirit on the other denominations, would have welcomed what was happening. As a consequence, it is surely likely that there would have been a far greater migration of new Christians into Pentecostal churches. The transfer would have been much easier to achieve because there would have been a smaller gap between the two church cultures. As a result, Pentecostal churches would have benefited enormously from an inflow of talent, finance and personnel in the 1960s. There would have been only a small charismatic fringe within the mainline denominations because of a greater shift into Pentecostalism. Yet, once these considerations are entertained it becomes clear that it would have been almost unthinkable for Pentecostals to have related to the traditional mainline churches without the intermediate fringe of a charismatic movement. In other words, the difference in the 1950s between Pentecostalism on the one hand and liturgical Christianity on the other was too great to bridge. Equally, the difference between biblical Pentecostalism on the one hand, and liberal Christianity, even of a non-liturgical kind, on the other was also too great to bridge.

To ask the question, then, about Pentecostals and the charismatic movement is probably to presume a course of development between the early 1920s and the 1950s which simply did not exist. The only way of re-thinking this is to presume that a cross denominational outpouring of the Spirit had taken place in the 1930s and that, in these circumstances, it would have been possible for Pentecostalism to have moved closer to the traditional denominations or indeed for the traditional denominations to have given rise to outward-looking fellowships, groups or agencies that might have pulled the separate expressions of Christianity together. Randall, in his analysis of the 1930s, points out that the Moral Re-Armament movement partly fulfilled these conditions and it is possible that had this movement been more biblical in its approach, it might have survived and played this useful role in the postwar period. As it was the Moral Re-Armament movement quickly went into decline at the end of the 1930s and was largely forgotten or treated as an inter-war aberration.

What would have happened if the Pentecostal churches in Britain had been more welcoming of Caribbean immigrants in the 1950s? This question presumes far less alteration to the general landscape for its answer. In order to have been more welcoming to Caribbean immigrants, Pentecostal churches would have had to have been more lively, more friendly and more alert to the plight of the new arrivals. All these alterations are much easier to put imaginatively into place. The 1950s were a very flat period in British Pentecostal history and so the churches were less active and alive than they subsequently became. They also, to their shame, probably partook of some of the negative racial attitudes prevalent in Britain at that time. As a result they were unable to put themselves in the shoes of the new arrivals who found themselves snubbed and derided by the culture of the 'mother country'. Had the Pentecostal churches opened their doors, it is possible to envisage a swathe of active Pentecostal churches, perhaps black but also of many races, within the areas where immigrants tended to settle, in the environs of Birmingham and in north London. If this wave of immigrants had been accepted and been allowed to contribute freely to established Pentecostalism in Britain, it is reasonable to suppose that the churches of the 1960s would have been much more ready to grow. They would have benefited from the contribution of Caribbean Christians in terms of social conscience and music. Moreover, and crucially, the help would have worked both ways. The Caribbean community would have been better able to retain the loyalty of their own young people who were born in England and whose experience of Britain all too often led to disaffection and, from there, to a rejection of Christianity itself.

Issues

Finally, having looked at the turning points of Pentecostal history, it is appropriate to comment on the current tensions within Pentecostalism, the issues that are unresolved within the matrix of beliefs, attitudes and institutional organisation.

Four broad areas can be identified: *relations* (including relations inside Pentecostal denominations, between Pentecostal denominations and between Pentecostals and charismatics), *spirituality* (including the role of experience in relation to a cognitive grasp of the biblical text and academic education in relation to patterns of training and spiritual gifting), *holiness* (including here the contrast between sacrifice and prosperity, conformity and non-conformity, the impact of the world upon the church and the church upon the world) and, finally, *mission* (including the relationship between church planting at home and mission abroad and, more widely, between risky growth and apparently safe stagnation).

Relations

Within Pentecostal denominations there is already considerable diversity. This diversity exists most obviously in the varied sizes of the different congregations. Congregations of more than 300 adults are very different from those with a mere 25 adults. Once congregations reach about the level of 200 adults they become capable of making an impact in the local area or of funding overseas missionaries or pastoral travels. The phenomenon of the megachurch already exists within the United States and such churches have little need for the help their denominations can give. Their pastors are well looked after, often supported by other junior ministers and secretarial assistance, complete with travel budgets and able to run their congregations, in some instances, like the executives of prosperous businesses. These ministers may find denominational politics boring and begin to withdraw themselves from local denominational gatherings or even from annual general conferences. In Britain megachurches may also take a similarly independent attitude and, when they do this, run their own in-house Bible schools or training schemes in order to recycle their people for new church plants in their area. It has to be said immediately that not all the British megachurches come to have no further use for their denominational roots, but the temptation to independence exists for them in a way that it does not exist for smaller churches which need all the help they can get from their denominational resources.

But diversity also exists in the realm of attitudes. Ministers may be divided into those who are middle of the road, who do the work they have been called to without innovation; those who are completely unimaginative and mechanical in their approach to their work, being unable even to change the time of meetings or to alter the shape or layout of their buildings; and those who are restless and always looking for the latest 'new thing that God is doing in our time'. Clashes tend to occur between the restless ministers, some of whom may have embraced every new idea since about 1970, and those who are rigidly mechanical and consider as many objections to change as they can find. The clashes most obviously take place within the forum of the annual general conferences which Pentecostal denominations utilise for major decision making.

Within Assemblies of God and Elim clashes have taken place in the past, most obviously over financial matters or the workings of the constitution, and what tends to happen is that the more middle-of-the-road ministers are willing to change their minds once they are persuaded by leaders they trust. Typically, the great majority of Pentecostal ministers *will* accept changes, but difficulties arise when the more radical and restless among them attempt to rush middle-of-the-road ministers into decisions with which they are uncomfortable. The more conservative ministers can rarely be persuaded to change their minds and may come to believe that minor alterations are matters of great principle – there were, for instance, men who felt it was a resignation matter when, by a democratic decision, the size of the Assemblies of God Executive Council increased and others who took a similar view when District Councils became Regional Councils.

Several types of meaningful unity within Pentecostal denominations can coexist with greater diversity. If Pentecostal denominations are to grow numerically in the new millennium, then they will only do so by retaining what they have already achieved and adding to it. Unity of organisation at least ensures that national offices, national officers and financial distributions work harmoniously; unity of theology ensures that conferences and conventions promote a common vision of the future; unity over issues of lifestyle ensures that bickering over moral and social matters does not occur. Ideally, each type of unity can be achieved but, in the nature of things, disunity of one type can have knock-on effects in the other areas.

Relationships between Pentecostal denominations appear to be easier to foresee. The main Pentecostal denominations are happy to collaborate with each other whenever necessary but, at the same time, to maintain their own distinctiveness and separate identity. Meetings between the Executive Councils of the Assemblies of God and Elim Church take place regularly, as a matter of policy, and are friendly. This constructive attitude permeates most local situations. Similarly, relationships between Elim and Assemblies of God and the Apostolics are good though collaboration is less common, partly because the Apostolics tend to be strongest in Wales where the other two Pentecostal denominations are less numerous. Relationships with Church of God are less developed, though well-known Church of God preachers have spoken at the Assemblies of God Annual Conference, a mark of the esteem in which they are held.

The Evangelical Alliance continues to be the main umbrella organisation under which Pentecostals are willing to sit. Although Kensington Temple, an Elim Church and the largest individual congregation in Britain, broke away from the Evangelical Alliance at one point in the 1990s, relationships were never allowed to deteriorate to the point of public polemics. Within the Alliance the acceptance of the authority of Scripture, the Trinity and the death and resurrection of Jesus, are sufficiently strongly held by Pentecostals, charismatics and evangelicals to become the overriding basis for collaborative fellowship even when they disagree on other matters.

There are already major events at which the whole Pentecostal and charismatic constituency is well represented. The Marches for Jesus that take place to raise the profile of the church either regionally or nationally have a strong Spirit-filled contingent. The banners, songs, balloons, prayer walking and proclamatory music attracts radical Pentecostals and the new churches. Similarly, the Mission to London, started in 1992 and originally spearheaded by Morris Cerullo, offered in 1999 a programme of morning seminars, afternoon street evangelism and evening rallies.[13] It has been jointly supported by Pentecostals and charismatics who supply most of the vision, drive and teaching.

Relationships between Pentecostals and charismatics need to be considered under two separate headings. Charismatics who occ;upy a place within the old-time denominations, for instance Anglican or Baptist charismatics, are separate from the charismatics who exist within the new churches. The old denominations continue to temper the mind-set of their charismatics so that, for example, Anglican charismatics will normally accept the validity of infant baptism whereas Baptist charismatics will find this an objectionable doctrine

By contrast, the new curches because they are new do not hold doctrinal positions sanctified by their own hallowed history. In most instances they grew up around the ministry of an outstanding individual whose own Christian convictions helped shape that of the network he formed. In almost every case these individuals were clear that they were definitely not founding a new denomination although definitions of the term 'denomination' were usually not made on a sociological basis. 'Denomination' was identified with committees and legalism rather than with the sociological notion which places it on a continuum between a 'church' and a 'sect'. In sociological terms a denomination is a religious organisation that

---

13 The Kensington Temple website (September 1999) spoke of the Mission to London being in its seventh year.

accepts the validity of other similar religious organisations.[14] Baptists, Methodists and Congregationalists belong to denominations in the sense that they believe that salvation is found within other expressions of Christianity that they recognise as being equally valid. A 'church', by contrast, usually makes universal claims and at the same time is less restrictive about its own membership. As a result a 'church' is usually friendly with its surrounding culture and sometimes identified with the secular governmental authorities.[15] A sect is usually hostile to its surrounding culture, and to other religious organisations and groups, and may be antagonistic to all forms of secular government without actually working politically for their overthrow. It is normally characterised by the belief that only it offers the true path to salvation.

Over time sects tend to become denominations and churches may give ground and accept denominational status, so that both ends of the continuum eventually meet in the middle. Since the start of the century Pentecostal groups have, by and large, moved from sect-like beginnings to their current denominational status. The new churches still retain sect-like qualities in the sense that their collaboration with other groups is less open and that organisational boundaries are more precise. Yet in another respect they are less sect-like since their attitude towards the surrounding culture is usually more open and friendly than that found in the less progressive Pentecostal congregations. The new churches accept modern clothes, communication, lifestyles and attitudes; they are not anti-world as archetypal sects are and, for this reason, are more open, flexible and adept at attracting newcomers. When Pentecostals, charismatics and new church believers adopt the same *social* attitudes, in contradistinction to the same doctrinal beliefs and organisational patterns, then collaborative ventures and transfer between them will become even easier. At the moment one of the psychological barriers between the three groups is found in the different orientations they have towards the surrounding secular culture.

Yet, there is sufficient similarity between Pentecostal, charismatic and new church beliefs and styles of worship for there to

---

14 Weber, 1930; Yinger, 1957; Wilson, 1963, 1976. See also Introduction.

15 Anglican bishops sit in the House of Lords.

be a small amount of traffic between them. Young people growing up in one environment find it easy to move across to another and, since the new churches usually enjoy younger ministers and congregations than the others, the migration of people is inclined to be in one direction. Similarly, new theological ideas travel across the spectrum *from* the new churches *to* the Pentecostals and charismatics. However, because irenic personalities among Pentecostals and charismatics have adapted their theology and approach as a consequence of new church criticism, the distinction between the three groups is less sharp than it was in the 1980s and the transfer of people, or in some instances of whole congregations, is less common.

The critical issue facing the new churches concerns the transfer of leadership to the second or third generation of ministers. Since there is no machinery for conferring leadership, it is not obvious how new charismatic leaders will arise within the networks that have been established. Two scenarios present themselves. The first is of a power struggle after the death of the original apostle. One man or a small caucus attempt to assume command, but this is unacceptable to others who refuse to recognise the new authority. Eventually small clusters of churches break free to form their own independent groupings. The second scenario is of a more orderly transition from the apostle to a chosen successor who manages to demonstrate all the drive and spirituality of the originator and so lead the network into expansion and prosperity. If the first scenario is played out and the networks of congregations established by the original apostles tear themselves apart then, presumably, disillusioned members and bewildered congregations may make a journey back to the traditional Pentecostal denominations.

Statistical analysis of churches across the world demonstrates the phenomenon of the post-Pentecostal or even the post-charismatic: someone who once belonged within a Pentecostal or charismatic congregation but who has since moved out to a traditional denomination, though probably one whose style of worship and pastoral relationships has been loosened up by earlier contact with the Pentecostal and charismatic scene.[16] In other words, the attraction of the liturgy and of the less demanding lifestyle of a traditional denomination has had an impact on Pentecostals and charismatics.

---

[16] Barrett, 1988; Barrett and Johnson, 1998.

Indeed, there are congregations within classical Pentecostal churches in the United States that are bathed in what at first sight appears to be a traditional Methodist or Episcopal ethos. Such churches may have a semi-liturgical form of worship, a robed choir, stained-glass windows and have not been the site of charismatic gifts for many years. These congregations retain a legal adherence to their Pentecostal denomination but, in all other respects, they have moved across the divide into a different denominational venue. They tend to attract elderly upper middle-class professionals.

The issue of cooperation between Pentecostals and other Christian groups is not new and was addressed by the first generation of Pentecostals who found their best spokesman in Donald Gee. He, at the conclusion of his history of Pentecostalism in Britain noted, 'the unity of the Spirit is vastly more important than a union of denominations', and addressing the issue of ecumenicism wrote:

> The new outbreak of glossolalia among the older denominations [was] something truly ecumenical, and [provided] a Pentecostal meeting-place among Christians ranging from Baptists to Roman Catholics, fraught with rich possibilities of a transcendent unity of the One Spirit.[17]

Gee believed fellowship between individuals was far more practical than fellowship between denominations. He spoke from his own experience. Most Pentecostals, particularly in the late 1950s and early 1960s, had very little time for Roman Catholics. Yet Gee had enjoyed a friendly correspondence with the Roman Catholic, Benedict Heron. Likewise most Pentecostals had no time for the World Council of Churches. Yet Gee had been invited to attend the 1961 meeting in Delhi and would have gone had Pentecostal officialdom not borne down upon him and persuaded him that it would have been impolitic to do so.[18] So Gee's position was that rules and bureaucracies, necessary though they might be for many purposes, got in the way of ecumenical fellowship and that genuine ecumenical fellowship only took place on the basis of a shared personal experience of God.

---

17 Gee, 1967, 309.

18 Thomas Zimmerman, the General Superintendent of American Assemblies of God, applied the pressure.

Spirituality

Pentecostal spirituality, like all spirituality, is prone to problems of definition and precision. Within the modern British context spirituality, partly because of its inclusion within the language of compulsory education, has become a term whose meaning has been adapted to make it acceptable to religious and non-religious groups.[19] Within this context it is permissible to speak about 'humanist spirituality' or 'spirituality' without any qualifying adjective. Spirituality in this context refers to a quality of mind and emotion, an ability to relate to human beings and to refer to the non-material side of life, often through appreciation of the arts.

Pentecostal spirituality, on the surface, appears to be characterised by embracing religious experience. This characterisation goes back to the beginnings of Pentecostalism when the critics of Pentecostal doctrine buttressed their case by pointing to the alarming behaviour of Pentecostal people who fell over, laughed, wept, became prostrate and even claimed to see visions and enjoy the charismatic gifts that had been removed from the church for centuries. So Pentecostal spirituality was really Pentecostal carnality and one interpretation of what happened when Pentecostal denominations became established was that genuine manifestations of the Holy Spirit were separated from their counterfeits by a clear and agreed interpretation of biblical principles. By this means Pentecostal carnality could be identified and subtracted and the experience and behaviours that remained were those that really originated with the Holy Spirit.

This analysis presumes that genuine spirituality must always be identified by a test derived from rational exposition of Scripture. This analysis may draw historical precedent from the writing of Jonathan Edwards whose remarks on the east coast revival after 1734 drew exactly this kind of conclusion.[20] Such an analysis would have been acceptable across a broad range of Pentecostal thinking. The role of the Pentecostal teacher, as Donald Gee argued, is to

[19] The 1988 Education Reform Act refers to the 'spiritual, moral, social and cultural' education of pupils.

[20] Edwards' *A Faithful Narrative of the Surprising Work of God* was written in 1737 and *The Distinguishing Marks of a Work of the Spirit of God* followed in 1741.

provide sound doctrine. While other ministries might stoke the ship's boiler and rev its engines, it was the job of the teacher to remain calmly on the bridge to steer the Pentecostal vessel away from rocks and icebergs.

But where did Pentecostals obtain their doctrine from and how did they obtain it? If the answer to this question was that Pentecostal doctrine came from the evangelical storehouse of knowledge that had been accumulated over the centuries, then why did this storehouse omit reference to the Pentecostal baptism? If the answer here was that Pentecostalism only emerged through the sovereign decision of God in the light of church history, Pentecostals still might be vulnerable to the charge that their own celebration of religious experience occupied a completely different place from that found within much traditional evangelical thought. And the more Pentecostals applied evangelical principles to their own religious lives, the more likely they were to exclude the vitality produced by the fervour of spiritually enthusiastic congregations. In other words, the danger was that Pentecostalism would fade out.

The most recent generation of Pentecostal scholars, equipped with all the advantages of an academic education, have begun to re-examine the connection between Pentecostal doctrine and Pentecostal experience. In an important book on Pentecostal spirituality Stephen Land has begun to re-analyse the past and rethink the future. He first of all describes Pentecostal spirituality and sees it has a 'passion for the kingdom' that arises from an apprehension of the eschatological purposes of God. One day the kingdom of God will dawn and human history is inexorably moving to this point. Pentecostals have appreciated these divine purposes and their spirituality is based upon the sense that:

> the kingdom is breaking through from the future and the Spirit was being poured out . . . the crisis experiences within this eschatological orientated development process were stages along the way, markers along the aisle, toward the altar and to the marriage supper. They were not experiences for experience's sake. They were necessary preparations for a kingdom . . .[21]

[21] Land, 1993, 80.

Each Pentecostal experience 'is a penultimate realisation of an aspect of the coming kingdom and is correlated with an attribute of God'.[22] Pentecostal experience is organised by three basic stages, each of which is related to God. The first is justification, the new birth. The second is sanctification, that sense of divine cleansing associated with a clear conscience. The third is Spirit baptism that equips the believer to do spiritual battle and to walk a straight path through the temptations of the world. These three experiences allow the believer to participate in some respects in the future kingdom within the present evil world. The tension between 'already' and 'not yet', between the kingdom now and the kingdom to come, is expressed particularly through the operation of spiritual gifts that follow Spirit baptism. And, since Pentecostals understand themselves to be moving towards the kingdom, it is natural for their lives to be narrated in terms of a journey that is typically witnessed to by verbal testimony. This journey unsurprisingly contains crisis points that are occasions when God breaks in again, but such crises are analogous to the sacraments more conventional Christians celebrate. The journey towards the kingdom is therefore marked by a crisis-development dialectic which needed to be matched by an action-reflective praxis. Or, put more simply, spiritual crises and experiences are integral to the journey and, after these occur, Christians are expected to reflect upon them and learn from them.

Speaking from an academically informed vantage point, Land is able to present the relationship between doctrine and experience in a fresh and original way. Instead of prising them apart Land shows how they belong together. Indeed, he argues that the role of theology is precisely to integrate Christian beliefs, actions and affections:

> Theology is the reflective, prayerful business of working at the interrelationship of orthodoxy, orthopraxy and orthopathy, or beliefs, actions and affections, respectively.[23]

Each part of the composite is necessary for the fashioning of the new theological unity. While the beliefs of Pentecostals are vital to their understanding of eschatology and salvation, affections are vital to

[22] Land, 1993, 82.
[23] Land, 1993, 184.

worship and witness as well as being correlated with the loving character of God.[24] And without orthopraxy Christian behaviour ceases to be an ethical walk and becomes disconnected from the righteousness of God.

The tension between Pentecostal spirituality and cognition is removed and resolved. Pentecostal spirituality is no longer the endless quest for fresh spiritual experiences. Nor need Pentecostal denominations split along lines between thoughtful academics who avoid experience and the thoughtless ministers who revel in it. Rather the role of cognition is widened and not simply reduced to the exposition of texts. Instead questions have to be asked about the kind of emotions Pentecostal experiences are generating and the morality they inspire. Holiness, seen in the light of morality, may be defined in terms of simplicity rather than in terms of power. Moreover, there is no necessary tension between academic approaches to Pentecostalism and the noisy life of Pentecostal congregations. Ministerial training can properly be academic and experiential.

In addition, because Pentecostalism is understood as a journey towards the kingdom that breaks in from the future, and breaks in through the operation of spiritual gifts, the place of spiritual gifts is safeguarded. Spiritual gifts are not a Christian option that happen to be written about in the Pentecostal literature. Rather, they are an integral part of the work of the Holy Spirit, essential for proclaiming and establishing the kingdom, and to be understood as having a purpose connected with the common good (1 Cor. 12:7). Seen in this way, Pentecostal training and charismatic gifting belong together and are not substitutes for each other.

Holiness

According to one legalistically inspired conception, holiness is the keeping of God's law, often defined in relation to parts of the Old Testament – though which parts is problematic and impossible to decide.[25] Pentecostalism has never easily mixed with this version of holiness but, when it does mix, it results in ordered and obedient

---

[24] Land, 1993, 133.

[25] Jas. 2:10. Distinctions between moral and ceremonial law are impossible to maintain in practice.

congregations, usually modestly dressed and stimulated only by eighteenth-century hymns and the exhortatory preaching of a forceful minister. Such holiness is visible on Sundays but more difficult to discover in the day-to-day lives of church members.[26]

According to another definition, holiness is to be equated primarily with spiritual power: seen in the healing of the sick and the proclamation of the gospel. The paradigms of such spiritual power are to be found in the high-profile evangelists whose ministries stretch across continents by means of television and satellite communications. Since the fall in 1987 of the televangelists Bakker and Swaggart such an equation of holiness and power has looked increasingly naïve, particularly since holiness of this kind is frequently (as it was in Bakker's case) linked with the doctrine of material prosperity.[27] If poverty is an undesirable state, prosperity is the blessing that removes it. Consequently the holiness which is much more readily found within the pages of the New Testament among the early disciples of Christ, that which is equated with simplicity of life and an ability to cope with social marginalisation, is invisible.

The tension between prosperity and sacrifice, between blessing and being blessed, between being accepted and being persecuted, may be resolved through a proper understanding of Pentecostal spirituality. It is, however, a tension that runs through modern western Christianity and is not confined to its Pentecostal expressions. It arises because of the attractions of western capitalism and the tendency of Christianity to conform to, and merge with, aspects of the dominant cultural milieu in the society where it finds itself.

According to a third conception of holiness, it is an apprehension of the transcendent glory of God through worship and prayer. It is the ability to reach out in the Holy Spirit to God and there draw upon the knowledge of the divine glory as it is seen in the face of Jesus Christ.[28] This kind of holiness infuses the mind and the emotions and has the effect of purifying the commitment of Christians for service. It is a form of holiness that is most likely to be

---

26 Personal observation.

27 Bakker's salary and bonuses for 1986–87 amounted to $1.6 million, Burgess, 1988.

28 2 Cor. 4:6.

communal in nature and may be transient in its effects. It is not rule-based or lifestyle-based and is associated with the cyclical renewal of the church that cannot be produced at will but results from the passion of preachers and church leaders, perhaps when they have been deeply stirred by tragedy or human need. Those who have participated in Pentecostal meetings where a preacher brings the text of Scripture to life with clarity and in the context of personal emotion will have seen whole congregations, and sometimes whole conferences, reduced to awe or tears. Such a conception of holiness transcends cultural expressions of Christianity.

At the moment, because of the present dominance of North American culture across the world, capitalistic versions of Pentecostalism are to be found in Asia and, to a lesser extent, in Latin America. Asian Pentecostalism is beginning to find its own voice, however, and to assert the importance of social concepts that are applicable to the Asian extended family rather than to the nuclear western family and, in asserting these concepts, a new theological vision can be glimpsed. Wonsuk Ma has worked out a model showing how Asian cultural customs that often exhibit sympathy with suffering and oppression may be theologically articulated.[29] Moreover since western Pentecostalism was first brought to Asia after the era of colonial powers when its original eschatological emphasis had been lost, Asian churches have always been more 'this worldly' than 'other worldly'. Additionally, Pentecostalism was preached at a time when Asian nations were exhausted by national struggles and the message brought by the missionaries was one of God's power and hope. This impetus has continued. Asian Pentecostal churches, as distinct from traditional churches, welcomed lay and female participation: theology was democratised – no longer the province of the élite few – and attentive to the human setting of Asia.

Latin American Pentecostalism, operating as it does against the background of Roman Catholicism, contains a mixture of streams and emphases. Martin marvels at the dynamism and energy of Pentecostal pastors, a 'buried intelligentsia' of men who run choirs, build churches, teach children, study law, preach impassioned sermons and even organise housing collectives.[30] Petersen daringly contends that

[29] Ma, 1998, 15–41.

[30] Martin, 1996, 52.

Pentecostals make a contribution to social theory.[31] Baptism in the Spirit transforms the passive victim into an agent of change; individual ethics become subsumed within the community of the church and so made effective without having to be placed into a trade union or workers' cooperative; the motive for social action derives from the apocalyptic expectation of God's kingdom of righteousness rather than from self-interest or party politics. Social action is carried out, then, not for Marxist reasons to assert the rights of the proletariat or to further the interests of the communist party but because God will ultimately be glorified through it.

Within a globalised world the impact of cultural norms is likely to follow the course of economic power since economic power also implies cultural power and cutting edge communications technology. Hollywood sells the American dream. Satellite communication carries American television and with it the English language. If, as expected, the Asian economies become proportionately more powerful in the first part of the twenty-first century as the Asian birth rate boom ensures that Asia holds a larger percentage of the world population, then Asian forms of Pentecostalism will become more prevalent and, with them, visions of holiness derived from a freshly minted Asian tradition.[32] Similarly, Latin American Pentecostalism will also begin to make an impact upon the west. Its representatives already question western intellectual movements, particularly post-modernism, and assert the primacy of issues of justice and politics.[33] Influenced by the concerns of Marxist Catholicism, Pentecostalism has begun to act in ways that seem radical to European and North American intellectuals. Holiness becomes a concern for the poor and a concern for the poor is ultimately expressed through political action. But to consider holiness as belonging within the arena of politics would be laughable to the cynical politicians of the west.

---

31 Petersen, 1996, 225.

32 'The West is overwhelmingly dominant now and will remain number one in terms of power well into the 21st century. Gradual, inexorable and fundamental changes, however, are also occurring in the balances of power amongst civilisations, and the power of the West . . . will continue to decline.' Rees-Mogg, *The Times*, 20 September 1999, quoting Huntington, *The Clash of Civilisations and the Remaking of the World Order*, Simon and Schuster.

33 Freston, 1997.

Neither Asian nor Latin American Pentecostalism has made an impact on British Pentecostalism, except in one respect. The 'cell church' principle has been widely promoted. Just as all living things are made up of countless cells, so the church, as a living body, is thought of as cellular. Each cell is a group of a dozen or so people. As each cell expands so, as in biological reality, it divides and by this means growth takes place. Holiness in the context of the cell church growth is subject to the scrutiny of other members of the group. Holiness can be equated with commitment to evangelism and care for fellow cell members.

Yet there are issues here that remain unresolved within the British Pentecostal community, particularly as it notices the patterns of committed behaviour held by Pentecostals overseas where churches are thriving and thousands meet to pray. The issues partly relate to the use of time: how can British Pentecostals whose working hours are among the longest in Europe give the time that is needed to church and family life? If they give the time which Korean Christians give, their jobs are at risk. If they fail to give this kind of commitment, British Pentecostal churches can hardly expect to see the same scale of church growth. Similar issues relate to Christian rock bands or Christian environmental concerns. If the Christian rock band is more Christian than rock, it becomes a pale imitation of the secular reality. If the Christian rock band is more rock than Christian, it loses its *raison d'être*. And environmental concerns can fall into the same trap, though here the possibility that a proper Christian theology of the environment may be taught and appreciated is much stronger. There is no need for Christian environmental concerns to ape new age environmental concerns. Rather, drawing upon the rich and time-honoured resources of Christian theology a doctrine of human stewardship awaits widespread dissemination.[34]

Mission

According to Barrett 'one quarter of the world's full-time Christian workers are Pentecostals/charismatics'.[35] In 1988 Pentecostals/charismatics were working in 80 per cent of the world's 3,300

[34] Orchard, 1997.

[35] Barrett, 1988.

large metropolises. Writing in the same year, Barrett was able to point out that over one hundred new charismatic mission agencies had recently been formed in the western world, and over three hundred more in the Third World. He welcomed the era of Pentecostal and charismatic global mission. These extraordinary figures which, when projected, suggest that approximately 8 per cent of world population will be Pentecostal or charismatic in the year 2025, appear to herald an evangelist harvest.[36] If the anticipated growth occurs – in other words if Pentecostal and charismatic churches continue as they are at present without being buffeted by waves of persecution or the backwash of political or economic conflicts on a global scale – then it is reasonable to ask what the impact of this will be upon Pentecostal churches in Britain.[37] Presumably they will wish to play their part in what is happening by continuing to send out missionaries, both long and short-term, by offering their services as itinerant teachers and by participating in aid and refugee programmes wherever and whenever they are necessary.

Assemblies of God in Britain began with a fully-fledged missionary agency attached to it (the Pentecostal Missionary Union) and has always had an overseas missionary work to which its ministers are emotionally and intellectual committed. Such commitment is shown in the voting patterns and in the response to missionary presentations at the Annual General Conference and in the welcome offered by most local congregations to itinerant missionaries looking for financial support before committing themselves to the field. Elim has been less prolific in its attention to missions. The Church of God in Britain, because it belongs to a worldwide organisation that has a strategy of promoting indigenous growth, is able to leave the planning of missionary work to the home church in the United States. The relatively small Apostolic Church in Britain can point to a huge and successful overseas work, the result of Apostolic labours and the guidance of the Holy Spirit. Yet, the balance of success between Pentecostal work in Britain and Pentecostal work overseas neatly illustrates a dilemma. If Pentecostal churches in Britain invest vast

---

[36] Barrett and Johnson, 1998.

[37] Such negative forces ought not to be discounted. Johnstone, 1998, points to the emergence of nationalism and ethnic conflict in the post-soviet world. Between 1990 and 1993, 23 new countries came into being.

efforts in overseas work, the churches at home will be depleted. If Pentecostal churches in Britain fail to respond to overseas need, they run the risk of becoming blinkered and callous.

Presumably the solution lies in striking a balance between overseas and domestic need. Yet who is to judge when this balance has been achieved? There is only one obvious criterion that might be brought into play, but it is a difficult one to apply and far too reliant upon human calculation to be appealing to most Pentecostal ministers. The criterion is this: there must be an optimum ratio between domestic and overseas investment; too much investment overseas and the domestic situation suffers; too much investment at home and the missionary work declines. A computation based upon historical analysis could begin to establish this ratio and by it the possibility of working out the maximum number of missionaries that might be supported while still allowing resources for growth at home. Yet, realistically, this is a fuzzy calculation since the cost of missionaries is dependent upon the standard of living in the countries where they go (missionaries to parts of Europe are usually more expensive than missionaries to Africa) and, moreover, the value of the pound sterling fluctuates so that, for example, at the beginning of the twentieth century when the pound was strong a large number of missionaries could be supported relatively cheaply. As the pound weakened missionaries noticed their economic circumstances worsen.

Prognosis

The future of British Pentecostalism is, like the future of Britain, bound up with its relations with Europe. If European integration continues and if monetary union leads to political union, then it is reasonable to expect that this will make an impact upon British culture. Positively, British Pentecostal churches may find themselves able to minister more readily all over Europe, their training and church planting activities may stimulate other Pentecostal denominations, the Baltic, Balkan and mid-European states are likely to benefit and, as is already happening through the ministry of Kensington Temple, satellite congregations in continental Europe may be established through broadcasting from London. Negatively, attempts to classify Pentecostals as cults and to legislate against them through the European Union are not improbable. Nor is the continued paganisation of Europe as, on the one hand, liberal Protestantism is transformed into a residual entity and, on the other, Islamic groups establish a militant presence that alienates middle-class intellectuals from all types of religion.

It is also possible to offer prognosis of the methodology adopted in this book. Theological ideas have been explored using sociological methods. Beliefs, both Pentecostal and non-Pentecostal, have been described and related to each other; beliefs have also been related to denominational statements of fundamental doctrines to discover whether there is a match between what Pentecostals officially believe and what they actually believe. Even without complicated social science analysis, basic trends identified here invite a future replication and a comparative analysis. Of greater service to the church in the long run, however, may be the construction of the more complicated models described here that included sociological and theological variables relating to the behaviour of ministers and the growth of congregations. The focus on particular variables, for example charismatic activity or personal devotion, would not have been made apart from a theological standpoint that identified them as important. Yet the assembling of these variables into a model that can be tested could not be made apart from a sociological standpoint; this is a job that theology on its own is not designed to do. Similarly, the relationship between personality variables, which are psychological in origin, and sociological and theological variables can only be properly made through a social science approach that straddles the three disciplines.[38]

In short, the information presented here could not have been fully understood without an interdisciplinary approach. Only an interdisciplinary approach can properly utilise historical and theological analysis and also make predictions based upon quantifiable social variables about likely future states of affairs. Thus, though history may tell the story of the past and attempt to project its narrative forward into the future, such a projection is considerably strengthened when it is able to draw upon the resources of data that are part of social scientific models. It is increasingly reasonable to suppose that in the future, as undergraduate courses become fully

---

[38] Francis, 1999, amplifies these points.

modular and diverse, academic research, carried out in a world of bewildering global communication systems that bring together hitherto unrelated bodies of knowledge, will operate on an interdisciplinary basis. To put this another way: the complexity of Pentecostalism requires a complex methodology of empirical and non-empirical components for its description and analysis. Iinterdisciplinary enquiry allows subject matter and method to converge.

Finally, the evidence provided by the survey of 930 Pentecostal ministers at the heart of this book shows the impact each minister can have on a congregation's charismatic activity, personal evangelism, growth, healing and compassionate social concern. What can be said of the minister and the congregation, can also be said of denominational leaders and their denominations. Leaders can make an impact for good on many thousands of lives. Consequently the training, identification and selection of denominational leaders becomes crucial. If Oliver Barclay's story of evangelical fellowships and agencies in Britain since the 1930s provides a lesson, it is that only a continued respect for the authority of Scripture ensures survival.[39] Similarly, if the story of British Pentecostalism since the Sunderland Conventions provides a lesson, it is that only continued respect for the radical and many-sided grace of God as displayed in charismatic gifts ensures congregational and denominational life. Future Pentecostal leaders will succeed if they are true to the best of their heritage. But future leaders depend on the quality and dedication of the local pastors, often unsung heroes, portrayed here by words and figures. The survey shows that these pastors, prior to their present calling, carried out between them at least seventy-five different jobs, including engineers, teachers, civil servants, librarians, pharmacists, farmers, fishermen, laundry workers, industrial chemists, driving instructors, nurses, machinists, bank clerks, milkmen and solicitors. All of them gave up the relative security of their secular jobs for the demanding and risky vocation of Pentecostal ministry. All of these felt they responded to the power of the biblically described Holy Spirit breaking into their lives to empower them in the service of Christ.

---

[39] Barclay, 1997.

Bibliography

Allen, D. (1994), *The Unfailing Stream: A charismatic church history in outline* (Tonbridge, Sovereign World)

Apostolic Church (1995), *The Apostolic Church World Wide Directory* (Swansea, The Apostolic Church)

Archer, K.J. (1996), 'Pentecostal Hermeneutics: Retrospect and Prospect', *Journal of Pentecostal Theology*, 8, 63–81

Arnold, S.E. (1992), *From Scepticism to Hope* (Nottingham, Grove Books).

Badham, P. (1998), *The Contemporary Challenge of Modernist Theology* (Cardiff, University of Wales Press)

Barclay, O. (1997), *Evangelicalism in Britain 1935–1995: A personal sketch* (Leicester, Inter-Varsity Press)

Barker, D., Halman, L. and Vloet, A. (1992), *The European Values Survey* (London, Gordon Cook Foundation)

Barker, D., Halman, L. and Vloet, A. (1993), *The European Values Study 1981–1990* (London/The Netherlands, European Values Group)

Barnes, L.P. (1995), 'Miracles, Charismata and Benjamin B Warfield', *Evangelical Quarterly*, 67 (3), 219–243

Barratt, T.B. (1909), *In the Days of the Latter Rain* (London, Elim Publishing Company, revised edition 1928)

Barrett, D.B. (1988), 'The Twentieth-Century Pentecostal/Charismatic Renewal in the Holy Spirit, with its goal of world evangelisation', *International Bulletin of Missionary Research*, July 1988, 118–129

Barrett, D.B. and Johnson T.M. (1998), 'Annual statistical table on global mission: 1998', *International Bulletin*, 22, 1, 26, 27

Barrie, R. (1949), 'How things began', *Redemption Tidings*, 11 November, 5

Barron, B. (1987), *The Health and Wealth Gospel* (Downers Grove, Ill., Inter-Varsity Press)

Basham, D. (1972), *Deliver us from Evil* (London, Hodder and Stoughton)

Bebbington, D.W. (1989), *Evangelicalism in Modern Britain* (London, Unwin Hyman)

Beit-Hallahmi, B. and Argyle, M. (1997), *The Psychology of Religious Behaviour, Belief and Experience* (London, Routledge)

Benvenuti, S. (1995), 'Anointed, Gifted and Called: Pentecostal women in ministry', *Pneuma*, 17 (2), 229–235

Berger, P.L. (1963), *Invitation to Sociology* (Harmondsworth, Penguin)

Berger, P.L. (1970), *A Rumour of Angels: Modern society and the rediscovery of the supernatural* (London, Allen Lane)

Berry, R.J. (1999), 'This cursed earth: Is "the Fall" credible?', *Science and Christian Belief*, 11, 1, 29–49

Blocher, H. (1984), *In the Beginning* (Leicester, IVP)

Bloch-Hoell, N. (1964), *The Pentecostal Movement* (London, Allen and Unwin)

Blumhofer, E.W. (1985), *The Assemblies of God: A popular history* (Springfield, Gospel Publishing House)

Blumhofer, E.W. (1993), *Aimee Semple McPherson: Everybody's sister* (Grand Rapids, MI., Eerdmans)

Bonnington, M.A. (1997), 'Charismatic Spirituality: Worship as sacrament, worship as story'. Unpublished paper given at the Pentecostal and Charismatic Research Fellowship, Regents College, Nantwich, December 1997

Bonnington, M.A. (1999), 'The New Churches'. Unpublished paper, St John's College, University of Durham

Boulton, E.C.W. (1928), *George Jeffreys: A ministry of the miraculous* (London, Elim Publishing House)

Brierley, P. (1997), *UK Christian Handbook Religious Trends no 1* (Carlisle, Christian Research Research/OM Publishing)

Brierley, P. (ed.), (1998), *Religious Trends no 1 1998/99* (London/Carlisle, Christian Research/Paternoster)

Brown, R.L. (1986), *The Welsh Evangelicals* (Cardiff, Tongwynlais Tair Eglwys Press)

Bruce, S. (1995), *Religion in Modern Britain* (Oxford, OUP)

Brumback, C. (1959), *God in Three Persons* (Cleveland, Ten., Pathway Press)

Budgen, V. (1985), *Charismatics and the Word of God: A biblical and historical perspective on the charismatic movement* (Welwyn, Evangelical Press)

Burgess, S.M. (1988), 'Jimmy Orsen and Tammy Faye Bakker' in S.M. Burgess, G.B. McGee and P.H. Alexander (eds.), *Dictionary of Pentecostal and Charismatic Movements* (Grand Rapids, Regency)

Canty, G. (1987), *The Practice of Pentecost* (London, Hodder and Stoughton)

Carr, E.H. (1986), *What is History?* (Basingstoke, Macmillan)

Carter, H. (1946), *Questions and Answers on Spiritual Gifts* (London, Assemblies of God Publishing House)

Carter, J. (1947), 'Editorial', *Redemption Tidings*, 25th April

Carter, J. (1979), *A Full Life* (Nottingham, Assemblies of God)

Cartledge, M.J. (1998), 'The future of glossolalia: Fundamentalist or experientialist?', *Religion*, 28, 233–244

Cartwright, C. (ed.) (1999), *George Jeffreys: A ministry of the miraculous* (Tonbridge, Sovereign World, revision of Boulton, 1928)

Cartwright, D.W. (1986), *The Great Evangelists* (Basingstoke, Marshall Pickering)

Cerullo, M. (1979), *Revelation, Healing, Power* (San Diego, Morris Cerullo World Evangelism Inc.)

Chambers, P. (1997), ' "On or off the bus": Identity, belonging and schism. A case study of a neo-Pentecostal house church' in S. Hunt, M. Hamilton and T. Walter (eds.), *Charismatic Christianity: Sociological Perspectives* (Basingstoke, Macmillan)

Chappell, P.G. (1987), 'Healing movements' in S.M. Burgess, G.B. McGee and P.H. Alexander (eds.), *Dictionary of Pentecostal and Charismatic Movements* (Grand Rapids, Regency)

Conn, C.W. (1966), Glossolalia and the Scriptures, in W.H. Horton (ed) *The Glossolalia Phenomenon* (Cleveland, Tenn., Pathway Press)

Conn, C.W. (1977), *Like a Mighty Army: A history of the Church of God 1886–1976* (Cleveland, Tenn., Pathway Press)

Conn, C.W. (1988), 'Church of God (Cleveland, Tenn.)', in S.M. Burgess, G.B. McGee and P.H. Alexander (eds), *Dictionary of Pentecostal and Charismatic Movements* (Grand Rapids, Mich., Zondervan)

Cooke, E. (1994), 'Jesus or Genesis?' *Redemption*, February, 42–43

Cooling, T. (1984), 'The evangelical Christian and RE' MA dissertation, Kings College University of London

Corcoran, K. (1995), 'Measuring burnout: An updated reliability and convergent validity study' in R. Crandall and P.L. Perrewé (eds.), *Occupational Stress: A handbook* (London, Taylor and Francis)

Corsie, E. (1977), 'The ministry gifts' in P.S. Brewster (ed.), *Pentecostal Doctrine* (London(?), Grenehurst Press)

Cotton, I. (1995), *The Hallelujah Revolution* (London, Little, Brown and Company)

Cox, H. (1996), *Fire from Heaven: The rise of Pentecostal spirituality and the reshaping of religion in the twenty-first century* (London, Cassell)

Crandall, R. and Perrewé, P.L. (eds.) (1995) *Occupational Stress: A handbook* (London, Taylor and Francis)

Currie, R., Gilbert, A. and Horsley, L. (1977), *Churches and Churchgoers: Patterns of church growth in the British Isles since 1700* (Oxford, Clarendon Press)

Cutten, G.B. (1927), *Speaking with Tongues: Historically and psychologically considered* (Yale, Yale University Press)

Dayton, D.W. (1987), *Theological Roots of Pentecostalism* (Peabody, Mass., Hendrickson Publishers)

Del Colle, R. (1997), 'Oneness and Trinity: A preliminary proposal for dialogue with Oneness Pentecostalism', *Journal of Pentecostal Theology*, 10, 85–110

Dewe, P.J. (1990), 'New Zealand ministers of religion: Identifying sources of stress and coping strategies' in L.J. Francis and S.H. Jones (eds.), *Psychological Perspectives on Christian Ministry* (Leominster, Gracewing)

Dicks, D.R. (ed.) (1986), *When the Vow Breaks* (Penygroes, Apostolic Publications)

Dixon, P. (1994), *Signs of Revival* (Eastbourne, Kingsway)

Dolan, S.L. (1995), 'Individual, organisational and social determinants of managerial burnout: Theoretical and empirical update' in R. Crandall and P.L. Perrewé (eds.), *Occupational Stress: A handbook* (London, Taylor and Francis)

Dorrien, G. (1998), *The Remaking of Evangelical Theology* (Louisville, Kentucky, Westminster John Knox Press)

Duane Collins, W. (1994), 'An Assemblies of God perspective on demonology (part 2)', *Paraclete*, Winter, 18–22

Dunn, J.G. (1970), *Baptism in the Holy Spirit* (London, SCM)

Dupree, S.S. (1996), *African-American Holiness Pentecostal Movement* (London, Garland Publishing)

Eaton, K. (1997), 'Beware the trumpet of judgement!: John Nelson Darby and the nineteenth-century Brethren' in F. Bowie (ed.), *The Coming Deliverer: Millennial themes in world religions* (Cardiff, University of Wales Press)

Edsor, A.W. (1989), *Set Your House in Order* (London, New Wine Press)

Evans, M. (1983), *Women in the Bible* (Exeter, Paternoster Press)

Eysenck, H.J. (1990), *Rebel with a Cause: The autobiography of Hans Eysenck* (London, W H Allen)

Faupel, W. (1993), 'Whither Pentecostalism? 22nd Presidential Address, Society for Pentecostal Studies', *Pneuma*, 15 (1) 9–27

Faupel, D.W. (1995), 'From the ends of the earth to the end of the earth: The scope of the new order of the Latter Rain'. Unpublished paper read at the Society for Pentecostal Studies/European Pentecostal and Charismatic Research Association conference at Mattersey Hall, Summer, 1995

Faupel, D.W. (1996), *The Everlasting Gospel: The significance of eschatology in the development of Pentecostal thought* (Sheffield, Sheffield Academic Press)

Fichter, J.H. (1996), 'The myth of clergy burnout' in L.J. Francis and S.H. Jones (eds.), *Psychological Perspectives on Christian Ministry* (Leominster, Gracewing)

Forster, R. and Marston, P. (1989), *Reason and Faith* (Eastbourne, Monarch)

Francis, L.J., Pearson, P.R. and Kay, W.K. (1983), 'Are religious children bigger liars?', *Psychological Reports,* 52, 551–4

Francis, L.J., Pearson, P.R. and Kay, W.K. (1988), 'Religiosity and lie scores: A question of interpretation', *Social Behaviour and Personality*, 16, 91–5

Francis, L.J. and Pearson, P.R. (1991), 'Personality characteristics of mid-career Anglican clergy', *Social Behaviour and Personality*, 19, 81–84

Francis, L.J., Gibson, H.M. and Lankshear, D.W. (1991), 'The influence of Protestant Sunday Schools on attitudes towards Christianity among 11–15 year olds in Scotland', *British Journal of Religious Education*, 14 (1) 35–42

Francis, L.J. and Thomas, T.H. (1992), 'Personality profile of conference-going clergy in England', *Psychological Reports*, 70, 682

Francis, L.J. and Lankshear, D.W. (1994), 'Survey response rate as a function of age: A study among clergy', *Psychological Reports*, 75, 1569–1570

Francis, L.J. and Kay, W.K. (1995), 'The personality characteristics of Pentecostal ministry candidates', *Personality and Individual Differences*, 5, 581–594

Francis, L.J. and Rodger, R. (1996), 'The influence of personality on clergy role prioritisation, role influences, conflict and dissatisfaction with ministry' in L.J. Francis and S.H. Jones (eds.), *Psychological Perspectives on Christian Ministry* (Leominster, Gracewing)

Francis, L.J. and Brierley, P.W. (1997), 'The changing face of the British churches: 1975–1995' in W. Shaffir (ed.), *Leaving Religion and Religious Life: Patterns and dynamics* (Greenwich, Connecticut, JAI Press)

Francis, L.J. (ed.) (1999), *Sociology, Theology and the Curriculum* (London, Cassell)

Freston, P. (1997), 'Charismatic Evangelicals in Latin America: Mmission and politics on the frontiers of Protestant growth' in S. Hunt, M. Hamilton and T. Walter (eds.), *Charismatic Christianity: Sociological Perspectives* (Basingstoke, Macmillan)

Funder, D.C. (1997), *The Personality Puzzle* (London, Norton)

Garrard, M.N. (1930), *Mrs Penn-Lewis: A memoir* (Leicester, The Excelsior Press)

Gasson, R. (1966), *The Challenging Counterfeit* (Plainfield, NJ., Logos)

Gee, D. (1930), *The Ministry Gifts of Christ* (Nottingham, Assemblies of God Publishing House)

Gee, D. (1937), *Concerning Spiritual Gifts*, (revised and enlarged edn., Missouri, Springfield)

Gee, D. (1952), *Trophimus I Left Sick* (London, Elim)

Gee, D. (1967), *Wind and Flame* (Nottingham, Assemblies of God Publishing House)

Gibbs, E. (1981), *I Believe in Church Growth* (London, Hodder and Stoughton)

Giddens, A. (1999), Reith Lectures, broadcast on BBC Radio 4 in May 1999

Gilbert, A.D. (1994), 'Secularization and the future' in S. Gilley and W.J. Sheils (eds.), *A History of Religion in Britain* (Oxford, Blackwell)

Gill, D.M. (1995a), 'The contemporary state of women in ministry in Assemblies of God', *Pneuma* 17 (1) 33–36

Gill, D.M. (1995b), 'The biblically liberated woman', *Paraclete*, 29 (2) 1–9.

Gill, R. (1993), *The Myth of the Empty Church* (London, SPCK)

Gilpin, G.W. (1976), 'The inspiration of the Bible' in P.S. Brewster (ed.), *Pentecostal Doctrine* (Published privately)

Greeley, A.M. (1973), *Unsecular Man: The persistence of religion* (London, SCM)

Greenglass, E.R., Fiksenbaum, L. and Burke, R.J. (1995), 'The relationship between social support and burnout over time in teachers' in R. Crandall and P.L. Perrewé (eds.) *Occupational Stress: A handbook* (London, Taylor and Francis)

Haley, J.M. (1999), 'Methodist circuit ministers' survey'. Unpublished doctoral dissertation, University of Wales

Hamilton, M.B. (1995), *The Sociology of Religion* (London, Routledge)

Hammond, T.C. (1961), *In Understanding Be Men* (London, Inter-Varsity Fellowship)

Harris, R. (nd, c. 1907), *The Gift of Tongues: A warning* (London, Pentecostal League)

Haskey, J. (1998), 'Families: Their historical context, and recent trends in the factors influencing their formation and dissolution' in M.E. David (ed.), *The Fragmenting Family: Does it matter?* (London, IEA Health and Welfare Unit)

Hastings, A. (1986), *A History of English Christianity: 1920–1985* (Glasgow, Collins)

Hathaway, M.R., (1995), 'The role of William Oliver Hutchinson and the Apostolic Faith Church in the formation of British Pentecostal Churches'. Unpublished paper read at the Society for Pentecostal Studies/European Pentecostal and Charismatic Research Association conference at Mattersey Hall, Summer, 1995

Hathaway, M.R. (1996), 'The role of William Oliver Hutchinson and the Apostolic Faith Church in the formation of the British Pentecostal Churches', *Journal of the European Pentecostal Theological Association*, XV, 40–57. [Note, as its errata slip points out, the journal is wrongly numbered XVI]

Hathaway, M.R. (1998), 'The Elim Pentecostal Church: Origins, development and distinctives' in K. Warrington (ed.), *Pentecostal Perspectives* (Carlisle, Paternoster)

Heslam, P.S. (1998), *Creating a Christian Worldview: Abraham Kuyper's lectures on Calvinism* (Carlisle, Paternoster)

Hocken, P.D. (1984), 'Baptised in the Spirit: The origins and early development of the Charismatic Movement in Great Britain'. Doctoral dissertation, University of Birmingham

Hollenweger, W.J. (1972), *The Pentecostals* (London, SCM)

Hollenweger, W.J. (1997), *Pentecostalism: Origins and developments worldwide* (Peabody, Mass., Hendrickson)

Hollenweger, W.J. (1998), 'Fire from Heaven: A testimony by Harvey Cox', *Pneuma*, 20 (2) 197–204

Hood jr., R.W., Spilka B., Hunsberger, B. and Gorsuch, R. (1996^2), *The Psychology of Religion*, (2nd ed.), (London, The Guildford Press)

Horrobin, P. (1998), *The Ellel Story: The story so far of an unfinished task*, (Ellel, Ellel Ministries Limited)

Horton, H. (1946^2), *The Gifts of the Spirit*, (Luton, Redemption Tidings Bookroom)

Hudson, D.N. (1998), 'Worship: Singing a new song in a strange land' in K. Warrington (ed.), *Pentecostal Distinctives* (Carlisle, Paternoster)

Hudson, D.N. (1999), 'A Schism and its Aftermath: An historical analysis of denominational discerption in the Elim Pentecostal Church, 1939–1940'. Unpublished doctoral dissertation, King's College, London

Hunt, S. (1997), ' "Doing the Stuff": The Vineyard connection' in S. Hunt, M. Hamilton and T. Walter (eds.), *Charismatic Christianity: Sociological perspectives* (Basingstoke, Macmillan)

Hurt, C. (nd), 'Can a Christian have a demon?', *Ministry*, 13, 1–3

Hunter, H. (1988), 'Shepherding movement' in S.M. Burgess, G.B. McGee and P.H. Alexander (eds.), *Dictionary of Pentecostal and Charismatic Movements* (Grand Rapids, Mich., Zondervan)

Inge, W.R. (1926), *Lay Thoughts of a Dean*, (London, G P Putnams's Sons)

Jackson, K. (1999), Unpublished Ministry Studies essay CHM 280, Regents Theological College

Jeffreys, G. (1929), *The Miraculous Foursquare Gospel* (vol. 1), (London, Elim Publishing Company)

Jeffreys, G. (1932), *Healing Rays* (London, Elim Publishing Company)

Johnstone, P. (1998), *The Church is Bigger Than You Think* (Gerrards Cross/Fearn, Christian Focus Publications/WEC)

Jones, B.P. (1995), *An Instrument of Revival: The complete life of Evan Roberts 1878–1951* (South Plainfield, NJ., Bridge Publishing)

Jones, G.E. (1997), *The Education of a Nation* (Cardiff, University of Wales Press)

Kay, W.K. (1977), 'Ideology and education with special reference to the USSR and Israel'. Unpublished MEd dissertation, University of Reading

Kay, W.K. (1989), 'A history of British Assemblies of God'. Doctoral dissertation, University of Nottingham, published as *Inside Story* (see below)

Kay, W.K. (1990), *Inside Story* (Mattersey, LifeStream/Mattersey Hall Publishing)

Kay, W.K. (1991), *Prophecy!* (Nottingham, LifeStream)

Kay, W.K. (1992), 'Three generations on: The methodology of Pentecostal historiography', *EPTA Bulletin* X.1 & 2, 58–70 [actually the 1990 issue published late]

Kay, W.K. (1993), 'Do doctrinal boundaries protect our identity or prevent fellowship?', *EPTA Bulletin*, XII, 38–48

Kay, W.K. (1997), 'Belief in God in Great Britain 1945–1996: Moving the scenery behind classroom RE', *British Journal of Religious Education* 20 (1) 28–41

Kay, W.K. (1998), 'A demonised worldview: Dangers, benefits and explanations', *Journal of Empirical Theology*, 11 (1) 17–29

Kay, W.K. (1999a), 'Pentecostalism: Charismata and church growth' in L.J. Francis (ed.), *Sociology, Theology and Curriculum* (London, Cassell)

Kay, W.K. (1999c), 'British Pentecostalism: Approaches to healing', *Journal of Pentecostal Theology*, 14, 113–125

Kay, W.K. (2000a), 'Pentecostal and Charismatic Movements in the British Isles' in S. Burgess and E. Van der Maas (eds.), *New International Dictionary of Pentecostal and Charismatic Movements* (2nd edn), Zondervan

Kay, W.K. (2000b), 'Job satisfaction in Pentecostal ministers', *Asian Journal of Pentecostal Studies*, January

Kay, W.K. (2000c), 'Society, Christian beliefs and practices: The large scale' in W.K. Kay and L.J. Francis (eds.), *Religion in Education (3)* (Leominster, Gracewing)

Kay, W.K. and Francis, L.J. (1995), 'Personality, mental health and glossolalia', *Pneuma*, 17 (2) 253–263

Kay, W.K. and Francis, L.J. (1996), *Drift from the Churches* (Cardiff, University of Wales Press)

Kay, W.K. and Francis, L.J. (1997), *Religion in Education (1)* (Leominster, Gracewing)

Kay, W.K. and Robbins, M. (1999), 'A woman's place is on her knees: The pastor's view of the role of women in Assemblies of God', *Journal of the European Pentecostal Theological Association*, 18, 64–75

Kidner, D. (1967), *Genesis* (Leicester, Inter-Varsity Press)

Kildahl, J.P. (1972), *The Psychology of Speaking in Tongues* (London, Hodder and Stoughton)

Kildahl, J.P. (1975), 'Psychological observations' in M.P. Hamilton (ed.), *The Charismatic Movement* (Grand Rapids, Eerdmans)

Koch, J. (nd), *The Devil's Alphabet* (W Germany, Evangelization Publishers)

Kuhn, T.S. (1967), *The Structure of Scientific Revolutions* (Chicago, University of Chicago Press)

Küng, H. (1994), *Christianity: Its essence and history* (London, SCM)

Kwilecki, S. (1987), 'Contemporary Pentecostal clergywomen: Female Christian leadership, old style', *Journal of Feminist Studies in Religion*, 3, 57–75

Lancaster, J. (1973), *The Spirit-filled Church* (Cheltenham, Genehurst)

Land, S.J. (1993), *Pentecostal Spirituality: A passion for the kingdom* (Sheffield, Sheffield Academic Press)

Lapsley, J.N. and Simpson, J.H. (1964), 'Speaking in tongues: Infantile babble or song of the self', *Pastoral Psychology*, 15, 16–24, 48–55

Lawson, S. (1991), 'Defeating territorial spirits' in C. Peter Wagner (ed.), *Territorial Spirits* (Chichester, Sovereign World)

Lewis, I.W. (1976), 'The rapture of the church' in P.S. Brewster, *Pentecostal Doctrine*. Published privately

Lillie, D. (1961), 'The emergence of the church in the service of the kingdom' in A. Wallis (ed.), *The Divine Purpose of the Church: An enquiry*. Privately printed

Linford, A. (1960), 'Editorial', *Redemption Tidings*, 6 May

Llewellyn, H.B. 'A study of the history and thought of the Apostolic Church in Wales in the Context of Pentecostalism'. Unpublished M.Phil dissertation, University of Wales

Louden, S.H. (1998), 'The greying of the clergy'. Unpublished doctoral dissertation, University of Wales

Lyon, D. (1985), *The Steeple's Shadow* (London, SPCK)

Lyseight, O.A. (1995), *Forward March: An autobiography* (Wolverhampton, George Garwood)

Ma, W. (1997), 'A "first waver" looks at the "third wave": A Pentecostal reflection on Charles Kraft's power encounter terminology', *Pneuma* 19 (2) 189–206

Ma, W. (1998), 'Towards an Asian Pentecostal Theology', *Asian Journal of Pentecostal Studies*, 1 (1) 15–41

Macchia, F. (1996), 'No laughing matter', *Journal of Pentecostal Theology*, 8, 3–6

Mackie, A. (1921), *The Gift of Tongues* (New York, G.H. Doran)

MacRae, D.G. (1974), *Weber* (London, Fontana)

Manwaring, R. (1985), *From Controversy to Co-existence: Evangelicals in the Church of England 1914–1980* (Cambridge, Cambridge University Press)

Martin, D. (1976), *A General Theory of Secularization* (Oxford, Blackwell)

Martin, D. (1996), *Forbidden Revolutions* (London, SPCK)

Marwick, A. (1982), *British Society Since 1945* (Harmondsworth, Penguin)

Maslach, C. and Schaufeli W.B. (1993), 'Historical and conceptual development of burnout' in W.B. Schaufeli, C. Maslach and T. Marek (eds.), *Professional Burnout: Recent developments in theory and research* (London, Taylor and Francis)

Maslach, C. and Leiter, M.P. (1997), *The Truth about Burnout: How organisations cause personal stress and what to do about it* (San Francisco, Jossey-Bass)

Massey, R.D., 'The Word of God: "Thus saith the Lord" ' in K. Warrington, *Pentecostal Perspectives* (Carlisle, Paternoster)

McClynn, F. (1996), *Carl Gustave Jung* (London, Bantam Press)

McCrae, R.R. and Costa, P.T. (1997), 'Conceptions and correlates of openness to experience' in R. Hogan, J. Johnson and S. Briggs (eds.), *Handbook of Personality Psychology* (London, Academic Press)

McGavran, D. (1955), *Bridges of God* (New York, Friendship Press)

McGavran, D. (1959), *How Churches Grow* (New York, Friendship Press)

McGavran, D. (1970), *Understanding Church Growth* (Grand Rapids, Michigan, Eerdmans)

McGavran, D. (1983), *Contemporary Theologies of Mission* (Grand Rapids, Michigan, Baker)

McGee, G.B. (ed.) (1991), *Initial Evidence: Historical and biblical perspectives on the pentecostal doctrine of Spirit Baptism* (Peabody, Mass., Hendrickson)

McGrath, A.E. (1988), *Understanding the Trinity* (Grand Rapids, Mich., Zondervan)

McGrath, A.E. (1992), *Bridge-building: Effective Christian apologetics* (Leicester, IVP)

McGee, G.B. (1988), 'Bhengu, Nicholas Bhekinkosi Hepworth' in S.M. Burgess, G.B. McGee and P.H. Alexander (eds.), *Dictionary of Pentecostal and Charismatic Movements* (Grand Rapids, Mich., Zondervan)

Middlemiss, D. (1996), *Interpreting Charismatic Experience* (London, SCM)

Moore, J.R. (1981), *The Post-Darwinian Controversies* (Cambridge, Cambridge University Press)

Moorman, J.R.H. (1980), *A History of the Church of England* (London, Adam and Charles Black)

Morris, H.M. (1974), *Many Infallible Proofs* (San Diego, Ca., Creation Life)

Morris, H.M. (1976), *The Genesis Record* (Grand Rapids, Baker)

Morris, H.M. (1977), *Evolution and the Modern Christian* (Grand Rapids, Baker)

Moule, H.C.G. (1907), The message: Its scriptural character' in C.F. Harford (ed.), *The Keswick Convention: Its message, its method and its men*, (London, Marshall Brothers)

Neil, A. (1997), *Full Disclosure* (Basingstoke, Pan)

Orchard, A. (1997), 'Assessing the relationship between three Christian theologies of creation and environmental concern', *Journal of Beliefs and Values*, 18 (1) 59–67

Osborn, T.L. (1959), *Healing the Sick*, (Oklahoma, T.L. Osborn Evangelistic Association Inc.)

Packer, J.I. (1958), *Fundamentalism and the Word of God* (Leicester, Inter-Varsity Press)

Packer, J.I. (1984), *Keep in Step with the Spirit* (Leicester, Inter-Varsity Press)

Parker, C.L. (1922), 'The Bible Reading Institute', *Keswick Week*, 1922

Parker, C.L. (1961), *Covert Earnestly* (London, Assemblies of God)

Parker, P.G. (1931), *Bible Study and Bible Problems* (London, Victory Press)

Parr, J.N. (1955), *Divine Healing* (Springfield, Gospel Publishing House)

Parr, J.N. (1972), *Incredible: The autobiography of John Nelson Parr* (Fleetwood, Private publication)

Pawson, D. (1997), *Jesus Baptises in One Holy Spirit* (London, Hodder and Stoughton)

Penn-Lewis, J. (nd), *War on the Saints* (Poole, The Overcomer Literature Trust)

Peretti, F. (1990) *Piercing the Darkness* (Eastbourne, Minstrel)

Petersen, D. (1996), *Not by Might nor by Power* (Oxford, Regnum)

Petts, D. (1993), 'Healing and the atonement'. Unpublished doctoral dissertation, University of Nottingham

Petts, D. (1998), 'The baptism in the Holy Spirit: The theological distinctive' in K. Warrington (ed.), *Pentecostal Perspectives* (Carlisle, Paternoster)

Plüss, J.D. (1997), 'The saviour, healer and the coming king I know, but who in the world is Jesus? Pentecostal hermeneutics reconsidered', *Transformation*, October, 14–20

Pollock, J.C. (1964), *The Keswick Story* (Hodder and Stoughton)

Poloma, M.M. (1989), *Assemblies of God at the Crossroads* (Knoxville, Tenn., University of Tennessee Press)

Poloma, M.M. (1996), *The Toronto Report* (Bradford, Terra Nova Publications)

Poloma, M.M. (1997), 'The "Toronto Blessing": Charisma, institutionalization, and revival', *Journal for the Scientific Study of Religion*, 36, 257–271

Poloma, M.M. (1998a), 'The Spirit Movement in North America at the Millennium: From Azusa Street to Toronto, Pensacola and beyond', *Journal of Pentecostal Theology*, 12, 83–107

Poloma, M.M. (1998b), 'Inspecting the fruit of the "Toronto blessing": A sociological perspective', *Pneuma*, 20 (1) 43–70

Powell, D. (1976), 'The doctrine of holiness' in P. Brewster (ed.), *Pentecostal Doctrine*. Published privately

Prince, D. (1976), *Discipleship, Shepherding, Commitment* (Ft. Lauderdale, Derek Prince Publications)

Ramm, B. (1955), *The Christian View of Science and Scripture* (Exeter, Paternoster)

Randall, I.M. (1995), 'Holiness and Pentecostal spirituality in inter-war England'. Unpublished paper read at the Society for Pentecostal Studies/European Pentecostal and Charismatic Research Association conference at Mattersey Hall, Summer 1995

Randall, I.M. (1999), *Evangelical Experiences: A study of the spirituality of English evangelicalism 1918–1939* (Carlisle, Paternoster)

Reed, D.A. (1988), 'Oneness Pentecostalism' in S.M. Burgess, G.B. McGee and P.H. Alexander (eds.), *Dictionary of Pentecostal and Charismatic Movements* (Grand Rapids, Mich., Zondervan)

Reed, D.A. (1997), 'Oneness Pentecostalism: Problems and possibilities for Pentecostal Theology', *Journal of Pentecostal Theology*, 11, 73–93

Reid, I. (1977), 'Sunday School attendance and adolescents' religious and moral attitudes, knowledge and practice', *British Journal of Religious Education*, 17 (1) 3–8

Rendle-Short, J. (1981), *Man: ape or image – the Christian's dilemma* (Sunnybank, Aus., Creation Science Publishing)

Richards, W.T.H. (1973), 'Demon possession', *Redemption Tidings*, 11 October, 10–13

Richter, P. and Francis, L.J. (1998), *Gone But Not Forgotten: Church leaving and returning* (London, Darton, Longman and Todd)

Riss, R.M. (1982), 'The Latter Rain movement of 1948', *Pneuma*, 4, 32–45

Riss, R.M. (1988), *A Survey of 20th Century Revival Movements in North America* (Peabody, Mass., Hendrickson)

Robeck, C.M. (1988), 'Azusa Street' in S.M. Burgess, G.B. McGee and P.H. Alexander (eds.), *Dictionary of Pentecostal and Charismatic Movements* (Grand Rapids, Mich., Zondervan)

Roberts, D. (1994), *The 'Toronto' Blessing* (Eastbourne, Kingsway)

Rowe, W.A.C. (1988), *One Lord One Faith* (Penygroes, Apostolic Publications)

Russell, B. (1918), *Mysticism and Logic*, (Harmondsworth, Penguin. Reprinted in 1953)

Russell, B. (1903), 'A Free Man's Worship' was first published in the *Independent Review*, in December, 1903 and then reprinted in *Mysticism and Logic* (see above)

Samarin, W.J. (1959), 'Glossolalia as learned behaviour', *Canadian Journal of Theology*, 15, 60–64

Samarin, W.J. (1973), 'Glossolalia as regressive speech', *Language and Speech*, 16, 77–79

Schatzmann, S. (1998), 'The gifts of the Spirit: Pentecostal interpretation of Pauline Pneumatology' in K. Warrington (ed.), *Pentecostal Perspectives* (Carlisle, Paternoster)

Shelbourne, M. (1990), 'Survey of Women's Ministries in Assemblies of God UK'. Privately circulated

Shelbourne, M. (1993), *Just Another Stepping Stone* (Nottingham, LifeStream Publications)

Smail, T., Walker, A. and Wright, N. (1995), *Charismatic Renewal* (London, SPCK)

Smith, J.K.A. (1997), 'The closing of the book: Pentecostals, evangelicals, and the sacred writings', *Journal of Pentecostal Theology*, 11, 49–71

Office for National Statistics (1995), *Social Trends* (London, HMSO)

Spittler, R.P. (1988), 'David Johannes du Plessis' in S.M. Burgess, G.B. McGee and P.H. Alexander (eds.), *Dictionary of Pentecostal and Charismatic Movements* (Grand Rapids, Mich., Zondervan)

Stevenson, H.F. (1959), 'The Spirit-filled life' in H.F. Stevenson (ed.), *Keswick's Authentic Voice* (London, Marshall, Morgan and Scott)

Storr, A. (1973), *Jung* (London, Fontana)

Strachan, G. (1973), *The Pentecostal Theology of Edward Irving* (London, Darton, Longman and Todd)

Stronstad, R. (1992), 'Pentecostal experience and hermeneutics', *Paraclete*, 26, 1, 14–30

Subritzky, B. (1986), *Demons Defeated* (Chichester, Sovereign World)

Synan, V. (1997), *The Holiness-Pentecostal Tradition* (Grand Rapids, Mich., Eerdmans)

Tee, A. (1976), 'The doctrine of divine healing' in P.S. Brewster (ed.), *Pentecostal Doctrine*. Published privately

Thomas, J.C. (1994), 'Women, Pentecostals and the Bible: An experiment in Pentecostal hermeneutics', *Journal of Pentecostal Theology*, 5, 41–56

Thomas, J.C. (1996), ' "An Angel from Satan": Paul's thorn in the flesh (2 Corinthians 12.7–10)', *Journal of Pentecostal Theology*, 9, 39–52

Thomas, J.C. (1998), 'Max Turner's The Holy Spirit and Spiritual Gifts: Then and now: An appreciation and critique', *Journal of Pentecostal Theology*, 12, 3–21

Thompson, W. (1997), 'Charismatic politics: The social and political impact of renewal' in S. Hunt, M. Hamilton and T. Walter (eds.), *Charismatic Christianity: Sociological perspectives* (Basingstoke, Macmillan), 160–183

Towler, R. (1968), 'The changing status of the ministry?', *Crucible*, May, 73–8. Reprinted in Robertson, R. (1969), *The Sociology of Religion* (Harmondsworth, Penguin)

Trexler, J.A. (1990), 'From chaos to order: G F Taylor and the evolution of southern pentecostalism'. Unpublished paper read at the Society for Pentecostal Studies, Dallas, November 8–10, 1990

Turnbull, T.N. (1959), *What God Hath Wrought* (Bradford, Puritan Press)

Turnbull, T.N. (1963), *Brothers in Arms* (Bradford, Puritan Press)

Turner, M. (1996), *The Holy Spirit and Spiritual Gifts: Then and now* (Carlisle, Paternoster Press)

Virgo, T. (1985), *Restoration in the Church* (Eastbourne, Kingsway)

Virgo, W. (1985), *Leading Ladies* (Eastbourne, Kingsway)

Vivier, L.M. (1960), 'Glossolalia'. Unpublished doctoral dissertation, Department of Psychiatry, University of Witwatersrand

Wagner, C.P. (1976), *Your Church Can Grow* (Glendale, California, Regal Books)

Wagner, C.P. (1984), *Leading Your Church to Growth* (Marc Europe, British Church Growth Association)

Wagner, C.P. (1987), *Strategies for Church Growth* (Marc, British Church Growth Association)

Wagner, C.P. (ed.) (1991), *Territorial Spirits* (Chichester, Sovereign World)

Walker, T.W. (1976), 'The Baptism in the Holy Spirit' in P.S. Brewster (ed.), *Pentecostal Doctrine* (Cheltenham, Elim Pentecostal Church Headquarters)

Walker, A. (1985), *Restoring the Kingdom* (London, Hodder and Stoughton)

Wallace, J.E. and Brinkerhoff, M.B. (1991), 'The measurement of burnout revisited', *Journal of Social Service Research*, 14 (5), 85–111

Wallis, A. (1961), 'The divine idea of the the local church' in L.D. Lillie (ed.), *The Divine Purpose of the Church: An enquiry*. Privately printed

Wallis, J. (1991), *Arthur Wallis: Radical Christian* (Eastbourne, Kingsway)

Wallis, R. and Bruce, S. (1992), 'Secularization: The orthodox model' in S. Bruce (ed.), *Religion and Modernization: Sociologists and historians debate the secularisation thesis* (Oxford, Clarendon Press)

Weaver, P.C. (1999), Survey carried out of all Assemblies of God ministers in the UK early in 1999; findings were presented at the Assemblies of God General Conference at Prestatyn, 17–24 April 1999

Weber, M. (1930), *The Protestant Ethic and the Spirit of Capitalism* (London, Unwin University Books)

Weber, M. (1954), *The Theory of Social and Economic Organisation* (New York, Free Press)

Wenham, G.J. (1987), *Genesis 1–15* (Waco, Tx., Word)

White, A.J.M. (1979), *What About Origins?* (Newton Abbot, Dunstone)

Whittaker, C. (1983), *Seven Pentecostal Pioneers* (Basingstoke, Marshall Morgan and Scott)

Wigglesworth, S. (1924), *Ever Increasing Faith* (Springfield, Mo., Radiant Books)

Williams, C.G. (1981), *Tongues of the Spirit* (Cardiff, University of Wales Press)

Wilson, B.R. (1961), *Sects and Society* (London, Heinemann)

Wilson, B.R. (1963), 'A typology of sects in a dynamic and comparative perspective', *Archives de Sociologie de Religion*, 16, 49–63

Wilson, B.R. (1966), *Religion in a Secular Society* (London, A C Watts and Co.)

Wilson, B.R. (1976), *Contemporary Transformations of Religion* (Oxford, Oxford University Press)

Winterson, J. (1991), *Oranges Are Not the Only Fruit* (London, Vintage)

Wolfe, K.M. (1984), *The Churches and the British Broadcasting Corporation 1922–1956* (London, SCM Press)

Woodford, L.F.W. (1956), *Diving Healing and the atonement: A re-statement* (Croydon, Victoria Institute)

Worsfold, J.E. (1991), *The Origins of the Apostolic Church in Great Britain* (Wellington, NZ, Julian Literature Trust)

Wulff, D.M. (1991), *Psychology of Religion: Classic and contemporary views* (New York, John Wiley and Sons)

Yinger, J.M. (1957), *Religion, Society and the Individual* (New York, Macmillan)

Yong, A. (1998), 'Whither systematic theology? A systematician chimes in on a scandalous conversation', *Pneuma*, 20 (1) 85–93

Young, M. and Willmott, P. (1975), *The Symmetrical Family* (Harmondsworth, Penguin)

Index